ALBEMARLE COUNTY

IN VIRGINIA

Giving some account of what it was by nature, of what it was made by man, and of some of the men who made it.

By Rev. Edgar Woods

"It is a solemn and touching reflection, perpetually recurring, of the weakness and insignificance of man, that while his generations pass away into oblivion, with all their toils and ambitions, nature holds on her unvarying course, and pours out her streams and renews her forests with undecaying activity, regardless of the fate of her proud and perishable Sovereign."—*Jeffrey*.

Notice

In many older books, foxing (or discoloration) occurs and, in some instances, print lightens with wear and age. Reprinted books, such as this, often duplicate these flaws, notwithstanding efforts to reduce or eliminate them. The pages of this reprint have been digitally enhanced and, where possible, the flaws eliminated in order to provide clarity of content and a pleasant reading experience.

Copyright © Edgar Woods, 1901

Originally published:
Charlottesville, Virginia: 1901

Reprinted:
Janaway Publishing, Inc.
2007, 2011

Janaway Publishing, Inc.
732 Kelsey Ct.
Santa Maria, California 93454
(805) 925-1038
www.janawaygenealogy.com

ISBN: 978-1-59641-124-1

Made in the United States of America

PREFACE

An examination of the records of the county for some information, awakened curiosity in regard to its early settlement, and gradually led to a more extensive search. The fruits of this labor, it was thought, might be worthy of notice, and productive of pleasure, on a wider scale.

There is a strong desire in most men to know who were their forefathers, whence they came, where they lived, and how they were occupied during their earthly sojourn. This desire is natural, apart from the requirements of business, or the promptings of vanity. The same inquisitiveness is felt in regard to places. Who first entered the farms that checker the surrounding landscape, cut down the forests that once covered it, and built the habitations scattered over its bosom? With the young, who are absorbed in the engagements of the present and the hopes of the future, this feeling may not act with much energy; but as they advance in life, their thoughts turn back with growing persistency to the past, and they begin to start questions which perhaps there is no means of answering. How many there are who long to ascertain the name of some ancestor, or some family connection, but the only person in whose breast the coveted knowledge was lodged, has gone beyond the reach of all inquiry. How many interesting facts of personal or domestic concern could have been communicated by a parent or grandparent, but their story not being told at the opportune season, they have gone down irrecoverably in the gulf of oblivion.

Public affairs are abundantly recorded. Not only are they set forth in the countless journals of the day, but scores of ready pens are waiting to embody them in more permanent form in histories of our own times. Private events—those connected with individuals and families—are less frequently committed to writing. They may descend by tradition through one or two generations, and then perish forever from the memory of mankind. Some general facts may be found in local records; but memorials of this kind are dry and monotonous in their nature, and never resorted to by ordinary readers. Their contents are soon lost sight of except by the antiquarian, or by those who are compelled by professional duty to unearth them from the forgotten past.

Such considerations induced the collection of the facts compiled in this volume. They were taken mainly from the county archives; in cases where they were derived from tradition, or where suggestions were made from conjecture, it is generally so stated. Except in a few particulars, the narrative was not designed to extend to the present generation.

Some matters that may be of interest to many, may be found in the appendix. To some now living in the county, and to others descended from those who once lived in it, the long list of names therein inscribed may show in some measure how their ancestors were employed, whither their wanderings led, or at what time they passed away from the present scene of action.

July 1st, 1900.

CHAPTER I.

The settlement of Virginia was a slow and gradual process. Plantations were for the most part opened on the water courses, extending along the banks of the James, and on the shores of the Chesapeake Bay and its tributaries. It was more than a century after the landing at Jamestown before white men made the passage of the Blue Ridge. As soon as that event was noised abroad, it was speedily followed up, and in the space of the next twenty years the tide of population had touched the interior portions of the colony, one stream pushing westward from the sea coast, and another rolling up the Shenandoah Valley from the wilds of Pennsylvania.

Besides the restless spirit animating the first settlers, the occupation of the country was hastened by the rage for speculation. The laws of the colony allotted fifty acres for every person transported into its territory; and men of wealth, in addition to availing themselves of this provision, largely invested their means in the purchase of land. While the wilderness was thus peopled, the institutions of civil government did not linger far behind. As growing numbers reached the frontiers, and were removed a great distance from the seats of justice and trade, these necessities of civilized life were soon established. One by one, the older counties were cut in two, the limits of the new ones stretching westward as far as the limits of the colony itself. Those recently formed were at first represented by public buildings made of logs, and by the scattered clearings and cabins of the pioneers; but men of knowledge and experience were always at hand to hold the reins of government and administer the laws. At once the courthouse was erected, and the power of the magistrate exerted to preserve peace and order in the community.

The county of Goochland was formed in 1727, a little more than ten years after Gov. Spotswood's expedition to the Blue Ridge. The first settlements within the present bounds of Albemarle were made while they were still parts of that county and Hanover. They ascended the courses of the South Anna, the James, the Rivanna and the Hardware, and were met by others proceeding from the foot of the Blue Ridge, and planted by immigrants who had come up the Valley, and crossed that mountain at Woods' Gap.

The first patents were taken out on June 16, 1727. On that day George Hoomes obtained a grant of thirty-one hundred acres "on the far side of the mountains called Chesnut, and said to be on the line between Hanover and Spotsylvania," and Nicholas Meriwether a grant of thirteen thousand seven hundred and sixty-two acres "at the first ledge of mountains called Chestnut," and said to be on the same line. That was the first appropriation of the virgin soil of Albemarle, as it is at present. These locations occurred in the line of the South Anna River, up which the increasing population had been slowly creeping for a number of years. The patent to Nicholas Meriwether included the present seat of Castle Hill, and the boundaries of the Grant, as it was termed by way of eminence, were marks of great notoriety to surveyors, and others interested in the description of adjacent lands, for a long period afterwards.

The next patent for twenty-six hundred acres was obtained nearly two years later by Dr. George Nicholas. This land was situated on James River, and included the present village of Warren. In the year following, 1730, five additional patents were issued: one to Allen Howard for four hundred acres on James River, on both sides of the Rockfish at its mouth; one to Thomas Carr for twenty-eight hundred acres on the Rivanna at the junction of its forks, and up along the north fork; one to Charles Hudson for two thousand acres on both sides of the Hardware, the beginning evidently of the Hudson plantations below Carter's Bridge; one to Secretary John Carter for nine thousand three hundred and fifty acres "on the Great Mountain on Hardware in the fork of the James," and to this day called Carter's Mountain; and one to Francis Eppes, the grandfather of Mr. Jefferson's son-in-law of the same name, for six thousand four hundred acres "on the branches of the Hardware, Rockfish, and other branches of the James"—one of the branches of Hardware being still known as Eppes Creek. The same year Nicholas Meriwether located four thousand one hundred and ninety acres more, adjoining his former tract, and running over the South West Mountain on Turkey Run, taking out an inclusive patent for seventeen thousand nine hundred and fifty-two acres in one body. From the recital of this patent, it appears that Christopher Clark was associated in the first grant, although it was made out to Nicholas Meriwether alone.

In 1731 only three patents were obtained within the present county: one by Charles Lewis for twelve hundred acres on both sides of the Rivanna, at the mouth of Buck Island Creek, one by Charles Hudson for five hundred and forty acres on the west side of Carter's Mountain; and one by Major Thomas Carr for two thousand acres "on the back side of the Chestnut Mountains." Several other patents were taken out the same year along the Rivanna within the present limits of Fluvanna County, one of which was by Martin King, whose name is still kept in remembrance in connection with the road which runs from Woodridge to the Union Mills, where was a ford also called by his name.

In 1732 were made eight grants, still confined to the James River, and the western base of the South West Mountain. One of these was made to Thomas Goolsby for twelve hundred acres "on the north side of the Fluvanna," that is, the James; another in the same region to Edward Scott for five hundred and fifty acres "at a place called Totier;" another for four hundred acres to John Key, the head of a family which subsequently owned all the land between the South West Mountain and the river from Edgemont to the bend below the Free Bridge; and another to Dr. Arthur Hopkins for four hundred acres "on the south side of the Rivanna, running to the mouth of a creek below Red Bank Falls, called Lewis' Creek." This last entry included the site of the future town of Milton.

Only four patents were taken out in 1733. None of them

reached further west than the west bank of the Rivanna under the shadow of the South West Mountain. One was obtained by Charles Lynch for eight hundred acres, which extended up the Rivanna from the mouth of Moore's Creek, and included the plantation of Pen Park.

In 1734 thirteen grants were made. These were mainly located near the bases of the South West Mountains on the Rivanna and Mechunk. One was obtained by Henry Wood, the first clerk of Goochland, and great grandfather of V. W. Southall, for two hundred acres on the south side of the Rivanna at the mouth of Buck Island Creek, increased subsequently to nearly three thousand in different tracts; and another by Edwin Hickman, Joseph Smith, Thomas Graves and Jonathan Clark for three thousand two hundred and seventy-seven acres on the north side of the Rivanna, running down form Captain MacMurdo's place and embracing the estates of Pantops and Lego. Another formed a notable exception to what had hitherto been the rule. It was the first to leave the streams, and strike out toward the middle of the county. It was obtained by Joel Terrell and David Lewis for twenty-three hundred acres, and shortly after for seven hundred more, lying on both sides of the Three Notched Road and extending from Lewis's Mountain, which it included to a point near the D. S. The Birdwood plantation was comprehended in this tract.

From this time the county was settled with greater rapidity. Most of the entries thus far noted were made in large quantities, and by wealthy men for the purpose of speculation. Few of those who have been mentioned occupied their lands, at least in the first instance. They made the clearings and entered upon the cultivation which the law required in order to perfect their titles, but it was done either by tenants, or by their own servants, whom they established in "quarters." Now, however, a new order of things began. Grants were more frequently obtained in smaller amounts by persons who left the older districts with the design of permanently residing in the new country. Accordingly in 1735 the number of patents rose to twenty-five. Not that this number was constantly maintained; in some years, on the contrary, it greatly diminshed. The population of the colony was yet comparatively sparse. The whole Piedmont region, and the fertile plains of the Valley were simultaneously opened, and held out strong inducements to settlers; and at the same time, inviting sections in the western portions of North and South Carolina were presented in glowing colors before the public eye, and soon drew largely on the multitudes given to change. Still the county steadily filled up. Patents were taken out this year on Green Creek in its southern part, on the south fork of Hardware near the Cove, on the south fork of the Rivanna, on Meadow Creek, on Ivy Creek, and on Priddy's and Buck Mountain Creeks in the north. Among the patentees were John Henry, father of the famous orator, to whom were granted twelve hundred and fifty acres situated on tributaries of the south fork of the Rivanna called Henry, Naked and Fishing Creeks, the same land afterwards owned by the Michies southwest of Earlysville; William Randolph, who was granted twenty-four hundred acres on the north side of the Rivanna and Mountain Falls Creek, including the present Shadwell and Edge Hill; Nicholas Meriwether, who was granted a thousand and twenty acres west of the Rivanna, embracing the plantation known as the Farm; Peter Jefferson, who was granted a thousand acres on the south side of the Rivanna, including Tufton; Abraham Lewis, who was granted eight hundred acres on the east side of Lewis's Mountain, then called Piney Mountain, including the present lands of the University; Thomas Moorman, who was granted six hundred and fifty acres, extending from the branches of Meadow Creek to the south fork of the Rivanna, "including the Indian Grave low grounds;" Michael Holland, who was granted four thousand seven hundred and fifty-three acres on both sides of Ivy Creek, including the present Farmington estate; and Charles Hudson, who was granted two thousand acres on Ivy Creek adjoining the Holland tract, and lying southwest of Ivy Depot.

In 1736 Robert Lewis obtained a patent for four thousand and thirty acres on the north fork of Hardware in the North Garden.

Nineteen patents were taken out in 1737. Michael Woods, his son Archibald, and his son-in-law, William Wallace, secured grants for more than thirteen hundred acres on Lickinghole, Mechum's River and Beaver Creek, embracing the present Mechum's Depot and Blair Park. The same day Michael Woods purchased the two thousand acre patent of Charles Hudson on Ivy Creek. These transactions took place at Goochland C. H., or more likely at Williamsburg; and this fact lends probability to the tradition that the Woods settlement occurred at the mouth of Woods's Gap in 1734. Crossing from the Valley into an unbroken forest, as Michael Woods did, it is almost certain that he made a clearing and built a cabin, and thus established his right to the estate the law gave, before he set himself to acquire a knowledge of the surrounding country and its owners, and to make large purchases. The axe had commenced to resound amidst the deep solitudes at the foot of the Blue Ridge, while yet no white settler had gone beyond the Rivanna at the South West Mountain. The same year, 1737, Henry Terrell, of Caroline, obtained a grant of seventeen hundred and fifty acres on the head waters of Mechums, including the present village of Batesville. As a suggestion of special interest, it may be mentioned that in October of that year a William Taylor patented twelve hundred acres lying on both sides of Moore's Creek. It can scarcely be questioned, that this was the tract of land which in process of time passed into the hands of Colonel Richard Randolph, which was sold by him to the county, and on which was laid out in 1762 the new county seat of Charlottesville.

It was not until 1739 that the first patent was located on Moorman's River. David Mills was by that instrument of writing granted twenty eight-hundred and fifty acres on its north fork. Two years later Dennis Doyle obtained the grant of eight hundred acres on the same stream, and from him was derived the name it has borne ever since. The same year, 1741, Thomas Moorman patented seven hundred and fifty acres lower down the main river, and as often as men now speak of it, they perpetuate the memory of his name.

All sections of the county had at that time been occupied in some degree, and the work of laying claim to its unappropriated lands constantly progressed from year to year. As late however as 1796, Matthew Gambell procured the grant of twenty-five thousand seven hundred and ninety-eight acres lying in Albemarle, Orange and Rockingham Counties near Seamond's Gap; and still later in 1798, John Davidson, who subsequently removed to Hardin County, Ky., took out a patent for eighteen hundred and seventy-seven acres on Buck's Elbow.

Reference has been made to the entry of bodies of land extending over a wide area. It may be further stated, that Major Thomas Carr patented altogether upwards of five thousand acres; George Webb, of Charles City, in 1737 upwards of seven thousand, near a mountain north of Earlysville still called by his name; Secretary John Carter in 1738, ten thousand within the present limits of Amherst; John Chiswell in 1739, nearly thirty thousand on Rockfish River, mainly within the present bounds of Nelson; William Robertson in 1739, more than six thousand on Naked and Buck Mountain Creeks; Robert Lewis in 1740, more than six thousand on Ivy Creek; Ambrose Joshua Smith in 1741, more than four thousand on Priddy's Creek; Samuel Garlick, of Caroline, in 1741 and 1746, thirty-six hundred on Buck Mountain Creek; Rev. Robert Rose in 1744, more than thirty-three thousand within the present counties of Amherst and Nelson; Rev. William Stith, President of William and Mary, from 1740 to 1755, nearly three thousand, and Dr. Arthur Hopkins in 1748 and 1765, nearly four thousand, on Totier and Ballenger's Creeks; and Allen Howard in 1742, more than two thousand on the lower waters of Rockfish.

Mr. Jefferson, in a brief sketch of his family, wrote of his father, "He was the third or fourth settler, about the year 1737, of the part of the county in which I live."

The act establishing the county of Albemarle was passed by the Legislature in September, 1744. It ordained its existence to begin from the first of January, 1745; and the reason alleged for its formation was the "divers inconveniences attending the upper inhabitants of Goochland by reason of their great distance from the courthouse, and other places usually appointed for public meetings." The dividing lines were directed to run from the point of fork of James River—that is, from the mouth of the Rivanna, where Columbia now stands—north thirty degrees east to the Louisa line, and from the same point a direct course to Brook's Mill, and thence the same course continued to the Appomattox River. These boundaries embraced the county of Buckingham, parts of Appomattox and Campbell, and the counties of Amherst, Nelson and Fluvanna, the Blue Ridge being the western line. That portion of the present county north of a line running past the mouth of Ivy Creek with the course of north sixty-five degrees west, remained in Louisa for sixteen years longer.

In accordance with a custom already begun of commemorating the governors of the Commonwealth, the name of Albemarle was given the new county, from the title of William Anne Keppel, second earl of Albemarle, at that time Governor General of the colony.

The organization took place the fourth Thursday of February, 1745, doubtless on the plantation of Mrs. Scott, near the present Scottsville, where the next court was directed to be held. The commission of the first magistrates was dated the second of the preceding January. Those present were Joshua Fry, Peter Jefferson, Allen Howard, William Cabell, Joseph Thompson and Thomas Ballou. Howard and Cabell administered the oaths to Fry and Jefferson, and they in turn to the others. The oaths taken were those of a Justice of the Peace, and of a Judge of a Court of Chancery, and the Abjuration and Test oaths were subscribed,— the former renouncing allegiance to the House of Stuart, and the latter affirming the receiving of the sacrament according to the rites of the Church of England. William Randolph was appointed Clerk by a commission from Thomas Nelson, Secretary of the Council, and Joseph Thompson, Sheriff, Joshua Fry, Surveyor, and Edmund Gray, King's Attorney, by commissions from William Gooch, the Governor; and all were sworn in. Patrick Napier and Castleton Harper were made Deputy Sheriffs, and Benjamin Harris, Deputy Clerk, the following May. As appears from the Deed Books, John Fleming was also Deputy Clerk. Thomas Turpin was appointed Assistant Surveyor, and John Hunter, Adrian Angle, John Hilton, John Harris, Robert White and Abraham Childress, Constables. The civil offices being filled, the military side of the organization was duly constituted. Joshua Fry received the appointment of Lieutenant of the county, Peter Jefferson of Lieutenant Colonel, and Allen Howard of Major. William Cabell, Joseph Thompson, Charles Lynch, Thomas Ballou, David Lewis, James Daniel, James Nevel, and James Martin were sworn as Captains. Charles Lynch, Edwin Hickman and James Daniel having been named magistrates, were subsequently inducted into office by taking the oaths. Of these officers, Jefferson, Howard, Cabell and Lynch had already been magistrates, and Jefferson had also acted as Sheriff, in Goochland. The William Randolph, who was the first Clerk, was unquestionably Colonel William Randolph, of Tuckahoe, who had some years before entered the tract of land known as Edge Hill.

The original attorneys who practiced in the courts of the county, were Edmund Gray, Gideon Marr, William Battersby—whose daughter Jane, the wife of Giles Allegre, was the mother-in-law of the eminent statesman and financier, Albert Gallatin—James Meredith, Clement Read and John Harvie. All except Harvie, and probably Meredith, resided on the south side of James River.

The routine of public business was at once begun and prosecuted with stated regularity. The location of the courthouse was a matter of deep interest. It was a conceded point that it should be fixed on James River. Jefferson, Howard, Lynch and Ballou were appointed to view the river and make a report; and as the result, Samuel Scott, son of Edward, agreed with proper security to erect at his own cost a courthouse, prison, stocks and pillory, as good as those of Goochland, the site to be selected by the Court, provided it was placed on his land. The site actually chosen was on the plantation of his brother Daniel, and is still pointed out about a mile west of Scottsville and a quarter of a mile north of the river bank.

During the next three years a number of ordinaries were licensed—Giles Allegre, to keep one on Mechunk; Daniel Scott and John Lewis each, one at the courthouse; William Battersby, opposite the courthouse; John Anthony, in the Glendower section; James Fenly, Isaac Bates and Gideon Marr, in Buckingham; William Morrison, in the Rockfish Valley; Charles Bond, on Briery Creek, a branch of the lower Hardware; Joseph Thompson, in the vicinity of Palmyra; Hugh McGarrough, not far from Afton, and John Hays, probably in the same neighborhood; and William Cabell, at his ferry at Warminster. Daniel Scott was licensed to establish a ferry from the courthouse landing to the opposite side of the river, and William Battersby, one from his land to the mouth of Totier Creek on Daniel Scott's land.

The roads received much attention. At that time they were not so much to be worked, as to be opened and cleared; and permission to this end was readily granted under the restriction, that they should not be conducted through any fenced grounds. John Henderson was summoned to show cause why a road should not be cleared through his land from the Three Notched Road to the Hardware River; that is, from near Milton to the vicinity of Mount Air. John Defoe was made Surveyor of the road from Number Twelve to Number Eighteen—numbers used to designate the distance, probably from the courthouse to certain trees, as mention is subsequently made of the road from the late Secretary's Ford to the Twelve Mile Tree. David Lewis was Surveyor of the road over Capt. Charles Lynch's Ford, or Ferry; this was a road which ran from some point on the Three Notched Road near the University, over the shallows of the Rivanna, a short distance southeast of the Pen Park mansion, and down the west side of the South

West Mountain. Andrew Wallace was Surveyor of the road from the D. S. to Mechum's River Ford—Archibald and Michael Woods, Jr. to assist in clearing it—and William Woods from Mechum's River to Michael Woods's Gap on the Blue Mountains. Benjamin Wheeler was Surveyor from his place into the "Four Chopped Road" to Woods's Gap. William Harris petitioned for a road from his plantation on Green Creek to the South River—that is, the James—on the lower side of Ballenger's Creek; and Robert Rose, Clerk, petitioned for one from his place on Tye River to Leake's, in the neighborhood of William Harris. The hands of Col. Richard Randolph, Rev. Mr. Stith and William Harris, were ordered to clear a road from the Green Mountain road near the head of Hog Creek, to the courthouse Road below Mr. Stith's Quarter. The tithables of the late Secretary at Clear-Mount—which must have been at Blenheim, or in that vicinity—were directed to work on the road from James Taylor's Ford to Martin King's Road, that is, from below Carter's Bridge to Woodridge; and his servants living above the mountains, together with the inhabitants on Biscuit Run, were to keep the road from David Lewis's to the late Secretary's Mill. This mill was on the north fork of Hardware, a short distance above its junction with the south fork. Fry & Lynch were appointed to apply to the Louisa Court, to continue the road over King's Ford on the Rivanna—at Union Mills—from the county line to Louisa C. H. These are a few instances of the care and energy devoted to this important object.

Howard and Daniel were appointed to list the tithables on the south side, and Lynch, Cabell, Hickman and Ballou, those on the north side, of the Fluvanna River. The number of tithables in 1745 was thirteen hundred and ninety-four, in 1746 fourteen hundred and seventy-nine, and in 1747 seventeen hundred and twenty-five. They were taxed twenty pounds of tobacco per poll. Taking Mr. Jefferson's calculations in his Notes on Virginia as a basis, this would make the whole population of the county as it then was, white and black, in 1745 about four thousand two hundred and fifty;

in 1746 four thousand five hundred; and in 1747 five thousand two hundred and seventy-five. According to the Census Reports; the progress of the population of the county within its present limits, has been as follows:

1790—12,585	1830—19,747	1870—25,800
1800—16,439	1840—22,618	1880—26,625
1810—18,268	1850—22,924	1890—27,554
1820—32,618	1860—32,379	1900—28,473

The population of Charlottesville was for the first time taken separately from that of the county in 1870. Its numbers are as follows:

1870—2.838	1880—2,676	1890—5,591	1900—6,449

Eleanor Crawley was sentenced to receive fifteen lashes on her bare back, well laid on, for stealing linen of the value of eleven pence—a little over fifteen cents—and Pearce Reynolds to receive twenty-one, for stealing a handkerchief of the same value. James, a negro of William Cabell, for stealing twelve pence, was burnt in the hand, and given thirty-nine lashes at the whipping post. In a suit James Fenly gained against Samuel Stephens, and Stephens choosing to be whipped rather than be imprisoned, the Sheriff was ordered to administer twenty-one lashes. The grand jury presented George McDaniel for profane swearing—two oaths within two months—and Abraham Childress for failing to clear the road of which he was surveyor. On motion of David Reese, the testimony of John and Stephen Heard, and of Patrick Nowlin, was recorded, certifying that a piece was bit out of Reese's left ear, in a fray with Nowlin. The testimony of Thomas Nunn and his wife Kate was recorded, showing that they had been imported about fourteen years before, and had never received their dues; and subsequently their two children, Mary and Lucretia, were directed to be bound out by the Church wardens of St. Anne's parish.

The Court was mindful to protect its own dignity. For misbehavior in its presence, Martin King was ordered into custody, and bound over for a year, and Martin King, Jr. and James Fenly were placed in the stocks.

HISTORY OF ALBEMARLE 13

The scalps of wolves were reported in large numbers. One hundred and forty pounds of tobacco were allowed for the scalp of an old wolf, and seventy-five for that of a young one, that is, one under six months old. When tobacco ceased to be a circulating medium, twelve and six dollars were given as the premiums. These reports continued with more or less regularity in subsequent years down to 1849; the last on record, when Isaac W. Garth was awarded twelve dollars for killing an old wolf. Jonathan Barksdale, Samuel Jameson, William Ramsey and Ryland Rodes, are names which appear most frequently in this connection. In 1835 Lewis Snow received a dollar and a half for the scalp of a red fox. The Court agitated the removal of these premiums once or twice after 1849, but there is no indication that their offer was ever made.

The foregoing particulars were compiled from the first order book of the County Court, a venerable relic of the past of great interest. Unhappily the records for many years following have been lost.

CHAPTER II.

Albemarle County has somewhat the shape of a lozenge. Its northwestern border follows the crest of the Blue Ridge. Its boundary on the southwest leaves the Ridge a little north of Rockfish Gap, runs a course of south thirty degrees east till it strikes the Rockfish River at the mouth of Green Creek, and then coincides with that river to its junction with the James. The angle at the south instead of coming to a point is irregularly truncated by the James, that river forming its border for about fifteen miles. The southeastern boundary starts from the lower end of Scottsville, and has a course of north thirty degrees east to the western side of the town of Gordonsville; whence that on the northeast runs north seventy-one degrees west till it intersects the top of the Blue Ridge. Its greatest length from north to south is about forty miles, and its greatest breadth about the same distance. It has an area slightly over seven hundred and fifty square miles.

Its surface is greatly diversified. Parallel with the Blue Ridge, the Southwest Mountain traverses its entire extent at an interval of eighteen or twenty miles. This range is continuous, except where it breaks to afford a passage for the Rivanna, Hardware and Rockfish rivers. Its highest point, Peter's Mountain, occurs where it enters the county on the northeast, having an altitude of perhaps fifteen hundred feet. In its course southward it maintains an elevation of ten to twelve hundred feet until it passes the Hardware, when it gradually declines, and exhibits a prominence but little different from the surface of the surrounding country. This mountain is for the most part a single ridge, and has none of the lateral offshoots so characteristic of the Blue Ridge, unless for a short distance on the west side of its northern portion. Here and there occur low depressions in its crown, which supply a natural and convenient way for roads. North of the Rivanna are three of these depressions—the most northerly, the Turkey Sag, so named from Turkey Run, a branch of Priddy's Creek which rises at its western base, the next, Stony Point Gap, opposite the village of that name, and the third, Hammock's or Thurman's Gap. Between the Rivanna and the Hardware there is but one, the Monticello Gap, which separates Monticello from the continuation of the range, called Carter's Mountain. South of the Hardware, the range bears the name of Green Mountain.

In the northwest part of the county, and still more in the southwest, irregular and massive formations raise their heads on high, which from their disorderly appearance pass under the name of the Ragged Mountains. Jutting from the Ridge near the western corner is a huge spur, denominated Buck's Elbow. Across Moorman's River to the north is another lofty spur, the Pasture Fence Mountain, called so without doubt because it contained one of the first enclosures for grazing. It is a peculiar feature of this spur, as it is of the whole Blue Ridge, that in summer it is covered with a luxuriant growth of blue grass; and in former days, large planters commonly owned farms on these mountains for the special purpose of pasturage. Along the eastern foot of the Pasture Fence lies a rich and beautiful valley, which from one of its first settlers is named Brown's Cove, and which is watered by an affluent of Moorman's River, called in early times its north fork, but now known as Doyle's River. Bordering the Cove on the east is a succession of smaller eminences, Pigeon's Top, Fox's Mountain and High Top, while scattered towards the northeast are numerous elevations, some having the appearance of ridges, and some rising as solitary peaks, and bearing the names of Currants, Long, Green, Buck and Piney Mountains.

Just west of where the University now stands is a small range with a higher summit at either end, which was originally called Piney Mountain. The north end has the name of Lewis's Mountain, and the south, Observatory Mountain, from its being the site of the astronomical department of the University. At a short interval southwest of this range, are heaped up for some miles great mountainous masses, rugged and broken, that may well be termed by way of eminence the Ragged Mountains. These heights are skirted on the east by a range which runs with a good degree of continuity to the extreme southwest of the county, called on the north side of the Hardware, Dudley's Mountain, and on the south, Gay's, Fan's and Appleberry's. Running off from the Ragged Mountains in a westerly direction is a range bearing the names of Martin's and Israel's Mountains, indented by Taylor's, Martin's and Israel's Gaps; while south and southeast of Israel's Gap, tower aloft some of the loftiest summits in the county, Castle Rock, High Top, Chalk and Heard's Mountains. Some views of these immense piles are truly grand and magnificent. In the midst of these gigantic heaps, are found reaches of comparatively level country of prime fertility, one lying along the north fork of the Hardware called the North Garden, another on the south fork called the South Garden, and a third, the Rich Cove, separated by a slight elevation from the South Garden on the south. The section north of James River is varied by gently sloping hills, and that east of the South West Mountain stretches away to the east as an extensive plain, and being covered with forest, is known as the Flatwoods.

Besides the James, the county is cut throughout its entire breadth by two streams, and is washed at its southwest corner by a third, all of considerable size. In the summer the volume of water they discharge is much reduced—so much at times, that during a remarkable drought in 1806, James O. Carr, who was then attending school at Milton was able to stop the entire current of the Rivanna with his hand; but being mountain streams, that is having their sources near the foot of the Blue Ridge, or its outlying spurs, they become speedily filled by heavy rains and the melting snows of winter, frequently rush down with the fury of a torrent, and overflow all the low grounds along their banks. The most northerly of these water courses is the Rivanna, which has two forks uniting about four miles north of Charlottesville, and forming the main stream. The north fork is made up near the north line of the county by the union of Swift Run and Lynch's River, both of which rise in Greene County near the Blue Ridge. It flows southeast and south to its junction with the south fork, augmented by Marsh Run, Herring's Run, Priddy's and Foster's Creeks, flowing into its north side, and by Beaverdam, Jacob's Run, and Flat Branch, coming from the south. The south fork is formed by the confluence of Moorman's and Mechum's Rivers, and being fed on its north side by Buck Mountain, Naked, Fishing and Powell's Creeks, and on its south by Ivy Creek, runs eastwardly about five miles to its junction with the north fork. Buck Mountain Creek has a large branch on its west side called Piney Run. Moorman's River rises in the deep ravine between the Blue Ridge and Pasture Fence Mountain, known as Sugar Hollow, and runs a south and then an east course, receiving on its north side Doyle's River, and Rocky and Ward's Creeks. Mechum's River has a greater length, some of its head waters springing beyond the county line in Nelson, and interlocking with branches of the north fork of Rockfish. It has also a more tortuous channel, but its general trend is east of north. It receives on its north side Virgin Spring Branch, Stockton's, Beaver and Spring Creeks, and on its south, Whitesides Creek, Pounding Branch and Broadaxe Creek. The Rivanna proper flows south, turns to the east in its passage through the South West Mountain for about four miles, and then runs southeast to the county line, when passing through Fluvanna County, it empties into the James at Columbia. In its course through Albemarle, it receives Red Bud, Mountain Falls, Carroll and Limestone Creeks on the north, and Meadow, Moore's, Henderson's and Buck Island Creeks on the south.

The Hardware divides into two forks, which join just above its passage through the Southwest Mountain. The north fork also divides not far from Red Hill Station, the south and middle prongs heading near each other on either side of Tom's Mountain, while the north prong rises in the vicinity of Taylor's Gap. Just before reaching the junction it receives on its north side Sowell's Branch. The south fork has its source south of Castle Rock, and northwest of Covesville. It makes its way in different directions among the mountains, but its general course is northeast. Its northern tributaries are Jumping Branch and Black Walnut, and its southern, Rapshin and Eppes Creeks. A well known branch of the latter is Beaverdam, which has recently acquired celebrity from the Soapstone Works successfully operated on its banks. After the union of its forks, the Hardware pursues a southeast course, crosses the country line about three miles north of Scottsville, and empties into the James in Fluvanna County. It is enlarged on its northern side by Murphy's and Turkey Runs, and on its southern by Harris's Creek, formerly known as Little Eppes, and by Cole's Creek, formerly called Hudson's.

The southwestern line of the county is intersected by the head waters of Lynch's, Taylor's, Hickory and Cove Creeks, all branches of Rockfish River. On the east side of Appleberry's Mountain are Ivy, Green and Hog Creeks, debouching into the same stream. Two creeks of moderate size water the southern part of the county, and fall into the James, one at Warren called Ballenger's, and the other about two miles above Scottsville called Totier. Both are fed by a number of branches. Mechunk Creek takes its rise not far from Gordonsville, flows southwest and southeast, and passing out of the county joins the Rivanna opposite Union Mills. The sources of the South Anna are also in Albemarle, located not far from that of Mechunk.

The character of the soil is various. The degrees of its fertility are distinguished by different colors, the richest exhibiting a deep red, and the less fertile a gray. The former prevails at the base of the mountains, and along the banks of the streams. Some parts of the county, especially in the mountainous localities, are stony; the more level lands are free from this incumbrance. The prevalent rocks are quartz and what is colloquially known as mountain granite. A single vein of limestone runs through the county, about four miles east of the Southwest Mountain. In a number of places slate and soapstone occur; both of fine quality. Gold is found in the southwestern corner. The soil and climate of Albemarle are well adapted to all the staple productions of the temperate zone, and are exceedingly favorable to the cultivation of fruit. The ravines and hollows of the mountains which might seem unfitted for the growth of any crop, are found to produce in perfection the Albemarle Pippins, the most highly prized apples in the world.

Most of the names given to the features of Albemarle scenery, belonged to them from the earliest times. In the patents first issued, the mountains and streams were already indicated by names, and they were generally those which they still bear. Who gave them, or why in many cases they were given, must now be reckoned among the things unknown. Sometimes they were suggested by natural circumstances, and sometimes derived from persons who were owners, or occupiers, of the neighboring lands. The latter have undergone more change than others, because with the lapse of years the names of former residents passed out of remembrance and those of their successors were applied in their stead. As settlements were made in different parts of the county at the same time, it has happened that names are frequently repeated.

The Southwest Mountain on which the first lands were entered, was originally called the Chestnut Mountains. It was also spoken of as the Little Mountain. Particular portions had local names, for the most part taken from owners or first settlers, as Peter's, Carter's, Lively's, Sugar Loaf, Monticello. Green Mountain no doubt derived its name from the color of its luxuriant vegetation. The Blue Ridge bore that name from the first planting of the country. The early inhabitants called it also the Blue Ledge, and the Blue Mountain. Sometimes it was designated the Great Mountains, in opposition to the Little Mountain, and occasionally the South Mountain, in opposition to the North Mountain on the west side of the Valley. Buck's Elbow and Pasture Fence—at first Smith's Pasture Fence—Mountain have always been so called. Brown's Gap and Brown's Cove were named from the family that largely settled the land in that region. Turk's Gap was first called Jameson's, and Jarman's bore the name of Woods'—all from families who lived near by. Rockfish Gap has always had that name, acquiring it from the river which rises in part at its base. Pigeon Top was once called Jameson's Mountain, and may have obtained its later name from a roost of that bird. Fox's Mountain tooks its name from a family that lived on it, and High Top from its lofty peak. Currant's and Webb's Mountains were named from persons who possessed the adjoining lands, and Buck Mountain, and the Creek of the same name, from the abundance of deer that roamed the forests. Piney Mountain was first called Poindexter's, from the man who entered the land at its foot. Yellow Mountain at one time went by the name of Epperson's. Castle Rock was so denominated from its huge towering form, Chalk Mountain from the light-colored rocks which face its crest, and Heard's, Appleberry's, Fan's, Gay's, Dudley's, from primitive settlers in their vicinity. In early times the Mountains north of Moorman's River, and south of Mechum's, were called Ragged, from their disordered appearances, and not from the garments of their inhabitants, as has sometimes been suggested.

The Hardware River has always borne that name. Rivanna was in use from the first, according to the fashion then in vogue, of honoring Queen Anne with the names of rivers recently discovered. In the earliest patents and deeds it was more frequently called the north fork of the James, as the James above the Rivanna passed under the name of the South Fork, or more euphuistically, the Fluvanna. In some instances the Rivanna was simply termed the North River, and the Fluvanna the South. The crossing of the Rivanna at the Free Bridge was known at the beginning of the century as Moore's Ford, or Lewis' Ferry, according to the stage of water, and its north fork was sometimes called, down to a quite recent date, the Little River. Red Bud was first named Key's Mill Creek, or Swamp. In early days, swamp seemed to be interchangeable with creek, no doubt from the rubbish of logs and leaves which for ages had obstructed the channels of the smaller streams. Priddy's, Buck Mountain and Rocky Creeks, and Jacob's and Piney Runs, had those designations from the beginning. The names of Meadow and Ivy Creeks obtained from the earliest times. Moorman's River was named from Thomas Moorman, one of the first patentees on its banks, and Mechum's, from a George Mechum, who was an owner of land near its head. The north fork of Mechum's was called Stockton's Creek, and its south fork, now regarded as the main stream, Stockton's Mill Creek, from a numerous family occupying their margins. The middle fork was always termed Virgin Spring Branch. Union Run was first named Mountain Falls Creek; afterwards, from being a favorite feeding place of the wagoners who brought their produce to Milton, it acquired the name of Camping Branch. Carroll's Creek was the original title of that stream. Limestone was first called Plum Tree Branch, then Scales Creek, and finally its present name, from washing the only vein of limestone in the county. Buck Island Creek was so designated from the beginning. It is a mistake to write it Buckeyeland, as if derived from the deer-eyed tree. The name was taken from an island in the Rivanna opposite its mouth, and as in the case of so many objects of natural scenery, was suggested by the great numbers of deer found everywhere in the country. There were two other tributaries of the Rivanna below Milton in early times, though their names are never heard at present, Henderson's and Miller's Branches. Moore's Creek has been so called from the first. The same is true of Biscuit Run; but the names of its branches, Plum Orchard on the east, and Cow Branch of the west, have slipped from the memory of men. A small prong of Moore's above Biscuit Run once had the name of Edge's Creek; it is forgotten now.

There were three Beaverdams in the county, one running into Mechunk, another into Lynch's River, and the third into Eppes Creek. Besides Ivy Creek that passes the depot of that name, there is another which empties into Rockfish. An affluent of Priddy's Creek, and one of Ballenger's, were both called Wolf Trap. Wolf Pit was a branch of Beaver Creek, and a cavity on the west side of South West Mountain had the same name. Piney Mountain was the designation, not only of the present mountain of that name, but also of Lewis's Mountain near the University and of an eminence near Afton. A branch of the lower Rockfish was called Buck Island, besides the stream so named that flows into the Rivanna. A Turkey Run empties into Priddy's Creek, and another of the name enters the Hardware. There were three Round Top Mountains, one of the Buck Mountain region, another not far from Batesville, and another near the University.

Whitehall was an election precinct under the successive names of Glenn's Store, William Maupin's Store, Maupin's Tavern, Miller's Tavern, Shumate's Tavern, till at length the present name was established about 1835. For a long time Batesville went by the name of Oliver's Store. Mechum's Depot was anciently known as Jarman's Mill, and afterwards as Walker's Mill. Ivy Depot was formerly called Woodville. The name of Glendower at first was Scott's Mill, then Dyer's, and then Dawson's. Woodridge was for many years denominated McGehee's Old Field. Besides Stony Point on the Barboursville Road, there was a Stony Point not far from Scottsville. Free Union formerly went by the name of Nixville, and is till so spoken of by the older citizens. Petersburg is the appellation of a hamlet on Priddy's Creek between the Southern Railroad and the Barboursville Road. Cartersburg is a straggling collection of houses on the hill south of Rio Bridge. Brownton and Lemon Hill stand for places not far from Glendower.

As already intimated, the former denizens of the forest were frequently alluded to in the names by which objects were distinguished. When the county was first occupied, game of every kind abounded. Traces of the buffalo still remained. A trail is said to have run up Rockfish River to the Gap of that name. It is also reported that the old Richard Woods road closely followed a buffalo trail. A tract of land belonging to the Webb entry, sold in 1769 to Isaac

Davis, and lying on the north fork of the Rivanna, is described as adjoining Buffalo Meadow. A branch of Buck Mountain Creek was called Elk Run. Deer were exceedingly plentiful. A tradition, which descended from one of the first settlers near the Blue Ridge, states, that by stepping from his door almost any morning, he was able to shoot a deer. From this circumstance it arose that the word Buck so frequently forms part of the names of the county. Lick Run was a branch of Beaverdam in its northern part. Bears were found, not only as they still are in the deep ravines of the Blue Ridge, but also in every neighborhood. Near the Rich Cove were Bear Creek, and Red Bear Hollow. Benjamin Brown devised to his son Bezalell the Bear cornfield. In a deed of 1789, conveying land north of Stony Point, one of the lines passed by "the Bear Spring on the road." As late as 1823, it was stated, that Henry Bruce with two other men, killed on the Blue Ridge twelve fine fat bears in fifteen days. As previously mentioned, an exterminating war was waged from the beginning against wolves. A prong of Green Creek bore the name of Black Fox Branch. Beaver and Beaverdam Creeks were connected with every leading stream of the county. In the first times flocks of turkeys thronged the woods, and every fall and spring wild ducks and geese darkened the rivers. Tradition refers to more than one pigeon roost, where great limbs of trees were broken down by the countless numbers of that bird. Before the construction of dams, fish of the best kinds, shad and herring, ascended the water courses. Dr. William Cabell derived a considerable revenue from his fisheries on James River, and fine shad, taken from the Rivanna, were often seen on the tables of the early inhabitants.

There is no evidence that Indians were resident in the county at the first approach of the white man, though they still passed through on their journeys from one part of the country to another. But memorials of their former occupation were not wanting. Mr. Jefferson mentions having often seen them in his boyhood, and refers in his Notes to a large band visiting the mound containing the remains of their ancestors on the Rivanna low grounds, and there expressing their customary signs of grief. In a description of land on Bremo Creek, in a deed of 1751, is noted a line that ran "up to the head of the branch that the Indian shot John Lawson at." The head stream of Buck Island that flows past Overton, was variously called Indian Creek, Indian Camp Creek, and Camping Branch, and the plantation at its source, once owned by William Short, and sold by him to David Higginbotham, bore the name of Indian Camp. Flint arrowheads, often of superior workmanship, are found in large numbers in many section of the county.

The first division of the county, besides its separation into the two parishes of Fredericksville and St. Anne's, was that made by the bounds of the militia companies. Each of the two regiments embodied in it contained eight companies, and thus there were sixteen of these divisions. The persons selected to perform the duty of Processioning, whilst that method of determining the boundaries of lands was practised, were chosen for these divisions, usually four persons for each. They were referred to by Mr. Jefferson as forming suitable district for stationing common schools, and appear in the records until quite a late period in connection with the appointment of patrolling parties.

For a long time the county seat was the exclusive locality for holding political elections. For electing Overseers of the Poor, there existed in the early part of the century four districts, for the northeast, the voting place was Trice's Tavern below Turkey Sag, and afterwards Stony Point; for the northwest, Fretwell's Store, or Free Union; for the southwest, Everett's Tavern, or the Cross Roads; and for the southeast, Dyer's Store. It was not until the second quarter of the century was considerably advanced that the number of election precincts was increased, and the convenience of the people thus consulted. As late as 1820, Charlottesville was the only post office for the county; subsequent to that date, mail facilities began rapidly to multiply.

In 1846, in accordance with an act of the Legislature, the county was divided into twenty-one School districts. A description of their limits is recorded in the Order Book for that year, page 312. In Deed Book No. Fifty, occurs the record of the boundaries of ten districts for election purposes, which were constituted in pursuance of an act of the Legislature passed in 1852.

The last division was effected by an act of the Legislature, under the requirement of the new Constitution, adopted in July, 1869. By this law, the county was laid off into five Townships, subsequently termed Districts. These were Rivanna, Whitehall, Samuel Miller, Scottsville and Charlottesville. In 1875 another was added, called Ivy, which was enlarged on its northern border in 1889.

Allusion has been made to the great misfortune sustained in the loss of the early records. The gap thus occasioned reaches from 1748 to 1783, a period of thirty-five years, and one intensely interesting in the history of the country at large. The loss was caused by the wanton ravages of the British troops near the close of the Revolutionary War. Many references to this event are met with in the subsequent proceedings of the County Court. In 1794 it recommended John Key, George Divers, Thomas Garth, Thomas W. Lewis, Garland Carr, Thomas Bell, Robert Jonett, W. W. Hening, and Cornelius Schenk as "Commissioners to reinstate such records as had been lost or destroyed." These persons or others were certainly appointed for this purpose, as the Court in one place ordered the transactions of the Commissioners "for reinstating the records destroyed by the enemy," to be recorded. A copy of Gideon Carr's will was proved before them, and directed to be placed on record. On a deed from Thomas Goolsby to Samuel Shelton dated July 1745, the following memorandum was inscribed: "February Court, 1788. This Indenture was produced to the Court, and it appearing from a certificate on the same, that it had been formerly recorded in this Court, the record whereof was destroyed by the British in the year 1781, on motion of Samuel Shelton it was ordered by the Court that it be recorded again, in pursuance of an act of Assembly for that purpose." The act here referred to may be found in Hening XII, 497. It is hard to conceive any conduct in an army more outrageous, more opposed to the true spirit of civilization, and withal more useless in a military point of view, than the destruction of public archives.

Other interruptions of the series however have happened since that time. The order books of the Court are missing from 1785 to 1791. Those for the years 1805 and 1827 are also wanting. It is difficult to account for these losses, except from want of due care in the removal of the books at different times from one office to another.

During the long interval posterior to 1748, two events transpired on which it is desirable to have as much light as possible, the change of location of the Court House, and the Revolutionary War. Materials fortunately exist to furnish some account of both.

The first occurrence was rendered necessary by the partition of the county in 1761. The territory on the south side of James River was cut off to form the county of Buckingham. That part which lay north of the James, and west of the Rockfish from its mouth up to the mouth of Green Creek, and thence west of a line running directly to the house of Thomas Bell, and continuing thence to the Blue Ridge, was constituted the county of Amherst. At the same time there was added to Albemarle that part of Louisa lying west of a line, beginning at the boundary between Albemarle and Louisa on the ridge between Mechunk and Beaverdam Swamp, and running along said ridge till intersected by an east course from the widow Cobb's plantation, and thence a direct course to the Orange line opposite the plantation of Ambrose Coleman. When this arrangement took place, it left the Court House on the extreme southern border, and rendered attendance thereat unnecessarily inconvenient to the people residing in the northern sections of the county.

What proceedings transpired to determine the site of the new Court House, whether it was fixed by the judgment of the County Court, or settled by a popular vote, there remains no means of knowing. Certain it is no more suitable place than the one selected could have been chosen. It occupies almost the exact centre of the county, it lies in the midst of a fertile country, and it is beautiful for situation. Lofty ideas were evidently entertained in relation to its establishment. A thousand acres were purchased from Colonel Richard Randolph, of Henrico, extending north and south from near Cochran's Pond to the south side of Moore's Creek, and east and west from the Chesapeake and Ohio Depot to Preston Heights. The title to this property was vested in Dr. Thomas Walker as Trustee, and he was empowered to sell and convey it to purchasers. The town was planned at the eastern edge of this tract, and consisted of four tiers of squares, each tier running east and west, and containing seven squares, and the four tiers extending from Jefferson Street on the north to South Street on the south. The public square for the courthouse was exterior to the limits of the town. The act of Assembly establishing the town was passed in November 1762. It is therein recited that fifty acres of land contiguous to the courthouse had already been laid off into lots and streets, and as it would be of great advantage to the inhabitants of the county if established a town for the reception of traders, it was so established, to be called and known by the name of Charlottesville. Dictated by the spirit of loyalty then prevalent, the name was given in honor of Princess Charlotte of Mecklenburg Strelitz, who had recently become Queen of England as the wife of King George III.

There being two half-acre lots in each square, the original town contained fifty-six lots. They were not disposed of with great rapidity. At the first sale in September 1763, about a year after the survey of the town, fourteen lots were sold to seven purchasers. Ten more were sold at intervals during the next year. Strange to say, the most of those alienated at first were remote from the courthouse, and lay on Main, Water and South Streets, although it is within the memory of some living since the Square ceased to be the business centre of the town. The next sale took place in October 1765, when twenty-three lots were disposed of, fourteen being purchased at once by Benjamin Brown and David Ross. By this time it may be supposed the courthouse was built, and the prospects of the new settlement being somewhat assured, the spirit of speculation began to operate. In the deed to John Moore of Lot No. Three in 1765, it was stated that the Court of the county was recently held thereon.

The residue of the public land was divided into fifteen parts, designated as outlots. They ranged in size from thirty-three to one hundred and fifty acres. The smallest of them lying north of the town and immediately on the public square, was sold to John Moore in April 1764. On this lot was a spring in the ravine behind Miss Ross' residence, which had already acquired the name of the Prison Spring. The latter part of the same year two others adjoining the town on the south, and containing seventy-three acres, were purchased by Richard Woods. In October 1765, eight more lying to the north, south and west, and aggregating upwards of six hundred acres, were bought by John Moore, Joel Terrell, and Richard and Samuel Woods. The last sale of outlots mentioned occurred in 1791, when the most northerly of them was sold to Dr. George Gilmer. The whole sum realized by the county from the sale of town lots and outlots averaged a pound an acre, amounting to thirty-three hundred and thirty-three dollars.

The improvements made in the town before the Revolution seem to have been few and scattered. One of the earliest was the residence of Joel Terrell, which was built on the corner of Market and Fifth Streets, where the City Hall now stands. Thomas West, a saddler by trade, lived on Main Street, on the square now occupied by the Letermans' Store. Samuel Taliaferro resided on the square to the east, on which afterwards stood the dwelling and store of Colonel Thomas Bell, occupied later by the family of Jesse Scott, and at present the seat of the Post Office. The first home of Dr. George Gilmer was on the south side of Main Street, near the present location of T. T. Norman's Store. John Day, a blacksmith, lived on the southeast corner of

Water and First Streets. Tucker Woodson, Deputy Clerk of the County, who married Elizabeth, daughter of John Moore, had his residence north of town, near the road to Cochran's Mill. A short time before the outbreak of the war, John Jouett built his public house, the Swan Tavern, on the east of the public square, where the house of the late Samuel Leitch now stands. The square on which is now erected the Perley Building, was known in those days as "the Grass Lot," and on a part of it was a house in which a Richard Scott lived, and which when sold during the war was reserved to him for his life. In a house on Lot Twenty-one, now marked by Huyett's Corner, a Mary Murphy lived the latter part of the war. Being afterwards married to Joseph Neilson, they sold it in 1784, and the same year it came into the possession of Robert Draffen, a former merchant of Charlottesville.

As the war of the Revolution drew near, the people of Albemarle were deeply aroused. Their opposition to the obnoxious measures of the British government was prompt and strong. Upon the first mutterings of the storm, an independent company of volunteers was formed, and by spirited resolves they devoted themselves to the public welfare. When the election of officers was entered upon, the choice fell upon Charles Lewis, of North Garden, as Captain, Dr. George Gilmer and John Marks, as Lieutenants, John Harvie, as Ensign, William Simms, William Wood, William T. Lewis, and John Martin, as Sergeants, and Frederick W. Wills, Thomas Martin, Jr., Patrick Napier and David Allen, as Corporals. As soon as the news was received of the removal of the powder by Lord Dunmore, without waiting for a call, eighteen men at once marched to Williamsburg. How long they remained under arms, does not appear. They returned home shortly after, in the midst of the prevailing uncertainty. But their eagerness to sustain "the cause of America," was unabated. In fact so enthusiastic was their warmth, that they were not disposed to listen to counsels which cooler minds deemed prudent. On receiving a message from Captain Hugh Mercer, to the effect that the Speaker and others thought the companies assembled should be dismissed, they were at a loss how to act. It was determined however that the matter should be submitted to the decision of the company. They voted to march again, and on July 11th, 1775, twenty-seven men under Lieutenant George Gilmer proceeded a second time to Williamsburg.

The Convention which met on July 17th of that year, formed sixteen districts in the colony, in which troops should be raised for its defence. In one of these Albemarle was associated with Buckingham, Amherst and East Augusta. The Committee of the district convened on September 8th, 1775, at the house of James Woods in Amherst. There were present from Albemarle, Charles Lewis and George Gilmer, from Amherst, William Cabell and John and Hugh Rose, from Buckingham, John Nicholas, Charles Patterson and John Cabell, and from Augusta, Sampson Matthews, Alexander McClanahan and Samuel McDowell. Thomas Jefferson was the other delegate from Albemarle, but was absent at the Continental Congress, of which he had been appointed a member the previous June. At this meeting it was resolved, that two companies of minutemen should be enlisted in each of the counties of Albemarle, Amherst and Buckingham, and four in that of Augusta, and that these ten companies should constitute a battalion under George Matthews, of Augusta, and afterwards Governor of Georgia, as Colonel, Charles Lewis, of Albemarle, as Lieutenant Colonel, Daniel Gaines, of Amherst, as Major, and Thomas Patterson, of Buckingham, as Commissary. This battalion was raised and went into camp November 11th, 1775, three miles from Rockfish Gap, and continued in training till December 6th. Inquiry fails to find any local tradition of the place of this camp, but it is said that grounds at that distance from the Gap, and admirably fit for military exercises, may be found on the main road between Hebron and Rodes' Churches. Charles Lewis appears as Colonel of a battalion the next year, and was ordered by the Convention in May to North Carolina. He was afterwards Colonel of the Fourteenth Virginia Regiment, and at the time of his death in 1779, Commander of the post at Charlottesville.

Soldiers from Albemarle fought on all the important battle fields of the war, Long Bridge, Trenton, Stony Point, Brandywine, Germantown, Saratoga, Monmouth, Savannah, Charleston, Camden, King's Mountain, Cowpens, Guilford, Eutaw and Yorktown. The most striking event connecting the county with the war, was the location within its bounds of the camp for the Convention Troops, as they were called; that is, the prisoners captured in October 1777, at Burgoyne's surrender. These troops were first sent to Boston, whence they were to be allowed to return to Europe on their parole not to serve again until exchanged; but Congress on account of its unsatisfactory relations with the British authorities, refused to ratify the terms of the Convention, and the next year directed the prisoners to be removed to Charlottesville. Being led by way of Lancaster, Pennsylvania, and Frederick, Maryland, they reached their new quarters about the first of the year 1779, and remained until October 1780. The camp was stationed on the northern bank of Ivy Creek, on what is now the farm of the late George Carr, and the place has ever since borne the name of The Barracks. There remain some interesting reminiscences of this episode of the war, derived from contemporary documents.

The prisoners arrived in the winter, when a spell of extremely bitter weather was prevailing. Such was the lack of preparation for their reception, and such their sufferings, that numerous remonstrances were presented by their officers to the Governor of the State, as well as to Congress. Demands were made for their immediate removal. In this state of affairs Mr. Jefferson wrote at much length to Patrick Henry, the Governor at that time, stating the circumstances, and urging that there was no necessity for a change. The letter, dated March 27th, 1779, is valuable for the interesting facts it preserves. In the course of it he says,

"There could not have been a more unlucky concurrence of circumstances that when these troops first came. The barracks were unfinished for want of laborers, the spell of weather, the worst ever known within the memory of man, no stores of bread laid in, the roads by the weather and the number of wagons soon rendered impassable; and not only the troops themselves were greatly disappointed, but the people of the neighborhood were alarmed at the consequences which a total failure of provisions might produce.

"The barracks occupy the top and brow of a very high hill; you may have been untruly told they were in a bottom. They are free from fog, have four springs which seem to be plentiful, one within twenty yards of the picket, and another within two hundred and fifty; and they propose to sink wells within the picket. Of four thousand people it should be expected according to the ordinary calculations, that one should die every day. Yet in the space of more than three months there have been but four deaths, two infants under three weeks old, and two others by apoplexy. The officers tell me the troops were never so healthy since they were embodied.

"The mills on James River above the falls, open to canoe navigation, are very many. Some of these are of great value as manufacturers. The barracks are surrounded by mills. There are five or six round about Charlottesville. Any two or three of the whole might in the course of the winter manufacture flour sufficient for the year.

"The officers after considerable hardship have procured quarters comfortable and satisfactory to them. In order to do this, they were obliged in many instances to hire houses for a year certain, and at such exorbitant rents as were sufficient to tempt independent owners to go out of them, and shift as they could. These houses in most cases were much out of repair. They have repaired them at considerable expense. One of the general officers has taken a place for two years, advanced the rent for the whole time, and been obliged moreover to erect additional buildings for the accommodation of part of his family, for which there was not room in the house rented. Independent of the brick work, for the carpentry of these additional buildings I know he is to pay fifteen hundred dollars. The same gentleman to my knowledge has paid to one person thirty-six hundred and seventy-dollars for different articles to fix himself commodiously. They have generally laid in their stocks of grain and other provisions. They have purchased cows, sheep, &c., set in to farming, prepared their gardens, and have a prospect of quiet and comfort before them.

"To turn to the soldiers. The environs of the barracks are delightful, the ground cleared, laid off in hundreds of gardens, each enclosed in its separate paling; these are well prepared, and exhibiting a fine appearance. General Riedesel alone laid out upwards of two hundred pounds in garden seeds for the German troops only. Judge what an extent of ground these seeds would cover. There is little doubt that their own gardens will furnish them a great abundance of vegetables through the year. Their poultry, pigeons and other preparations of that kind present to the mind the idea of a company of farmers, rather than a camp of soldiers. In addition to the barracks built for them by the public, and now very comfortable, they have built great numbers for themselves in such messes as fancied each other; and the whole corps, both officers and men, seem now happy and satisfied with their situation."

Besides this narrative of Mr. Jefferson, there is extant an account of the Barracks, and of the condition of affairs in the surrounding country, in the published letters of Major Thomas Anbury, a British officer, and one of the prisoners. These letters were despatched from time to time to his friends in England, and exhibit a detail of his experiences and observations, from Burgoyne's march from Canada, till near the close of the war. They were written in a free, dashing style, and while his descriptions are sprightly and entertaining, they present things in such aspects and colors as would naturally be expected from a British point of view. Most of those written from Albemarle were dated at Jones's Plantation, and the circumstances to which he refers make it evident that the place was that of Orlando Jones, situated north of Glendower, and now bearing the name of Refuge. Respecting matters concerning the prisoners, he writes,

"On our arrival at Charlottesville, no pen can describe the

scene of misery and confusion that ensued; the officers of the first and second brigades were in the town, and our arrival added to their distress. This famous place we had heard so much of, consisted only of a courthouse, one tavern, and about a dozen houses, all of which were crowded with officers; those of our brigade were therefore obliged to ride about the country, and entreat the inhabitants to take us in. As to the men their situation was truly horrible, after the hard shifts they had experienced in their march from the Potomac. They were, instead of comfortable barracks, conducted into a wood, where a few log huts were just begun to be built, the most part not covered over, and all of them full of snow. These they were obliged to clear out and cover over, to secure themselves from the inclemency of the weather as soon as they could, and in the course of two or three days rendered a habitable, but by no means comfortable, retirement. What added greatly to the distress of the men was the want of provisions, as none had as yet arrived for the troops, and for six days they subsisted on the meal of Indian corn made into cakes. The person who had the management of everything, informed us that we were not expected till spring.

"Never was a country so desitute of every comfort. Provisions were not to be purchased for ten days; the officers subsisted upon fat pork and Indian corn made into cakes, not a drop of spirit of any kind; what little there had been, was already consumed by the first and second brigades. Many officers to comfort themselves put red pepper into water to drink by way of cordial. Upon a representation of our situation by Brigadier General Hamilton to Colonel Bland, who commanded the American troops, he promised to make the situation of the men as comfortable as possible, and with all expedition. The officers upon signing a parole might go to Richmond and other adjacent towns, to procure themselves quarters; accordingly a parole was signed, which allowed a circuit of near a hundred miles. After they had drawn lots, as three were to remain in the barracks with the men, or at Charlottesville, the principal part of them set off for Richmond, while many are at plantations twenty or thirty miles from the barracks. On the arrival of the troops at Charlottesville, the officers what with vexation and to keep out the cold, drank rather freely of an abominable liquor called peach brandy, which if drunk to excess, the fumes raise an absolute delirium, and in their cups several were guilty of deeds that would admit of no apology. The inhabitants must have thought us mad, for in the course of three or four days there were no less than six or seven duels fought.

"I am quartered with Major Master and four other officers of our regiment at this plantation, about twenty miles from the barracks. The owner has given up his house and gone to reside at his overseer's, and for the use of his house we pay him two guineas a week. It is situated upon an eminence, commanding a prospect of near thirty miles around it, and the face of the country appears an immense forest, interspersed with various plantations four or five miles distant from each other. Informing the Commissary of provisions where we were quartered, he gave us an order on a Colonel Coles, who resides about four miles distant, to supply us, he being appointed to collect for the use of Congress in this district; who upon application sent us about a month's provision of flour and salt pork for ourselves and servants. Cattle, horses, sheep and hogs followed the cart, to lick the barrels containing the salt meat.

"The house where General Phillips resides is called Blenheim. It was erected shortly after that memorable battle by a Mr. Carter, Secretary of the Colony, and was his favorite seat of residence. It stands on a lofty prominence, commanding a very extensive prospect. Colonel Carter, its present proprietor, possesses a most affluent fortune, and has a variety of seats surpassing Blenheim, which he suffers to go to ruin. When General Phillips took it, it was crowded with negroes, sent to clear a spot of ground a few miles off. The extent of his land is immense, and he has fifteen hundred negroes on his different plantations.

"The Congress must be acquitted of the bad treatment of the prisoners; they were misguided and duped by a Colonel

Harvie, a member from this province. When Virginia was fixed on as a depot for the prisoners, Colonel Harvie proposed to Congress to remove the Convention army to a tract of land belonging to him, about six miles from Charlottesville, about four from the Blue Mountains, and near two hundred from the sea coast; and if Congress approved, he would engage to build barracks and lay in provisions by the ensuing spring. The resolution was passed the latter end of June. Colonel Harvie immediately resorted to Virginia, and set all his negroes, and a number of the inhabitants, to build the barracks and collect provisions; and after having planned everything, he left its completion to the management of his brother, and returned to Congress. His brother not possessing so much activity, and not being perhaps so much interested in the business, did not pay proper attention to it; and this was the cause why the barracks were not finished, and affairs were in such confusion on our arrival. Colonel Harvie supposed all would be ready by Christmas.

"Colonel Bland, who commands the American troops, was formerly a physician at a place called Petersburg on the James River, but at the commencement of the war, as being in some way related to Bland, who wrote a military treatise, he felt a martial spirit arise within him, quitted the Esculapian art, and at his own expense raised a regiment of light horse. As to those troops of his regiment with Washington's army, I cannot say anything; but the two the Colonel has with him here for the purposes of express and attendance, are the most curious figures you ever saw; some like Prince Prettyman with one boot, others without any; some hoseless, with their feet peeping out of their shoes, others with breeches that put decency to the blush; some in short jackets, and some in long coats, but all have the fine dragoon caps, and long swords swung about them; some with holsters, some without, but, gramercy, pistols, they haven't a brace and a half among them; but they are tolerably well mounted, and that is the only thing you can advance in their favor. The Colonel is so fond of his dragoons, that he reviews and maneuvers them every morning, and when he rides out, has two with drawn swords before, and two behind. It is really laughable to see him thus attended by his ragged regiment, which looks, to borrow Shakespeare's idea, as if the gibbets had been robbed to make it up; then the Colonel himself, notwithstanding his martial spirit, has all the grave deportment as if he were going to a consultation. He greatly amused some of us calling to see him not long since. He had just mounted his horse to ride out, and seeing us approach, and wishing to air his french, he called out very pompously to his orderly, *'Donnez moi—donnez moi—eh—mon scabbard!'* "

In May 1779, he wrote,

"A few days ago Madame Riedesel, [who with her husband, Baron Riedesel, was living at Colle, near Simeon] with two of her children had a narrow escape. As she was going to the barracks in her post chaise, when the carriage had passed a wooden bridge—which are of themselves very terrific, being only so many rough logs laid across beams, without any safeguard on either side—an old rotten pine fell directly between the horses and the chaise, but providentially did no other damage than crushing the two fore wheels to pieces, and laming one of the horses.

"I am filled with sorrow at being obliged to relate the death of W—, a relative of Sir Watkin Williams Wynne. He had been drinking peach brandy till he became insane; and riding from Charlòttesville to the barracks, he contrived to escape his companions, and next morning was found dead in a by-place five miles off, being tracked by the foot-prints of his horse in the snow."

From the Barracks, to which he had removed in the early part of 1780, he wrote later,

"The log huts of the men are becoming dangerous from the ravages of insects, that bear the appellation of Sawyers, and are infested with rats of enormous size. The prisoners are deserting in great numbers, especially the Germans, and duels have become very frequent among the German officers."

On November 20th, 1780, he wrote from Winchester,

"About six weeks ago we marched from Charlottesville

barracks, Congress being apprehensive that Cornwallis in overrunning the Carolinas might by forced marches retake the prisoners. The officers mumured greatly at the step, having been given to understand that they were to remain till exchanged. Many had laid out considerable sums to render their huts comfortable, particularly by replacing the wood chimneys with stone, and to promote association, they had erected a coffee house, a theatre, a cold bath, &c. My miserable log hut, not more than sixteen feet square, cost between thirty and forty guineas in erecting. The woods had been cleared away for the space of six miles in circumference around the barracks. It had become a little town, and there being more society, most of the officers had resorted thither. After we quitted the barracks, the inhabitants were near a week in destroying the cats that were left behind; impelled by hunger, they had gone into the woods, and there was reason to suppose they would become extremely wild and ferocious, and would be a great annoyance to their poultry. We crossed the Pignut Ridge, or more properly the Blue Mountains, at Woods's Gap, and though considerably loftier than those we crossed in Connecticut, we did not meet with so many difficulties; in short, you scarcely perceive until you are upon the summit that you are gaining an eminence, much less one that is of such a prodigious height, owing to the judicious manner that the inhabitants have made the road, which by its winding renders the ascent extremely easy. After traveling near a mile through a thick wood before you gain the summit of these mountains, when you reach the top, you are suddenly surprised with an unbounded prospect that strikes you with amazement. At the foot of the mountain runs a beautiful river; beyond it is a very extensive plain, interspersed with a variety of objects to render the scene still more delightful; and about fifty miles distant are the lofty Alleghany mountains, whose tops are buried in the clouds."

As Anbury's work is out of print, it will no doubt prove acceptable to give a few extracts, in which are presented the condition of the country, and the state of society, as viewed by a stranger occupying his peculiar circumstances.

"The plantations are scattered here and there over the land, which is thickly covered with timber. On these there is a dwelling house in the centre, with kitchen, smoke house, and other outhouses detached, and from the various buildings each plantation has the appearance of a small village. At some little distance from the houses are peach and apple orchards, and scattered over the plantations are the negroes' huts, and tobacco barns, which are large and built of wood for the cure of that article. The houses are most of them built of wood, the roof being covered with shingles, and not always lathed and plastered within; only those of the better sort are finished in that manner, and painted on the outside; the chimneys are often of brick, but the generality of them are wood, coated on the inside with clay; the windows of the better sort are glazed, the rest have only wooden shutters.

"All taverns and public houses in Virginia are called Ordinaries, and 'faith, not improperly in general. They consist of a little house placed in a solitary situation in the middle of the woods, and the usual method of describing the roads is, From such an ordinary house to such a one, so many miles. The entertainment you meet with is very poor indeed; you are seldom able to procure any other fare than eggs and bacon with Indian hoe cake, and at many of them not even that. The only liquors are peach brandy and whiskey. They are not remiss however in making pretty exorbitant charges. Before the war, I was told, one might stop at any plantation, meet with the most courteous treatment, and be supplied with everything gratuitously. Gentlemen hearing of a stranger at an ordinary, would at once send a negro with an invitation to his house.

"Most of the planters consign the care of their plantations and negroes to an overseer; even the man whose house we rent has his overseer, though he could with ease superintend it himself; but if they possess a few negroes, they think it beneath their dignity; added to which, they are so abominably lazy. I'll give you a sketch of this man's general way of living. He rises about eight o'clock, drinks what he calls a julep, which is a large glass of rum sweetened with sugar, then walks, or more generally rides, round his plantation, views his stock, inspects his crops, and returns about ten o'clock to breakfast on cold meat or ham, fried hominy, toast and cider; tea and coffee are seldom tasted but by the women. He then saunters about the house, sometimes amusing himself with the little negroes who are playing round the door, or else scraping on a fiddle. About twelve or one he drinks a toddy to create him an appetite for dinner, which he sits down to at two o'clock. After he has dined he generally lies down on the bed, rises about five, then perhaps sips some tea with his wife, but commonly drinks toddy till bed time; during all this time he is neither drunk nor sober, but in a state of stupefaction. This is his usual mode of living which he seldom varies; and he only quits his plantation to attend the Court House on court days, or some horse race or cock fight, at which times he gets so egregiously drunk, that his wife sends a couple of negroes to conduct him safe home.

"Thus the whole management of the plantation is left to the overseer, who as an encouragement to make the most of the crops, gets a certain portion of his wages; but having no interest in the negroes any further than their labor, he drives and whips them about, and works them beyond their strength, sometimes till they expire. He feels no loss in their death, he knows the plantation must be supplied, and his humanity is estimated by his interest, which rises always above freezing point. It is the poor negroes who alone work hard, and I am sorry to say, fare hard. Incredible is the fatigue which the poor wretches undergo, and it is wonderful that nature should be able to support it. There certainly must be something in their constitution as well as their color different from us, that enables them to endure it. They are called up at daybreak, and seldom allowed to swallow a mouthful of hominy or hoecake, but are drawn out into the field immediately, where they continue at hard labor without intermission till noon, when they go to their dinners, and are seldom allowed an hour for that purpose. Their meal consists of hominy and salt, and if their master is a man of humanity, touched by the finer feelings of love and sensibility, he allows them twice a week a little fat, skimmed milk, rusty bacon and salt herring to relish this miserably scanty fare. The man of this plantation in lieu of these, grants his negroes an acre of ground, and all Saturday afternoons, to raise grain and poultry for themselves. After they have dined, they return to labor in the field till dusk in the evening. Here one naturally imagines the daily labor of these poor creatures was over. Not so. They repair to the tobacco houses where each has a task of stripping allotted, which takes up some hours, or else they have such a quantity of Indian corn to husk; and if they neglect it, they are tied up in the morning, and receive a number of lashes from those unfeeling monsters, the overseers, whose masters suffer them to exercise their brutal authority without restraint. Thus by their night task it is late evening before these poor creatures return to their second scanty meal, and the time taken up at it encroaches upon their hours of sleep, which for refreshment of food and sleep together can never be reckoned to exceed eight. When they lay themselves down to rest, their comforts are equally miserable and limited; for they sleep on a bench or on the ground, with an old scanty blanket, which serves them at once for bed and covering. Their clothing is not less wretched, consisting of a shirt and trousers of coarse, thin, hard, hempen stuff in the summer, with an addition of a very coarse woolen jacket, breeches and shoes in winter. But since the war the masters, for they cannot get the clothing as usual, suffer them to go in rags, and many in a state of nudity. The female slaves share labor and repose just in the same manner, except a few who are termed house negroes, and are employed in household drudgery. These poor creatures are all submissive to injuries and insults, and are obliged to be passive. The law directs the negro's arm to be cut off, who raises it against a white person. Notwithstanding this humiliating state and rigid treatment to which they are subject, they are devoid of care, contented and happy, blest with an easy, satisfied disposition. They always carry out a piece of fire, and kindle one near their work, let the weather be ever so hot and sultry.

"There were, and still are, three degrees of rank among the inhabitants, exclusive of the negroes; but I am afraid the advantage of distinction will never exist again in this country, in the same manner it did before the commencement of hostilities. The first class consists of gentlemen of the best families and fortunes, which are more respectable and numerous here than in any other province. For the most part they have had liberal educations, possess a thorough knowledge of the world, with great ease and freedom in their manners and conversation. Many of them keep their carriages, have handsome services of plate, and without exception keep their studs, as well as sets of handsome carriage horses.

" The second class consists of such a strange mixture of character, and of such various descriptions of occupation, being nearly half the inhabitants, that it is difficult to ascertain their exact criterion and leading feature. They are however hospitable, generous and friendly; but for a want of a proper knowledge of the world, and a good education, as well as from their continual intercourse with their slaves, over whom they are accustomed to tryannize, with all their good qualities they are rude, ferocious and haughty, much addicted to gaming and dissipation, particularly horse racing and cock fighting. In short, they form a most unaccountable combination of qualities, directly opposite and contradictory, many having them strangely blended with the best and worst of principles, many possessing elegant accomplishments and savage brutality; and notwithstanding all this inconsistency of character, numbers are valuable members of the community, and very few deficient intellectual faculties.

"The third class, which in general composes the greatest part of mankind are fewer in Virginia in proportion to the inhabitants, than perhaps in any other country of the world; yet even those who are rude, illiberal and noisy, with a turbulent disposition, are generous, kind and hospitable. We are induced to imagine there is something peculiar in the climate of Virginia, that should render all classes of so hospitable a disposition. The lower people possess that impertinent curiosity so disagreeable to strangers, but in no degree equal to the inhabitants of New England. They are averse to labor, much addicted to liquor, and when intoxicated extremely savage and revengful. Their amusements are the same with those of the middling sort, with the addition of boxing matches.

"We found many gentlemen of the province very liberal and hospitable to the British officers, among whom I may mention Messrs. Randolph, of Tuckahoe, Goode, of Chesterfield, and Cary, of Warwick. In conversing with the prisoners, they carefully refrain from politics. So warm and bigotted was the prevailing spirit, that those who exercised such courtesy incurred much criticism and censure. Some went so far on this account as to threaten to burn Colonel Randolph's mills. He however treated the matter with an easy independence, offering on the other hand five hundred pounds for the discovery of those who made the threat.

"There is a place called Kentucky, whose soil is extremely fruitful, and where an abundance of buffaloes is found. The emigration of the people to that place is amazing, seeking thereby to escape the tyranny and oppressions of the Congress, and its upstart dependents.

"In this neighborhood I visited Colonel Walker, a member of Congress, and found his home a hospitable house, but unpleasant, because the family chiefly conversed on politics, though with moderation. His father is a man of strong understanding, though considerably above eighty years of age. He freely declared his opinions of what America would be a hundred years hence, and said the people would reverence the resolution of their fathers, and impress the same feeling on their children, so that they would adopt the same measures to secure their freedom, which had been used by their brave ancestors."

As can be seen by every intelligent reader, some of the information Anbury received from others was erroneous, or misunderstood, many of his observations were no doubt hastily formed, and all related to a country, and people, suffering under the hardships of war, and were tinctured by the prejudices and mortification of a vanquished enemy. Still his account is full of interest to those now living, inasmuch as it exhibits the views of a young man of cleverness and education, and especially of one who spent nearly two years of that memorable era on the soil of the county, and among the men who were then conductors of its affairs. Copies of his Travels, as his book was called, are now rarely to be found.

Not long before the removal of the prisoners, an unhappy tragedy occurred at the Barracks, James Garland, Jr., an officer of the guards, was killed by Lawrence Mansfield while on duty as a sentinel. According to all traditions connected with the case, it was a justifiable homicide. It was owing to a refusal to halt and give the countersign. The motive of Garland is differently explained. One account represents him as designing to test the competence and fidelity of the guard. Another version has it, that he was indulging a spirit of frolic. With a number of companions he had been invited to an entertainment in the neighborhood. As they mounted their horses, he announced that he would have a little fun with the sentry. He preceded the others, and approaching the station was hailed. He continued to ride on heedless of the warning. The sentinel raised his gun, and intended, as he said afterwards, to fire above the offender; but just as the gun was discharged, Garland's horse reared, and the ball struck the rider's head with fatal effect. His remains were buried on his farm some miles west of Batesville, and but a few years ago his grave was pointed out near the cabin of a negro, who in the changes of the times had become the owner of the place. The will of the unfortunate man is on record, and from the serious spirit with which it is pervaded, one would judge that the first account more probably indicates the reason of his conduct.

The Tarleton Raid upon Charlottesville took place in June,

1781. With two hundred and fifty horse, the British commander was passing Louisa C. H. at a rapid rate, when they were seen by John Jouett, who at the time was a temporary sojourner at the place. Suspecting their object, he leaped on his horse, and being familiar with the roads he took the shortest cuts, and soon left the enemy behind. He obtained a considerable advantage in addition by the detention Tarleton underwent at Castle Hill, where he stopped for breakfast, and for the capture of several members of the Legislature who were visiting Dr. Walker. Meeting an acquaintance near Milton, he despatched him to Monticello to warn Mr. Jefferson, who was then Governor of the State, while he pushed on to give the alarm at Charlottesville. By this means the Legislature which had just convened at that place, was notified in time to adjourn, and make a precipitate retreat to Staunton. After a short interval Tarleton and his troop entered the town. Though disappointed in their main object, they remained a part of two days, and it is said destroyed a thousand firelocks, four hundred barrels of powder, together with a considerable quantity of clothing and tobacco. The most important as well as most useless waste they committed, was the destruction of the public records already mentioned —a great contrast to the orders given the officer detailed to Monticello, to allow nothing on the premises to be injured. It is stated that Captain John Martin, a son-in-law of old David Lewis, was stationed in the town with two hundred men. Had they been seasonably apprised of the real state of the case, they might have lain in ambush in the gorge below Monticello, and sent the enemy on their return more quickly than they came. But the suddenness of the alarm, the uncertainty respecting the numbers approaching, and the widespread terror of Tarleton's name, probably led Captain Martin to think that the most prudent course was to withdraw from the scene.

While at Charlottesville, Tarleton made his headquarters at the Farm, the residence of Nicholas Lewis. The story is told, that in living on the enemy, the British soldiers speedily made way with a fine flock of ducks belonging to Mrs. Lewis, at the same time for some reason laying no hands on its veteran leader. When after Tarleton's departure she was informed of her loss, she promptly ordered a servant to take the forlorn drake, and riding after the Colonel to present it to him with her compliments. Appreciating the courteous irony of the fact, the Colonel bade the servant present his mistress in return his profoundest thanks. It is also related, that Mrs. Lewis was not as bitter in her feelings towards the invaders of her country as the other members of her family, and that the arm chair in which Tarleton sat while an inmate of her house was ever after cherished as an object of special veneration.

As the buildings of Charlottesville were not numerous at that period, it is a question of some interest where the Legislature held its sessions. It is rather singular that no authentic tradition in regard to it has been handed down. It has been claimed, that they convened in the tavern which stood on the corner of Market and Fifth Streets, where the City Hall now stands. The same claim has been made respecting the old Swan Tavern. The house, which is situated in the rear of the late Thomas Wood's, and which is said to have been removed from the public square in front of the court house as a cottage of the Eagle Tavern, has also been pointed out as the building; but it is not likely that the Eagle Tavern was built as early as the Revolutionary War. The strong probability is that the courthouse was the place of their meeting. It may have been this circumstance that brought Tarleton's vengeance on its contents; and for nearly fifty years subsequent to that date, it afforded accommodation to almost all the public assemblies of the town, both civil and ecclesiastical.

The anecdote is recounted by the historians of Augusta County in regard to Patrick Henry flying with breathless haste, when a rumor of Tarleton's approach created a panic in Staunton. The same story is told, with the scene laid in Albemarle, and a sturdy Scotch Irish matron of the Blue Ridge section as the great man's devoted admirer. The orator with two companions in their flight to Staunton, alighted at a house near the Ridge to procure the means of refreshing their weary frames after their hard ride. The mother of the household, while superintending a supply for their wants, learned that they were members of the Legislature, and were escaping from the dreaded Tarleton. She eyed them with evident contempt, and at length declared her firm belief, that if Patrick Henry had been there, he never would have quailed before the foe. "Why, madam," said one of his friends, laughing, "there is the man himself!" The announcement received no credit, till the silence of the distinguished fugitive brought about a reluctant assent. The looks of the woman betrayed her utter amazement, and she no doubt thought that things were indeed fast rushing to ruin, when the idol of her trust had so wofully failed.

It seems that the owners of land in Albemarle, whose sympathies ran on the British side during the Revolution. Under the law confiscating the property of such persons to the State, six inquisitions were held in the year 1779 before Peter Marks, the public escheator. One of these referred to eight hundred acres of John Lidderdale on Buck Mountain Creek, and was held on the premises; another to Lot Twenty-Two in Charlottesville, on which the former Presbyterian Church stands, and which belonged to Robert Bain; another to seven and a half acres adjoining Charlottesville on the east, belonging to Donald Scott & Co., the property afterwards owned by Judge Dabney Carr, and later the home of Ira Garrett; both of these inquisitions were held in Charlottesville. Another referred to more than three thousand acres on Ivy Creek, and fifty-two negroes, the property of Francis Jerdone, including the Farmington estate, and was held at the house of his steward, James Garland, Jr.; another to two hundred acres on the south fork of Hardware, and the last to four hundred and fifty acres on James River, both tracts belonging to Henderson, McCaul & Co., the inquisition on the former being held on the premises, and that on the latter at the house of Charles Irving. In all these cases the juries rendered a verdict of condemnation. Robert Bain however appears to have made his peace with the State, as in 1781 the

Legislature by a special act restored his estate, or made compensation for whatever part had been sold, on condition of his taking the oath of allegiance. Francis Jerdone too must in some way have made proper amends in the public eye, as he himself sold the same property to George Divers in 1785. It may be interesting to mention the names of the jury which sat in Charlottesville: James Kerr, foreman, James Marks, Thomas Garth, Bennett Henderson, Charles Lilburn Lewis, Benjamin Dod Wheeler, Richard Woods, Charles Statham, John Key, Benajah Gentry, Isham Lewis, William Grayson and Jacob Oglesby. In this connection it may be stated, that in August 1785 a deed from Thomas Meriwether, heir-at-law of Captain David Meriwether, to Chiles Terrell was ordered to be recorded, and a note was entered at the same time, that the same deed had been presented at November Court 1777, but its record had been refused, because of the suspicion that Mr. Terrell had not taken the oath of allegiance. In all ages, such differences of opinion have occurred in the trying ordeals of warm political strife.

CHAPTER III

A weather-beaten stone lies near the centre of Maplewood Cemetery in Charlottesville, inscribed with the name of Letitia Shelby, and the statement that she departed this life on September 7th, 1777. This Cemetery was not laid out until 1831. Previous to that time families of the town were generally in the habit of interring their dead in their own lots. A public graveyard however is said to have existed on the road to Cochran's Mill, about where the residence of Drury Wood now stands, and from this place this stone was removed after Maplewood was established. It is declared by descendants of the Shelby family, that this Letitia was the wife of General Evan Shelby, and mother of General Isaac Shelby, the first Governor of Kentucky. A curious inquiry arises how she came to be in Charlottesville, or in Almarle County, at the time of her death.

Evan Shelby was an immigrant from Wales, and at first settled in Maryland, near Hagerstown. There his son Isaac was born in 1750. In the year 1771 father and son were both in southwestern Virginia, in the neighborhood of Bristol; and there the home of Evan Shelby continued to be during his life. It is natural to suppose that his wife, whose maiden name was Letitia Cox, accompanied them to their new home in the West. Whether she was visiting friends in Albemarle, or was passing through on a journey, at the period of her last sickness, it is perhaps impossible now to ascertain. But the plain, well preserved inscription on her tombstone leaves no doubt that this vicinity was the place of her death. A tradition in the Floyd family states, that about 1680 a Nathaniel Davis, who was also a native of Wales, married a child of Nicketti, a daughter of the Indian Chief, Opechancanough, the brother of Powhatan. Robert Davis was a son of these parents, and an ancestor of Jefferson Davis, President of the Confederacy; and a granddaughter of Robert

Davis was the wife of Evan Shelby. Probability is lent to this account by the fact, that Robert Davis had a son named Samuel, who would thus be the uncle of Letitia Shelby; and Samuel Davis was the owner of several tracts of land in Albemarle, on the north fork of the Rockfish, on Green Creek, and on both sides of Moore's Creek, adjoining the Carter lands. At the time of her death, Mrs. Shelby may have been visiting the family of this man.

General George Rogers Clark, the famous conqueror of the North West Territory, first saw the light in Albemarle. His grandfather, Jonathan Clark, of King and Queen County, joined with Hickman, Graves and Smith, as already mentioned, in patenting more than three thousand acres of land on the north side of the Rivanna, opposite the Free Bridge. In the division of this land, the upper portion fell to Clark; and in a house situated a short distance from the present residence of Captain C. M. McMurdo, John Clark, the son of Jonathan, lived, and George Rogers was born. The wife of John Clark, and mother of George, was Ann Rogers, a sister of Giles, George and Byrd Rogers, all of whom possessed land in Albemarle, in the Buck Mountain region. The birth of George Rogers Clark occurred in 1752, and when he was about five years of age his father removed to Caroline, where a kinsman had devised to him a handsome estate. It is not known that in his active and eventful life, the General was ever again in the county of his birth but once. In the fall of 1777 he travelled from Kentucky to Richmond, to procure means for setting on foot the expedition to Illinois, which he had already conceived, and which he carried out the next year. His route lay through Cumberland Gap, and the Holston country. He came down the Valley, and crossed the Blue Ridge at Rockfish Gap, or one of the gaps just above. He states in his diary that he spent the night at a Mr. Black's, who was beyond question James Black, a son of the old Presbyterian minister, who kept a tavern on the place afterwards owned by Alexander Garrett, and his son, Dr. Bolling Garrett. On his way to Richmond next day he passed through Charlottesville, where he tarried long enough to purchase a pair of shoes. During this visit to Richmond he became acquainted with Mr. Jefferson, and deeply impressed him with his vigorous and heroic qualities. In a letter Jefferson wrote to Judge Innes, of Kentucky, in 1791, he says, "Will it not be possible for you to bring General Clark forward? I know the greatness of his mind, and am the more mortified at the cause which obscures it. Had not this unhappily taken place, there was nothing he might not have hoped; could it be surmounted, his lost ground might yet be recovered. No man alive rated him higher than I did, and would again, were he to become again what I knew him. We are made to hope he is engaged in writing the account of his expedition north of Ohio. They will be valuable morsels of history, and will justify to the world those who have told them how great he was."

William Clark, who was associated with Meriwether Lewis in his exploring tour across the Rocky Mountains, was a brother of George, but he was born in Caroline in 1770.

Albemarle was the place of residence of Doctor Thomas Walker, one of the most remarkable men of his day. With his expeditions to southwest Virginia were connected some interesting and romantic facts of personal history. In the course of these travels he made the acquaintance of William Inglis, who married a Draper, planted the first white settlement west of the Alleghanies at Draper's Meadows, near the present site of Blacksburg, and subsequently spent his remaining days at Inglis's Ferry on New River. Inglis and his family suffered the common penalty of those who led the way in peopling the wilderness. His wife and children were captured by the Indians, his wife marvellously escaped the same year, but his son Thomas was retained among them for a period of thirteen years. Being in the plastic season of childhood, the latter became so thoroughly inured to the habits of Indian life, that it was difficult to break their power; in fact, it was never wholly broken. However, when his father penetrated the remote forests of Ohio to effect his ransom, he seemed to feel the promptings of natural affection, and returned with him to the old home. After being taught his native language, and the rudiments of learning, he was sent to Castle Hill, and placed under Doctor Walker's care. Here he continued for three or four years, and made considerable progress in the elementary branches of education. But here he was also brought under a spell, which softened him far more than all the endearments of parental love, and all the mollifying influence of letters. He fell in love with a young woman of the neighborhood named Eleanor Grills. A John Grills in 1745 and subsequent years, became the owner by patent and purchase of more than two thousand acres of land in the county, part of it lying on Moore's Creek, where he built a mill, and where one has continued ever since, on the present site of Hartman's Mill. He was also the original purchaser of Lot Eighteen in the new county seat, the western half of the square on which Lipscomb's stable stands. Although he seems to have sold his possessions in Albemarle about the time Thomas Inglis came to the county, it is likely he continued to reside here or in *Louisa*, and that Eleanor was his daughter. At all events young Inglis, when he returned to his father's house in 1772, was bound to her by promise of marriage. He was a Lieutenant in Colonel Christian's regiment in the battle of Point Pleasant in 1774; and the next year, crowned with the laurels of successful warfare, he returned to Albemarle, and secured the hand of his bride. He first settled on *Wolf Creek* of New River; but unable to repress the roving disposition contracted during his sojourn among the Indians, he soon removed to Burke's Garden, where in an incursion of the savages he nearly lost his wife, then to Knoxville, and finally to Natchez in Mississippi, where at length he closed his wanderings with the close of his life.

Another incident of personal history may be noted, illustrating the progress of the early settlements, and the fortunes of individuals. As previously stated, a Dennis Doyle patented in 1741 eight hundred acres of land on the north fork of Moorman's River, and from him the stream acquired its name. In 1749 Doyle conveyed to William Battersby, the law-

HISTORY OF ALBEMARLE 53

yer, a tract of four hundred acres on Biscuit Run, another of four hundred in North Garden, and another of eight hundred on Totier Creek. He appears to have been a man of means, and to have been still living in the county in 1760; as in that year was born within its limits John Doyle, who was in all probability a son of Dennis. At the age of eighteen, John accompanied the march of General George Rogers Clark into the North West Territory. Returning to Albemarle, he joined the army, and served to the close of the Revolutionary War. The year after the surrender at Yorktown, he was a private in Colonel Crawford's disastrous expedition against the Ohio Indians, but fortunately got back to the settlements in safety. In 1786 he went to Kentucky near Maysville, was a friend of Simon Kenton, and for three years occupied the post of captain of scouts on the Ohio River. He was in service with General Harmar in 1790, and under Scott with General Wayne in 1794. He then settled in what is now Lewis County, Kentucky, where he discharged the duties of a magistrate for more than twenty years. But his active and adventurous life was not yet ended. In 1813 he enlisted again under General Shelby, and took part in the battle of the Thames. He survived until May 1847, having nearly completed his eighty-seventh year, and blest with the vigorous exercise of his powers to the end. In all his long life he was seldom sick, and in all his exposure to peril he was never wounded.

The depreciation in the paper money of the country at the close of the Revolution, was apparent in the enormous prices paid for land. One hundred acres in the southern part of the county, not far from Heard's Mountain, sold for five thousand pounds, fifty acres on Buck Mountain Creek for four thousand, and a hundred and eighty-eight acres on Moorman's River for six thousand. Samuel Dedman sold to James Lewis ten acres on the Ragged Mountains beyond the University, for ten thousand pounds, while Samuel Muse sold to Andrew Monroe, a brother of the President, two hundred and seven acres at the head of Mechum's River for twenty thousand, the same tract which two years before, also in war times, brought eight hundred and thirty, and which sixteen years before, with two hundred acres in addition, brought only thirty-five. At the same time John Curd sold to John Coles two hundred acres for fifty pounds "hard money," and Matthew Mills, of Guilford County, North Carolina, sold to William Leigh five hundred and seventy-five acres, not far east of the Miller School, for two hundred pounds sterling. All these sales took place in the latter part of 1781. The story is told by tradition, that George Divers rode from Philadelphia to Albemarle, and broke down five horses in the ride, to purchase Farmington with paper money, and that the purchase had scarcely been consummated when the money became worthless; but as this transfer did not occur till 1785, the story may admit of some doubt.

A large part of the business of the County Court immediately after the Revolution consisted in certifying to bills for supplies furnished the Army and the Barracks prisoners, to the value of articles taken for public use, and to pensions for soldiers disabled in the service. The location of the prison camp in the county proved a great pecuniary benefit to the inhabitants. From a long distance in the surrounding country they carried thither, and to the different places where the officers lodged, quantities of corn, flour, meal, beef, pork and wood. In the prostration of business, and the consequent hard times occasioned by the state of hostilities, the demand for these commodities afforded a convenient market, of which most other parts of the country were destitute. It is said that Colonel William Cabell mainly paid for the fine Oak Hill estate in Nelson with the various kinds of produce furnished the Barracks, the land having been confiscated because the former owners were alien enemies. Colonel John Coles was allowed three hundred pounds for horses taken by Baron Steuben. Hastings Marks received remuneration for horses and wagons employed in the service. Joseph Morton was allowed five pounds, six shillings, and eight pence for his gun, "taken for the militia in 1781," and Edmund Woody was recompensed for his, "taken during the late invasion." Captain John Martin was awarded an allowance for conducting the Convention troops, that is, the Barracks prisoners, to Frederick, Maryland. The detachments of the army mentioned as having been supplied in this vicinity, were Baron Steuben's Command, Colonel Armand's Legion, and Captain Walker's Company. John Burton and Richard Marshall were assigned pensions at the rate of forty dollars a year. For the purpose of establishing proper lines of inheritance, it was certified that Charles Goolsby, corporal, and James and John Goolsby, privates, died in the service, Charles and James having been taken prisoners at Germantown, and that William Hardin was killed at Ninety Six, and John Gillaspy, of the Ninth Virginia, at Germantown.

The statute guaranteeing religious freedom having been enacted, the law which required all marriages to be solemnized by ministers of the established Church was abolished, and the courts were authorized to license ministers of all denominations to perform that ceremony. In accordance with this provision, William Irvin, Presbyterian, was licensed to celebrate the rite in 1784, and Matthew Maury, Episcopalian, and William Woods, Benjamin Burgher and Martin Dawson, Baptists, the next year. The first Methodist minister mentioned as receiving such a license, was Athanasius Thomas, who lived near the present site of Crozet. This occurred in 1793, and was followed in 1797 by the licensing of William Calhoun, Presbyterian, and John Gibson, Methodist. John Shepherd, Methodist, was licensed in 1798.

The migratory spirit which characterized the early settlers, was rapidly developed at this period. Removals to other parts of the country had begun some years before the Revolution. The direction taken at first was towards the South. A numerous body of emigrants from Albemarle settled in North Carolina. After the war many emigrated to Georgia; but a far greater number hastened to fix their abodes on the fertile lands of the West, especially the blue grass region of Kentucky. For a time the practice was prevalent on the part of those expecting to change their domicile, of applying to the County Court for a formal recommendation of character, and certificates were given, declaring them to be honest men and good citizens. Among those who were thus commended to the people of Georgia, were James Marks, one of the magistrates, Abraham Eades, William Sandridge, Christopher Clark, Bennett Henderson, and William and Samuel Sorrow. James Marks was not long after followed by his brother, Colonel John Marks, who removed during his incumbency in the office of sheriff. An act of the Legislature was passed in November 1788, which recited that no sale of lands in Albemarle County for delinquent taxes for the years 1786 and 1787, was legally possible, because John Marks, Sheriff of said county, removing some time within those years to Georgia, and which therefore authorized William Clark, one of his deputies, to make such sales.

The increasing business of the colonies, the desire to develop their resources, and perhaps the threatening aspect of their relations with the mother country, led to early efforts to manufacture iron in this county. Three men from Baltimore, Nathaniel Giles, John Lee Webster, and John Wilkinson, bought land for this purpose in the latter part of 1768. Giles and Webster disappear after the first purchase. The next year Wilkinson was joined by John Old, from Lancaster County, Pennsylvania, and they made further purchases along the Hardware in the vicinity of North Garden and the Cove. In 1771 the Albemarle Furnace Company was formed, with a capital of two thousand pounds, the following gentlemen being stockholders, James Buchanan to the amount of three hundred pounds, Dr. William Cabell of two hundred, Colonel William Cabell of two hundred, Joseph Cabell of one hundred, Edward Carter of three hundred, Allen Howard of two hundred, Thomas Jefferson of one hundred, Nicholas Lewis of one hundred, John Scott of one hundred, John Walker of one hundred, and Dr. Thomas Walker of three hundred. Larger areas of mineral land were purchased on the lower Hardware, and among the Ragged Mountains. As far as can be ascertained, three furnaces were built, one about a mile below Carter's Bridge, giving to a colonial church erected near by the name of the Forge Church, another where the old Lynchburg Road crosses the north fork of Hardware, long known as Old's Forge, and the third on the south fork of Hardware below the Falls, and south of Garland's Store. The last still remains in a tolerable state of preservation, though covered with a thick growth of bushes and small trees. Local traditions yet linger, that ore was excavated near North Garden and the Cove during the Revolutionary War. Mr. Jefferson states in his Notes, that among the iron mines worked in Virginia at the time of their composition, was "Old's, on the north side of James River in Albemarle." The enterprise however appears not to have been successful. Colonel Old soon became a farmer, instead of an iron-master. A suit instituted in the County Court under the style of Cabell v. Wilkinson to wind up the affairs of the Company, was determined in 1796, and Andrew Hart and Samuel Dyer as Commissioners made sale of all the lands, Nicholas Cabell becoming the purchaser. Of all the mines opened by Wilkinson and Old, the only one now remaining is that known as the Betsy Martin Mine in Cook's Mountain, near North Garden; and though its ore seems rich and plentiful, it has not been worked for a number of years, because of some foreign ingredient which impairs its utility.

In 1789, and the years succeeding, an eager ambition was manifested to build up towns in the county. At the first mentioned date an act of the Legislature was passed, vesting one hundred acres of the land of Bennett Henderson at a place on the Rivanna called the Shallows, in Wilson C. Nicholas, Francis Walker, Edward Carter, Charles L. Lewis, William Clark, Howell Lewis and Edward Moore, to be laid out as a town, and sold in half acre lots, and to be called Milton. More than twenty lots were sold in the next ten years. The first disposed of was bought by Christian Wertenbaker, and among others who became lot holders were Joel Shiflett, Edward Butler, Richard Price, James and John Key, William Clark, Jacob Oglesby, George Bruce, and Joseph J. Monroe. The village was soon in a thriving state, rapidly growing, and transacting a prosperous business. Up to the war of 1812 it was the chief commercial centre of the county. Except in time of freshets, it was the head of navigation on the Rivanna, and became the shipping port of perhaps three-fourths of the county, and of a large section of the Valley. some who have but recently been gathered to their fathers, could remember the long lines of wagons that formerly passed over Swift Run and Brown's Gaps, and crossed the South West Mountain at Hammock's (Thurman's) Gap, bringing their loads of grain, flour and tobacco to the warehouses of the newly erected town. The brook on the north side of the river, which at first bore the romantic name of Mountain Falls Creek, became at this time Camping Branch, from the multitude of wagoners who camped with their teams along its banks. Milton was the seat of a public Tobacco Warehouse, called Henderson's, long after the Henderson family had removed to Kentucky, and regularly equipped with a corps of inspectors; for many years William D. Fitch, Jacob Oglesby, John Fagg and Richard Gambell discharged the functions pertaining to that office. A large merchant mill was also erected by the Hendersons. A number of firms conducted the trade of the place, and in some cases laid the foundation of large fortunes; among these were Fleming and McClanahan, Henderson and Conard, Peyton and Price, Divers, Rives & Co., Brown, Rives & Co., Martin Dawson, William and Julius Clarkson, David Higginbotham & Co. Its business gradually declined as Charlottesville grew; and when the town of Scottsville was established, and the site of the University fixed near the county seat, its prestige was completely broken, and it quietly subsided into the straggling hamlet which now crowns the river hill.

About the same time Warren was projected by Wilson C. Nicholas on James River, at the mouth of Ballenger's Creek. A few lots were sold and a few houses built. An extensive mill and distillery were erected and carried on for some years by Samuel Shelton & Co. A large stone tavern was built by Jacob Kinney, afterwards of Staunton, rented for some time, and finally sold to William Brown, under whose management it made a prominent figure in its day. At this village was located another Tobacco Warehouse called Nicholas's, which in the early part of the century shipped about as many hogsheads as Henderson's. The first inspectors were Clifton Garland, Abraham Eades, Samuel Childress, Robert Moorman and John T. Holman. Beyond these enterprises Warren never made much progress.

At the beginning of the century plans were outlined for four other towns, of which even the memory has perished from among men. One was North Milton, laid out by Thomas Mann Randolph on the north side of the Rivanna, opposite Milton. It was established by the Legislature and placed in the hands of trustees. Those appointed to that office were Francis Walker, William D. Meriwether, Edward Moore, James Barbour, William Bache, George Divers, Hore Brouse Trist, Edward Garland and David Higginbotham. It appears the only lot ever sold was Lot numbered Eight, and that was conveyed to John Watson in 1802. Still another Tobacco Warehouse was established here, and for a short period conducted under the same inspection that had the oversight of the warehouse at Milton. But the place was over shadowed by its neighbor across the river, and from all indications, never had more than a name.

The other three attempts were private speculations. Traveller's Grove, a name suggestive of refreshment and repose, was planned by Colonel John Everett at the junction of what are now known as the Lynchburg and the Taylor's Gap Roads. Four lots formally numbered, but apparently unmarked by improvements of any kind, were sold to a Paul Apple, and subsequently underwent two other transfers, There their history terminates. Not long after Colonel Everett disposed of the environs of the new town, and removed to Cabell County. He was succeeded in the possession of Travellers' Grove by James Kinsloving, Jr., in whose time the name was changed to Pleasant Grove. In later years the place was purchased by the Methodist churches of the adjacent circuit for a parsonage, and though held now by other hands, it still goes in the neighborhood by that name.

Another of these mushroom creations was New York, or as it was colloquially spoken of, Little York. It was established by James Hays at the foot of the Blue Ridge, a few hundred yards north of the present road to Staunton. At the time it was laid out, the road passed along its main street. Like Charlottesville it was divided into lots and out lots. Its first inhabitants were for the most part Germans from Pennsylvania, Greegors, Spieces, Hallers, Landcrafts. Its manufactories were a smith's shop, and a tanyard. It was once the seat of a postoffice, and had a meeting house. More than that, it had a place on the map of Virginia, published in 1824. At present no sign of buildings or streets can be seen, its very ruins have disappeared, and its site is a fertile field, on which a late proprietor raised the most abundant crop of corn he has ever gathered.

In some respects the most remarkable of these temporary municipalities was Morgantown, a place well known, but not by that name. It was a pretentious city on paper, laid off into at least two hundred and fifteen lots, and wood lots, as they were called. It was situated on the main road to Staunton, about a mile west of Ivy Depot. It was planned by a man named Gideon Morgan, and sold by lottery at the rate of fifty dollars a ticket. The special attraction was Lot One Hundred and Seventy-six, on which were built a large brick house and stable, and this attraction had such power that tickets were purchased by persons, not only in Albemarle, but also from the surrounding counties, Frederick, Shenandoah, Rockingham, Bath, Augusta, Rockbridge, Fluvanna, and even places as far distant as Henrico and Lancaster Counties and the city of Philadelphia. Among those who participated in the affair from Augusta were Chesley Kinney, Jacob Swoope, and Judge John Coalter; while from Albemarle were Peter and John Carr, Isaac Miller, Elijah Garth, Richard Gambell, Andrew Kean and Thomas Wells. The fortunate ticket-holder was George Anderson, of Greenbrier, who sold that place to Benjamin Hardin. In 1821 Anderson's widow, then living in Montgomery County, conveyed her interest in the property to Hardin, to whom Morgan also sold his remaining land. Hardin kept tavern there down to 1827 or 1828, when the place was sold for his debts. As the

HISTORY OF ALBEMARLE 61

other lots lay on bare fields and forest, running up on Turner's Mountain, the owners most probably quietly abandoned them, and allowed them to lapse into Hardin's possession. In 1814 however, Micajah Woods and wife conveyed to Hardin two lots which had been drawn by William Davenport, and Taylor and Newbold, of Philadelphia, conveyed to him another in 1821. Altogether one hundred and nine persons bought tickets, and Morgan derived from his few acres, nearly twice as much as the county derived from the thousand acres on which Charlottesville was built. Intoxicated by his success, he went over to Rockingham and projected another town not far from Port Republic, which he named New Haven; but in this attempt he was not so highly prospered. The last heard of him, he was living in Rowan County, Tennessee. As will be readily conjectured, the brick house and stable are still standing, the same that Francis McGee occupied as a tavern after Hardin, and that was recently the residence of his daughter, Mrs. John J. Woods.

It may be stated, that another town, called Barterbrook, spread itself in the books more extensively that it did on the face of the earth. Its situation was on the west side of the road to Stony Point, just where it crosses the branch opposite Liberty Church. It contained a tanyard, and a tavern, which had the significant appellation of Pinch'em-slyly. A muster ground was contiguous, where the militia company of the district assembled to perform their exercises, and where Joshua Key, a neighboring magistrate, was often called upon to exert his authority for the preservation of the peace. According to the records, Lot Fifty-Six in Barterbrook was conveyed by William Smith to Thomas Travillian's heirs, by said heirs to Pleasant Sandridge, of Green County, Kentucky, and by Sandridge to Dr. John Gilmer, when it became a part of the Edgemont estate. A successor in some sort, possessing the same name, and consisting principally of a tanyard conducted by Bernard Carr, was at a later date located in the western part of the county, near Mechum's River.

An impression has prevailed with many, that the celebrated statesman and philosopher, Benjamin Franklin, was once a visitor in Albemarle, and while here purchased a plantation for his son. There is no real ground for this impression. A Benjamin Franklin did live in the county in its early days, but he came from Orange, and died in 1751. Franklin, the philosopher, appears never to have been South but once, and then he visited Charleston, South Carolina, making the journey most probably by sea. He had but one son who lived beyond maturity, who in all likelihood was never South at all, and who was the Tory Governor of New Jersey, obliged at the close of the Revolution to leave the country, *never to return. But it is true, that a grandson of Franklin came to Albemarle, bought property, and resided on it for a short time.* His name was William Bache, the son of Franklin's daughter, and already referred to as one of the trustees of North Milton. In 1799 he purchased from James Key the farm which is known as the old Craven place, and which still bears the name of Franklin. The letters of the Jefferson household about that period make mention of him and his family. His son, Benjamin Franklin Bache, a distinguished surgeon in the navy, is stated in Appleton's Biographical Cyclopedia to have been born at Monticello, February 7th, 1801. William Bache was evidently not blest with prosperity. He incurred many debts, was harassed with many lawsuits, gave a deed of trust to Thomas Mann Randolph to sell Franklin, and left the State. He was a physician by profession. His place was sold to Richard Sampson in 1804. Dr. Bache while here also invested in Charlottesville lots. He bought from David Ross Lots Forty-three and Forty-four, now cut in two by the track of the Chesapeake & Ohio Railroad; and in 1837 they were conveyed to Dr. Hardin Massie by his son B. F. Bache and his wife, and his daughter Sarah and her husband, who was Rev. Dr. Charles Hodge, the eminent professor of theology at Princeton.

John Blair, Justice of the United States Supreme Court, was also a land owner in Albemarle. The old Michael Woods place, Mountain Plains, at the mouth of Woods' Gap, descended to his son William, who sold it to Thomas Adams, a resident, the latter part of his life, of the Pasture District of Augusta County. Adams, who died in 1788, made title by his will to this and other parcels of land he had bought in the neighborhood, amounting to nearly a thousand acres, to Judge Blair—"To my honorable friend, John Blair, Esq., Chancellor, all the lands he purchased of me in Albemarle County, known by the name of Mountain Plains, and for which he has long since honestly paid me." From him the place has since acquired the name of Blair Park. Judge Blair devised it to his two daughters, through whom it came to their two sons, James P. Henderson and John Blair Peachy. In 1831 Peachy sold his interest to Henderson. After Henderson's death in 1835, it passed into other hands.

A still more distinguished jurist Chief Justice Marshall, owned land in the county. He was once the proprietor of the old D. S. place. He purchased it from Henry Williams about 1809, and in 1813 sold it to Micajah Woods.

When the county was organized, settlements had been making within its present limits for twelve or thirteen years. Williamsburg being the capital of the colony, and its public business being transacted there, it was natural that the first great roads of the country should tend in that direction. There can be little doubt that one was opened along the river James; but that leading to the more northerly portions of the county was the Three Notched Road. It was cleared on the track it pursues now, following the watershed between the South Anna and the James, and still bearing the name, though the tree marks on account of which it was given, have not been seen for three or four generations. It passed the county line where it does now, not far from Boyd's Tavern, came up the Rivanna on its north side, crossed at the Secretary's Ford, coincided with what is now the main street of Charlottesville, crossed Ivy Creek and Mechum's River where it does still, but at that point diverged from what is the main road at present. It continued in a straight line to Woods's (now Jarman's) Gap, instead of striking the Ridge at Rockfish Gap. At the mouth of Woods's Gap was the first settlement in that part of the county, and for some years the chief route of travel passed over it to the Valley. In the diary of Thomas Lewis, dated 1746, in which he describes his journey to Orange County to join the surveyors appointed to run the line between the Northern Neck and the rest of the colony, he states that he crossed from Augusta at Woods's Gap, and stopped with Michael Woods both on his departure and return. As late as near the close of the Revolution, when Rockfish Gap was much used, the prisoners of the Convention army, as already mentioned, were upon their removal taken across the Blue Ridge at Woods's Gap. The Three Notched Road was the dividing line between the parishes of Fredericksville and St. Anne's.

Another road had the name of Three Notched in early times. It was the cross road leading from Carter's Bridge to Red Hill Depot. At present it is only a neighborhood road; but when the county seat had its location near Scottsville, being the highway thither for all the northwestern part of the county, it occupied a place of the highest importance, and was one of the earliest cleared. As settlements extended up the James in what is now Nelson and Amherst, they necessarily sought a way of access to the Court House. Accordingly one of the first roads established was that which was known as the River Road, crossing the Rockfish at Limestone Ford near Howardsville, and at another higher up, called Jopling's, and proceeding along the brow of the river hills to the county seat. In 1746 Rev. Robert Rose petitioned the County Court for the clearing of a road from Tye River to the Rockfish.

The Buck Mountain Road was made in the primitive times. This name was applied to the series of roads which start from Rockfish Gap, bend along the base of the Ridge and Buck's Elbow to Whitehall, pass over Moorman's River at Millington to Free Union and Earlysville, cross the north fork of the Rivanna at the Burnt Mills, and enter the Barboursville road at Stony Point. It still follows the route on which it was originally laid out, except slight deviations for short distances to avoid some obstacle, or gain an easier grade. The Barboursville Road ran from the beginning, much as it does now. Just after the county was formed, old David Lewis was appointed Surveyor of the road from his place south of Birdwood to Lynch's Ferry; at that point the Rivanna was crossed, instead of as now at the Free Bridge. This road must have intersected the Three Notched Road some distance west of Charlottesville, the existence of which at that time had not entered the thought even of the most sagacious. The hill at the old Craven place was in all probability always ascended where it is at present. The trade of the upper part of the county, and the adjacent sections of the Valley, being then carried on with Fredericksburg, both of these roads, and the Three Notched also as far as the fork at Everettsville, possessed in common the name of the Fredericksburg Road. In early times the Barboursville Road was continued down the river on the eastern side, and probably ran across the hills through the Haxall and Pantops plantations to the Secretary's Ford.

When the Court House was removed to Charlottesville, it of course became the centre of the county roads. The Three Notched Road running along its main street, afforded a ready approach both from the east and the west. One outlet towards the north was the Barboursville Road by way of Lynch's Ferry. Another was by a connection with the Buck Mountain Road at David Wood's old place, which was at or near the late Colonel Bowcock's. The road making this connection left the west end of High Street, ran to the foot of the hill near Clay Michie's thence over Meadow Creek past the place recently occupied by the late Harvey Hull, and crossed the south fork of the Rivanna at Carr's old Ford on the Carrsbrook plantation. Shortly after another road was opened, branching from the last mentioned north of Harvey Hull's, crossing the south fork at the Broad Mossing Ford, and continuing thence to the Burnt Mills.

The Barracks Road was laid out during the Revolution, and has since been a noted way, though much deflected from its original course. It started from the west end of High

Street, ran on the highland south of the ravine crossed by the present road near Kellytown—remains of the stone fences lining it can still be seen—passed over Preston Heights not far from the mansions of Colonel Preston and General Rosser, forking on the summit with the road to Carr's Ford, continued past Colonel Duke's and the colored settlement of Georgetown to the ridge east of Ivy Creek, and descended to the ford of the creek past the old Ivy Creek Church. Near town a branch of the Barracks road diverged from its main course on the eastern slope of Preston Heights, and ran into the Three Notched Road not far from the Junction Depot. The present location of the Barracks Road immediately west of Charlottesville, was fixed about the beginning of the Century. A contention respecting it arose between Isaac Miller and John Carr, Clerk of the District Court, owners of the adjoining lands. After several views and reports on the subject, it was finally determined according to the ideas of Mr. Miller, whose residence at the time was either at Rose Valley, or near the house of Mason Gordon.

The course of the road from Brown's Gap was always much the same as it is at present. It crossed Mechum's River where it does now, coming down through the rocky defile on the west, then known as the Narrow Passage. After passing Ivy Creek, it turned southeast and ran over to the Three Notched Road—passing on its way the old D. S. Church— entering it where the old Terrell, or Lewis's, Ordinary stood, the location of which must have been near the site of Jesse Lewis's blacksmith shop. This road went for many years by the name of Rodes's Road. The connecting link between Rodes's and the Barracks Roads was made about the first of the century. It wound round Still House Mountain as it does now, and then turned south and continued down the ravine in which the outflow of what was called Wade's Spring was carried off. The old Poor House was built immediately upon this road. Somewhat later Governor Nicholas petitioned for the opening of a road from the D. S. Church to his plantation on the Rivanna, the present Carrsbrook; but it does not appear that anything was ever done.

The road that crosses the river at Rea's Ford was opened about the close of the last century. The people of the northwest section of the county petitioned for a more convenient way to the courthouse. It was decided after several views, that a new road should start at Fretwell's Store, which was at or near Free Union, cross at Rea's Ford, fall into the Barracks Road and continue with it to the top of the ridge east of Ivy Creek, and there branching off run to Meadow Creek at the plantation of Bernard Carter, now F. B. Moran's, uniting at that point with the road from Carr's Ford.

The Richard Woods, or Dick Woods Road, as it was frequently called, is one of the oldest in the county. It diverged from the Three Notched just west of the D. S., passed Richard Woods' place at the mouth of Taylor's Gap to the little stream called Pounding Branch, crossed Mechum's river at the Miller School, and continued thence to Rockfish Gap. The place of Pounding Branch went in the early times by the name of little D. S. A tanyard was located there, which at first was named Simpson's, and afterwards Grayson's. Near that point the road turned off, described in old deeds as the road to Amherst C. H., the same that still exists, running through Batesville, and passing the Nelson line at what was formerly known as Harlow's Tavern on Lynch's Creek. Tradition relates that Richard Woods, in laying out the road called by his name, followed a well marked buffalo trail, and the fact of its being established by those sagacious engineers of nature accounts for the gentle grade for which it has been distinguished. It seems that the road through Israel's Gap was not made till near the end of the last century. At that time William Woods, Surveyor Billy, was summoned by the County Court to show cause why he had not opened a road from Israel's Gap into the Richard Woods Road.

The outlets from Charlottesville to the south were mainly the same as now exist. The road by which the people of Fluvanna south of the Rivanna reached the county seat, passed through Monticello Gap, then called the Thoroughfare, crossed Moore's Creek where it does now, and joined the Three Notched Road at the top of the hill near the junction of the macadamized road recently made by Mr. Brennan; for the Three Notched Road then came from the Secretary's Ford along the ridge now followed by the Chesapeake and Ohio Railroad, over the low grounds of Moore's Creek in the rear of the Woolen Mills. The road from town to Carter's Bridge has always pursued the present route. It was formerly described as passing by a place, well known as the Colt's Pasture, and the Plum Orchard Branch of Biscuit Run. The Old Lynchburg Road has been in use from the first settlement of the town. It commenced at the foot of Vinegar Hill, reached the top of the Ridge beyond the Dry Bridge, and continued along its crest to the branch at its south end, then called Haggard's, and afterwards West's Saw Mill Run. It crossed the north fork of Hardware where it does at present, the place long known as Old's Forge, turned around the end of Gay's Mountain past Andrew Hart's Store, and crossing Jumping Branch and the south fork of Hardware as at present, united with the present Lynchburg Road at the end of Persimmon Mountain a short distance north of Covesville. Near town it went by the name of Haggard's Road, from a Nathaniel Haggard, who owned the land on its course from the end of the Ridge to Moore's Creek. In those days the present Lynchburg Road was a mere farm road bearing the name of Wheeler's, from a family who lived at the head of Moore's Creek.

The Secretary's Road has frequent mention in the early records. It set out from Carter's Mill on the north fork of Hardware, shortly above its union with the south fork, ran on the north side of that river to Woodridge, and thence pursued the watershed between it and the Rivanna to Bremo on the James. From its lower terminus it was sometimes called the Bremo, corrupted to Brimmer, Road. Near Woodridge the Martin King Road branched from it, crossing the Rivanna at Union Mills, and thence proceeding to Louisa. The road which passes over the Green Mountain west of Porter's Precinct was established at an early date. For many years it was known as the Irish Road, as far as can be ascertained from a man name James Ireland, who was a patentee of land in that neighborhood.

The first turnpike in the county was built in 1806. It crossed the Blue Ridge at Brown's Gap, descended Brown's Cove, and joined the Three Notched Road at Mechum's Depot. It was made and owned by William Jarman and Brightberry Brown. It received a formal acceptance by inspectors appointed by the County Court, though the tolls were taken by the owners. In 1819 Jarman's share was sold by James Jarman to Ira Harris; and in 1867 the title as individual property was relinquished, and it lapsed into an ordinary road of the county. It was known as Brown's Turnpike.

About 1830, a few years before and after, a number of turnpikes were undertaken. The first was the Staunton and James River, having a charter of incorporation, and extending from the place first named to Scottsville. It crossed the Ridge at Rockfish Gap, and ran through Batesville and Israel's Gap, following for the most part the course of old roads. As far back as 1790 a lottery was authorized by the Legislature, to be managed by Francis Walker, William Clark, Nicholas Lewis, John Breckinridge, George Divers, William D. Meriwether, Charles Irving and Isaac Davis, to raise not exceeding four hundred pounds for the purpose of cutting a road from Rockfish Gap to Nicholas's and Scott's Landings; what was accomplished in pursuance of this act is not known. The Staunton and James River Turnpike was for a number of years the route of heavy transportation, passing from the Valley to connect with the James River and Kanawha Canal. Later, when plank roads became the fashion of the day, it was converted into a Plank Road Company. Under its auspices some alterations were made in the grades, particularly avoiding the hills between Kidd's Mill and North Garden, and between Hart's and Garland's Stores, and an inconsiderable portion near Hughes's Shop was covered with plank; but the coming of the railroads, and the temporary nature of the construction, destroyed the public interest in its maintenance. The building and support of good roads over which the produce of the farm is to be hauled, and rapid and comfortable transit to be enjoyed, constitute a lesson the people have yet to learn. The Staunton and James River Turnpike was abandoned in 1867, and taken back by the county as a common road.

The next was the Blue Ridge and Rivanna River Turnpike, which ran from Meriwether's Bridge on the Rivanna to the Turnpike last mentioned at Brooksville. Its construction occasioned the laying out of the straight road from the Woolen Mills to the east end of Market Street. Not many years before, Mrs. Mary Lewis, of the Farm, petitioned for a more convenient approach from her residence to Charlottesville, as previously her only way lay directly south to the Three Notched Road. Opie Norris was the Secretary and Treasurer of this Turnpike, and advertised for bids for its construction. Its route west of town mainly coincided with the Three Notched Road to Mechum's River, and generally with the old road from that point to its termination. Toll gates were erected and for some years its business was regularly transacted. The first gate west of town was immediately opposite the large oak tree on Jesse Lewis's place, under which General Washington is said once to have lunched, and which was blown down by a violent storm in September 1896; its keeper was Patrick Quinn. In 1857 the road was purchased by the county for fifteen hundred dollars, John Wood, Jr. being appointed to receive the purchase money for distribution among the stockholders. When this Turnpike was first projected, an urgent petition was presented to the Legislature for the establishment of a similar one from Meriwether's Bridge to Boyd's Tavern, but nothing further was ever effected.

About the same time the present Lynchburg Road was opened. The Legislature passed an act, granting permission to the counties of Amherst, Nelson and Albemarle, to co-operate in the construction of a road from Lynchburg to Charlottesville, each county to make the road within its own bounds. Amherst declined to engage in the work, but at the request of the Albemarle Court reconsidered its action, and decided to join forces with the other counties. John Pryor surveyed the route, and William Garland made the roadbed in Albemarle. Advantage was taken of country roads already existing, but the line was then first run by way of the old Suddarth Mill, and the Cross Roads, and on the old Wheeler Road down Moore's Creek, instead of the east side of Dudley's Mountain.

The Harrisonburg and Charlottesville Turnpike was laid out shortly after. Col. T. J. Randolph, Alexander Garrett and Achilles Broadhead, Surveyor of the county, were appointed to determine its course, Dr. Gilly M. Lewis recording his protest against its construction. It crossed the Blue Ridge at Swift Run Gap, entered the county at Nortonsville, fell into the Buck Mountain Road west of Earlysville, ran from Colonel Bowcock's to Rio Mills, ascended the hill south of the river by the present easy grade, and continued by way of Rio Station and Cochran's Mill to town.

Many efforts were put forth about the same time to build a turnpike from Scottsville to Rock Spring in Nelson, and thence to the head waters of Rockfish River, but the project was never consummated.

The first bridges, built within the present county, were undoubtedly those over the main Hardware at Carter's Bridge, and over its north fork, just above its junction with the south fork. That river was the largest stream between the old Court House and the greater part of the northern section of the county; and the north fork, besides being crossed by one of the great highways to the county seat, was passed by many to reach Carter's Mill, one of the first erected in the newly-settled country. Owing to the loss of the records, no account exists of the original building of these bridges; but when rebuilt towards the close of the last century, it is recited that there had been one—and in all likelihood more than one—before, at each of those places. Both have since been often renewed, not so much because of use and decay as because of the freshets, which from time to time have swept down from the mountains with terrible violence.

A great flood in James River and its branches occurred in 1771, so remarkable for its enormous and wide-spread destruction as to become the special occasion of action by the

Legislature that year; and in an application Mr. Jefferson made for a writ of *ad quod damnum* in order to erect his mill at Shadwell in 1795, he states that the former one had been carried off by the flood of 1771. It is presumable the Hardware bridges met the same fate. Certainly Carter's Bridge was rebuilt in the years 1795, 1800, 1812, 1859, and 1876. Inasmuch as these improvements are one of the chief signs of civilization, and are so indispensable to the convenience and prosperity of communities, experience teaches us that it is true economy to build them substantially, and put them beyond the reach of all contingencies, in the first instance. In such cases it is better to spend more once, than less often.

The first bridge over Moore's Creek was erected in 1798, and it would seem its location was on the old Lynchburg Road. In 1801 another was built over the same stream, apparently on the Monticello Road. As far as appears, there was no structure of the kind near Meriwether's Mill, now Hartman's, till 1848.

The same Legislature which established the town of Charlottesville, passed an act authorizing any person to erect a bridge over the Rivanna near that town, and as a remuneration allowing him to take tolls, the reason assigned being that the river was often rendered impassable by freshets; but no one availed himself of the permission. For many years the passage of the stream was made either at the Secretary's Ford, or near the Free Bridge by what was known according to the amount of water as Moore's Ford, or Lewis's Ferry. It was not until 1801 that the County Court took the matter in hand. Then they passed an order that George Divers, Thomas M. Randolph, John Watson, Nimrod Bramham, Joshua Key and Achilles Douglass should let the erection of a bridge at the latter point, the cost not to exceed two thousand dollars. Against this action Thomas Garth entered his protest. Since that time it has been rebuilt in 1831, 1846, 1865 and 1870. It stood safe in the flood of 1877, but the causeway on the west side with its stone retaining walls was washed away, and the wooden approach on trestles which still remains, was then constructed.

A bridge was built at the Woolen Mills in 1825 by William H. Meriwether. Being on the line of the Three Notched Road, the main thoroughfare through the county, it was at once a great convenience and a desirable means of safety. Some four or five years before in the month of May, a wagon and six horses belonging to a Mr. Collins, of Augusta County, in attempting to cross the river at the Secretary's Ford on their return from Richmond, were swept down and lost, the driver making his escape with the greatest difficulty. It was most likely in consequence of this disaster, and the constant threatening of others, that Col. T. J. Randolph soon after sought the establishment of a ferry at that point. Meriwether's Bridge obviated such perils, and proved a signal benefit to the community for something like twenty years. In 1843 the County Court was compelled to make some provision by reason of the Free Bridge having been destroyed, and deliberated whether to rebuild, or purchase the Meriwether Bridge. They adopted the former alternative. In the course of a year or two Meriwether sold his bridge to Thomas Farish, and shortly after it was swept away by a flood.

The bridge over the south fork of the Rivanna near Rio Mills was first erected in 1836. Those Mills had a few years before been built by William H. Meriwether, and in 1833 the Harrisonburg Turnpike had been located to cross the river at that place. These were beyond question the constraining reasons for the erection of the bridge. Previously the stream had been passed from time immemorial at two fords near by, one called Carr's Ford, and the other the Island Ford. Rio Bridge has been built twice since, in 1860 and 1865. The latter year G. F. Thompson and M. S. Gleason obtained the contract for replacing it for nineteen hundred dollars, and the Free Bridge also for twenty-six hundred and sixty.

The first bridge across the Rockfish at Howardsville seems to have been erected in 1839. Prior to that time the river had been crossed at the neighboring fords.

CHAPTER IV.

The County Court continued to supervise the affairs, and guard the interests, committed to its trust. In 1783 James Stowers for stealing a horse from Joseph Chapman was examined and sent on to Richmond, where at that time all felonies were tried. John Mullins, son of William, was acquitted of burglary, but sent on for stealing leather from the tan vats of John Watson, of Hightop. Crimes of every class perpetrated by negroes, were entirely under the jurisdiction of this Court. Sam, a slave of James Kerr, for attempting to assault a daughter of David Humphreys, was punished with thirty-nine lashes; the same day however he was cleared of stealing fifty pounds in specie from his master's desk. Ben, a slave of Charles Rodes, was burnt in the hand for poisoning James, a slave of Thomas Smith, under pretence of giving him medicine.

Not only did it punish evil doers, but it interposed in behalf of the weak and oppressed. Daniel Dunavan, a servant of James Lewis, probably a redemptioner, made complaint that his master furnished him with insufficient food and raiment. It promptly required security that suitable provision should be made in future. George Bruce, the jailor, charged Richard Woods with compelling his boy Tom, an orphan child, to wear a collar; it at once ordered the degrading appendage to be removed. It especially exercised a judicious care over apprentices, protecting them from improper treatment, yet refusing to lend an ear to groundless representations. Samuel Burch was summoned to show cause why his apprentice, Abraham Gaulding, should not be discharged from his service, and William D. Hunt why Fielding and William Starke should not have their bonds cancelled. When James Robinson sought to obtain the release of his sons Matthew and Moses as apprentices of Bartlett Dedman, it decided there was no just reason for interference in the case. In like manner, Newberry, son of Thomas Stockton, was continued under the charge of his master, Nathaniel Landcraft.

The Court likewise vindicated its own dignity, and strictly quelled the bold spirit of insubordination that sometimes displayed itself. Martin Marshall for profane swearing in open court was fined five shillings, and William Thurmond for the same offence committed twice was fined and placed under bonds. Daniel Thacker was bound over for making an affray, and breaking the peace in the presence of the court. A fine of eight dollars was imposed on William Alcock for refusing in open court to serve as a juror.

The first instance of capital punishment that appears in the records, occurred at the beginning of the century. Aaron, a slave of Hugh Rice Morris, for breaking into the store of Philip Moore, and stealing seven sides of leather, was condemned to be hanged on the second Friday of February, 1801. Though this punishment seems severe, yet forcibly entering any building on the curtilage, especially at night, was always viewed with jealous sternness. Aaron too was an old offender, having been previously convicted and punished for breaking into the lumber room of Andrew Hart. In this case he had the advantage of being defended, the Court appointing James Brooks as his counsel.

An event of pathetic and tragical interest happened sometime in 1802 or 1803; and it is specially remarkable, as it furnished the only case in which a white man has ever been judicially hanged in the history of the county. James Hopkins was the son of Dr. Arthur Hopkins, who was one of the earliest and largest landholders in Albemarle. He was a man of fine education and considerable wealth. Making choice of his father's profession, he travelled abroad and studied medicine in the University of Edinburgh. On his return to this country, he settled in what is now Nelson County under the shadow of Sugar Loaf Mountain, where for many years he was occupied with an extensive practice. He was possessed not only of great learning, but also of great piety. He had an only child, a daughter, who was married to a Captain Richard Pollard. One evening while the doctor was kneeling in the act of conducting family worship, he was shot through the window of the room, and died in the course of an hour. After a careful measurement of tracks made in the snow by the shoes of the guilty person, a man named Lewis McWane was arrested for the crime, examined by the Amherst County Court, and sent on for trial in the District Court of Charlottesville. In due time he was convicted and executed at that place. On the scaffold he denied having performed the deed. He avowed that he had been employed by Pollard to commit the murder, and had approached the window of the house for that purpose, but when he saw the old man kneeling in prayer, his heart failed him, and he returned to Pollard a short distance off, and declared he could not perpetrate the act; that Pollard, after forcing him to exchange shoes, went to the window and shot his father-in-law with his own hand; and that his motive in desiring his death was to prevent him from making a will, having in some way formed the impression that he was to be excluded from all interest and control in the estate. On the ground of this statement Pollard was arrested and tried, but in the absence of all other testimony was acquitted; yet the belief was widely prevalent that McWane's declaration was true. Pollard lived to a great age, but never by word or act in the slightest degree betrayed his guilt. His purpose, if he had formed it, was in vain. Dr. Hopkins had already made his will. He provided for the gradual emancipation of his slaves, and devised his estate to his daughter, and his grandson, Dr. Arthur Pollard, requiring the name of the latter to be changed to Hopkins, which was duly effected by the County Court of Amherst.

About this time Dr. John T. Gilmer was placed under bonds for an alleged offence in inoculating for smallpox. Legislation on this subject had been enacted in Virginia. Rules had been prescribed for its regulation, and the superintendence of it committed to the County Courts. The milder and safer mode of preventing the disease by vaccination had not yet been fully developed. The interest of Dr. Gilmer in the matter was so great, that he had established a hospital for the special treatment of those who sought exemption from the dreaded malady. The immediate cause of his being summoned before the Court was the occurrence of a fatal case, after the operation had been performed. A panic ensued, and complaint was made against the philanthropic leech. The sympathies of the Court, as well as of all enlightened men, must have been exerted in his favor; for he was required to give bond only for three months "for his good behavior, especially in not alarming the neighborhood in which his hospital is established, unless he first obtain the consent of the citizens." The doctor's residence—and presumptively, his hospital—was at Edgemont, on the Barboursville Road.

An interesting point of law came before the Court in the early part of the century. Mrs. Elizabeth Henderson, widow of Bennett Henderson, on whose land the town of Milton was laid out, sued out a writ of dower against those who had purchased lots within its limits. The decision was that the widow was barred by the Act of Assembly authorizing the establishment of the town, vesting its lands in trustees, and giving them power to sell. The case was appealed to the District Court. What its decision was, cannot be known, as its records have disappeared; but it can hardly be supposed the lower court was not sustained. Mrs. Henderson's counsel was George Poindexter, who was a Louisa man, settled for a time in Milton, removed to Mississippi while it was a Territory, became successively Judge, Aide to Jackson at the battle of New Orleans, Representative in Congress, Governor, United States Senator, and died in 1853.

President Monroe was one of the magistrates of the county, as Mr. Jefferson also was. When Jefferson was appointed cannot be definitely known, as no record of the event exists. From his prominence, even while a student of law, it may be conjectured he received the appointment shortly after his attaining his majority, in 1764 or 1765. It does not appear that he ever sat upon the bench. The only official act he ever performed as Justice of the Peace apparent in the records, was taking the acknowledgment of Mrs. Elizabeth Eppes in 1777 to a deed of her husband and herself, conveying three thousand acres of land on Green Mountain to John Coles; this acknowledgment, and the memorial of respect entered in the minutes of the court at his death, are the only indications the records show, that he ever was a magistrate. The truth is, that until his Presidential term expired, he was comparatively speaking rarely at home. The same thing is largely true of Mr. Monroe. He was frequently absent on public business. But when at home he often attended court. The latter half of 1799, just before he became Governor of the State, he sat upon the bench regularly every month.

A feeling of regret may naturally be indulged, that the old County Court system has passed away. It was a peculiar feature in the history of Virginia from a very early period, and in many respects a most valuable institution. It is hard to conceive how justice could be administered in a less burdensome form. In large measure the rights of the people were secured, and their convenience promoted, absolutely free of expense. It possessed a high degree of dignity, and was regarded by the community with sentiments of veneration and respect. Its members for the most part occupied the most reputable standing in society. They generally fulfilled the requirement of the law, that they should be "able, honest and discreet." Their wealth placed them above temptations to corruption and rapacity, their integrity inspired general confidence, while their honorable character and gentlemanlike bearing presented an example worthy of imitation, and were not without effect in imparting a chivalrous tone, and disseminating habits of politeness, among the public at large. And it may be affirmed with truth, that their cheap administration did not produce cheap results. Their work was usually well done. They spared no pains in promoting the peace of their neighborhoods. If business was sometimes delayed by the presence of private claims, perhaps on the whole it amounted to no more than the interruptions necessarily incident to all human affairs. Their official duties were often performed with no little trouble. Men of the highest position would ride for miles across mountain ranges, and over almost impassable roads, to receive the acknowledgment of a poor neighbor's wife, whose infirmity or want of means prevented her from travelling to the county seat. Nor was there a failure in respect to their judicial decrees. Guided by their own intelligence and sound sense, and the aid of the Commonwealth's attorney, they attained substantial righteousness in their conclusions. Their decisions were not often reversed; and it happened more than once that they were sustained by the Court of Appeals against the counter-adjudications of such eminent jurists as Archibald Stuart and Lucas P. Thompson.

For some years after the Revolution, all persons charged with felony, were sent to Richmond for trial before the General Court. To remedy this arrangement which was both inconvenient and expensive, a law was passed in 1788, forming judicial districts throughout the State, and appointing a court for each district. Three judges were to preside in each court, two of them to form a quorum. One of these districts comprised the counties of Louisa, Fluvanna, Albemarle and Amherst, and its court was called the District Court of Charlottesville. Who were its judges is not known, its records being lost. John Carr, son of Major Thomas Carr, was its Clerk. This Court was abolished in 1809, and the Circuit Superior Court of Law for the county was organized, with Archibald Stuart, of Staunton, as Judge, and John Carr as Clerk. Mr. Carr resigned in 1818, and Alexander Garrett was appointed in his stead. During this time the Court of Chancery having jurisdiction of such cases arising in this county, was held in Staunton. In 1830 the Circuit Superior Court was invested with the jurisdiction of all cases, both of Law and Chancery, and this scheme continues to the present day. In that year Judge Stuart was appointed to the bench of the Court of Appeals, and was succeeded by Lucas P. Thompson, of Amherst. Judge Thompson continued in office until 1852, when he was promoted to the Court of Appeals, and was succeeded by Richard H. Field, of Culpeper. Judge Field sat for the last time in October 1864, and soon after died. When the confusion consequent upon the war somewhat subsided, Egbert R. Watson was made Judge of the Circuit Court in 1866 by the United States military authorities. He was superseded in the beginning of 1869 by the appointment of Henry Shackelford, of Culpeper, who held the office until his death in 1880, when Daniel A. Grimsley, of Culpeper, was chosen. In 1882 he gave place to George P. Hughes, of Goochland, until 1886, when he was again elected, and continues to occupy the position at the present time.

Before the Constitution of 1850 the Circuit Judges had the appointment of the Attorneys for the Commonwealth practising in their courts. When Judge Stuart took his seat on the Albemarle bench in 1809, he selected Dabney Carr to represent the State. Upon Mr. Carr's resignation in 1811, he appointed John Howe Peyton, of Staunton, who held the office until 1839 when he resigned. Thereupon Judge Thompson appointed Thomas J. Michie, of Staunton, whose incumbency was terminated by the provisions of the new Constitution. Under those provisions the office became elective, and the person who filled it practised in all the courts alike.

Nothing is known concerning the first building occupied as a courthouse, except that it was erected by Samuel Scott on the land of his brother Daniel, near Scottsville. It afforded accommodation to those transacting the public business for seventeen years, when the removal to Charlottesville took place. Nor does any record remain, giving an account of the building of the first courthouse at the new county seat. The edifice erected however answered the purpose of a hall of justice for a little more than forty years. It must have had some pretension to architectural display in the shape of an ornamental cover to its entrance, as we learn that in 1800 Richard Thurmond was bound over for "a fray in the portico of the courthouse." This courthouse, and the early jails, were evidently of slight and temporary construction; with the course of years they required almost continual repairs. The first jail appears to have been built by William Terrell, and the second by Henry Gambell about the close of the

Revolutionary War. Trouble was encountered in settling with the latter contractor, on account of the imperfect manner in which his work was done. In 1785 a stone prison was built, sixteen feet by sixteen, and two stories in height, and lasted until 1798. A new jail was then erected, the cost of which was a thousand pounds, or three thousand, three hundred and thrity-three dollars. Thomas Whitlow was the builder. This structure continued in use, with repairs from time to time—particularly in 1846, when three thousand dollars were expended in its improvement—until the present jail was built in 1876.

The court square was first enclosed in 1792. Thomas Bell, James Kerr and Thomas Garth were directed to have a railing put up at a distance of not more than forty-five feet from the courthouse. A large space was consequently left as open ground. The subject of selling a part of this unoccupied space was seriously agitated. In 1801 the justices of the county were specially convened to deliberate in regard to the matter; fortunately, after due consideration they came to the conclusion, that it was inexpedient that any part of the public grounds should be sold.

In 1803 it was determined that a new courthouse was necessary. George Divers, William D. Meriwether and Isaac Miller were appointed to draw a plan for the edifice, and Messrs. Divers, Miller, Thomas Garth, William Wardlaw and Thomas C. Fletcher were directed to solicit bids for its erection, the cost not to exceed five thousand dollars. The building committee was also directed, when the new house was finished, to remove the old one, together with the rubbish incident to the work. From this circumstance it is inferred, that the old building was located not far from the site of the present Clerk's Office. The house then erected is substantially the one which now exists. Iron bars were placed in the office windows in 1807. The cupola was repaired in 1815. After a consultation to devise some means of protecting the public buildings from fire, the Court ordered lightning rods to be put up on the courthouse; this was done in 1818. These safeguards then went by the name of Franklins. James Leitch furnished the iron necessary for fifty dollars, and Jacob Wimer did the work for seventy-five. The building was covered with tin in 1825. In 1849 an inquiry was made as to the propriety of embellishing the front with a porch and pillars, but was attended with no result until ten years after. At that time a contract was entered into with George W. Spooner to construct a front addition designed by William A. Pratt, a former Proctor of the University, he giving bond for the faithful performance of the work in the sum of nine thousand four hundred dollars. This addition was flanked with towers and crowned with gables. While this work was in progress, the Court held its sessions in the old Town Hall. After the war the gables and towers were removed, and the pediment with its supporting pillars, as they appear at present, was erected by Mr. Spooner. These improvements were deemed sufficient untol the recent alterations in 1897.

At the organization of the county, the pillory, stocks and whipping post were regarded as necessary accompaniments of the courthouse, and court proceedings. In 1807 order was given to repair these important means of correction. In process of time they seem to have disappeared by natural decay. In 1820 they were all directed to be restored in the public square. Subsequent to that period the first two receive no further mention, but James Lobban and Andrew Brown were appointed to select a place for the whipping post as late as 1857.

In 1811 a brick and stone wall was ordered to be erected on the Square forty-five feet from the courthouse. John Jordan contracted to perform the work. In 1816 the trustees of the town were allowed to sink a well on the Square, exterior to the wall. In 1824 V. W. Southall obtained permission to build an office on the southeast corner of the Square, and F. B. Dyer one on the southwest corner. At the same time an office was directed to be built on the northeast corner for the use of the County Clerk's assistant, and William H. Meriwether was allowed to build one adjoining it on the west;

but after a month or two the entire order was rescinded. The next year a commission, consisting of Joseph Coffman, John M. Perry, John Winn, Alexander Garrett, Micajah Woods and Opie Norris, was directed to have two offices erected on the northeast corner of the Square for the Commonwealth's Attorney and the Sheriff, the brick wall taken down, the front yard paved with the materials, and a light railing placed around the Square. These two offices were occupied in 1830 by V. W. Southall and T. W. Gilmer at a rent of fifty dollars. In 1841 permission was again given for the erection of offices on the front corners of the Square; but it was evidently withdrawn, though no notice of the countermanding order appears. The same year the Charlottesville Lyceum had leave to hold their meetings in the courthouse. Authority was given in 1855 to Messrs. Strange and Jones, to ring the courthouse bell for the uses of their school, but it was soon after recalled.

In 1847 in answer perhaps to some ebullition of public spirit, James W. Saunders, John R. Jones and William A. Bibb were directed to enclose and improve the public square, provided the expense of the work was borne by private subscription. What was effected in pursuance of this movement is not known. Two years later Allen B. Magruder and W. T. Early asked leave to build offices on the Square, and the petition was so far taken into consideration that Malcolm F. Crawford and Thomas Wood were appointed to examine and report on the subject. In 1855 the town was granted liberty to erect an engine house on the west side of the Square, in a line with which Drury Wood and W. T. Early were allowed to build offices on the east side. The next year an order was passed, directing the enclosing and paving of the Square according to a plan submitted by William S. Dabney, and it was no doubt in agreement with the provisions of this plan, that shortly after the stone wall and iron railing now existing were ordered to be erected, not to exceed the cost of fifteen hundred dollars.

Not long after the beginning of the century an effort was made to secure the transportation of the produce of the county by water. The need of a cheaper and more expeditious mode of reaching a market had long been felt. Farmers had been obliged to move their crops, first to Fredericksburg, and then to Richmond, by wagons; and the goods of merchants had been conveyed to their stores by the same slow and expensive process. The course of James River was then unobstructed, and the question arose whether the Rivanna might not be rendered useful for the purposes of commerce. The scheme was attempted of turning to account these water courses, which nature had placed at the door to be outlets of such admirable convenience. The Rivanna Navigation Company was formed, and a charter procured. In 1810 George Divers, Williams D. Meriwether, Nimrod Bramham, John Kelly and Dabney Minor were its Directors, and Peter Minor its Treasurer. The original methods of procedure were simple enough. They aimed to keep the channel of the river clear of snags and hammocks, and to provide flat-bottomed boats called batteaux, for the carriage of freight. Advantage was taken of freshets to load the boats, and run them down, while the stream was at high water mark. As at such times the water rushed with the speed of a torrent, the navigation was often dangerous; but the management of the boats became a special business, and the men employed acquired an intelligence and skill which were seldom baffled by accidents. A family named Craddock bore for many years a high reputation as adroit and successful watermen.

In 1827 books were opened for an enlarged subscription of stock, and eleven hundred and fifteen shares were taken at fifty dollars a share. A list of the subscribers remains on record in Deed Book Twenty-Seven. This money was raised to improve still further the channel of the river. The improvement consisted in the erection of dams at shoal places, to increase the depth of water, and thus secure slack water navigation, locks being provided to raise or lower the boats at the different levels. Some of the locks were handsomely faced with hewn stone, and built in a substantial manner. Besides the dams located in Fluvanna, there was one erected at Milton, three at Shadwell, one at the Woolen Mills, one at the Three Islands, two at the Broad Mossing Ford, and two at Rio Mills. It was no doubt in preparation for this effort, that commissioners, were appointed by the County Court in 1825 to consider the practicability of clearing out the south fork from the mouth of Ivy Creek to the "Little River." The court also in 1841 directed an examination of the improvements on the south fork with the view of allowing additional tolls. Some still living remember boats bound for the James River Canal at Columbia, which carried from eighty to one hundred barrels of flour, and from forty to fifty hogsheads of tobacco. The value of this work was entirely destroyed by the advent of the railroads; yet it seemed hard to abandon an enterprise, on which so much had been expended, and from which such great benefits had been derived. Since the war another attempt was made to renew its usefulness. Two dams were constructed, one above Milton, and the other above Shadwell, but both being damaged by sweeping floods, the whole matter has been finally dropped.

The early settlers of Albemarle amidst all the distracting labors of founding new homes, set no small value on the advantages of education. Both those who pushed their way up from the tidewater section, and the Scotch Irish element who came over from the Valley, made it their care to build the schoolhouse. Soon after the formation of the county, Rev. James Maury, Rector of Fredericksville parish, opened a classical school on the borders of Albemarle and Louisa, which he superintended for many years with eminent success. In this nursery of learning Mr. Jefferson received in part his mental training. At the same period Rev. Samuel Black, whose home was on Mechum's River below the Miller School, was also engaged in teaching. Rev. Matthew Maury, son of James, succeeded his father in the school as well as in the parish. In fact, it was generally the case that ministers of the gospel, whose salaries were small, joined the work of instruction to their regular professional duties. In the early deeds, it is not uncommon to find in the description of places sold, the incidental mention of the schoolhouse, or the schoolhouse spring. It was also customary in setting forth the parties to deeds, to state their residence and occupation, a matter of no slight importance in a historical point of view. We learn in this way that about 1760 a James Forbes, who bought land at the head of Ivy Creek, was a schoolmaster, and that William Coursey, Jr., who lived in the northern part of the county, pursued the same vocation. David Rodes, who resided on Moorman's River, mentions in some notes still remaining, patronizing from 1766 to 1768, the schools of Charles Lambert, William Coleman and William Harris.

In consequence of Mr. Jefferson's repeated suggestions, seconded by the active efforts of Joseph Cabell in the Legislature, a State law was passed in 1818 in which it was provided, that Commissioners should be appointed in every county, not less than five, nor more than fifteen in number, who should give attention to the children of families unable to bear the expense of their education. These appointments were made in Albemarle every three years for a considerable time. Those who constituted the first commission were Martin Dawson, James Clark, Francis Carr, John Goss, Thomas Wood, James Jarman, John A. Michie, Isaac A. Coles, William Harris, Allen Dawson, William Woods, Samuel L. Hart, Charles Yancey, Christopher Hudson, and Henry T. Harris.

In the early part of the century John Robertson, a native of Scotland, and father of Judge W. J. Robertson, taught a classical school on the east side of the South West Mountain. His library, a catalogue of which is recorded in Will Book No. Seven, contained a more complete set of the Greek and Latin authors than perhaps could be found in any other private collection in the State. The first numbers of the Central Gazette supply some information in regard to the educational facilities of the county during the decade of 1820. In that year was commenced the Charlottesville Female Seminary, the site of which was what is now the Leterman lot, corner of High and Third Streets. Its first principal was a Mrs. George. Is was subsequently presided over by Mr. and Mrs. Littleford, of Baltimore, Mrs. G. K. Taylor, and Mrs. Egan. Mr. Gerard E. Stuck, who was accredited by most flattering testimonials, taught the Charlottesville Academy, designed for boys. Allen Dawson had a school, first at his farm on the Scottsville Road, then at his house on Main Street, west of Third, and still later at a schoolhouse that once stood on J. W. Marshall's lot on Park Street. In this house Thomas Woodson taught some years later. The small brick near the east end of Main Street, now occupied by William Durrett, accommodated successively the schools of George Carr, Thomas W. Maury and Rev. Mr. Hatch. Mr. Carr afterwards taught in connection with Christopher Hornsey, and Mr. Maury removed his school to his residence west of the University, now owned by Samuel Emerson. Mrs. Charles Spencer gave instruction to small children on the south side of Main Street at the foot of Vinegar Hill, and to the same class of pupils Mrs. Ebenezer Watts devoted her labors at a subsequent period. Mrs. Rebecca Estes had a school for young ladies in the large brick on the top of Vinegar Hill. About 1829 Mrs. Blaetterman opened an academy for young ladies in the large brick, south of where the Lynchburg road passes under the Chesapeake and Ohio Railroad. S. Overton Minor taught at the Farm, and later in the basement of the old Baptist Church. In the old brick next east of the Opera House on West Main Street, a classical school was conducted by Bartholomew Egan and Victor Ferrow. William A. Bowen taught near Ivy Depot, holding his examinations in Mountain Plains Church, and afterwards near Batesville, making a similar use of Mount Ed Church. Thornton Rogers had a classical academy at his place at Keswick. Joseph Mills gave instruction near Earlysville, and William J. Wilkerson two miles west of Michie's Old Tavern. Mason Frizzell, a graduate of Williams College, had charge of a school on Chestnut Ridge, and John Duggins of one near H. Martin's, presumably south of Covesville. T. L. Terrell was a teacher at James H. Terrell's on the east side of the South West Mountain. Samuel Harrison taught at Piney Grove. A school in Brown's Cove was instructed by William Brander, and a Female Seminary in the same place by Miss Sarah P. Catlett. When Jonathan B. Carr retired from the practice of the law, he opened a school at his place, the Retreat, north of Dunlora. Rev. Ovid A. Kinsolving received part of his early education at Plain Dealing, the residence of Samuel Dyer.

During the next decade was built the house where Dr. William S. White taught for some years, now the Presbyterian Manse, and shortly after the brick at the corner of Maple and Seventh Streets was erected as a Female Seminary. Midway, first opened as a hotel under Louis A. Xaupi, became the seat of a flourishing academy taught by Duke and Powers—Alexander Duke and Pike Powers—and afterwards by Duke and Slaughter—Alexander Duke and Charles Slaughter.

These were some of the places of instruction which existed at that time, and which for the most part might be styled high schools. In them were imparted the elements of a classical education. They were the forerunners of those admirable preparatory seats of learning which arose in the next generation, and still exist in living memory, those of Franklin Minor at Ridgeway, of Charles Minor at Brookhill, of Professor Gessner Harrison at Cocke's Tavern, of William Dinwiddie at Greenwood, of Col. J. B. Strange on the Ridge at Charlottesville, and of Brown and Tebbs at Bloomfield; and at a later period, those of Major Horace Jones in Charlottesville, of the Wood Brothers at Cocke's Tavern, and of John R. Sampson at Pantops.

A project was conceived of establishing at or near Charlottesville a large academy, to be organized and managed on the plan of the German Gymnasium. Its great design was to insure a more exact and thorough drill in the rudiments of learning, and thus afford a more adequate preparation for entrance into the University. In prosecution of this idea, a long prospectus was published in 1829, signed by a large number of the most eminent men in all sections of the State, but nothing tangible ever resulted. Things still seem to be shaping themselves more and more in agreement with the wonderful foresight of Mr. Jefferson, forming that gradation which constituted the ideal of his mind, each step rising higher from the common school to the University, at which all the last and most finished results of every branch of learning could be obtained.

Jefferson well deserves the title of Father of the University of Virginia. The whole establishment was the outgrowth of his views upon education. These views occupied his mind while acting as one of the Revisors of the Laws of Virginia in 1776, were constantly revolved in his thoughts, and were from time to time expressed in legislative bills, and correspondence with his friends, until they finally assumed permanent form in the noble institution which is the chief ornament of Albemarle, and one of the chief ornaments of the State. His fundamental maxim was, that the stability and happiness of the republic depended on the general diffusion of knowledge through the mass of the people; hence the attainment of this object was perhaps more the dictate of his patriotism, than of his literary tastes. The instrumentality to be employed comprehended common schools, grammar schools or acadamies, and a university as the head of the system. An act containing these general ideas was prepared and presented to the General Assembly in 1779, but amidst the turmoil of the Revolution attracted but little attention. The same views were expressed in his Notes on Virginia, in which he proposed that William and Mary should be enlarged, and made to occupy the place of a university. In 1796 the Legislature passed an act which approached as near the attainment of free schools in Virginia, as was ever realized until after the war.

This act provided that a majority of the acting justices of each county should determine whether they should be established; that in case they came to this conclusion, they should elect three officers called aldermen, who should divide their county into hundreds, in imitation of the political divisions of old English times; and that the people of each hundred should tax themselves for the erection of a school house in the most convenient place, and for the support of a teacher. According to Mr. Jefferson, the common schools were to be wholly supported by local taxation, the academy was to be assisted by the State, and the University was to receive a larger measure of State assistance, in conjunction with the benevolent contributions of the friends of education. But his conceptions were far in advance of his age. The magistrates were as little inclined as the people, to levy a special tax for general education. Although before the system was introduced by the present constitution, the counties and cities of the state were allowed by special enactment to adopt free schools for themselves, it is doubted whether a single county availed itself of the privilege, and whether more than one or two cities were liberal minded enough to enter upon the work. A meeting of the magistrates of Albemarle was called to consider the subject in 1797, the year after the act referred to was passed, at which were present Francis Walker, Samuel Murrell, Rice Garland, Wilson C. Nicholas, George Divers, Bernard Brown, Thomas C. Fletcher and Thomas Bell. The decision at which they arrived was, "that no election of aldermen shall be held this year"—nor was any ever held thereafter. Under the law of 1818 which required not less than five nor more than fifteen Commissioners to be appointed in every county, the full number was appointed in this county. They disposed of the quota of the State Literary Fund apportioned to the county, and provided for free education as far as this means would allow. Children thus aided were admitted to the schools upon certificate from one of the magistrates. In 1849 a memorable debate on the question took place before the people of the county, and an election was held. Dr. William H. McGuffey, of the University, took the stump in behalf of free schools, and General William F. Gordon and Col. T. J. Randolph against them. By the popular vote it was decided, that the time for public schools had not yet come.

As early as 1783, just after the Revolutionary War, a movement was begun to establish a grammar school in Albemarle. This appears from a letter of Mr. Jefferson, written the last day of that year. In it he narrates the efforts he had made to secure a teacher, some literary character of the Irish nation, or some person from Scotland—"from that country we are sure of having sober, attentive men." A charter was obtained for the Albemarle Academy in 1803, but though trustees were elected, nothing further was accomplished. Mr. Jefferson was President of the United States, and had the affairs of the country in his hands; the mainspring was therefore wanting. In 1814 he was appointed a trustee. Agitation at once commenced, plans were devised, a site was pitched upon, the town of Charlottesville was selected. But the project was soon enlarged. Albemarle Academy grew into Central College. The Legislature made this change of name in 1816, and provided for the appointment by the Governor of six visitors, who should choose professors, and superintend the affairs of the new institution. The visitors were Thomas Jefferson, James Madison, James Monroe, Joseph C. Cabell, David Watson and John H. Cocke. The next year land was bought from John M. Perry, the present site of the University, and on October 6th, 1817, the corner stone of Central College was laid.

The design had received a start, and like the letting out of waters could not be stopped. Matters ripened fast. In February 1818, the Legislature enacted that the Governor should appoint the Commissioners, one from each Senatorial district of the State, who should meet in the month of August in that year at a tavern in Rockfish Gap on the Blue Ridge, and settle the site for a university, a plan for its construction, the sciences to be taught, the number of professors, and a legislative bill for organizing and managing the institution. That body was appointed, and consisted of the following gentlemen: Thomas Jefferson, James Madison, Spencer Roane, Creed Taylor, Peter Randolph, William Brockenbrough, Archibald Rutherford, Henry E. Watkins, Armistead T. Mason, Hugh Holmes, John G. Jackson, William H. Cabell, Nathaniel H. Claiborne, William A. E. Dade, William Jones, James Breckinridge, Philip C. Pendleton, Archibald Stuart, Thomas Wilson, M. C. Taylor, Philip Slaughter, John Johnson, R. B. Taylor, and ——— Faulkner. All except the last three met at the tavern designated, which was the predecessor of the present Mountain Top, and was kept at the time by two brothers named Leake, kinsmen of the late Hon. Shelton F. Leake. Their hall of assembly was a low, whitewashed room, furnished with a deal dining table and split-bottom chairs. The Commissioners were men of distinction, yet with them as with others local predilections had their weight. Jefferson, who was chosen president, strongly endeavored to secure Central College as the site. Two other places were proposed, Staunton and Lexington. After mature consideration the vote was taken, and stood sixteen for Central College, three for Lexington, and two for Staunton. The work was virtually accomplished. On January 25th, 1819, Central College was by the Legislature transmuted into the University of Virginia.

The erection of buildings which had been begun by the authorities of Central College, was already in a good degree of forwardness. The plan of the whole group, as well as the styles of the particular edifices, had been designed by Mr. Jefferson himself. All the residences, or pavilions, as they were called, and all the dormitories, on the West Lawn were put up, and the interior wood work and plastering were in progress. This was true also in regard to the first and second pavilions, that is, the two most northerly, and ten dormitories, on East Lawn. No contracts had yet been let for the remaining buildings, the three southern pavilions and the other dormitories on East Lawn, and the hotels and dormitories on the East and West Ranges. Nor was any mention yet made of the erection of the Rotunda. The first pavilion designed in the Doric order, with the four adjoining dormitories, on West Lawn was built, the brick work by Carter and Phillips, and the wood work by James Oldham. Matthew Brown did the brick work, and James Dinsmore the wood work, of the second pavilion in the Corinthian order. The third pavilion in the Ionic order, with the seven nearest dormitories, was erected, the brick work by John M. Perry, and the wood work by Perry and Dinsmore. The fourth pavilion in the Doric order, with fifteen dormitories adjacent, was built, the brick work by Matthew Brown, David Knight and Hugh Chisholm, and the wood work by John M. Perry. The fifth pavilion and one dormitory were built, the brick work by Carter and Phillips, and the wood work by George W. Spooner and John Neilson. The entire work of pavilions one and two, with the ten adjoining dormitories, on East Lawn, was contracted for by Richard Ware.

According to Mr. Jefferson's report in 1821, the cost of the ten pavilions was estimated at eight-six thousand dollars, of the one hundred and nine dormitories at sixty-five thousand, and of the six hotels at twenty-four thousand. The entire sum for land, buildings and labor was placed at two hundred and seven thousand. The construction of the Rotunda proved to be an expensive undertaking. An estimate published in Niles's Register in 1826, set down the cost of the complete establishment at about four hundred thousand dollars.

The scholastic duties of the University began at length on March 7th, 1825. The number of students present at the opening was forty; the whole number matriculated during the session up to the last of September, was one hundred and sixteen. The Central Gazette issued on the seventh of March noticed the opening, and stated "that many were said to have been prevented from being present by heavy rains and bad roads."

In the early days of the University there was a greater tendency to disorder among the students than has since been apparent. In 1836 wild and boisterous spirits prevailed to such an extent that the firm hand of Benjamin Ficklin was required to repress their effervescence, and in 1840 the deplorable death of Prof. John A. G. Davis occurred by the rash violence of a student. But the height of these excesses produced a reaction, and led to a more quiet and rational line of conduct. It may be safely affirmed, that in the history of the institution as a whole, there have been as little turbulence and destructive riot as in any assemblage of like kind in the country. In truth, notwithstanding reports to the contrary, the most healthful moral influences have been in operation from the beginning. In 1828 the faculty by their formal action invited Rev. F. W. Hatch and Rev. F. Bowman, the only resident ministers in the town, to preach alternately every Sunday at the University. In 1830 a Temperance Society, holding regular sessions, was formed among the students. Its first officers were J. W. C. Watson, President, Thomas H. Hamner, first Vice President, Socrates Maupin, second Vice President, and Samuel Scott, Secretary, and a hall was erected for its special use in 1856. About 1830 a chaplain was chosen by the faculty to officiate regularly in the institution, and for more than sixty years this office was stately filled, and supported by the voluntary contributions of the professors and students; and in 1854 a comfortable house was built on the University grounds as the chaplain's residence. During the period when the scenes of greatest disorder occurred, a weekly prayer meeting was maintained among the students by the energetic zeal of such men as Dr. Frank Sampson and Rev. Dennis Dudley, then prosecuting their academic studies; and later a Young Men's Christian Association was formed within its walls, which was the first organized body of the kind in the country.

In those early days the students of the University wore a uniform. It consisted of a suit of grayish cloth, called Oxford Mixed, specially imported from year to year by John Cochran, the coat braided on the collar, and the pantaloons striped at the sides. This badge of distinction gave rise to an extensive industry in Charlottesville. From a hundred to a hundred and twenty journeyman tailors were engaged in its manufacture, and the firm of Marshall & Bailey, Shoemakers, employed from thirty-five to forty hands in their business.

The Public Hall annexed to the Rotunda, and destroyed by the fire of 1895, was commenced in 1851, and in 1859 Dawson's Row was erected. These buildings were constructed with the proceeds of a farm devised by the will of Martin Dawson, a citizen of the county, who died in 1835. By the sale of this farm, the sum of fourteen thousand dollars was realized. The Chemical Laboratory was erected in 1870, the Brooks Museum in 1875, and the buildings of the McCormick Observatory in 1881. In 1859 a parcel of land belonging to Mrs. Sophia Johnson, containing several springs, and lying in a ravine north of Observatory Mountain, together with the right of way for pipes, was condemned for the use of the University. A reservoir was formed in the ravine to furnish the institution with a supply of water.

CHAPTER V.

The only reference to the war of 1812 in the records occurs in 1866, where an enumeration of the family of James Michie, Jr., was presented to the Court. It was there stated, that in that contest that gentleman was a corporal in the company of Captain Estes, of the Virginia militia, and that a land warrant for one hundred and sixty acres was issued to his descendants on that account. It is ascertained upon inquiry that a cavalry company from the county commanded by Colonel Samuel Carr, and of which Dr. Frank Carr was Surgeon, and an infantry company of which Achilles Broadhead was Captain, were also called into service. From the same source it is learned that William Wertenbaker was a private in Captain Estes's company, and Henry Turner, the father of the venerable William H. Turner, served in the cavalry. To what point these troops were marched is not known; but as the enemy never landed on the soil of the State, no occasion happened for their employment in action. In a letter dated September 1814, and written by William Wirt, who commanded an artillery company in camp on York River, he says, "Frank Gilmer, Jefferson Randolph, the Carrs and others, have got tired waiting for the British, and gone home."

Captain Estes above mentioned was Triplett T. Estes, who for many years kept the Stone Tavern on the square on which Lipscomb's livery stable stands. In the appointment of Processioners in 1811, he is designated as Captain of the militia company in the district immediately south of Charlottesville, and to which the inhabitants of the town belonged. He was unfortunate in his business affairs. He purchased the Stone Tavern with its surrounding square, but was unable to make the payments. At one time he also owned the farm on Biscuit Run which Martin Dawson afterwards devised to the University; but that together with all his property was sold under deeds of trust. About 1819 he removed from Charlottesville to Fredericksburg, and in 1832 was living in Dinwiddie County, probably in Petersburg.

In 1816 the County Court received a communication from the State authorities, requesting a survey of the County to be made in order to the preparation of an accurate map of the State. In compliance with this request they appointed Dabney Minor, Dr. Frank Carr and Dr. Charles Brown to arrange for the survey; and in answer to their overtures William H. Meriwether proposed to undertake the work. It is supposed he carried it into effect; but no details of the time or manner of its accomplishments have been found. The results of this and other similar surveys throughout the State, were committed to John Wood, an eminent engineer of the day. He however died in 1822, before the completion of his task. The fruits of his labors, with all the materials which had been collected, were then entrusted to Herman Boye. By the contract entered into with him, the map was to have been finished on the first of April 1824, and in all likelihood it was published during the course of that year. A well preserved copy formerly hung in the University Library in the Rotunda, but it no doubt perished in the fire of 1895. Two or three other copies in private hands, much defaced by time and want of care, have been met with in the county.

The Legislature passed an act in January 1818, establishing the town of Scottsville on James River. This point had been well known from the beginning of the county. In its proximity the first courthouse had been located, and for seventeen years was the centre of public business for all the surrounding country. In can hardly be questioned that the people of the neighborhood looked upon it as a heavy blow, when the seat of justice was removed, and they were obliged to repair to Charlottesville in discharge of their public functions.

It continued nevertheless to be a place of considerable notoriety. As Scott's Ferry, it was a point of chief importance in crossing the river James, and maintaining the means of communication between the inhabitants north and south of that stream; and as Scott's Landing, it was a station of some consequence in the business of its navigation. When the Tobacco Warehouses were established at Milton and the mouth of Ballenger's Creek in 1792, liberty was also given for the erection of one on John Scott's land at Scott's Ferry, but restricted by the conditions, that the proprietor should construct an edifice of brick or stone, with roof of slate or tile, and with gates of iron, and that until the County Court entered upon their records the fact of such construction, no tobacco should be received, and no inspectors appointed. As no fact of the kind was made a matter of record, it would appear the proprietor regarded the conditions too burdensome to fulfil.

The desire for the founding of a town at this place was undoubtedly stimulated by the progress of the James River improvement, and the further extension of the canal. An abortive attempt seems to have been made in 1816 by private efforts of the Coles family, who sold a number of lots with that end in view. Two years later the sanction of the Legislature was obtained for the project. Fifteen acres of land belonging to John Scott were vested in Samuel Dyer, Sr., Samuel Dyer, Jr., Christopher Hudson, Tucker Coles and John Coles as Trustees, to be laid out in half acre lots, to be conveyed to purchasers, and to be called the town of Scottsville. Thirty-three lots and four outlots were sold the same year for upwards of thirteen thousand dollars. About 1830 an addition was made on its western boundary by Peyton Harrison, who had since its origin purchased the Belle Grove plantation, which lay just above the town, and on which the old courthouse formerly stood.

In 1824 the Staunton and James River Turnpike was commenced, and Scottsville was its river terminus. Because of its fine shipping facilities, it was not long before great numbers of huge, old-fashioned wagons thronged its streets, large consignments of produce from the west, and of merchandise from the east, filled its warehoues, and it became the emporium of a busy commerce, and rapidly rose to great prosperity. A tobacco warehouse was now successfully established, and its first inspectors were James B. Holman, James Thomas, Fleming Moon and Richard Omohundro. It enjoyed the brightness of these palmy days until about 1850, when its flourishing trade was greatly diminished by the advent of the railroads. It continued however to possess the benefits of the canal, and when that was relinquished, those of the railway which succeeded in its stead.

No newspaper was published in Albemarle during the first seventy-five years of its existence, nor until the fifty-seventh year after the establishment of Charlottesville. People depended on Richmond and Washington for information of events transpiring in the world, and as in those days the mail was received but once a week, it is probable but few dailies were taken. At the close of the last century the Courts directed their orders to be published in the Virginia Gazette in Richmond, and after the beginning of the present century, sometimes in a paper of Staunton, and sometimes in one of Lynchburg.

But in a county where so much of intellectual cultivation existed, where Charlottesville Academy had merged into Central College, and Central College was merging into the University of Virginia, it was high time that a step so indicative of mental and literary activity should be taken. The first paper issued in its bounds was the Central Gazette, its first number appearing on the twenty-ninth of January, 1820. Its proprietors were Clement P. and John H. McKennie. It became the medium of advertisements for this and the contiguous counties. Some original communications were contributed, but the main part of its literary matter consisted of extracts from other papers, setting forth the political events of the day, and the news from foreign countries. After a time Thomas W. Gilmer was associated with its editorial staff. It is not certainly known how long its publication continued, but it probably ceased about 1827 or 1828. A number of its volumes bound, and running perhaps through its whole course, were deposited in the University Library, but all except the first were unfortunately consumed in the fire of 1895.

The Virginia Advocate was the next journal that appeared. It began simultaneously with the cessation of the Gazette. Its first editors were Thomas W. Gilmer and John A. G. Davis. Nicholas P. Trist subsequently took part in its management. It then passed into the hands of Dr. Frank Carr, and was sold by him in 1830 to E. W. Reinhart. After an interval of some years it was under the control of William W. Tompkins and Alexander Moseley, the latter of whom afterwards became the distinguished editor of the Richmond Whig. Later it was conducted by Robert C. Noel, William J. Shelton and James C. Halsall, and still later it was edited successively by John L. Cochran and James C. Southall.

In the meantime, about 1829 or 1830, James Alexander came to Charlottesville from Massachusetts through the agency of Colonel T. J. Randolph, to undertake the printing of Mr. Jefferson's correspondence. When that work was completed, Mr. Alexander commenced in 1836 the publication of the Jeffersonian Republican, avowedly as a Democratic organ. Some years before the opposition to General Jackson had assumed positive form, and between the Whig and Democratic parties lines of demarcation had been distinctly drawn. The Advocate had taken sides with the former, and to further the interests of the latter the Jeffersonian was set on foot. Mr. Alexander was the ostensible editor as well as publisher, though he was constantly supplied with articles written by such active members of the party as Colonel Randolph, Frank Ruffin, Shelton F. Leake and others. These two papers ran side by side until both were suspended by the disorganizing influences of the civil war. During their continuance a periodical of some sort, exhibiting the title of The Idea, was started by Thomas W. Michie, but apparently it proved ephemeral in its duration. A few months before the war began, a new journal appeared under the name of the Charlottesville Review, but owing to the disastrous pressure of the times it survived but a short season. A religious paper, the Christian Intelligencer, was published for a time in Charlottesville by Rev. James Goss.

All papers had discontinued their issues by May 1862. While the period of suspension lasted, orders of Court were directed to be published in Lynchburg or Staunton. In October 1864 James C. Southall commenced the publication of the Chronicle, and in 1868 disposed of it to Bennett Taylor and John W. Foster. They were succeeded by Littleton Waddell, and he, by H. B. Michie. Some years after the war the Jeffersonian Republican was recommenced by R. P. Valentine, with A. R. Blakey as editor. It was afterwards transferred to James Blakey, who conducted it several years. The present paper of the county, the Progress, was launched as a Daily in 1890 by J. H. Lindsay, and it was not long before it absorbed both of the other papers. The Chronicle was published as a Tri-Weekly, and all the other journals mentioned except the Progress as Weeklies.

Besides the Correspondence of Mr. Jefferson which has been mentioned, a Gazetteer of Virginia was published in Charlottesville in 1835 by Joseph Martin. It was an octavo of more than six hundred pages. It contained a collection of statistics, valuable at the time, a description of each county, with an enumeration of its post offices, a history of Virginia, written expressly for the work, and a map of the State as it then was. Quite a corps of collaborators was engaged in its execution. William H. Brockenbrough, a member of the Albemarle Bar, and subsequently Judge of the United States District Court of Florida, was editor, Moseley and Tompkins printers, Joseph Martin binder, and E. C. Morse general aid.

In early periods the people of the county seem to have been animated by a stronger public spirit than prevails at present. This was manifested in their frequent co-operative action for attaining important results. For sometime prior to 1820 the Albemarle Agricultural Society was accomplishing a successful work, its members publishing accounts of their individual experiments, maintaining a correspondence with kindred bodies, and holding annual exhibitions of their products, with the award of liberal premiums to competitors who excelled. An idea of the powerful influence it exerted for good, may be formed from the list of those who took a leading part in its affairs. James Madison was its President. Its first Vice President was Thomas Mann Randolph, its second, John H. Cocke, its Treasurer, Nimrod Bramham, and its Secretaries, Peter Minor and Dr. Frank Carr. Its Committee of Correspondence were T. M. Randolph, James Barbour, Dr. Thomas G. Watkins, William D. Meriwether and Peter Minor, and its Committee of Accounts, Dabney Minor, Dr. Thomas E. Randolph and John J. Winn. Among the excellent disquisitions published on these subjects, Colonel Randolph described his experiments with clover, John H. Craven how he reduced the great gullies with which Pen Park was furrowed when it came into his possession, and Peter Minor the results of different methods of corn-planting on high lands. At one of its yearly exhibitions, the first premium for the best tilled farm in the county was assigned to John Rogers, and the second to John H. Craven. On these occasions George W. Kinsolving and William Woods, Surveyor, displayed their fine blooded horses, the latter supplying his stables with purchases from the choice stock of John Randolph of Roanoke. Beyond question the agency of this Society gave a powerful stimulus to the improvement of the live stock of the county as well as to the better cultivation of its soil.

In those days a Colonization Society existed, of which Jonathan B. Carr was Treasurer, and which held an annual meeting on the first Monday of October. In furtherance of its objects Rev. Francis Bowman preached a sermon on the Fourth of July 1824, and in May 1830 the ladies of Charlottesville and the county held a fair at Fitch's Tavern.

The Albemarle Bible Society was organized in August 1828. Nathaniel Burnley acted as Secretary when they first convened, and the first Monday of August was appointed as the time of the annual meeting. A full staff of officers was elected for a thorough canvass of the county, and for the energetic prosecution of its work. Hugh Nelson was President, John Kelly, Vice President, Rev. F. W. Hatch, Secretary, Rev. F. Bowman, Treasurer, and Dr. Hardin Massie,

William Woods, Surveyor, Nimrod Bramham, G. W. Kinsolving and John Rogers, Managers. Agents were likewise chosen to awaken interest in the different battalion districts. George Wood and Allen Dickerson served in the first battalion of the Eighty-Eighth Regiment, John J. Bowcock and M. Fretwell in the second, Dr. Harris and John B. Hart in the first battalion of the Forty-Seventh, John L. Thomas and Matthew Pilson in the second, and Dr. H. Massie in the town of Charlottesville. It is a matter of interest to know who at that time were leaders in so praiseworthy a cause.

A Debating Society was maintained in Charlottesville, which, besides kindling the talents and directing the studies of the young men of the town, quickened the patriotism of the community by occasionally celebrating the Fourth of July. On that day 1830, they assembled in the Presbyterian Church, where Dr. Frank Carr read the Declaration of Independence, and Nathaniel Wolfe, a member of the bar, delivered an oration.

In 1830 the Albemarle Temperance Society was formed with Dr. Frank Carr as President, Dr. H. Massie, Vice President, J. W. C. Watson, Secretary, and Edward S. Watson, Treasurer.

Nor should it be omitted, that as a means of promoting the mental life and culture of the community, a meeting was held in 1823 for the establishment of a public library. A committee was appointed to draft a constitution, and another consisting of Mr. Jefferson, Rev. F. Bowman and John Ormond, a member of the bar, to prepare a catalogue of appropriate books for purchase. The next year the Albemarle Library Association was organized. V. W. Southall was its President, John J. Winn its Vice President, Ira Garrett its Secretary, William Wertenbaker its Treasurer, and William H. Meriwether its Librarian. Its doors were to open Mondays and Fridays, from eleven A. M. to three P. M. Like many other beneficent projects, it has passed away among the things that were, and its books scattered to the four winds. Occasionally an odd volume may still be met with, marked with the label of the Association.

The visit of Lafayette to this country occurred in 1824, and Albemarle was particularly honored with his presence. In November of that year he came from Richmond to exchange greetings with Mr. Jefferson. Special preparations were made for his reception. At the Fluvanna line a troop of cavalry, named in his honor the Lafayette Guards, met him on Thursday the eleventh, to escort him to Monticello. The officers of this detachment were John H. Craven, Captain, George W. Kinsolving, First Lieutenant, Richard Watson, Second Lieutenant, and Thomas W. Gilmer, Cornet. On its arrival at that point, the carriage containing Lafayette was halted, and he was addressed by William C. Rives, who in the course of his remarks mentioned, that he was held in lively and affectionate remembrance by the people of Virginia, and that not far from where they stood there remained a memento of him and his gallant services in their behalf during the Revolution, as the road by which he led his army to protect the old Court House from Cornwallis's approach, still bore the name of the Marquis's Road.

When the cortege arrived at Monticello, the troop was drawn up, on each side of the southern lawn. Lafayette alighted a short distance from the portico, from which Jefferson descended with tottering steps to meet him as he approached. As they drew near, the one exclaimed with choking emotion, "Lafayette," and the other with the same tender pathos, "Jefferson," and for a season they were locked in each other's embrace, while tears freely coursed down their cheeks. So affecting was the scene that there was scarcely a dry eye among all the spectators. At length the venerable friends turned and entered the house. Before they were seated however, word was brought to Lafayette that a company of youth, styled the Junior Volunteers, who had been a part of his escort from the Fluvanna line, wished to offer him the tribute of their respect. He immediately returned to the portico, where he was saluted in an admirable and manly address by Egbert R. Watson, then fourteen years of age. When the conclusion was reached, he approached the youthful orator, and taking both his hand in his own, assured him and his companions of his hearty appreciation of their reception.

On Friday the twelfth, he was conveyed to the Central Hotel in Charlottesville, where he was addressed by Thomas J. Randolph. A public reception followed. At noon a procession was formed and marched to the University, where on the portico of the Rotunda he was again addressed by William F. Gordon. In the Rotunda, then in an unfinished condition, a large number of guests sat down with him to dinner. According to the programme, Governor Randolph was to have presided on this occasion; but being necessarily absent, his place was happily filled by V. W. Southall. At six o'clock Lafayette returned to Monticello, accompanied by Jefferson and Madison, with whom he quietly spent the interval until Monday the fifteenth. On that day he was again taken in charge by the Guards, and conducted as far as Gordonsville on his way to Montpelier.

At this period, and for some time previous, many persons visited the county to obtain the sight of Monticello, and its distinguished occupant. They came from all parts of the country, and even from foreign lands. Mr. Jefferson was obliged largely to pay the penalty of greatness. Some of his visitors were animated by a just admiration of his brilliant gifts and services, others moved by a curiosity both low and annoying. An Englishman, who spent some time in the country toward the end of 1824, left on record his great delight with the aged statesman, with Charlottesville, and with the whole state of Virginia; and as an instance of the unbounded hospitality he had experienced, he states, that the evening before his departure from Charlottesville he was obliged to sup with three different families. Another stranger, in a letter dated March 1825, expresses himself in the following enthusiastic terms over the beauty of Albemarle scenery:

"The site of the village [Charlottesville] is upon the summit of a gentle elevation which begins to rise from the foot of Monticello. In contains a courthouse, a half finished church, and three or four taverns, which constitute the whole of its public buildings. It covers a limited portion of ground, and from its appearance, though I cannot positively affirm the fact, may number six hundred inhabitants. When a traveller arrives in the village, he is struck with the sublime, beautiful and picturesque scenery which everywhere surrounds him, and he pauses to contemplate with eager curiosity the magnificent prospect which meets his view. He forgets there is such a place as Charlottesville in existence, when he casts his eye upon mountain after mountain rising in regular succession, and whose lofty summits mingle with the sky till they are lost in the distance. At one time the tops of these lofty hills are enveloped in clouds, and at others when the glorious King of day sinks behind them, and tinges with golden rays their elevated heads, it calls forth an unfeigned burst of admiration. The pure, unadulterated air which descends into this village, surrounded with these mountains, gives infallible token that the best of all earthly blessings, health, dwells among them."

Besides the public buildings referred to above, Charlottesville had at that time a market house. In October 1829, Opie Norris advertised the "old" structure of that name for sale, and required the removal of all the materials from the ground. Its site was on Market Street immediately east of Third. Soon after the war another edifice of the kind was taken down at the west end of Market Street; whether it was erected just after the demolition of the first is not known. It was an advanced period in the history of the county before banking facilities were enjoyed. In the earlier years when a business man wished to remit money in the long intervals of a payment in person, it was a common practice to cut in two a bank note of high denomination, and send a half by mail, and when the receipt of that was acknowledged, to send the other half. In one instance this mode of remittance led to an unhappy episode in the life of one of the citizens.

In 1820 Solomon Ballou advertised to run a hack to and from Richmond once a week, leaving Charlottesville on Wednesdays at the tavern of G. W. Kinsolving, and Richmond on

Saturdays at Saunder's Tavern. His design was to transport passengers, and also to carry the mails. Sometime after Opie Norris in the course of business sent the half of a fifty dollar note to a correspondent in Richmond. Hearing nothing in reply, he had the other half mailed from Nelson County to go by a different route, accompanied with the explanation that he had already sent the first half. Assured that the latter had not been received, he had Ballou arrested and searched, and the missing piece was found on his person. In consequence he was convicted of robbing the mail, and sent for a term of years to the penitentiary. What seemed a prosperous career, was thus brought to a sad end. Ballou was doubtless the son of a man of the same name, who in 1780 bought a large plantation between Ivy Creek and Mechum's River from Rev.William Woods. After his fall, Frank B. Dyer sold under a deed of trust Lot Twenty-Nine—the most easterly lot of the old town on the south side of Main Street—of which he was the owner; and in 1832. when his imprisonment had probably ended, he and his wife Philadelphia sold to John Lee the south end of the lot on which the Perley Building stands.

It was still some time before a banking house was opened in the county. The first concern of the kind was founded during the decade of 1830. This was the Savings Bank of Charlottesville, of which John H. Bibb was Cashier, and which, when its business had grown to large proportions in later years, had its office in the building of the Monticello Bank. In the beginning of 1840, a branch of the Farmers' Bank of Virginia was located in Charlottesville, at first on the west side of the Square. John R. Jones, James W. Saunders and T. J. Randolph were its Presidents in succession, William A. Bibb its Cashier, and Kemp Lowry and Edlow Bacon its Tellers. It was here the venerable John M. Godwin received his financial training, being connected with the bank during the whole of its existence. The present City Hall on the corner of Market and Fifth Streets, was erected for the prosecution of its business.

Shortly after the establishment of the Farmers' Bank, the

Monticello Bank was commenced. Its place of business was the large edifice on the corner of Main and Fourth Streets, which was especially built for its use. N. H. Massie was its President, B. C. Flannagan its Cashier, and Alexander P. Abell its Teller.

All these institutions were permanently closed by the civil war. The one last mentioned had a somewhat romantic prolongation of its proceedings after the cessation of hostilities. When towards the termination of the war apprehensions were entertained of the Sheridan Raid, it was deemed advisable to remove the specie of the bank from its vaults. Protected by a detachment of the Provost Guard, several boxes of gold and silver coin were taken from the bank to the residence of B. C. Flannagan, now in the occupancy of Judge Lyon. The same night the bank officers, accompanied by a friend and a negro in whom confidence was reposed, transported them across the country to the brow of the hill on the east side of Ivy Creek, near the point where it is crossed by the Whitehall Road. In the evidence detailed before the Court, a graphic description was given of the journey, made toilsome by their heavy burdens, amidst the gloom of the nocturnal darkness, over the face of the land unmarked by any object in the shape of enclosure or fence, all having been swept away by the ravages of the war. Reaching the place proposed, they hastily dug holes for the reception of the boxes. They found the ground frozen and stony, so that their work was difficult. They were likewise hampered by the fear, that the noise of their picks striking upon the rocks might attract the ears of some belated passenger. The result was that the boxes were partly buried in shallow excavations, and partly covered with leaves under the trunk of a fallen tree. After the return of peace it was discovered that the money buried in the earth was gone, while that concealed under the leaves remained undisturbed.

In searching the surrounding locality, an envelope was found addressed to George W. Bailey. Inquiry revealed the fact, that he and several friends had been fishing along Ivy Creek a few days before. Bailey was arrested, and no other evidence appearing at his examination, was discharged. He thereupon brought suit against B. C. Flannagan, who had procured his arrest. The case was tried at the October term of the Circuit Court in 1866, and excited intense interest in the community, both from the mysterious incidents involved, and from the brilliant array of legal talent on both sides. The jury came to the conclusion that the defendant had not acted unjustly or unreasonably.

After the war the Charlottesville National Bank was organized in place of the Monticello Bank, with the same officers. In 1867 the Farmers' and Merchants' Bank opened its doors on the north side of Main Street below fifth, its President being John L. Cochran, and its Cashier John M. Godwin. About the same time the Virginia Loan & Trust Company was projected, but was not long after transformed into the Citizens' National Bank, under Doctor Henry Howard as its President, and W. W. Flannagan as its Cashier. On the death of Doctor Howard in 1874, this institution was consolidated with the Charlottesville National Bank. In consequence the financial panic which swept over the country in 1873, and of discounts granted beyond safe limits, both of the remaining banks collapsed, entailing upon the community no little loss, and causing a serious disturbance of its business. In the lack of banking facilities thus occasioned, the Albemarle Insurance Company, which was established in 1854, and had been managed with great profit, became a place of deposit in charge of John Wood, Jr.; but it shortly failed under the stringency of the times. To meet the requirements of trade, B. H. Brennan, who had recently come to the county from Buffalo, New York, opened a private bank, with his son Frederick, as Cashier, and Daniel Harmon, as Teller. It likewise suffered from adverse conditions, and soon succumbed.

At the close of this season of commercial disaster and gloom, the present monetary institutions, the People's National Bank, and the Bank of Albemarle, entered upon their career, and by careful and skilful supervision, it is believed, are fixed on firm foundations.

The Courts, besides discharging the ordinary routine of business committed to their charge, maintained a vigilant oversight of the morals of the people. Some of the former generations of the county appear to have been much more addicted to the vice of gambling than the present. It pertained to the country as well as the town; and the gamesters, by resorting to the country taverns, frequently brought their hosts into the clutches of the law, as its prohibition was levelled at the place no less than the person. The magistrates sought to repress the evil with a steady hand. In 1807 Ferrell Carr was presented before the County Court for this offence, and was bound over to abstinence. Joshua Grady, Daniel Farley and Henry Chiles were frequent transgressors. In 1812 Martin Thacker was held under bonds in the Circuit Court "to abstain from the infamous practice of gambling." In fact a large portion of the cases coming before Judge Stuart during his early occupancy of the bench, were trespasses of this kind; and no doubt the rigid sternness with which he pursued the delinquents, greatly diminished their number, and the frequency of their misdeeds.

The Courts were also firmly resolute in keeping in check the impetuous spirits, that became unduly heated in the conflicts of the bar, or the competitions of daily life. Not to cover great names with reproach, but to show that the most eminent are men of like passions with the mass of mankind, records of this nature may be recalled. Dabney Carr, *"clarum et venerabile nomen,"* and George Poindexter were placed under bonds to keep the peace in 1801. So were John T. Hawkins and Richard Terrell the next year. In 1828 Charles A. Scott was bound over for a breach of the peace against Isaac A. Coles. In 1833 Thomas W. Gilmer and William C. Rives were obliged to give security to live peaceably with each other, and the sum of one thousand dollars specified in the bonds indicated the sharpness of their contention. In this case John Gilmer became surety for the former, Peter Meriwether for the latter, and James Clark for both. Alexander Rives was held under bonds in 1836 with Alexander Moseley, and in 1846 with Willis H. Woodley.

In 1841 John S. Moon and Jesse L. Heiskell were placed under similar restraint; and so strained were the relations between the two, that the same year they were presented for attempting to fight a duel. Many instances happened in the past history of the county, in which these barbarous encounters proceeded as far as design; but fortunately through the vigilance of the magistrates, or the opportune intervention of the police, they were suffered to proceed no further. Among these was the case of the irrepressible Lewis T. Wigfall in 1835, while a student of the University, and subsequently a member of the United States Senate from Texas. For contempt of Court in 1850, a fine of fifty dollars was imposed on Roger A. Pryor, at that time a practitioner of the Albemarle bar.

At the October term of the Circuit Court in 1818, a presentment of a different character took place. Andrew Hart Sr., Alexander Blain, William B. Harris, James Hart, Andrew Hart Jr., James Robinson Sr., Jesse Hamner and James Robinson Jr., were summoned to answer to the charge of the unlawful assembling of slaves, and teaching them at the Cove Meeting House, on the Sundays of September twenty-seventh and October fourth. This presentment was based on the information of Henry T. Harris, Isaac Hays Jr., William Suddarth and Samuel W. Martin. James Robinson, Pastor at the Cove, was also presented individually for words spoken in addressing the negroes. He was reported, on the information of Isaac Hays, Jr. alone, as having said, "You have been disappointed in your school, but do not be disheartened. Come and attend to me. I will instruct you, and I have no doubt that in fifteen of twenty years you will be as free as your masters." It is impossible now to obtain an exact knowledge of all the particulars of this case, as all the parties connected with it have long since passed from the land of the living, and a recollection of the faintest tinge as to the mere fact remains in the minds of their descendants. That there was a technical offence, cannot be gainsaid. Nor is it unikely that some logical excitement was aroused by the occurrence, as the language of Mr. Robinson, if he really uttered it, was inexcusably indiscreet. It happened too that James Robinson, the son, abused Elijah Brown, who was a Grand Juror in the case, for which he was summarily brought before the Judge and fined one hundred dollars; though upon his poverty being proved it was reduced to fifty. But it may well be conjectured there were considerations of an extenuating nature. Mr. Robinson was probably in bad health, as he died within the next two years. He was himself a slave-holder. In 1834 two negroes belonging to his estate, were on account of age or disease exempted from taxation. Henry T. Harris was one of his elders, and William Suddarth perhaps one of his members, certainly a member of his congregation. No doubt these persons testified simply in obedience to their summons. But the strongest apology was the nature of the work in which the accused were engaged. Instruction from the word of God, even when given against the letter of the law, was an act which not only no Christian, but no reflecting and right-thinking, mind would condemn. Every enlightened conscience would arise to speak in its behalf. At any rate such observant guardians of the law as Judge Stuart and John Howe Peyton permitted it quietly to drop. The case was continued for two or three terms, and then dismissed.

Near the latter part of 1822 a brutal murder was committed in the Ragged Mountains, not far from Taylor's Gap. A man named Hudson Sprouse killed Susan Sprouse, a woman nearly related to him by the ties of kindred. He was tried for the crime of the October term of the Circuit Court, 1823, and though defended by Rice Wood, Frank Dyer and V. W. Southall, was convicted of murder in the first degree. In the examination of persons summoned on the venire, as to whether they had formed opinions respecting the guilt of the accused, Abraham Wiant declared that he had formed a substantial opinion on the subject. Judge Stuart directed his enrollment as a juror, when he was peremptorily challenged by the prisoner's counsel. This order of the Judge was made the ground of an appeal, and the Court of Appeals holding that a substantial opinion was tantamount to a decided opinion, granted a new trial. The prisoner being arraigned again at the October term 1824, it was found impossible to obtain a jury, the whole community appearing to have adjudged him guilty. The judge immediately removed the case to Rockingham County, where he was tried on the nineteenth of the same month, and convicted. He was hanged at Harrisonburg on the tenth of the ensuing December, utterly hardened to his fate, and repelling every approach on the part of others, except towards a Mr. Best, who had made kind and earnest efforts to prepare him for his end. It ought not to be questioned that the Court above acted, as they were obliged to act, according to the rules of law; but it can be as little questioned, that these are the proceedings that occasion the enforcement of the Lynch law. It is difficult to see how, if the Legislature should make final a certificate of the Judge, that the accused had a fair, impartial trial, and was convicted on sufficient testimony, it would militate against the most scrupulous dictates of justice, or in any way abridge the rights and safety of mankind.

Another shock was given the community in 1833 by a murder perpetrated on the person of Peter U. Ware. He was a tinner by trade, and had his shop on Fifth Street below the old Advocate office. He was a quiet, inoffensive man, and had only a year or two before been married to Elizabeth Mayo. In compliance with some call of convenience or business, he had gone to the Buck Island neighborhood, where he was assailed by two negroes, and killed, as was supposed, for the purpose of robbery. Circumstances of a suspicious kind led to the arrest of Peter, a servant of Isaiah Stout, and Leander, who belonged to Elizabeth Dean, and they were speedily brought to trial. Egbert R. Watson, who had been recently admitted to the bar, was assigned as their counsel, and put forth his maiden advocacy in their defence. They were however condemned, and in the following October executed on the hill above Schenk's Branch opposite Mudwall, which at that time had become the Gallows Hill of the town.

The most unhappy event in the history of the University occurred in November 1840. Some of the students had for a time been participating in scenes of disorder, contrary to the regulations of the institution. In attempting to quell the disturbance one night, Prof. John A. G. Davis laid hold of a young man who was present, and when seized turned upon the Professor and shot him. The wound proved fatal. Joseph G. Semmes, a student from Georgia, was arrested for the deed, and after arraignment before the examining Court was sent on for trial. At the succeeding May term of the Circuit Court, the case for some reason was continued. Efforts were then made to procure the liberation of the prisoner on bail. Judge Lucas Thompson, who was then on the bench, positively refused to accede to the motion. Application was thereupon made to the General Court, and on receiving the testimony of Drs. Carter, Massie and James L. Jones as to the prisoner's health, bail was allowed in the sum of twenty-five thousand dollars. Reuben Grigsby and B. F. Porter, of Rockbridge, and William Porter, of Orange, became sureties for his appearance in that amount. When the time for trial arrived, the prisoner failed to appear, and the bail was forfeited. The report was believed, that Semmes fled to Texas, and a few years later died.

An event happened in 1846, which was the occasion of much regret both in the community and at the University. A menagerie was holding its exhibition on the open space between the lot of Mrs. John Kelly and the Cemetery. One of its features consisted in a showman riding in a car drawn by a lion. The route to be traversed extended through two or three of the cages, the ends of which were opened and connected together. A rope was stretched a short distance in front to keep the spectators back, and an address given, exhorting them to the observance of quietness and silence during the performance. Just as it began, a student named John A. Glover, from Alabama, who was leaning against the rope, threw a lighted cigar at the animal between the bars of the cage. The performer, enraged by the reckless act, leaped from the cage, and seizing a tent pin struck Glover on the head, and felled him to the ground. Glover was taken up unconscious, and borne to the Farish House, where a day or two after he died. His remains were interred in the University Cemetery, where a monument, erected by his fellow students, still commemorates his untimely end. The man who gave the blow, during the confusion that ensued, made his escape. George Nutter, a proprietor of the show, was arrested for the murder, and sent on by the examining magistrates. He was tried at the May term of the Circuit Court, and defended by Judges Watson and Rives; but the evidence produced failing to connect him with the fact, he was acquitted.

In March 1853 John S. Mosby, whose family at the time were residents of the county, shot George W. Turpin, the son of a tavern keeper in Charlottesville, in the course of an altercation; but his adversary, though severely injured, fortunately recovered. For the offence Mosby was prosecuted. At that period Judge W. J. Robertson was Attorney for the Commonwealth, and Watson and Rives defended the accused. Mosby was convicted and sentenced to pay a fine of five hundred dollars, and to suffer imprisonment in the county jail for twelve months. During the term of his confinement his counsel loaned him the necessary books, and he improved his enforced leisure by devoting himself to the study of law. Two years later he was admitted a member of the Albemarle bar. Shortly after he removed to Abingdon, where he was practising his profession when the civil war broke out, in which he was destined to achieve such brilliant renown.

The old Louisa Railroad, afterwards the Virginia Central, and now the Chesapeake and Ohio, was extended to Charlottesville in 1848. The line was continued westward and reached Staunton in 1854. For some years while the tunnel through the Blue Ridge was in progress, trains were moved over the summit of the mountain on tracks laid in a zigzag manner, one of the most remarkable feats of civil engineering ever accomplished. It was performed by Colonel Claude Crozet, formerly a professor in the Military Academy at West Point, and the distinguished engineer of the road. During the process of construction west of Mechum's River, the Colonel was presented by the Grand Jury for obstructing the Mountain Plains Road; but no doubt because the inconvenience was temporary, and the benefit immeasurable and permanent, it was judged best not to push the matter to extremity.

The Orange and Alexandria Railroad, then the Washington City, Virginia Midland and Great Southern, later the Richmond and Danville, and now the Southern, was opened between Charlottesville and Lynchburg during the war, in 1863. The link between Charlottesville and Orange C. H. became a line of travel in 1881. Before that time its trains were run over the Chesapeake and Ohio track between Gordonsville and Charlottesville. By the intersection of these roads, Charlottesville is made a prominent railroad centre, with arms radiating to all the cardinal points of the compass.

For some time previous to the civil war, symptoms of uneasiness were apparent in the community. A man named Rood was tried in 1859 on a charge of conspiring against the Southern people, and endangering the safety and perpetuity of the Union. He was acquitted. Rumors that the negroes were plotting to rebel were circulated in various sections of the county. Chapman, a servant of Mrs. Frances Estes, was apprehended, but no serious charge against him was substantiated. Patrolling parties were sent out more frequently, and were more vigilant in observing the state of things in every neighborhood. A person so sedate as Miss Rebecca Leitch was fined and bound over, for permitting her servant John to hire himself out according to his own pleasure. Owing to vague anticipations of evil, free negroes in some instances voluntarily subjected themselves to slavery, and made choice of masters. In this manner John Martin placed himself under the sheltering wing of J. E. Huckstep, Sachel Grayson of John Wood Jr., and Anderson Hutton of B. F. Abell. But notwithstanding all these disquieting tokens, a benignant Providence maintained peace between the people and their servants. In Albemarle, as generally throughout the South, the kindly relations between the races were manifested by the absence of any insubordination during all the trying circumstances that arose.

Because of the demoralizing influences of the war, much more trouble was experienced from a certain class of white people. Numbers deserted from the army, and to evade the officers seeking their arrest, took refuge in the hollows and secluded places of the Blue Ridge. Sallying forth from time to time from their secret haunts for purposes of plunder, they became a terror to the neighboring districts. It is said that more than once the people were constrained to form themselves into vigilance committees, to pursue these marauders into the mountains, and to make them the objects of their quiet but determined vengeance. During the last years in which hostilities continued, and those immediately succeeding, the courts were busy with prosecuting transgressors of this description. Indictments for larceny, assaults, obtaining property on false pretenses and horse-stealing, were frequent, and indicated the vicious and depraved spirit which was rife.

As soon as the tocsin of war sounded, steps were at once taken to raise money and arm men for the conflict. At a special meeting of the County Court, it was proposed to authorize a levy of fifty thousand dollars for the purchase of arms. The Nineteenth Virginia was mainly formed of men enlisted within the bounds of the county. A large portion of the Second Virginia Cavalry consisted of Albemarle men. Many were scattered in other divisions of the army, especially the Forty-Sixth Virginia, of which R. T. W. Duke became Colonel. The older men were disposed into companies of Home Guards. The county authorities displayed their zeal in such important measures as procuring supplies of salt, and preventing the spread of smallpox and other contagious diseases. They answered the call of the general government in sending the servants of the county to perform work on the defences of Richmond. Three drafts for this purpose were made in 1862 and 1863, the first for five hundred and forty laborers, the second for two hundred, and the third for one hundred and ninety. In connection with the last draft, W. T. Early drew on himself the animadversion of the Court. He refused to comply with the order. He was consequently fined ten dollars for contempt, and one hundred and eighty for failing to furnish a servant according to the allotment made, for sixty dollars at three dollars a day. Both fines were immediately paid in open court; and those who remember the Captain, can readily imagine the odd mixture of scorn and good humor with which the sentence must have been discharged.

Early in the war Charlottesville was designated as the seat of a large military Hospital. Two spacious frame buildings were erected just south of the present Junction, and furnished with cots and other appliances for ministering to the sick and wounded. Great numbers of these afflicted classes were conveyed thither for treatment throughout the war. The medical professors of the University devoted their time and skill to this benevolent work, and the ladies of the town and surrounding country exhibited a laudable interest in providing supplies of necessaries and delicacies, and many of them in exercising the soothing and efficient care of the nurse.

As an illustration of the manner in which the South suffered loss from their deranged currency, some of the public payments may be mentioned. In early times the ordinary daily allowance made to the county jailor for maintaining a prisoner in his custody, was twenty cents. As the war progressed, it rose to eighty cents, then to a dollar, in June 1863 to a dollar and a quarter, in December 1863 to two and a half, in May 1864 to three and a half, and in August 1864 to four dollars. The ordinary amount for which the Sheriff gave his bond for the faithful performance of his duty was sixty thousand dollars. During the war the amount required rose to two hundred and twelve thousand, and in September 1864, L. S. Macon was directed to increase his bond to five hundred thousand.

At the close of the war no courts were held from May till August 1865. The county was then under military government. The State of Virginia had been transformed into Military District No. One, and General John M. Schofield was the first military ruler. An officer of the United States army was stationed in Charlottesville, with the style of Military

Commissioner of Albemarle County, and through him the orders of the commander at Richmond were carried out. For the most part these military rulers were fair and broadminded men. Captain William Linn Tidball first occupied this office in Albemarle. He was ordered to Mississippi in July 1867, and was suceeded by Lieutenant A. F. Higgs, Sixteenth United States Infantry. Lieutenant Higgs was subsequently ordered to Georgia, and was followed by Lieutenant Town. The people generally acknowledged that they had reason to congratulate themselves, that posts justly esteemed odious and repulsive, were filled by men who evidently tried to discharge their duties in the least odious and repulsive way.

By the force and sharp practice of Federal authority, Francis Pierpont, of Marion County, was at the time Governor of the State, though his tenure of the office was merely nominal. All real government proceeded from Headquarters. An order from this source permitted an election to be held for county officers under William W. Gilmer as Commissioner of Elections, and in August 1865 he swore in the magistrates chosen, mainly those who had occupied the office before. Egbert R. Watson was appointed Judge of the Circuit Court, but because of his connection as counsel with numerous cases on the docket, Judge Sheffey, of Staunton, frequently sat on the bench in the way of exchange.

Affairs moved on with tolerable smoothness until the early part of 1869. In the meantime the Underwood Convention was held in Richmond, in the Hall of the House of Delegates, sitting from December 1867 till April 1868. The representative in this body for the District composed of Louisa, Albemarle and Augusta, was James C. Southall, and those for the county of Albemarle, James T. S. Taylor, colored, and Clifton L. Thompson. This Convention was largely made up of members holding the most extreme radical views. More than twenty were ignorant negroes. The constitution they formed *not only disfranchised all who had ever served in any civil or military capacity, even down to the most unimportant county position, but it prescribed the iron clad test oath to be taken by every one before he could enter upon* any office. This was virtually turning over the whole State government in all its ramifications to negroes, or to unscrupulous white men, who thronged into the State in great numbers from every section of the country, to profit by this wholesale disqualification of the native population. By the direction of the Convention, a vote was to be taken on the adoption of the Constitution in the ensuing July, at which time State officers and members of the Legislature were also to be elected.

Both parties immediately bestirred themselves. A Radical Convention assembled in Richmond on May sixth, and nominated Henry H. Wells, for Governor, James H. Clements, of Portsmouth, for Lieutenant Governor, and George W. Booker, of Henry County, for Attorney General. A Conservative Convention met at the same place the next day, and nominated Robert E. Withers for Governor, James A. Walker, for Lieutenant Governor, and John L. Marye, for Attorney General. During the same month the Radicals made nominations for the county. C. L. Thompson was to be State Senator, and J. T. S. Taylor, Franklin Nelson—both negroes—and John B. Spiece were to be members of the House of Delegates. The Conservatives proceeded so far as to nominate Dr. Robert S. Beazley, of Greene, who had been a member of the Convention, for the State Senate. Their greatest efforts however were put forth to have the Constitution voted down. Fortunately the higher authorities intervened. General Schofield, who had paid a formal visit to the Convenion, and strongly advised against their policy of disfranchisement, ordered the election for July both as to the Constitution and State officers, to be indefintely postponed. This afforded opportunity for the initiation of other measures. General Grant was elected president in November 1868. On the last day of that year, at the suggestion chiefly of Alexander H. H. Stuart and John B. Baldwin, of Staunton, a Convention assembled in Richmond to devise some plan of obviating the difficulties of the situation. As a result of their deliberations, a Committee of nine persons was selected to confer with the authorities in Washington. This Committee consisted of Mr. Stuart, Mr.

Baldwin, John L. Marye, Wyndham Robertson, William T. Sutherlin, William L. Owen, James F. Johnson, James Neeson and J. F. Slaughter. They were successful in gaining the ear and good will of General Grant. It was arranged that the provisions of the Constitution, especially that of negro suffrage, should stand, but that a few of its clauses, embracing particularly the sweeping disfranchising section and the iron clad test oath, should be submitted to a separate vote.

While matters were thus working for better days, present troubles seemed to be growing thicker and darker. In July 1868 General Schofield was appointed by President Johnson Secretary of War, and gave place to General George Stoneman as Commander of District No. One. Governor Pierpont's term had expired, and by an order from Headquarters, H. H. Wells was appointed Governor of Virginia. January twenty-third 1869 the crushing blow fell. On that day Congress, maddened by the idea that any of the people of Virginia should presume to oppose the radical Constitution, passed an act that swept out of office all incumbents, who could not take the iron clad oath, and allowed none to be appointed but those who could. Accordingly on March twenty-sixth came an order from Richmond, ejecting the Clerk, Commonwealth's Attorney, Commissioners of the Revenue, and all the magistrates. As the term of L. S. Macon as Sheriff had ended, a new Sheriff, J. C. Childress had already been appointed. By military authority, W. J. Points was made Clerk, George F. Jones and Angus A. McDonald Commissioners of the Revenue, the former for Fredericksville parish, the latter for St. Anne's, William F. Worthington, Commonwealth's Attorney, and the following persons magistrates, Henry N. Harrison, William G. Merrick, John Thornley, Thomas Garland, John W. Porter, William H. Hotopp, Edward S. Johnson, John W. Williams, Charles Goodyear and Charles A. Goodyear. About the same time Wells was removed as Governor, and the entire power of directing affairs, nominal as well as real, rested in General Stoneman.

How completely at this period the laws were silent, and the

force of arms had absolute sway, may be seen in the records of the County Court. Indictments were forwarded to Headquarters for the inspection of the General commanding, and orders were returned from the General commanding, directing them to be quashed. In other cases when grand juries found indictments for such crimes as robbery, and they were brought to the notice of the Court, one of the justices states to his brethren that there was no ground for them, and his mere word was enough for the Commonwealth's Attorney to ignore, and the Court to dismiss them.

But the better days were coming. In May of this year, 1869, the third Commander, General Edward Canby, was sent to occupy Headquarters. By his order the election was held in July. The new Constitution was adopted, but all the clauses on which a separate vote was taken were rejected. Gilbert C. Walker, a New Yorker, was elected Governor, John F. Lewis Lieutenant Governor, and James C. Taylor, Attorney General. The State and county were rescued from negro control. Things gradually returned into their proper channels. Henry Shackelford became Judge of the Circuit Court, and the year following John L. Cochran, Judge of the the County Court, the new Constitution dispensing with the service of the magistrates in this respect, and requiring the office to be filled by a man learned in the law. Ira Garrett was appointed to his old office of Clerk, and James S. Barksdale was made temporary Sheriff. At that time Virginia, and the County of Albemarle, were relieved from military rule, and all functions of government have since been discharged according to the usual provisions of law.

During the era of general confusion consequent upon the war, a foul murder was committed on the west side of the South West Mountain, not far from Stony Point. John H. Salmon, instigated by the desire of becoming sole owner of a small farm which had descended from his father, killed his mother and brother, the other joint tenants. The evidence was wholly circumstantial, but such as left no doubt of the guilt of the accused. He was brought to trial in the County Court in July 1870, and after a hearing protracted through a large portion of the month, was convicted and sentenced to be hanged in the ensuing November. Meanwhile his counsel appealed the case to the Circuit Court on some points excepted to in the trial, with the result that a new trial was awarded. The prosecution was accordingly continued in the County Court the following May. A venire was summoned from Lynchburg, a jury was empaneled, and the trial was about to begin, when the prisoner's counsel moved for his discharge on the ground that the number of the terms of Court prescribed by the statutes had been suffered to pass since his indictment without a trial. The jury was discharged, and argument on the motion heard. It turned out that in the prevailing derangement of affairs, and because of several interferences of the General commanding at Richmond, the ground alleged was true. The Court took the matter under advisement, and finally discharged the prisoner. So intense was the feeling of indignation awakened throughout the community by the crime, that the man at once fled, and according to report made his way to Texas.

CHAPTER VI.

EPISCOPAL

By the old law of Virginia, the Anglican, or Episcopal, was recognized as the Church of the State. The territory of the State was divided into parishes for ecclesiastical government, just as it was divided into counties for civil government. The officers of the parishes were styled vestrymen, twelve honest and discreet men for each, originally elected by the freeholders of the parish, and vacancies afterwards occurring to be filled by themselves. They had charge of the erection and preservation of the church buildings, the choosing of the rectors, and the care of the poor. The two parishes which Albemarle contained were Fredericksville in the north, and St. Anne's in the south. The dividing line between them was the Three Notched Road, entering the present limits of the county near Boyd's Tavern, and running to Woods's Gap. Before the formation of the county, the scattered inhabitants of the southern part, being still in Goochland and the parish of St. James Northam, were the objects of the spiritual care of Rev. Anthony Gavin. He was the rector of that parish from about 1736 until his death in 1749. From the description of him given by Bishop Meade, and a letter of his quoted by him, he was evidently a man of devoted industry and zeal. Though his residence was in the neighborhood of Dover Mills, and the present bounds of Goochland afford a large field of labor and travel, yet he made frequent visits to the people living "up in the mountains." In these remote parts he had seven places of service, and in his journeys within the space of two years had forded the North and South Rivers, that is, the Rivanna and the James, nineteen times.

In St. Anne's parish two churches were built in early times, the Church on Ballenger's Creek and the Forge Church. The former is still standing, and has been altered and occupied as a private residence. It is situated near the creek, between the road from Warren to Howardsville, and that passing through Porter's Precinct. The Forge Church stood on the north side of the Hardware River, about a mile or two below Carter's Bridge. From an act of the Legislature passed in 1777, directing the Sheriff to summon the freeholders of the parish to meet "at the new church on Hardware," to elect a new vestry, it is inferred that it was built but a short time before. Bishop Meade describes a service held in it with Bishop Moore, not long after the latter came to Virginia, which must have been about 1814; and the account he gives of its dismantled condition, and the open crevices through which wind and rain were wont to drive, touches the heart with its pathos. At a meeting of the Convention in Charlottesville in 1822, they adjourned to meet at the Forge Church on Friday, and at Walker's on Saturday. The Forge Church was still standing a few years ago, but reduced to ignoble uses. Converted into a barn, and filled with the fodder, in some way it caught fire, and burned to the ground. The glebe of St. Anne's was bought from William Harris in 1751 by Samuel Jordan and Patrick Napier, Church Wardens of the parish. It consisted of four hundred acres, and was located on the south fork of Totier Creek, where it is crossed by the road from Scottsville to Howardsville. After the glebes were declared public property, it was sold in 1779 by Thomas Napier, George Thompson and John Harris as Commissioners, to Joseph Cabell. He gave it to his daughter Mrs. Breckinridge, and it was the residence of her husband till his removal to Kentucky in 1793. The proceeds of the place, as well as of all the glebes of the county, were eventually applied to the erection of the University buildings.

The first rector of St. Anne's was Rev. Robert Rose. His residence was in what became Amherst County, not far from New Glasgow, but he occasionally preached in the churches of Albemarle. He was succeeded by Rev. William Camp, who in a short time went west, and was killed by the Indians near Vincennes. He was followed by Rev. John

Ramsay, who in 1759 purchased from Jacob Eades three hundred acres of land on the south fork of Totier. It is judged from his will, which is on record, that he died in 1770. He left his whole estate to his wife Barbara, who the same year sold the land on Totier to Abraham Eades, Jr., and bought more than four hundred acres on Hardware, adjoining the lands of the Carters and Hudsons. This land is described as being near Scratchface Mountain, which it is impossible now certainly to identify. Mrs. Ramsay subsequently sold to John Wilkinson for the Iron Company, was married to Thomas Richards, and removed to Bedford County. Rev. Charles Clay, a cousin of Henry Clay, was the next incumbent. He was an earnest minister, preaching not only in the churches, but also in private houses and at the Prison Barracks. He unhappily became involved in lawsuits both with his vestry and with individuals, and this occasioned his removal about 1784. He finally settled in Bedford County, where he died, and by the directions of his will an immense heap of stones, twenty feet in diameter and twelve feet high, was piled up upon his grave. Rev. Isaac Darneille succeeded Mr. Clay. He seems to have lived in Nelson. Incurring heavy debts, he became a lawyer, and finally escaping his liabilities as well as forsaking his family, he went South.

Fredericksville parish at first occupied Louisa County; but when in 1761 the western portion of Louisa was annexed to Albemarle, the parish was divided by the county lines, the part remaining in Louisa receiving the name of Trinity. Two churches were erected in this parish, one on either side of the South West Mountain. That on the east side was first called Belvoir Church, then in common speech Walker's, but is now known as Grace. When it was first built does not appear. It already existed in 1769, as in that year John Walker conveyed to Thomas Walker, Mosias Jones, Isaac Davis, William Barksdale, Thomas Carr, Nicholas Lewis, Nicholas Meriwether, John Rodes, Mordecai Hord, Thomas Jefferson and William Simms, Church Wardens and Vestrymen of Fredericksville parish, two acres "whereon the

Belvoir Church is situated." The church on the west side of the mountain was the Buck Mountain Church. It originally stood on the Buck Mountain Road, west of Earlysville. The date of its construction is unknown. Bishop Meade mentions that in 1745 it was determined to build three churches in the parish, the third to be erected on the Buck Mountain Road between the mountains. Its first mention in the records occurs in 1797, when Lucy Mills, Executrix of David Mills, conveyed to David Michie thirty-three acres, "whereon the Buck Mountain Church was built." The edifice, having fallen into disuse, was occupied by the Baptists in 1801. They held services in it till 1833, when the Episcopalians, being increased in numbers, asserted their right, and resumed possession. In subsequent years the church was rebuilt in Earlysville.

Rev. James Maury became the rector of Fredericksville parish in 1754, and continued until his death in 1768. He was succeeded by his son Rev. Matthew Maury, who served until his death in 1808. Neither of these ministers occupied the glebe, choosing rather to reside on their own farms. This glebe on the east side of the mountain, consisting of four hundred acres, was sold in 1809 to Nathaniel Ragland by Edward Garland, Stephen Moore and others, who at the time were acting as Overseers of the Poor. There was also a glebe on the west side of the mountain, which was situated between the Burnt Mills and Earlysville, and which was sold in 1780 by Thomas Johnson and William Simms, Church Wardens, to Epaphroditus Rhodes.

For many years after the death of Rev. Matthew Maury, there was no Episcopal preaching in the county except occasionally by ministers, who in passing held services in the courthouse in Charlottesville. In 1818 Rev. John P. Bausman was settled in the neighborhood for a short time. He was followed by Rev. Frederick W. Hatch in 1820, who lived in Charlottesville till 1830. He was an active and earnest minister, and a zealous mason. During his incumbency the Episcopal Church in town was built. The memory of the older inhabitants differs in regard to the manner of its erection, some affirming that it was built solely as an Episcopal Church, and others as a Union Church. The truth seems to be that the affair began as a union effort, but that the house was at last erected as an Episcopal place of worship. Bishop Meade states, that while the project of a union church was agitated, it was opposed by Mr. Hatch. An advertisement appeared in the Central Gazette on January twenty-third, 1824, proposing to purchase a lot for the building of a church, and it was discontinued on April sixteenth. On March nineteenth another appeared, inquiring for a lot for an Episcopal Church. Doubtless the change of plan took place in the interval between January and March. The building was commenced that year. As already stated, a letter dated in March of the ensuing year mentions that the town contained "a half finished church." After the removal of Mr. Hatch, and a short period of service by Rev. Zachariah Mead, Rev. Richard K. Meade, son of the Bishop, became rector, and the termination of his long pastorate is a somewhat recent event.

Mr. Hatch, in addition to his busy ministerial labors, preaching frequently at Buck Mountain and Walker's as well as in town, was a school teacher. He erected as his residence the brick house on the northeast corner of Market and Seventh Streets, and taught in the one story brick near the east end of main, now occupied by William Durrett. A ludicrous incident is told of him in connection with his celebrating the rites of matrimony. In performing this useful work, he often rode miles in the country in every direction. On one occasion he was called to unite a couple in the Ragged Mountains. When the ceremony was finished, the groom announced with some confusion that he was unable to remunerate him for his trouble. Mr. Hatch, observing a long string of gourds festooned on the wall of the room, proposed accepting a number of them. The young man was overjoyed at discharging his obligation so easily. He cut off a goodly array, and to relieve the parson from the inconvenience of carrying them, tied them around his horse's neck. Thus accoutred, he started on his return. As he approached the top of Vinegar Hill, the horse took fright at something by the wayside, and set off at full speed. The clash and rattle of the gourds increased his panic, and made him dart ahead at a still wilder rate. Down the hill he dashed, with his rider thrown forwards, and clinging around his neck with both hands, the gourds all the while keeping up their discordant clatter. The mad race continued through the whole length of the street, before the gaze of the astonished townsmen; nor was the rider released from his perilous position, until the panting steed drew up at the stable door. While Mr. Hatch was a resident of Charlottesville, a son was born to him, who received his own name, became a distinguished physician, and died a few years ago in Sacramento, California.

Besides the meeting of the Convention in 1822, it met again in Charlottesville in 1829, and during its session Rev. William Meade was elected Bishop of the Diocese of Virginia.

PRESBYTERIAN

Presbyterians were settled in the county while it was yet a part of Goochland. The colony of Scotch Irish who came over the Blue Ridge in 1734 under the auspices of Michael Woods, brought with them the faith of their fathers. Among these were the families of Wallace, Kinkead, Stockton, McCord and Jameson. Further to the south along the base of the Ridge were the Morrisons, McCues, Montgomerys, Reids and Robertsons. These last were the founders of Rockfish Church, located in the forks of Rockfish River. About 1746 James McCann, who had patented the land in 1745, conveyed to John Reid, James Robertson and Samuel Bell one acre and thirty-five poles, for the Rockfish Church, and for a school for the inhabitants of that vicinity.

Among the families first mentioned two churches were established. The first was Mountain Plains, which was built near the confluence of Lickinghole Creek and Mechum's River, and called after Michael Woods's plantation, and which still exists as a Baptist Church. The second was the D. S. Church, which was situated on the southwest face of the hill, on the summit of which S. W. Caulbeck recently resided. These communities, and others in Virginia and North Carolina, received the visits of several Presbyterian ministers in early times, beginning with that of Rev. James Anderson in 1738. In 1745 John Woods was sent to the Presbytery of Donegal in Pennsylvania, to prosecute a call for the services of Rev. John Hindman in the churches of Mountain Plains and Rockfish, but his errand seems to have been unsuccessful. Mr. Hindman was no doubt the same man who became an Episcopalian, and was the first rector of Augusta parish, dying there a year or two after entering upon the office. A call is still extant, dated March 1747, and signed by fifty-seven persons, which solicited the labors of Rev. Samuel Black in the church of Mountain Plains, and among the inhabitants of Ivy Creek. The place of worship for the people last mentioned was the D. S. Church, which was probably erected shortly after, as Mr. Black accepted the call. He was the first Presbyterian preacher who settled in the county. In 1751 he purchased from Richard Stockton four hundred acres on both sides of Stockton's Creek, and there he resided until his death in 1770. Descendants bearing his name still live on a part of the old place.

About the time of Mr. Black's settlement in Albemarle, Rev. Samuel Davies commenced his work in Hanover County. He had at first no little trouble with the State authorities, whose intervention was invoked by some bigoted ministers of the establishment under the old repressive laws against non-conformity. He however boldly and skilfully appealed to the provisions of the English Act of Toleration, which he claimed applied to the colonies no less than to the mother country, and was soon able to pursue his labors without molestation. He gathered several congregations, reaching from Hanover through Louisa and Goochland to Charlotte County. In 1755 the Presbytery of Hanover was formed. At their first meeting, they received a petition from the people of Albemarle near Woods's Gap, asking for preaching, and Mr. Davies himself being appointed spent with them the second Sunday of March 1756. From that time through a number of years, they had, besides the services of Mr. Black, those of Mr. Davies, John Todd, John Brown, John Martin, Henry Patillo and others. These ministers occasionally preached to the people on Buck Island at Mr. Lewis's—unquestionably at Monteagle—to those living between the Secretary's Ford and the mountains—no doubt in the Charlottesville courthouse, and at D. S. Church—to those at North Garden at Mr. Garland's, and to those at the Cove at George Douglas's.

As years passed on, ministers born and educated in Virginia were settled in the county. In 1769 Rev. William Irvin, who had been a pupil at Mr. Todd's school in Louisa, became pastor of the Cove Church. In 1770 Rev. Samuel Leake accepted a call to the D. S. Church. The next year Mr. Irvin extended his labors to Rockfish and Mountain Plains.

The Presbytery of Hanover convened with considerable frequency in the churches of the county. It met at Rockfish in 1772, 1773 and 1775, at the Cove in 1793, 1794, 1799, 1800, and 1803, and at the D. S. in 1771, 1772, 1775 and 1792. The last time it met at D. S. was in October 1809, holding night sessions at the house of John R. Kerr. At that meeting Rev. Thomas Lumpkin, a young minister, who had taught school for a short time in the neighborhood, was to have been ordained, and installed as pastor, but unhappily he had died the preceding month. The membership of this church was so much reduced by deaths and removals, that two years later its organization was dissolved. The ground on which it stood, and which had been conveyed to the congregation in 1773 by Joel Terrell, passed into the hands of Jesse Lewis, who within the memory of some now living removed the old dwelling. Two meetings of the Presbytery were held in Walker's Church. The first occurred in 1814, when they convened at night at the house of Captain Meriwether. At that time it received under its care John Robertson, the father of Judge W. J. Robertson, as a candidate for the ministry. The second meeting took place in 1819, and night sessions were held at the house of John Rogers. It met at Mountain Plains in 1778, and for the last time in October 1828, when they held night sessions at the house of the elder William Woods, of Beaver Creek.

South Plains Church was established in 1820, as the result of the labors of Rev. William Armstrong, and Rev. James C. Wilson. John Kelly, of Charlottesville, was one of its first elders. A branch of the same church worshipped on the west side of the South West Mountain at Bethel. It was not until 1870, that Bethel was set apart as a separate organization. Rev. Francis Bowman began preaching at South Plains in 1822, preaching occasionally also at the courthouse. Under his ministry the first Presbyterian house of worship in Charlottesville was built in 1827. In that year the lot on which it stood, on the southeast corner of Market and Second Streets, was conveyed by James Dinsmore to John Kelly, James O. Carr, Francis Bowman, Thornton Rogers, William Woods, Surveyor, Thomas Meriwether and Dr. John Holt Rice, as trustees of the new organization. It was not constituted a distinct organization until 1839, when it was under the ministry of Dr. William S. White.

The Presbyterian Church of Scottsville was founded in 1827, chiefly through the agency of Rev. Peyton Harrison. He had settled there as a young lawyer in 1825. Having been converted by the preaching of Rev. Asahel Nettleton, he became actively interested in religious work, and rested not till a church was formed. Shortly after he relinquished the law, and studied for the ministry. When he became a preacher, he returned to Scottsville, and was settled as pastor over the church for a brief period. Dr. William S. White succeeded him, and continued his labors there until he removed to Charlottesville.

BAPTIST.

The first Baptist Church in the county was organized in January 1773. This event took place in Lewis's Meeting House, which stood on old David Lewis's place, on the elevated ground south of the Staunton Road, about where the house of Mrs. Humbert now stands. The church commenced

HISTORY OF ALBEMARLE 133

with a membership of forty-eight persons. George Twyman, who lived just south of Earlysville, was one of its original members, and at a meeting held two months later presided as Moderator. The influence of the Presbyterian polity, under which doubtless many of the members had grown up, was apparent in their earliest proceedings. The original organization was effeced by two ministers and an elder, and at a subsequent meeting it was determined that "the feeling of the church concerning elders and deacons should be made known." It was several years without a pastor, but was occasionally supplied by such ministers as John Waller, and Elijah and Lewis Craig. This church was variously called by the names of Albemarle, Buck Mountain and Chesnut Grove. In 1801 they took possession of the old Buck Mountain Church of the Establishment, which had been disused by the Episcopalians. When that place of worship was claimed by its former owners, they removed to the union church in Earlysville in 1833, and in 1879 erected their present building a mile west of that place.

Andrew Tribble was chosen their pastor in 1777, and was ordained by Lewis Craig and others. How long Mr. Tribble continued in that relation is not known. He purchased a farm of one hundred and seventy-five acres a short distance below the D. S. Tavern, which he sold in 1785, and it is likely he performed his pastoral duties until that time. William Woods, distinguished as Baptist Billy, was ordained at Lewis's Meeting House by Messrs. Tribble and Benjamin Burgher in 1780, and became the pastor when the work of Mr. Tribble ceased. In 1798 Mr. Woods became a candidate for the Legislature; and as the law of Virginia at that time prohibited a minister from holding a civil office, he relinpuished his ministerial calling at Garrison's Meeting House in November of that year.

When the church was first formed, it was in the bounds of Dover Association, which then embraced the whole State. In 1791 the Albemarle Association was constituted, including the territory south of the Rapidan, and west of a line running from Barnett's Ford on the Rappahannock to the mouth of Byrd Creek on the James. Up to this time eight other churches had been founded, four of which lay within the present limits of the county, Totier in 1775, Ballenger's Creek probably about the same time, Priddy's Creek in 1784, and Whitesides now Mount Ed, in 1788. Martin Dawson became a minister soon after 1774, and preached for many years at Totier, which was situated near Porter's Precinct, and was then commonly known as Dawson's Meeting House. His labors however extended largely over the whole county. Benjamin Burgher, who lived on the headwaters of Mechum's River, was for a long period the pastor of Mount Ed. In 1822 he, Benjamin Ficklin and John Goss had advertised to begin a protracted meeting on a certan day at Mountain Plains, but on the very day of the appointment Mr. Burgher rested from his earthly labors. John Goss came to the county from Madison in 1802.

In 1820 Daniel Davis, Jr., a Baptist minister, preached occasionally in Charlottesville, sometimes in the courthouse, and sometimes in a large room of John Burrus. An organization seems to have existed in town at that date, as Mr. Davis, advertised that he would baptize those who had made a declaration of their faith to the church. Yet it appears that the formal establishment of the Charlottesville Church did not take place until August 1831. On that occasion four ministers were present, John Goss, Valentine Mason, Reuben L. Coleman and Charles Wingfield. Dr. Hardin Massie was appointed its Clerk. In October 1835, Dr. Massie conveyed to Nimrod Bramham, William Dunkum, Isaac White and Lewis Teel as trustees, a part of Lot. No. Five, on which, it was stated in the deed, the Baptist Church "stands." In 1853 the Circuit Court granted permission to sell the old church property, and appointed as trustees for the new church, William P. Farish, Lewis Sowell, James Lobban, John T. Randolph, John Simpson, James Alexander and B. C. Flannagan.

METHODIST.

The first mention of a Methodist Church in the county occurred in 1788 in a deed from James Harris to Thomas

Jarman, whereby seventy-five acres on the north side of Moorman's River were conveyed, surrounding two acres before given, on which "the Methodist Episcopal Church stands." This was beyond question the predecessor of Mount Moriah at Whitehall. The lot on which the latter was built, three and three fourths acres, was conveyed in 1834 by Daniel and Hannah Maupin to Jesse P. Key, William Rodes, Thompson and Horace Brown and David Wiant. Many years anterior to the date just mentioned this church was commonly known as Maupin's Meeting House, and was a favorite place for holding camp meetings. Henry Fry, a former Deputy Clerk of the county, speaks in his autobiography of Bishop Asbury preaching at an early day at Tandy Key's, who lived north of the Cove, at the junction of the Austin Gap and Lynchburg Roads; and in that vicinity, probably on Key's land, was located a building, which went by the name of Key's Meeting House, but of which no trace now remains. In 1795 Henry Austin conveyed a parcel of land to Thomas Stribling, Samuel Wills, Joseph Hardesty, Bernis Brown, Daniel Maupin, John Gibson, George Bingham, William Oliver and Basil Guess, of Orange, for a church, which was then called Austin's Meeting House, and is no doubt the same as that now known as Bingham's Church. In 1808 Bland Ballard donated one-fourth of an acre for a Methodist Church, which was the old Ivy Creek Church on the Barracks Road.

The first Methodist preacher on record was Athanasius Thomas, who was licensed to celebrate the rites of matrimony in 1793. This gentleman was the purchaser of several small tracts of land in the vicinity of Mountain Plains Church, where in all probability he made his home. In 1811 he disposed of this property, and presumably removed to another part of the country. Following him were Bernis Brown in 1794, John Gibson in 1797, John Goodman in 1802, and Jacob Watts in 1806. About the beginning of the century, there came to the county from Maryland two men, who although laymen filled the place of local preachers, John B. Magruder and George Jones. For many years they did a good work, and exercised a strong influence in behalf of their own church, and of true religion. In November 1823 a District Conference met in Charlottesville, of which James Boyd was President, and Walker Timberlake, Secretary.

The Charlottesville Church was established in 1834. In June of that year William Hammett purchased from Mary Wales, and other representatives of Thomas Bell, Lot No. Fifty-Five, and in the ensuing October conveyed in to Gessner Harrison, Nathan C. Goodman, Stapleton Sneed, Matthew and Thomas F. Wingfield, Ebenezer Watts and Thomas Pace as trustees, for a Methodist Church.

During the twelve years from 1825 to 1837 there was a great accession of church buildings in the county. In the first of these years were built the Charlottesville Episcopal Church, and a Methodist Church near Hammock's Gap; in 1827, the Charlottesville Presbyterian Church; in 1828, Mount Zion Methodist Church, and Mount Pleasant Methodist, near Hillsboro; in 1830, the Scottsville Presbyterian Church; in 1831, the Buck Island Methodist Church; in 1832, the Scottsville and Shiloh Methodist Churches; in 1833 Wesley Chapel, Earlysville Free Church, and the Charlottesville and Milton Baptist Churches; in 1834, Bethel, Presbyterian, Charlottesville and Mount Moriah Methodist, and Hardware Baptist Churches; in 1835, Cross Roads Episcopal Church; in 1836, Charlottesville Disciples Church; and in 1837, Free Union Free, and Piney Grove Baptist Churches.

CHAPTER VII.

ACCOUNT OF FAMILIES.

ABELL.

The first Abell in the county was Caleb, who came from Orange near the end of the last century. In 1798 he purchased what is still known as the old Abell place on Moore's Creek. It originally consisted of six hundred and ninety-four acres, comprising three different grants, but all bought from the executors of Henry Mullins, of Goochland. Caleb conveyed it to his son, John S. Abell, in 1808. John S. entered the Baptist ministry about 1830, and died in 1859. In 1816 he married Lydia Ralls, and his children were Alexander P., who was magistrate under the old regime, was first a merchant in Charlottesville, then Teller in the Monticello and Charlottesville National Banks, married Ann, daughter of William McLeod, and about 1876 removed to Greenville, S. C.; George W., who was one of the early ministers of the Disciples Church; and J. Ralls, whose wife was Susan, daughter of William Dunkum.

Besides John S., there were Joshua Abell, who married Caroline, and Richard, who married Emily, daughters of Benjamin Martin, of North Garden; Caleb, who married Jane, daughter of William Black; and Benjamin F., whose wife was Elizabeth, daughter of Joseph Grayson.

ALPHIN.

John Alphin began to purchase land in the county in 1778, when he became the owner of two hundred and fifty acres on Meadow Creek between the Staunton and Whitehall Roads. He continued his purchases till he acquired more than a thousand acres in one body. He conducted a noted hostelry, situated nearly opposite the residence of Jesse Lewis, and for many years a favorite resort for men of the turf. He furnished excellent accommodations, a prime cuisine, large stables, and a track for training horses. His house was a place of wide notoriety at the beginning of the century.

He married Martha, daughter of Christopher Shepherd, and his children were Julius, Sarah, the wife of William Chapman, Jane, the wife of David Owen, Nancy, the wife of William Fagg, Mary, the wife of Blake Harris, and Elizabeth. He sold to the county in 1806 the land on which the old Poor House was built. He died in 1818. Most of his family disposed of their interests in his estate, and removed to the West, some of them to Blount County, Tennessee.

ANDERSON.

David Anderson and his wife Elizabeth, came from Hanover County, and lived on a plantation in Albemarle, not far from Scottsville. David died in 1791, and his wife in 1804. They had eight sons, William, Nathaniel, Thomas, Richard, David, Matthew, Edmund and Samuel, and three daughters. Of the daughters, Ann was married to Dabney Minor, of Hanover, Sarah, to Christopher Hudson, and the third to a Barrett, whose son Anderson Barrett lived in Richmond, and was an executor of both his grandparents. One of the sons, Nathaniel, had his residence on the old glebe of St. Anne's on Totier, which he bought from John Breckinridge in 1796. He married Sarah, daughter of John Carr, of Bear Castle, and sister of Dabney, Mr. Jefferson's brother-in-law. He died in 1812, and left four children, William, Nathaniel, Mary, the wife of a Mosby, and Elizabeth, the wife of a Lawrence. Nathaniel married Sarah Elizabeth ———, and his children were Martha, the wife of Stephen Woodson, Mary, Dabney Minor and Overton. Edmund, son of David, is thought to be the same person who married Jane, daughter of William Lewis, and sister of the celebrated explorer, Meriwether Lewis. He died in 1809, leaving two sons and four daughters, William, Dr. Meriwether, who married Lucy Harper, Ann, the wife of Thomas Fielding Lewis, Jane, the wife of Benjamin Wood, Lucy, the wife of ———, Buckner, and Sarah, the wife of Gabriel Harper.

Richard Anderson, son of David, married Ann Meriwether, sister of Lucy, the wife of William Lewis. He at one time owned an interest in the land on Ivy Creek on which the Prison Barracks were built, and which he sold to John Harvie about a year before their building took place. His son David was living at Milton at the beginning of the century, and represented Brown, Rives & Co., one of the firms doing business in that town. In 1801 David was appointed a magistrate of the county, but resigned the next year. Some time after he removed to Richmond. He married Susan, daughter of Reuben Moore, of Culpeper, and his children were Meriwether L., Richard, Catharine, the wife of Jefferson Trice, of Richmond, and Helen, the wife of a Porter. In 1829 he returned to Albemarle, and married again Mary, daughter of Thomas W. Lewis, and widow of James Leitch, and two years later his son Meriwether married Eliza Leitch, daughter of his step-mother. Their home was at Pantops. David Anderson died in 1841, and Meriwether in 1872.

It is believed Richard Anderson had two other sons, Edmund and Jasper. Edmund married first Frances Moore, sister of his brother David's first wife. Some years later he married Ann, daughter of William Cole, of North Garden, and not long after Jasper married her sister, Susan Cole. In 1813 Edmund purchased from Clifton Rodes, executor of John Jouett, sixty acres of land lying east and north of Charlottesville, and extending from the present Ninth Street east to the hill overlooking Schenk's Branch, and laid it out in town lots. This tract was known as Anderson's Addition. He sold a number of lots, chiefly on East Jefferson and Park Streets, during the decade of 1820, and in 1831 conveyed to John J. Winn and Alexander Garrett Lot Thirty-Four, the present Maplewood Cemetery. In the meantime he removed to Richmond, and entered into business under the firms of Anderson & Woodson, and of Anderson, Woodson & Biggers, but the business failing, he transferred all his property in Albemarle to John R. Jones as trustee, who in 1829 sold it for the payment of his debts. A son, Charles Anderson, was a Druggist in Richmond, and a few years ago removed to Roanoke, where he died.

BALLARD.

Ballard was one of the first names of the county in the order of time. As early as 1738, Thomas Ballard obtained a patent for three hundred and twenty acres near the foot of Piney Mountain. His descendants became numerous, all having large families, and occupying farms in the stretch of country between Piney Mountain and Brown's Cove. Thomas died in 1781, leaving six sons and three daughters, Thomas, William, John, David, Bland, Samuel, Ann, the wife of Gabriel Maupin, Frances, and Susan, the wife of William Pettit. The second Thomas died in 1804. His children were John, James. Anne, the wife of a Bruce, Mary, the wife of a Davis, Lucy, the wife of Joseph Harvey, Elizabeth, the wife of Frost Snow, and Martha, the wife of Thomas Pettit. John married, it is believed, Elizabeth, daughter of Roger Thompson, and died in 1829, leaving seven sons and one daughter, Edward, James, David, John, Nicholas, William, Wilson, and Elizabeth, the wife of Pleasant Jarman. James, brother of John, married Ann, daughter of David Rodes, and died in 1853. His children were Garland, Thomas, David, Susan, the wife of Thomas L. Shelton, Selina, the wife of Thomas Bohannon, Judith, the wife of Nimrod Day, Frances, the wife of Porter Cleveland, Sophia, the wife of Hudson Oaks, and Mary, the wife of William Thompson. William the son of the first Thomas, married a daugher of William Jarman, and lived below Mechum's Depot; and his son John P., after occupying a position with Valentine, Fry & Co. in Charlottesville, removed to Richmond, where he founded the Ballard House, formerly one of the most popular hotels of that city. Bland married Frances, daughter of John Shiflett, and died in 1809. His family consisted of five sons and ten daughters. He donated the ground on which the old Ivy Creek Methodist Church was built.

BARCLAY.

Robert Barclay and his wife Sarah lived, in the early part of the century, on the south side of the road leading from the Cross Roads to Israel's Gap, at the place where James B.

Sutherland now resides. There Barclay died in 1818, and his widow was afterwards married to John Harris, of Viewmont. He left two sons and two daughters, Mary E., who became the wife of John D. Moon Sr., Thomas J., James T., and Ann Maria, the wife of Edward H. Moon. Thomas died unmarried in 1828. About the same time James came to Charlottesville, and opened a drug store. He lived in the brick house on the northeast corner of Market and Seventh Streets, which he bought in 1830 from Rev. F. W. Hatch. This place and some other property he sold to T. J. Randolph, and the same year purchased from him Monticello, containing five hundred and fifty-two acres, then valued at seven thousand dollars, the transaction being in all probability an exchange. He resided there till 1836, when he sold it with two hundred and eighteen acres to Commodore Uriah P. Levy. He then became a Disciples minister, and sailed as a missionary to Jerusalem, where he remained for many years. As the result of his researches there, he published a large work descriptive of the place, entitled The City of the Great King. He and his wife Julia had several children, among them a son, who was appointed by Mr. Cleveland in his first term Consul to Algiers, where a kinsman of the same name had discharged the same functions a hundred years before. The latter part of Mr. Barclay's life was spent in this country with a son in Alabama, where he died a few years ago.

BARKSDALE.

William Barksdale is noticed in the records of 1765. He was for a number of years a buyer of land, chiefly on the south fork of the Rivanna north of Hydraulic Mills, and on the upper part of Mechum's River. He and his wife Ann were the parents of eleven children, Nathan, Goodman, Samuel, Jonathan, John H., Nelson, ———, the wife of John Douglass, Ann, the wife of Alexander Fretwell, Sarah, the wife of William Warwick, of Amherst, Lucy, the wife of Richard Burch, and Elizabeth. William Barksdale died in 1796, and some years later his widow was married to Philip Day.

Nathan seems to have died young, leaving two sons,

Achilles and Douglass, to whom their grandfather gave a tract of land on Mechum's River above the Depot of that name. Goodman and Jonathan were settled in the same neighborhood. Goodman died in 1832. Jonathan married Lucy, daughter of Giles Rogers, and died in 1831. His children were Nancy, the wife of George W. Kinsolving, Lucy, the wife of Richard Rothwell, Ralph, Nathan, who married his cousin Elizabeth, daughter of Parmenas Rogers, and whose children were Ralph, Lucy, Mary and George, and William G., who married Elmira, daughter of John Wood. Jonathan formerly owned the land on which the village of Hillsboro stands.

Samuel Barksdale lived between the old Lynchburg Road and Dudley's Mountain. He was twice married, first to Mary, daughter of Jeremiah Hamner, and secondly to Jemima, daughter of Charles Wingfield Sr. His children by the first marriage were Elizabeth, the wife of William Watson, long the keeper of the county jail, and Mary, the wife of William Douglass. Those by the second were Rice G., whose wife was Elizabeth White, whose children were John H. Jr., and James S., and who died in 1879, John, who was a Presbyterian minister, one of the first set of Students at Union Theological Seminary, but who died in Charlottesville in 1829, just after entering upon his work, Jane, the wife of Willis Day, and Sarah, the wife of Richard Fretwell.

John H. Barksdale resided north of Hydraulic Mills. His children were Hudson, Elizabeth, the wife of Charles Overstreet, and Orlando, who some years ago lost his life on the railroad near the Burnt Mills, in the act of saving Edward Gilbert from being crushed by a passing train. Nelson was the most active and thrifty of the family. His home was also north of Hydraulic Mills. For many years he farmed the Sheriffalty of the county, and was Proctor of the University while it was yet in its humbler guise as Central College. He died in 1861. He married Jane, daughter of Jesse Lewis, and his children were Mary Jane, the wife of J. Frank Fry, Sarah, the wife of John J. Bowcock, Sophia, the wife of James Fray, John T., Eliza, the wife of Albert Terrell, and secondly of Robert Durrett, Caroline, the wife of T. J. Eddins, and Margaret, the wife of Dr. H. O. Austin.

BIBB.

The Bibbs came to Albemarle from Louisa. In 1821 William A. became associated in the mercantile business with his father-in-law, Nimrod Bramham. He was appointed a magistrate in the county in 1832. When the Branch of the Farmers' Bank of Virginia was established in Charlottesville, he was appointed its Cashier, and managed its affairs with eminent skill until all business was interrupted by the war. In 1836 he purchased from the trustees the square on which the old Female Seminary stood, the present site of the Leterman mansion, and made it his residence until his death in 1865. He married Sarah Bramham, and his children were Henry, Angeline, the wife of Edward J. Timberlake, Dr. William E., Horace, Cornelia, the wife of George W. Thornhill, Emma, the wife of Professor H. H. Harris, James T., Sarah, the wife of Robert Williams, and F. Gillett, the wife of George Willingham, of South Carolina.

John H. Bibb, a nephew of William A., commenced his business life as a clerk in the house of Valentine, Fry & Co. It was not long however before he became a merchant on his own account, conducting his affairs with success until the war. He was also the first Cashier of the Charlottesville Savings Bank. He built the brick house on the west side of Ridge Street, now in the possession of Dr. George Scribner, and resided there for some years. His home was afterwards at Branchland, where Major Bolton now resides, and he finally purchased the large brick on Jefferson Street, formerly the dwelling of John R. Jones. He married Harriet, daughter of French Strother, of Culpeper, and his children were Helen, the wife of William P. Louthan, A. Pendleton, and Catharine, the wife of Dr. William Du Bose, United States Navy. Mr. Bibb died in 1888.

BISHOP.

A William Bishop was the grantee of a small parcel of land on the south fork of Hardware in 1756, which his descendants sold in 1774 to George Eubank. In 1782 James Bishop entered four hundred acres on the Blue Ridge in the Afton neighborhood, which he and his wife Elizabeth subsequently sold to other parties. About the end of the last century Joseph Bishop began to purchase land in the county, and continued to purchase from time to time in various localities, particularly in the Biscuit Run Valley and the vicinity of D. S. In 1803 he bought from John Carr twelve acres bordering on the west side of Charlottesville, and extending from the Staunton to the Whitehall Road; with this tract his name was more intimately connected. He established the tanyard at the west end of Main Street. He erected the first buildings in Random Row, and gave lots on Vinegar Hill to most of his children. The largest part of this land he sold not long before his death to John Neilson, an Irishman, who was one of the contractors for the University buildings. Joseph Bishop died in 1825. He left nine children, John T., who married Mary Ann, daughter of James Jeffries, and removed to Dearborn County, Idiana, Joseph, James, Ann, the wife of Johnson Pitts, Patience, the wife of Gustavus Parsons, Mary, the wife of William Young, Frances, Jonathan, A. J., who removed to Missouri, and Lucy Jane, the wife of Ezra M. Wolfe. Joseph Bishop's wife was Jane, daughter of Edmund Terrell, and his wife, Margaret Willis, a granddaughter of Henry Willis, the founder of Fredericksburg, and his wife, Mildred Washington Gregory, sister of General Washington's father. His son, Joseph, was an active dealer in Charlottesville real estate. He was one of the original trustees of the Disciples Church.

BLACK.

Samuel Black was a native of Ireland, and coming to this country as a student of theology, was licensed to preach by the Presbytery of New Castle. He was settled as pastor over two churches in Donegal Presbytery in Pennsylvania. In 1743 he began to visit Virginia as a missionary, and in 1747 received a call from Mountain Plains Church, and the people of Ivy Creek, who formed the congregation of D. S.

In 1751 he purchased from Richard Stockton four hundred acres on Mechum's River, where he made his home until his death in 1770. For a time he taught school in connection with his ministerial duties. His wife's name was Catharine Shaw, and his children were Samuel, James, Margaret, Mary, Sarah, John and William. James became the owner of six hundred acres on Stockton's Creek not far from Rockfish Gap, where he kept a public house, and where in the fall of 1777 he had as a guest General George Rogers Clark. He and his wife Eleanor sold out in 1780, and seem to have removed from the county. John and his wife Elizabeth, in 1789 sold to Menan Mills one hundred and thirty acres adjoining the home place. After this time the only member of the family whose course can be traced is Samuel, the eldest son.

He became a man of prominence, prospered in his affairs, was active as a magistrate for some years, and died in 1815. He and his wife Mary had six sons and three daughters, Samuel, William, Dorcas, the wife of Charles Patrick, Catharine, Mary, the wife of John Ramsay, James, John, Joel and Daniel. The second son, William, married Matilda Rowe, and died in 1809, leaving seven children, Samuel, who died unmarried in 1846, Jane, the wife of Caleb Abell, Andrew, James, Thomas, who died unmarried in 1878, John and Mary. Andrew died in 1875. His wife was Sarah, daughter of Nicholas Merritt, and his children, William, Nicholas, Mary, the wife of Willis Piper, Elizabeth, the second wife of James H. Rea, and Cynthia. James married Rosanna, sister of Andrew's wife, and died in 1876. His children were Samuel, Nicholas, Elizabeth, the wife of Richard Robinson, and Sarah Ann, the first wife of James H. Rea,

BOWCOCK.

The first of the Bowcock family in the county was Jason. The records mention indeed a Samuel Bowcock, but nothing more is known of him except that he died in 1783. A daughter of Alexander McKinzie, who from 1742 to 1799 owned part of the land now possessed by the University, was the wife of a Bowcock, and left a daughter who was living at the beginning of the century. The husband here referred to may have been Samuel, and he may possibly have been the father of Jason. The latter lived on the Barboursville Road north of Stony Point, and died in 1816. He and his wife Judith had six children, Ann, the wife of Achilles Douglass, Douglass, Achilles, Tandy, Mildred, the wife of John Douglass, and John, who succeeded his father on the old place. In December 1822, Achilles Bowcock, while sitting at table at Nathaniel Burnley's in Stony Point, apparently in perfect health, fell dead from his chair.

Douglass lived at the junction of the Earlysville and Piney Mountain Roads, and kept tavern there for some years before his death in 1825. His wife was Mildred Blackwell, and his children Catharine, the wife of Dr. John F. Bell, who removed to Kentucky, and John J. John J. occupied a large place in the hearts of the people of the county. His early advantages in point of education were slender, and his natural gifts not brilliant, yet few men exercised a wider or more beneficial influence in the community. His powers of perception were clear, his judgment sound, and his integrity without spot or suspicion. He inherited his father's farm, and followed him in the conduct of a public house; but almost immediately he espoused the views which had then begun to prevail on the subject of temperance, and turned the tavern into a house of entertainment. The disputes of the surrounding country were largely referred to his arbitration, and his decision was accepted as an end of strife. His neighbors often desired that he should be the guardian of their children, and settle their estates. He was a magistrate under the old regime, and among the first elected under the new constitution; and four times in succession he was made by the choice of his fellow justices presiding magistrate of the County Court. For many years he served as Colonel of the Eighty-Eighth Regiment, his farm by the way being the regular place of its muster. He was a member of the House of Delegates, and according to a friend of opposite politics, such was the universal regard in which he was held, that no competitor could stand before him, and he might have been reelected as often as he wished; but his unambitious temper soon declined the honor. He was for a long period a ruling elder in the South Plains Presbyterian Church. He died full of days in 1892, and was followed to the tomb by the high esteem and sincere regrets of all who knew him. His wife was Sarah, daughter of Nelson Barksdale. Of his five sons and two daughters, Dr. Charles, who for many years practised his profession at Everettsville, did not long survive him.

BOWEN.

Four brothers named Bowen bought land in Albemarle. James M., William, Peter and Thomas C. They came from the vicinity of Jeffersonton, Rappahannock County. In 1817 James and William together made their first purchase of five hundred acres from Benjamin Ficklin—the old White place southwest of Batesville. James must have relinquished his interest to William, since in 1829 the latter with his wife, who was Eliza George, of Fauquier, sold this land to Roland H. Bates. William was a teacher, having had a school near Ivy Depot, and afterwards near Mount Ed church. He finally returned to Rappahannock. Peter, who was a physician, never resided in the county, though he more than once purcased land in the Greenwood neighborhood. Besides farming, James for some years prosecuted business as a merchant. He prospered in his affairs, and in 1835 bought the old Ramsey place, with its Mill, building the large brick mansion which still stands, calling it Mirador, and making it one of the finest seats in the county. He married Frances Starke, and his children were Ann, the wife of Dr. John R. Baylor, Mary, the wife of Dr. O. R. Funsten, of Clarke and Eliza, the wife of her cousin, Dr. George M. Bowen, son of Peter. James died in 1880. His grandson, James Bowen Funsten, was recently consecrated Episcopal Bishop of Boise, Idaho.

When Thomas first came to the county, he also engaged in the vocation of teaching. One of his schools was located beside the old Mount Pleasant Methodist Church, which stood on the hill three of four hundred yards west of Hillsboro, and there he had Slaughter Ficklin as one of his pupils. In 1837 he purchased from John Pilson the place which he occupied till his death, which had been the old home of Isaac Hardin, and which consisted of three tracts, Huntsmans, so called by a former owner who removed to Kentucky, Hard Labor, and Greenwood, which gave name to the Depot subsequently established. Thomas Bowen acted a more prominent part in the affairs of the county than his brother, and served as a magistrate prior to the Constitution of 1850. He was twice married, first to Miss Wheatley, of Culpeper, and secondly to Margaret Timberlake, of Clark County. He left two daughters, Mary Eliza, the wife of Colonel Grantham, of Jefferson County, and Julia, the wife of John Shirley. His death occurred in 1886. Thornton W. Bowen, who lived north of Whitehall, was a brother of these gentlemen.

BRAMHAM.

Nimrod Bramham first appears, when he commenced business as a merchant at the point where the road over Turkey Sag comes into the Barboursville Road. His store there was a noted centre for many years. He purchased the place in 1797 from James Sebree and Gravett Edwards. He was highly esteemed both for his commercial skill and energy, and for his civil and military abilities. In 1800 he succeeded William Wirt as Lieutenant in the militia, and in 1806 Francis Walker as Colonel of the Eighty-Eighth Regiment. In 1801 he was appointed a magistrate. He represented the county in the Legislature in 1812. In 1805 he gave the ground for the Priddy's Creek Baptist Church, and was one of the first trustees of the Charlottesville Baptist Church. He probably removed to Charlottesville in 1806, as he then bought part of the lot on the west side of the Square, where for years he did business under the firms, first of Bramham and Jones, and afterwards of Bramham and Bibb. In 1818 he purchased from Jesse W. Garth the place southwest of Charlottesville, on which he built the large brick house, the present residence of Herndon Fife, where he spent the remainder of his life. He died in 1845. His wife was Margaret Marshall, of Culpeper, and his children, Sarah, the wife of William A. Bibb, Nimrod, James, Lucy, the wife of John Simpson, Gilly, the wife of William Eddins, and Jane, the wife of Dr. Wyatt W. Hamner.

BRAND.

Joseph Brand came from Hanover County, and in 1779 bought from John Clark seven hundred and seventy-three acres of land on Mechunk Creek. Some years after he purchased a tract of more than six hundred acres on the Rivanna opposite Milton. He also owned property in Hanover, and land in the North Western Territory on the Miami. He died in 1814. He and his wife Frances had twelve children, Benjamin, Sarah, William, James, Joseph, Chiles, David, Robert, Eliza, George, John, and Frances, the wife of David Huckstep. What became of most of this large household is not known. One of the sons, William, it is believed, emigrated to New Orleans, where he prosecuted a successful business. The year after her father's death, Sarah was married to John Robertson, a native of Scotland, who had taught school in the county for some years, and who in 1814 was taken under the care of Hanover Presbytery as a candidate for the ministry. Chiles married Elizabeth Bryan, and died in 1861. His children were Ann Eliza, the wife of Thomas R. Bailey, Mary Jane, the wife of Richard Pinkard, Sarah, Richard, Catharine, who was for many years a teacher in Charlottesville, and became the wife of William Bell, of Augusta, Maria, William, James, and Lucy, the wife of R. H. Munday, who still occupies the house on University Street which was conveyed to her grandmother by John M. Perry in 1825. William D. Meriwether and James Lindsay were the acting executors of Joseph Brand, and according to the instructions of his will sold the land opposite Milton to Martin Dawson in 1815, and that on Mechunk to Joseph Campbell in 1833.

BROCKMAN.

One of the early land holders in the northeast part of the county was Samuel Brockman. He diel in 1779, leaving two sons, Samuel and William, and probably a third named Jason. William was apparently prosperous in his affairs. He lived on Priddy's Creek, owned a considerable quantity of land, and had one of the first mills erected in that section. He died in 1809. A Baptist church, the precursor of the Present Priddy's Creek Church, was on his land, and he devised it to the congregation using it as a place of worship. His children were Frances, the wife of a Taylor, Elizabeth, John, Margaret, the wife of a Henderson, Thomas, William, Ambrose, Samuel and Catharine, the wife of a Bell. Ambrose married Nancy, daughter of Captain William Simms, and became a Baptist preacher. Samuel married Ann Simms, a sister of Ambrose's wife, and his son Samuel, who died in 1847, was the father of Richard Simms, Bluford, Tandy, Simpson, Tazewell, and Agatha, the wife of Thomas Edwards. Richard Simms married Martha, the daughter of Wiley Dickerson, and removed to Amherst. Among his children were Fontaine D., Harriet, the wife of William Jeffries, Tandy, and Willis Allen, who removed to Atlanta, Georgia.

In the early part of the century many of this name emigrated to Kentucky, a Tandy Brockman going to Christian County, and Elizabeth, a widow, with a large family of children, to Boone.

BROOKS.

James Brooks was a lawyer of the early Albemarle bar. He married Elizabeth, daughter of Richard Woods, and lived on a parcel of land on Mechum's River below the Miller School, given him by his father-in-law. He died in 1815, comparatively young. His children were Robert, Elizabeth, James and Richard. He, and after him his son Robert, had charge of the estate of Thomas West.

In 1808 Robert married Elizabeth, daughter of James Hays, the founder of New York, and at first resided in Nelson County. In 1812 he became a resident of New York, purchasing Lot Thirty-One, on which stood at the time a one-story framed house. In 1817 he made from David Hays the first purchase of what was subsequently the Brooksville plantation in the same vicinity. The next year his brothers and

Shelby County, Kentucky, in 1809. Benajah also disposed of his interests, and removed to Buckingham.

Bernard had his home at the foot of Buck's Elbow, not far from Whitehall. He was the first of the family to depart this life, dying in 1800. He and his wife Elizabeth had twelve children, Robert, Reuben, Bernard M., Charles, Thomas H., Ira B., Asa B., Benjamin H., Bezaleel, Francina, wife of John Rodes, Lucy, the wife of Nathaniel Thompson Sr., and Sarah. Robert and Reuben emigrated to Sumner County, Tennessee. Bernard M. married Miriam, daughter of David Maupin, and had nine children, among whom were Thompson Brown, Sarah, the wife of Clifton Brown, and Pyrena, the wife of Tilman Maupin. Charles practiced medicine in Charlottesville in the early part of the century. He lived where Dr. W. G. Rogers now resides till 1822, when he removed to the farm on the waters of Ivy Creek which he bought from Crenshaw Fretwell, and on which his son Ezra still resides. He married his cousin Mary, daughter of Bezaleel Brown, and had six children. He died in 1879, having attained the remarkable age of ninety-six years. Thomas H. married first Mildred Brown, and secondly Lucy, daughter of Horsley Goodman. By his first marriage he had a daughter Emaline, who was the wife of W. G. Fretwell. Ira B. married Frances Mullins, and had six children, among them Burlington D. Brown. Benjamin H. married Judith, daughter of Hudson Fretwell. Bezaleel married Elizabeth, daughter of John A. Michie, and his children were Cynthia, the wife of William H. Brown, Frances, Addison, Williamson, Mary, the wife of George W. Kemper, Martha, the wife of Charles H. Parrott, and John A. M. He was cut off in the prime of his days in 1825. The family of Bernard Brown was remarkable in one respect. He an his three sons, Charles, Thomas H., and Ira B. were magistrates of the county, and two of them served as Sheriff, Charles in 1841, and Thomas H. in 1849.

Bernis was one of the early Methodist preachers in the county and country, entering the ministry some years before the close of the last century. He married Henrietta, daughter of John Rodes, and died in 1815, leaving eight children, Sarah, the wife of Thomas Jones, Henrietta, the wife of John Ruff, Ann, the wife of John Dickerson, Bernis, Tyree, Benjamin T., who married Lucy Richards, Elizabeth, the wife of Charles Carthrae, and John R.

Bezaleel was an officer in the Revolutionary army at Yorktown, was a magistrate of the county, and served as Sheriff in 1805. He died in 1829. He and his wife Mary had six children, William T., Bezaleel, Elizabeth, the wife of Jesse Garth, Lucy, the wife of her cousin Reuben, Bernard's son, Sarah, the wife of Charles Parrott, and Mary, the wife of Dr. Charles. William T. married Mary, daughter of James Jarman, and died in 1877. His children were Lucy, Sarah, the wife of John R. Early, and Mary, the wife of Dr. William E. Bibb. Bezaleel was appointed a magistrate in 1835, was a member of the House of Delegates from 1844 to 1847, and died in 1878.

Brightberry and his wife Mary had five sons, Horace, Clifton, William, Nimrod, and Brightberry. He died in 1846. Horace lived at the head of the Cove, just beneath Brown's Gap, and his house, on account of its bracing air, quiet seclusion and generous fare, was a favorite resort of the Methodist clergy during the heat of summer.

This family of Brown, from their early settlement, their prominent part in public affairs, the high character generally prevalent among them, and the lasting impress they have made on the natural scenery of the county, is one of the most noted in its history.

A numerous family of the same name began with Andrew Brown, who in 1789 bought land in North Garden from John Everett. He lived in a house which is still standing, about a quarter of a mile west of North Garden Depot. He died in 1804, and the place was well known for many years after as the residence of his wife Mary. His children numbered thirteen, Elizabeth, the wife of Joel Yancey, John, James, Anderson, Nancy, Lucy, the wife of Ralph Thomas, Sarah, the wife of Absalom Johnson, Nelson, Mary, the wife of Martin Moore, Margaret, the wife of James Kinsolving, Williamson, Maurice and Damaris, the wife of Benjamin W. Wheeler. John married Martha, the widow of John P. Watson, who had devised to her his real estate, nearly five hundred acres lying east of North Garden Depot; she however in 1816 joined with her second husband in a deed to James Leigh, that it might be reconveyed to him. He died in 1845 and his children were John A., William, Catharine, the wife of Jerome B. Wood, Sarah, the wife of John M. Carr, Ann, the wife of George W. Rothwell, Charles, Martha, the wife of Benjamin F. Ammonett, and Marietta, the wife of Elijah J. Bettis. Anderson and his wife Susan had ten children, among whom were Sarah, the wife of D. C. Rittenhouse, Mary Jane, the wife of James A. Watson, and the late Andrew J. Brown, of Charlottesville.

A Benjamin Brown was associated with David Ross in the purchase of a large number of lots in Charlottesville, when they were originally sold. He died about 1799, and John Brown, of Louisa, was his executor. It is probable Benjamin lived in Louisa, and he may have been the eldest son of Benjamin Sr., of Brown's Cove.

Another Benjamin Brown was a lawyer of the Albemarle bar at the beginning of the century. He was the owner at different times of the plantations of Meadow Creek and Mooresbrook, at which latter place his son, Robert M., a prominent attorney of Amherst, was born. He married Sarah E. W., daughter of Colonel Charles Lewis, of North Garden. After selling Mooresbrook to R. B. Streshley in 1812, he removed to Amherst County.

Matthew Brown, who it is said was not related to the last mentioned Benjamin, married Ann, the sister of Benjamin's wife. For a few years subsequent to 1804, he resided on a thousand acres which he purchased from John M. Sheppard, of Hanover, and which were situated in North Garden on the north side of Tom's Mountain. He also removed to Amherst. At a later date he was a contractor for erecting the buildings of the University. He was the grandfather of Judge Thompson Brown, of Nelson.

BURCH.

In 1763 Thomas Burch, of Caroline County, together with Ritchins Brame, purchased from Francis Jerdone four hundred acres on Ivy Creek, a part of the Michael Holland tract, of which another part is the present Farmington. He died in 1775, leaving his widow Sarah, and fourteen children, Mary, the wife of a Howlett, Cheadle, John, Benjamin, Keziah, the wife of a Cook, William, Sarah, the wife of a Bowles, Ann, Frances, Samuel, Joseph, Richard, Jean Stapleton, the wife of John Rodes, son of the first Clifton, and Thomas. His widow and James Kerr were designated executors of his will. As to what became of most of this large family, no sign remains.

Samuel was shot by George Carter in his own door on Main Street in Charlottesville in 1800. His house was situated about where the store of T. T. Norman now stands. His wife, who was Mary, daughter of James Kerr, with her daughter Sarah, who became the wife of Robert Andrews, removed to Fleming County, Kentucky, and their interest in the lot on which Samuel had lived, was sold to William Thombs in 1828. Two sons, Thomas D. and James Kerr settled in Wake County, North Carolina, James K., whose wife's name was Helen, became a Presbyterian minister, preached at one time in Kentucky, and in his last years removed to Missouri. His daughter, Catharine was the wife of the distinguished divine of Kentucky, Dr. Nathan L. Rice.

Joseph Burch in 1786 married Mary, daughter of the elder Clifton Rodes and his wife Sarah, daughter of John Waller, of Pamunky. He removed to Kentucky. A son of Joseph was the Rev. Clifton R. Burch, whose daughter was the wife of John C. Breckinridge, the Vice President; and a daughter of Joseph was the wife of Waller Bullock, and mother of the late Rev. J. J. Bullock, of Baltimore and Washington.

Richard Burch married Lucy, daughter of William Barksdale in 1791. He was the owner of what is now known as the Ivy Cottage plantation, which was no doubt a part of his father's place. In 1793 he entered upon a contest with Moses Bates in regard to the erection of a mill on Ivy Creek; and in 1813 the Court decided that the right to the bed of the creek belonged to Burch. Meanwhile he devoted himself to tavern keeping. He conducted a public house at Stony Point, then at Michie's Old Tavern, and still later at the Swan in Charlottesville. In 1821 he was engaged in the same business in Lovingston, Nelson County.

BURNLEY.

John Burnley, an Englishman, who lived in Hanover County, returned to England in 1771, leaving in Virginia a will of that date, but making another in England in 1778. In both of these he bequeathed property to a son Zachariah, and to daughters, Elizabeth and Keziah, who were both married to Dukes. A litigation followed respecting these bequests, and was protracted through a period of fifty years. Hardin Burnley, a brother or son of John, obtained patents for land in Albemarle from 1749 to 1764. Zachariah, probably the one already mentioned, and a citizen of Orange County, purchased in 1767 from Dr. Arthur Hopkins nearly fifteen hundred acres on Hardware and Totier, which Hardin had patented, but forfeited for non-payment of quit rents. In 1788 he also purchased upwards of four hundred acres at the mouth of Priddy's Creek, which he shortly after sold to Peter Clarkson. Nicholas Mills, of Hanover, in 1786 conveyed to James Burnley, of Louisa, a considerable tract of land on Beaver Creek, north of Mechum's River Depot, and from the nominal consideration specified it is likely he was Mill's son-in-law. He fixed his residence there, as did his son John also; but toward the close of the century they appear to have sold to other persons, and removed elsewhere.

A Reuben Burnley was the owner of Lots Seventy-Three and Seventy-Four in Charlottesville, the square on which Dr. W. G. Rogers resides, and with his wife Harriet conveyed them in 1806 to Dr. Charles Everett. A James Burnley purchased about eighty acres north and northeast of the University in 1803, but dying before the deed was made, the property was conveyed to his wife Ann. He left a daughter Mary, who was married first to John L. O'Neal, and secondly to Daniel Piper, and in the decade of 1820 she and her second husband sold this land to different persons, in part to the University. When the estate of Cornelius Schenk was sold, Ann bought Lots Sixty-Seven and Sixty-Eight, immediately west of the Episcopal Church, and lived there for many years, selling them in 1837 to Alonzo Gooch. From her the spring at the foot of the hill, at the junction of the extension of High Street with the Whitehall Road, formerly went by the name of Burnley's Spring. There can hardly be a doubt that all these Burnleys, as well as those mentioned hereafter, derived their descent from the same stock.

Of eight brothers of the name belonging to Louisa County, two, and the descendants of two others, settled in Albemarle. Seth Burnley lived north of Hydraulic Mills, married Ann, daughter of Horsley Goodman, and died in 1857. He was succeeded by his son James H., who married Mildred, daughter of John J. Bowcock. Nicholas, who lived in the Beaver Creek neighborhood, married Susan, daughter of James Harris. He left two sons, James Harris and Joel, who removed to Pickaway County, Ohio, and a daughter Mary, who was the wife of John T. Wood. Samuel, the son of Henry Burnley, pursued for many years the calling of a teacher. He married, Martha, the daughter of his cousin Nathaniel, and spent his last days on his farm on Mechunk, not far from Union Mills. He died in 1875. A sister of Samuel, Mildred, became the wife of Crenshaw Fretwell, and four of his neices the wives of Judge George P. Hughes, James F. Burnley, A. J. Wood and J. R. Wingfield. Nathaniel, the son of John Burnley, settled in the early part of the century at Stony Point, where he kept tavern for many years. In 1829, in partnership with Rice W. Wood, he bought from John M. Perry the Hydraulic Mills, where he transacted the milling and mercantile business until his death in 1860. In 1811 he married Sarah, daughter of the elder Drury Wood, and his children were James F., William, Horace, Drury, Martha, the wife of Samuel Burnley, Lucy, the wife of Charles Vest, Mary J., the wife of Dr. Garland A. Garth, Emily, the wife of Burwell Garth, and Cornelia, the wife of James P. Railey.

Nathaniel's sister Elizabeth was married in 1816 to Hudson Fretwell.

BUSTER.

A family named Buster, occasionally spelled in the records Bustard, was settled in the county at, or soon after, its formation. Its head was William, who lived in North Garden on the north fork of Hardware, near where the old White mill stood. He was one of the signers of the call to Rev. Samuel Black. A bridge called by his name spanned the stream near by, and was a landmark in the vicinity up to the end of the last century. As early as 1749, his wife Elizabeth was left a widow. He had certainly two sons, John and Claudius, who were the owners of more than three hundred acres on the Hardware. Both also bought land on the head waters of Mechum's River. John was for a time a citizen of Augusta County. About 1785 he established himself on Moore's Creek, a mile or two south of Jesse Maury's residence. He was a ruling elder in the D. S. Church, and died in 1820, aged eighty-three. He was twice married, first to Elizabeth Woods, and secondly, to Alice, daughter of John Gilliam. His children were Ann, the wife of John Wingfield, Martha, the wife of Matthew Wingfield, Sarah, the wife of Dixon Dedman, Margaret, the wife of William Foster, Elizabeth, the wife of George Moore, Patience, the wife of Levi Wheat, Claudius and David.

Claudius about 1785 purchased the D. S., where he kept tavern until his death in 1807. He and his wife Dorcas had eleven children, John, Mary, the wife of James Hays, the founder of New York, William, Claudius, Thomas, Benjamin, Patience, the wife of Charles Bailey, Nancy, the wife of William Garland, Robert, Charles Franklin, and Elizabeth. Claudius, whose wife's name was Ann, and Thomas removed to Kanawha, where Thomas was a Justice of the Peace in 1819. Another of the sons, thought to be Charles Franklin, removed to Loudoun County, whence his descendants afterwards went to Greenbrier, of which county one of them was recently the Clerk.

A Buster, no doubt another son of William and Elizabeth,

sisters appointed him their attorney to sell nine thousand acres of land in Harrison County, Kentucky. For a long period he kept a tavern at Brooksville, held in high esteem among travellers for its capital good cheer. He was a magistrate of the county, and a ruling elder in the Mountain Plains Church. He and John Pilson were the only justices who appeared to enforce the law against profane swearing, both paying over to the Poor Fund fines which they had imposed for that offence. His children were Elizabeth, Mary Frances, William, Robert, Ira, Henry and Maria Antionette. But though possessing a fine farm, and conducting a popular hostelry, his affairs became greatly embarrassed. In 1836 he was compelled by his debts to sell his place to James P. Tyler, and removed to Kentucky.

BROWN.

The Browns of Brown's Cove were a Hanover family. Its head, Benjamin, and his eldest son Benjamin, patented a large area of land in Louisa County, both before and after its establishment in 1742. They began to obtain grants in Albemarle also soon after its formation. From 1747 to 1760 they entered more than six thousand acres on both sides of Doyle's River. Benjamin Sr., married Sarah Dabney, who according to Dr. Charles Brown's will, was descended from the Jennings that left the enormous estate in England, which such a multitudinous posterity in the country has coveted, and which prompted Dr. Charles to cross the great sea twice in his old age. Benjamin died in 1762, leaving eleven children, Benjamin, William, Agnes, Barzillai, Benajah, Bernard, Bernis, Bezaleel, Brightberry, Elizabeth, the wife of John Price, and Lucretia, the wife of Robert Harris. Passing these names under review, one can imagine the delight of the old gentleman in the iterating alliteration of B. B., and how assiduously he searched the Scriptures and the Lives of the Saints, to attain his pet ideal.

Benjamin and William were their father's executors, and appear to have had their portions and residence in Hanover or Louisa. Barzillai sold out in Albemarle, and settled in married Mary, daughter of Thomas Smith, and had two sons, John and David. These brothers in 1784 bought a tract of land on the old Richard Woods Road southwest of Ivy Depot, part of which they sold to William Gooch. John also owned the land in North Garden east of Israel's Gap, which he sold in 1799 to Thomas Carr, and which was the home of his son Dabney Carr for more than three score years. John Buster in 1786 married Lucy, daughter of Mask Leake, and about the beginning of the century removed to Charlotte County.

CARR.

Major Thomas Carr, of King William, commenced entering land within the present bounds of Albemarle in 1730. Up to 1737 he had patented more than five thousand acres along the north fork of the Rivanna, and on the west side of the South West Mountain. The most of this land he gave to his son John, of Bear Castle, Louisa. John, who died about 1769, was twice married, first to Mary Dabney, and secondly to Barbara Overton. His children were Thomas, Dabney, Samuel, Overton, Garland, and Sarah, the wife of Nathaniel Anderson, who resided on the old glebe of St. Anne's. Thomas married Mary Clarkson, and his children were John Manoah, Dabney, Thomas, Samuel, and Mary, the wife of Howell Lewis, of North Garden. He lived on the south fork of the Rivanna, and died in 1807. John M. was the Clerk of the District Court of Charlottesville, and the first Clerk of the Circuit Court of Albemarle, which office he filled till 1819. His home was at Belmont, the residence of the late Slaughter Ficklin. His wife was Jane, the daughter of Colonel Charles Lewis, of North Garden, and his children Charles Lewis, a physician, who married Ann, widow of Richard P. Watson, and practised in North Garden, John H., who married Malinda, daughter of Manoah Clarkson, Nathaniel, Willis, a physician, who married Mary Ann Gaines, and practised in the vicinity of Ivy, and Jane. Most of this family, it is believed, emigrated to Kentucky. Dabney married Lucy, daughter of John Digges, of Nelson, lived in the southwest corner of North Garden, near the foot of Israel's Gap, and died in 1862, about ninety years of age.

Dabney, the second son of John, was the rising orator of Revolutionary times, mentioned by Wirt in his Life of Patrick Henry. He married Martha, sister of Mr. Jefferson. He lived in Goochland, but died in 1773 in Charlottesville, whither he had come on business. He was buried at old Shadwell, but in consequence of an agreement made in youthful friendship, Mr. Jefferson had his remains removed to Monticello, where it was the first of a long list of distinguished interments in the present cemetery. His children were Peter, Samuel, Dabney, Martha, the wife of Richard Terrell, Jane, the wife of Miles Cary, and Ellen, the wife of Dr. Newsom, of Mississippi. Peter studied law, was some time Mr. Jefferson's private secretary when President, married Hester Smith Stevenson, a young widow of Baltimore, lived at Carrsbrook, was appointed a magistrate, but soon resigned, and died in 1815. He left three children, Dabney, minister to Turkey six years from 1843, Ellen, wife of William B. Buchanan, of Baltimore, and Jane Margaret, wife of Wilson M. Cary. Samuel lived at Dunlora, was a magistrate, Colonel of cavalry in the war of 1812, member of the House of Delegates and State Senate, married first his cousin Ellen Carr, and secondly Maria, sister of Major William S. Dabney, was the father of James Lawrence, of Kanawha, and Colonel George, of Roanoke, and died in Kanawha in 1849. Dabney began life as a lawyer in Charlottesville, married his cousin Elizabeth Carr, lived where Ira Garrett so long resided, and after being Chancellor of the Winchester District, became Judge of the Court of Appeals in 1824. He died in Richmond in 1837.

Samuel, the third son of John Carr, was an officer in the Navy, married a Mrs. Riddick, of Nansemond, and died without children. He devised his place Dunlora to his nephew and namesake, Samuel.

Overton, fourth son of John, married a Mrs. Anderson, and resided in Maryland. His two daughters, Ellen and Elizabeth, became the wives of Colonel Samuel and Judge Dabney. A son, Jonathan Boucher, came to this county, married his cousin Barbara, daughter of Garland Carr, settled in Charlottesville as a lawyer, was Commonwealth's Attorney for eleven years from 1818, bought Dabney Carr's place, and sold it to Ira Garrett when he moved to the country, lived where Dr. H. O. Austin recently resided, and finally emigrated to Missouri. He was the father of Mary Ann, wife of Hugh Minor. Another son, Overton, was for many years Doorkeeper of the House of Representatives at Washington.

Garland, youngest son of John, was a magistrate of the county, and lived at Bentivar, where he died in 1838. He married Mary, daughter of William Winston, of Hanover, and his children were Francis, Daniel Ferrell, James O., Barbara, the wife of J. Boucher Carr, Elizabeth, the wife of Rev. John D. Paxton, of Rockbridge, and Mary, the wife of Achilles Broadhead, who succeeded William Woods as County Surveyor, removed to Missouri, and was the father of the late Hon. James O. Broadhead, of St. Louis, and Professor Garland C., of the University of Missouri. Francis was in many ways a useful man, a physician, a teacher, an editor, Secretary of the County Agricultural Society, Secretary of the Faculty of the University, and for many years an active magistrate. He also served as Sheriff in 1839. He married first Virginia, daughter of Richard Terrell, and secondly Maria, daughter of Richard Morris. He had two sons, Peter, who removed to Missouri, and the late F. E. G. He lived in town in the one story frame in the rear of the late Thomas Woods's and in the country at Red Hill, where he died in 1854. Daniel Ferrel succeeded his father at Bentivar, married Emily, daughter of William Terrell, and died in 1847, leaving his estate to his son, Dr. W. G. Carr. James O., married Mary, daughter of Richard H. Allen, lived at the Meadows, the present residence of H. C. Michie, and near the close of his life removed to Amherst, where he died in 1864.

William Carr was the patentee of upwards of four thousand acres on the north fork of the Rivanna, above that entered by Major Thomas Carr, and embracing the region lying west of the Burnt Mills. He was also granted a tract of four hundred acres on Buck Mountain Creek. These entries were made from 1737 to 1740. After the death of William, his widow Susan was married to Lodowick O'Neal. He had a son Thomas, and a daughter Phoebe, the wife of Walter Chiles; these persons who sold portions of the land above mentioned, belonged to Spotsylvania. A part of this land also was the property of Mordecai Hord, during his residence in the county. It is likely William had another son named Charles, as in 1780 a part of the same land that William had entered, and that "had formerly belonged to Charles Carr," was sold by Walter Carr (presumably a son of Charles) and his wife Elizabeth.

Three other Carrs, heads of families, lived on the west side of the South West Mountain, south of Stony Point. What relation they bore to each other, or to those already mentioned, is not known; but there can scarcely be a question that they were all derived from the same source. Their names were Gideon, Micajah and John. Gideon died in 1795. His children were William, Thomas, Mary, the wife of Thomas Travillian, John, Gideon, Nancy, the wife of Benjamin Thurman, Micajah, Elizabeth, the wife of John Fitch, and Meekins. It is probable most of the descendants of this family emigrated to the West. A notice of the death of Thomas Carr is extant, in which it is stated that he was the son of Gideon Carr, a pioneer settler on the Little Mountain in Albemarle, that he removed to Wilson County, Tennessee in 1807, and that he died in 1821 in the seventy-ninth year of his age.

Micajah died in 1812. He was at one time the owner of Colle. He and his wife Elizabeth had ten children, Mary, the wife of W. J. Blades, Martha, the wife of Daniel Shackelford, Mildred, the wife of James Travillian, David, James, John, Henley, the wife of Gideon C. Travillian, Sarah, the wife of John H. Maddox, George, who in early life taught school in Charlottesville, and at the time of his death in 1886 was the Nestor of the Albemarle bar, and Burton, who removed to Green County, Kentucky.

John Carr was a successful man. He became the owner

by purchase of more than fifteen hundred acres in different parts of the county. He died in 1809. He and his wife Elizabeth had nine children, David, who married Eliza, daughter of Achilles Bowcock, Thomas D., Mary, the wife of Wiley Dickerson, Malinda, the wife of Drury Wood, Nancy, the wife of Allen Jones, Elizabeth, the wife of Thomas Salmon, Sarah, the wife of James Early, Anderson, who removed to Montgomery County, Tennessee, and John F., who removed to Nelson County.

CARTER.

John Carter obtained in 1730 the grant of nine thousand, three hunrded and fifty acres, which embraced the whole of what is still called Carter's Mountain. It seems strange he should have taken up a rugged mountain, when the whole country lay before him to choose from, the Biscuit Run valley, the fair campaign between Moore's and Meadow Creeks, the fertile lands of Ivy, the North and South Gardens, and the Rich Cove; but perchance, having spent all his days in the tidewater district, wearied with its flatness, and languid from its malaria, the breezy summits of the mountains had a peculiar charm in his eyes. He was the eldest son of Robert (King) Carter, and was made Secretary of the Colony in 1721; for which appointment it is said he paid fifteen hundred pounds sterling. He also patented ten thousand acres on Piney and Buffalo Rivers in Amherst. He died in 1742, about two years before the formation of Albemarle; hence the title frequently given him in the early records in connection with places associated with his name, the late Secretary's Ford, Road, Mill, &c. He never lived in the county, but had in it two establishments, both furnished with a large number of servants, the Mill improvement on the west side of the mountain, on the north fork of Hardware, and the other on the east side called Clear Mount, perhaps the same with Redlands, or Blenheim. His eldest son Charles succeeded to his patrimonial estate in Lancaster, but his lands in Albemarle were given to his son Edward. Edward married Sarah Champe, and in his early life lived in Fredericksburg, but in his latter years spent much of his time at Blenheim. He represented the county in the House of Burgesses with Dr. Thomas Walker from 1767 to 1769, and in the House of Delegates with George Nicholas in 1788. He died in 1792. His children were John, Charles, Edward, William Champe, Hill, George, Whitaker, Robert, Elizabeth, the wife of William Stanard, uncle of Judge Robert Stanard, Sarah, the wife of her cousin George Carter, Jane, the wife of Major Verminet, Mary, the wife of Francis T. Brooke, Judge of the Court of Appeals, and Ann W. Troup.

Charles married Elizabeth, daughter of Fielding Lewis, and among his children was Maria, the wife of Professor George Tucker, of the University, and mother of Eliza, wife of Professor Gessner Harrison, and Maria, second wife of George Rives.

Edward married Mary R., daughter of Colonel Charles Lewis, of North Garden, and had among other children by this marriage Dr. Charles Carter. His second wife was Lucy, daughter of Valentine Wood and Lucy Henry, sister of the famous orator. He sold his possessions in Albemarle, and removed to Amherst.

William Champe married Maria Farley, lived at one time at Viewmont, which he purchased from Governor Edmund Randolph, and subsequently removed to Culpeper. His daughter Elizabeth became the wife of Samuel Sterrow, of that county. Hill lived in Amherst, and married there, it is said, a Miss Rose.

George became insane, and was no doubt suffering from mental derangement, when in 1800 he was bound over for challenging James Lewis, and a few day later killed Samuel Burch. Mr. Jefferson in a letter to his daughter dated July fourth refers to this event: "A murder in our neighborhood is the theme of present conversation. George Carter shot Burch of Charlottesville in his own door, and on very slight provocation. He died in a few minutes. The examining Court meets tomorrow." As the result of the trial, he was sent to the Asylum, where he continued until his death in 1816.

Whitaker never married, and squandered his property by dissipation. He died in Charlottesville in 1821. A year or two before his death he conveyed to his sister-in-law, Mrs. Mary Eliza Carter, one-seventh and one-twelfth of a parcel of land in Fluvanna, about twenty-five acres near Scott's Ferry, devised by Edward Carter to his seven youngest sons; in the consideration for this fag-end of a handsome estate, "for kindness, pecuniary and other favors," there was something sadly pathetic.

Robert married Mary Eliza, daughter of John Coles. He lived at Redlands, just east of Carter's Bridge, where he died comparatively young in 1810. His children were John Coles, who married Ellen Monroe Bankhead, was a magistrate, was once the owner of Farmington, and moved to Missouri. Robert H., who succeeded his father at Redlands, was admitted to the bar, was appointed a magistrate, and married Margaret Smith, a granddaughter of Gov. W. C. Nicholas, Mary, the first wife of George Rives, and Sarah, the wife of Dr. Benjamin F. Randolph.

CLARK.

Christopher Clark was a large land owner in Louisa, and obtained grants within the present limits of Albemarle in 1732. He was a Quaker, and with his son Bowling was overseer of a Friends' Meeting House, which was situated on land he had entered near the Sugar Loaf peak of the South West Mountain. He and Bowling also took out patents on Totier Creek. Numerous tracts in the eastern part of the county were owned by the Clark family. John in 1778 purchased from Robert Nelson, of Yorktown, more than two thousand acres on Mechunk, which were patented in 1733 by Thomas Darsie, and which Clark sold the same year to James Quarles and Joseph Brand. As well as can be ascertained, Christopher and his wife Penelope had five sons and four daughters, Edward, Bowling, Micajah, John, Christopher, Elizabeth, the wife of Joseph Anthony, who entered two thousand and forty acres in Biscuit Run valley, and moved to Bedford County, and a number of whose descendants intermarried with members of the Cabell family, Sarah the wife of Charles Lynch, Rachel, the wife of Thomas Moorman, and the wife of Benjamin Johnson.

The most of the family removed to Bedford, now Campbell County. In 1754 Edward and Bowling were overseers of the Friends' South River Meeting House, located on Lynch's Branch of Blackwater Creek, three of four miles from Lynchburg. Micajah married Judith, daughter of Robert Adams, and his children it is believed were Micajah, Robert, Jacob and William. Robert married Susan, daughter of John Henderson Sr., and followed his relatives to Bedford; his children were Robert, the first manufacturer of iron in Kentucky, James, Governor of Kentucky when he died in 1839, and Bennett, the father and grandfather of the two John Bullock Clarks, who were both members of Congress from Missouri, and both Generals in the Confederate army. William was deputy sheriff for John Marks in 1786, and was empowered by the Legislature on account of his chief's removal to sell lands delinquent for taxes. He was also a magistrate of the county, and died in 1800. His sons were Jacob, James and Micajah, and his widow Elizabeth (Allen) Clark is remembered by many as the proprietor of Clarksville, an excellent house of entertainment near Keswick, recently the country seat of James B. Pace, of Richmond. James was a magistrate, married Margaret, daughter of Thomas W. Lewis, of Locust Grove, and in 1836 with most of the Lewis family emigrated to Missouri. Micajah became a physician, and was for many years a successful practitioner in Richmond.

CLARKSON.

Five Clarksons filled a considerable space in the early history of the county, Peter, John, William, James and Manoah. There is documentary evidence that three of these were brothers, John, William and James, sons of David Clarkson, who came from Amherst; it is probable the other two were also brothers in the same family. There seems moreover to have been three sisters, Mary, the wife of Thomas Carr, Susan, the wife of John Lewis, the father of Jesse, and Letitia, the wife of Zebulon Alphin.

Peter began to purchase land in 1770, buying two hundred and fifty acres from John Senter, not far from the present Rio Station, which he and his wife Ann sold soon after to Thomas Carr. Possessing apparently a large amount of money just after the Revolution, he purchased during the decade of 1780 nearly three thousand acres, lying on Spring Creek near Whitehall, south of Ivy Depot, and in the neighborhood of the Burnt Mills. On this last tract he made his home until his death in 1814. His children were Elizabeth, William, Julius, Mary, the wife of Richard Harrison, David, and Ann, the wife of Mann Townley. William and Julius were merchants in Milton, but the former removed to Bourbon County, Kentucky. Julius married Mary, daughter of Jesse Lewis, and died in 1812. His widow afterwards became the wife of John H. Craven, and his only child, Elizabeth, the wife of Thomas W. Maury. David received a part of his father's place at the mouth of Priddy's Creek, where he died early. He and his wife Lucy, daughter of Joseph Morton, had four children, Joseph Morton, who emigrated to Alabama, Elizabeth, the wife of Richard D. Simms, Mary, the wife of James Collins, of Madison, and Nancy, the wife of Francis Catterton. Ann, the venerable widow of Peter, died in 1822, in the eighty-eighth year of her age.

John and William settled beside each other, west of the road between Hydraulic Mills and the Bowcock place. John bought upwards of five hundred acres from Major John Wood, and William upwards of four hundred from David Wood. A place of business existed somewhere on their land, known as Clarkson's Store, in all likelihood conducted by both, as both were alike overtaken by business disaster. In 1807 they conveyed their farms to the same trustees to secure debts due William Brown & Co. of Richmond, and within nine years both farms were sold by the trustees, that of William to George Crank, and that of John to Nelson Barksdale. In 1820 John and his wife Nancy made another conveyance to Barksdale, perhaps to dispose of the dower, in consideration of a life estate in fifty-nine acres. It is not known whether either of the brothers had children, but it is thought that

James Clarkson, who married Maria, daughter of David Wood, was the son of John and Nancy.

James Clarkson made his home in the forks of Hardware, his place embracing the mouth of Eppes Creek, and being the same afterwards owned by the young patriot, Roberts Coles, and now in the possession of Tucker Coles. He bought it from William Champe Carter in 1799. He suffered from the burden of debt, and to secure it placed his property under a deed of trust; but he must have arranged his affairs successfully, as in 1828 he and his wife Elizabeth sold his farm to Thomas Maupin, son of William. He died in 1829 at the advanced age of ninety-five. A son Reuben removed to Meade County, Kentucky, and another, Julius, married Margaret M., daughter of John Thomas. Julius died about 1835, and in 1838 his widow was married to Robert Cashmere.

Manoah Clarkson advanced in the course of life more slowly, but more surely. In 1777 he bought nearly three hundred acres on Ivy Creek near the Barracks, which he sold two years later to John Harvie. He then rented from Garland Carr in the forks of the Rivanna. At length he purchased from David Anderson six hundred acres three or four miles south of Charlottesville, a part of the old Carter tract, where he lived until his death in 1829 in his eighty-eighth year. He was twice married, and had twelve children, Mary, the wife of Jeremiah A. Goodman, Nancy, the wife of Jesse Lewis, Jane, the wife of Thomas Ammonett, Mildred, the wife of Nathan Goodman, who went to Kentucky, James, Anselm, who moved to Kentucky, Frances, the wife of M. C. Darnell, Dorothy, Malinda, the wife of John H. Carr, Elizabeth, the wife of William Watkins, Charlotte, the wife of Edmund Hamner, and Martha, the wife of Dudley Jones.

COCHRAN.

John Cochran came to Charlottesville from Augusta County about 1825. For years he was one of the leading merchants of the town, occupying the store on the southwest corner of Jefferson and Fifth Streets, and residing in the building immediately to the west. He was a man of energy and sound judgment, and achieved great success. In 1829, at a sale of lots in Anderson's Addition, he purchased a parcel of ground on Park Street, where he erected the large brick mansion, in which he lived until his death in 1883, at the age of eighty-six. He was appointed a magistrate of the county in 1843. His wife was Margaret Lynn, daughter of Major John Lewis, of Sweet Springs, and his children were Judge John L., Margaret, the wife of John M. Preston, Howe P., Henry K., William Lynn, and George M. Mr. Cochran owned the mill on Meadow Creek that had formerly belonged to John H. Craven, and has left his name associated with it, and the adjoining pond, which however in the ever-changing movements of time has already become a thing of the past.

COCKE.

James Powell Cocke, of Henrico, went to Augusta County in 1783, and bought from Rev. James Waddell, the blind preacher, Spring Hill, the old Patton place, that lay at the west foot of the Blue Ridge. In 1787 he came over to Albemarle and purchased from Robert Nelson, son of President William Nelson, sixteen hundred acres, situated where the south fork of Hardware breaks through the mountain, one of the tracts patented in the name of Mildred Meriwether. He fixed his residence on the east side of Fan's Mountain, and the west edge of the Eppes Creek valley, on the place recently owned by J. Henry Yates. He first built the mill which has ever since continued in that vicinity, and which for many years went by his name. His death occurred in 1829. He was twice married, first to Elizabeth Archer, and secondly to Lucy Smith, and his children were James Powell, who married Martha Ann Lewis, but died without children in 1811, Smith, who died unmarried in 1835, Chastain, who also died unmarried in 1838, Mary, the wife of Dr. Charles Carter, and Martha, the second wife of V. W. Southall.

Charles Cocke, a nephew of the elder James P., came from Southampton County in 1815, and bought from Rezin Porter the farm about two miles west of Porter's Precinct, on which he lived during his life, and which is now in the possession of the Lane brothers. He was a physician, though it is believed he never practised in this county. He was an active politician, and from 1822 to 1843 was at times a member of the House of Delegates, and afterwards of the State Senate. He was appointed as magistrate in 1819, and was serving as Sheriff at the time the Constitution of 1850 became operative, and the office of Justice of the Peace was made elective. It is said he sued the county for the salary which would have accrued, had his term reached its usual end; but it is hardly supposable the sovereign power of a popular convention could not cut short any office. After some change in his politics, he was defeated as a candidate, and at a Fourth of July dinner occurring shortly after, the circumstance gave rise to the following toast: "Dr. Charles Cocke, of Albemarle, a dead cock in the pit, killed in wheeling." His wife was Sarah Taylor, and he had one daughter, Charlotte, who became the wife of William Gordon, of Nelson.

The distinguished and eccentric General John H. Cocke, of Fluvanna, though never a citizen of this county, was yet much interested in its affairs through his connection with the University. He was prominent among those who labored for its establishment, and was one of its first Board of Visitors. He was an earnest promoter of the cause of Temperance, and in his efforts to this end, especially to guard the students from temptations to inebriety, he purchased nearly fifty acres of land on the south side of University Street, extending from the corner near the Dry Bridge to the Junction Depot, and built a large hotel in which no liquor was to be allowed, and which he named the Delavan, from his eminent friend and coadjutor in the cause, of Albany, N. Y. The hotel had a wall in front, flanked with heavy pillars, and covered with stucco stained with the tawny hue of the Albemarle clay; and from this peculiarity it acquired the popular soubriquet of Mudwall. The hotel has long since gone, but its site is occupied by the Delavan Colored Church; and to this day there is a struggle for the pre-eminency between the names of Delavan and Mudwall. The public-spirited scheme of the good General was premature; like many other well-laid plans of mice and men, it went agley.

Another person of the same name, prominent in the Greenwood neighborhood, was John S. Cocke. He was settled in that section as early as 1824. In 1827 he bought from Elijah May the tavern which had been well known from the beginning of the century under the conduct of Colonel Charles Yancey and May, but which under Cocke's management became still more widely celebrated for its admirable fare among the throngs journeying to the Virginia Springs. As in the case of many noted hostelries in the county, the advent of the railroads destroyed his business. He was a magistrate under the old system, and was active in public affairs. Pecuniary troubles overtook him in his old age, and his last days were spent in Charlottesville; where he died in 1879.

COLE.

In 1778 William Cole, a citizen of Charles City County, purchased from John Jones upwards of a thousand acres in North Garden, just north of Tom's Mountain. His wife was Susanna Watson, a sister it is believed of William Watson, who settled in North Garden in 1762. His children were William, John, Mary, the wife of Thomas Woolfolk, Nancy, the wife of Edmund Anderson, Sarah, Susan, the wife of Jasper Anderson, Richard, Joseph and Elizabeth, the wife of Joseph H. Irvin. The most of the sons never lived in the county, their father leaving them portions of his large estate below Richmond. He devised to Joseph his Albemarle land, on which he, his mother and sisters appear to have had their dwelling. The father died in 1802, Joseph in 1812, and his mother in 1814. In 1815 the land was sold, part to Norborne K. Thomas & Co., of Richmond, and part to Stephen Moore; a considerable portion of it subsequently came into the possession of Atwell and Philip Edge. For many years after the estate had passed into the hands of strangers, Miss Sarah Cole, whose residence was in Richmond, was accustomed to pay annual visits to the old home, where the remains of many of her kindred lay buried.

COLES.

The main body of land on which the Coles family resided, was granted to Francis Eppes in 1730, who received a patent for six thousand, five hundred acres. He devised it to his sons Richard and William. They sold three thousand acres to John Coles, but their deed was never admitted to record, because proved by only two witnesses. In 1777 Francis Eppes, son of Richard, with his wife Elizabeth, made a conveyance of the tract to Mr. Coles, and acknowledged it before Thomas Jefferson and George Gilmer as magistrates.

John Coles' father, John, came to this country from Enniscorthy, Ireland, and established himself in Hanover County, Virginia, where he married Mary Winston. His children were Walter, Sarah, Mary, the wife of John Payne, and mother of Dorothy, President, Madison's wife, John, and Isaac, who lived in Halifax County, and was a member of Congress from that district. John settled in Albemarle on the land above mentioned. He married Rebecca E. Tucker, who first drew the breath of life in the historic city of Jamestown. His children were Walter, John, Isaac, Tucker, Edward, Rebecca, the wife of Richard Singleton, of South Carolina, Mary Eliza, the wife of Robert Carter, Sarah, the wife of Andrew Stevenson, Elizabeth, and Emily, the wife of John Rutherford, of Richmond. John Coles died in 1808, and his wife in 1826.

Walter was a magistrate of the county, but soon resigned. His home was at Woodville, the present residence of Charles Shaw, where he died in 1854, at the age of eighty-two. He married first Eliza, daughter of Bowler Cocke, of Turkey Island, and secondly Sarah, daughter of John Swann, of Powhatan. His children were Walter, who succeeded his father at Woodville, who married Ann E. Carter, and who was the father of Dr. Walter, of St. Louis, and of Sarah and Elizabeth, still residing near the old home, and Edward, who was given a farm about five miles south of Charlottesville, which his father bought from William T. Henderson in 1806, who married Letitia, daughter of Rezin Wheat, and who died in 1883.

John married Selina Skipwith, of Mecklenburg. His home was Estouteville, where he died in 1848. He left three sons, John, who lived near Warren, Peyton, who married his cousin Isaetta, and succeeded his father at Estouteville, where he died in 1887, and Tucker, whose present residence is Viewmont.

Isaac A. was a member of the Albemarle bar, for a time President Jefferson's private secretary, and a member of the House of Delegates. He lived at Enniscorthy, married Mrs. Julia Stricker Rankin, widow of Hon. Christopher Rankin, of Louisiana, and had two children, Isaetta and Stricker. He died in 1841, and his wife in 1876. Tucker also represented the county in the House of Delegates. He married Helen Skipwith, of Mecklenburg, and died without children at Tallwood in 1861.

Edward, the youngest son of John Coles, was the private secretary of President Madison, sold the plantation on Rockfish River left him by his father, and in 1881 removed to Illinois, carrying with him all his slaves, giving them their freedom, and settling them by families on farms near Edwardsville. He was appointed by Mr. Monroe first Governor of the Territory of Illinois, was elected its second Governor when it became a State, and having made an earnest and successful struggle against a party seeking to make it a slave State, he removed to Philadelphia in 1832. He there married Sarah L. Roberts, and died in 1868. He had three children, one of whom, Roberts, came to Virginia, lived on the old Clarkson farm on the south fork of Hardware, was a Captain in the Confederate army, and fell on Roanoke Island in 1862. His remains were brought for interment to the Coles cemetery at Enniscorthy.

CRAVEN.

The parents of John H. Craven belonged to Bucks County, Pennsylvania. He himself came to Albemarle from Loudoun County in 1800; in that year he became a renter from Mr. Jefferson of the land that now comprises the farm of Tufton. The lease was evidently drawn by Mr. Jefferson in the clear and exact language with which he usually wrote, mentioning the fields each by its own name, and the order of their crops, and providing for the payment of the rent in gold and silver, and the continuance of the ratio between them at that time existing, even though it might be changed by law during the term of the lease. Before its expiration—it was to run for five years— Craven began to purchase land from Isaac Miller, and from Tucker and Samuel H. Woodson, till he was the owner of more than six hundred acres lying north and northeast of Charlottesville. In 1819 he bought from Richard Sampson, Pen Park, then containing four hundred acres, and two years later from the same person nearly five hundred acres on the east side of the Rivanna; so that his possessions extended from the top of Rich Mountain to Meadow Creek, opposite the present residence of H. C. Michie. He owned the mill now known as Cochran's, but then called the Park Mills. He was considered one of the best farmers of the county. After the death of his first wife Elizabeth, he married Mary, widow of Julius Clarkson, and daughter of Jesse Lewis. His children were John D., who married Jane Wills, George W., who married Susan, daughter of Alexander St. C. Heiskell, William, who married Ellen Craven, his cousin, removed to Illinois, and died in Jacksonville in that State in 1868, Elizabeth, the wife of Stapleton C. Sneed, Amanda, the wife of Malcolm F. Crawford, and Sarah, the wife of Robert W. Lewis. All these were the parents of large families, and their descendants have for the most part emigrated to other sections of the country. The old home of John D. Craven on Rose Hill, still occupied by his remaining children, is the only portion of the great estate now belonging to the name. John H. Craven died in 1845.

DABNEY.

In 1759 John Dabney, of Hanover, bought from Joel Terrell and David Lewis four hundred acres, and from Joel Terrell four hundred more, which included the present Birdwood plantation, and the oldest tavern perhaps in all the section, called at the time Terrell's Ordinary. In 1764 William Dabney, a brother, purchased from Archibald Woods four hundred acres on Mechum's River, above the Depot of that name. John soon returned to Hanover. William sold his place in 1768 to William Shelton, and John having died in the meantime, his trustees sold his land in 1773, six hundred acres of it to James Kerr, and the remainder to Robert Anderson.

In 1803 William S. Dabney came to the county, and bought from William C. Nicholas nearly nine hundred acres on the head waters of Ballenger's and Green Creeks, now in the possession of Edward Coles. He died in 1813. His wife was Sarah Watson, of Green Spring, Louisa, and his children were Maria, the wife of Colonel Samuel Carr, James, Walter, William S., May Senora, the wife of Benjamin M. Perkins, and Louisa, the wife of William M. Woods. Walter removed to Arkansas. William S. succeeded his father in the possession of the farm. He was a man of decided efficiency and success, both in his private business and in matters of public concern. He was appointed a magistrate in 1835, and entrusted with many affairs of importance by his brethren of the county bench. His taste was relied on as well as his judgment. In 1856 when improvements to the courthouse were contemplated, a plan reported by him was adopted, according to which the present enclosure and pavements of the Square were made. In 1846 he purchased Dunlora, Colonel Samuel Carr's old place, whither he removed, and where he died in 1865. He married Susan Gordon, and his family had the unusual distinction of having two sons occupy leading professorships in the University of Virginia, William C. in the Medical Faculty and Walter in that of Law.

Mildred, daughter of Samuel Dabney and his wife Jane Meriwether, of Hanover, was the wife of Dr. Reuben Lewis, brother of the celebrated explorer. She died at her home near Ivy Depot in 1851.

DAVIS.

Isaac Davis in 1769 bought from the Webb family, of New Kent County, eight hundred acres on the north fork of the Rivanna, near Webb's Mountain. His deed for this land was witnessed by the great orator, Patrick Henry, and was probably drawn by him. He was one of the early magistrates of the county. Dr. George Gilmer in a letter to Mr. Jefferson at the outbreak of the Revolution, refers to him; mentioning his leading the Albemarle company to Williamsburg, he speaks of old Isaac Davis marching at the head of the troop, as an indication of the determined and zealous spirit that animated the people. Many years were allotted the old patriot after the close of the war, his death not occurring till 1805. His children were William, Elizabeth, the wife of Richard Durrett, Isaac, who married Harriet, daughter of Garland Garth, and Robert.

John A. G. Davis, came to Albemarle from Middlesex, and engaged in the practice of law. In 1828 he was associated with Thomas W. Gilmer in the publication of the Virginia Advocate. In 1830 he was chosen to occupy the professorship of Law in the University of Virginia, as the successor of John T. Lomax. His death took place in 1840. He married Mary Jane, daughter of Richard Terrell and his wife Martha, who was the daughter of Dabney Carr and Martha, sister of Mr. Jefferson. His children were Eugene, Dr. John Staige, Rev. Dabney C. T., Rev. Richard T., and Caryetta, wife of Robert C. Saunders.

DAWSON.

The name of Dawson has place in the records from the beginning of the county. At the first meeting of the County Court, Martin Dawson was appointed to appraise the estate of Charles Blaney in the vicinity of the Cove. In 1747 he patented three hundred acres on Buck Island, which he sold in 1761 to John Burrus. He lived on Ballenger's Creek, and was no doubt the father of Rev. Martin Dawson, one of the earliest Baptist preachers of Albemarle. The son commenced preaching during the Revolutionary War, and as soon as the statute of religious freedom was passed, giving to non-Episcopal ministers a license to solemnize the rite of marriage, he was greatly in demand in this respect as well as in the pulpit. He supplied the Baptist churches throughout the county, but his labors were chiefly given to the Totier Church, which was commonly called by his name. His home was on a farm of more than five hundred acres, which lay southeast of Hughes's Shop, and there he finished his earthly course in 1821. His wife's name was Elizabeth, and of his twelve children, Martin, the eldest, removed to Gallia County, Ohio, John in 1812 to Mississippi Territory, and Elijah, who married Martha, daughter of Benajah Gentry, to Missouri. Another son, Allen, married Lucy, daughter of Christopher Wingfield, and was for a number of years a citizen of Charlottesville, a magistrate, clerk of the town trustees, and deputy Surveyor of the county. He also taught school, first on his farm four or five miles south of town, and afterwards at his house on Main Street near east Third, which from his institution, and the Female Seminary, being located thereon, received its former name of School Street. Notwithstanding his multifarious occupations, he was unsuccessful. Accumulated debts constrained the sale of his property piece by piece, till all was gone. A daughter of Rev. Martin, Elizabeth, was the wife of Reuben Elsom, who lived in the southern part of the county.

As early as 1757, John Dawson, whose wife was Sarah Carroll, was living on the water of Carroll Creek. Did he remove to Amherst, now Nelson, and was he the father of Martin, the well known merchant of Milton? Certain it is, that Martin's father was named John, that his place was in Nelson, not far from Faber's Mills, and that he was the brother of Rev. Martin's father. Martin was one of nine children. He established himself in Milton shortly after it was founded, at first apparently connected with Brown, Rives & Co.; and he continued to be associated with the village, until its business was wholly absorbed by Charlottesville and Scottsville. By his diligence, thrift and good judgment, he amassed a considerable fortune. About 1822 he purchased Bellair on the north side of Hardware below Carter's Bridge, which had before belonged to Charles Wingfield Jr., and there he made his residence until his death in 1835. He left a will so elaborately indited, that it was twice taken before the Court of Appeals for construction. In his desire to promote popular education, he directed that an academy should be established at each of the three places, Milton, Bellair, and his father's old homestead in Nelson; that suitable buildings should be erected both for teachers and scholars; and that their advantages should be assigned in the first place to the boys of Albemarle and Nelson. Having a premonition that these provisions might be adjudged invalid, he directed that in case they were set aside, his property at the places mentioned should be sold, the proceeds transferred to the Literary Fund of the State, and the interest devoted to the cause of education in the two counties specified. The latter bequest was approved by the judgment of the Court. He also prescribed the enclosing of ten acres at the old homestead in Nelson as a family burial place, where he enjoined his own remains to be interred. Besides his private business, he was much employed in that of the county. He was appointed a magistrate in 1806, and frequently occupied a seat on the bench of the County Court. He never married.

A brother, Pleasant Dawson, was the owner of nearly fifteen hundred acres on the lower Hardware. He was engaged in milling operations, in the prosecution of which he was involved in a long litigation with Littlebury Moon. He died unmarried in 1826. A sister, Nancy, was the wife of Rev. Hugh White, a Baptist minister, who was for a time a lot holder both in Charlottesville and Milton.

Another brother was John S. Dawson, the father of seven children, some of whose representatives are at present residents of the county. His son, Benjamin, married Dorothy Childress, and of their children Benjamin H. lives at the western foot of Still House Mountain, and Andrew, and Agnes, the wife of Peter Turner, about two miles south of Porter's Precinct. Another son of John S., was Pleasant L., whose daughter Jane, the wife of Dr. Isaac F. Forbes, recently died in Charlottesville, at the house of her son-in-law, Harrison Robertson, and whose son, John L., still lives on the lower Hardware, where he has long and usefully discharged the office of Justice of the Peace. Pleasant's widow, Mahala, survives in the enjoyment of a green old age, and forms a link between this and former generations.

DEDMAN.

Samuel Dedman came to Albemarle from Louisa in 1768. He settled in the Ragged Mountains, about a mile below the Reservoir, where he purchased two hundred acres from William T. Lewis. He died in 1800. He and his wife Mary had a large family, John, Samuel, Richmond, Bartlett, Nathan, who married Elizabeth, daughter of William Gooch, and from whom are descended Rev. Neander Woods, of Memphis, and Rev. William H. Woods, of Baltimore, Dixon, Sarah, the second wife of John Everett, Susan, Nancy, the wife of Moses Clack, and Mary, the wife of John Simms. They all eventually emigrated to the West, some to southwest Virginia, and others to Kentucky. Bartlett lived for a few years in Charlottesville. He built a dwelling on a lot he purchased from John Nicholas at the foot of Fourth Street east, which he sold in 1801 to William Waller Hening. Dixon was the last to remain in the county. He succeeded to the property below the Reservoir. He was twice married, first to Sarah, daughter of John Buster, and secondly to Sarah Drumheller. He finally sold out about 1828, and went West.

DICKERSON.

John Dickerson was settled in the north part of the county, while yet it belonged to Louisa. He lived on the north fork of the Rivanna, not far from Piney Mountain. He died in 1788. He and his wife Mary had three sons, John, William and Thomas. Thomas died in 1807. His wife's name was Mildred, and his children were Frances, the wife of Rev. John Goodman, the wife of William Thurman, the wife of John Crossthwait, Thomas, Wiley, who married Nancy, daughter of Rev. Jacob Watts, Griffith and Lucy. Another Wiley, son of one of the other brothers, married in 1789 Mary, daughter of John Carr. He died in 1847. His children were William, Willis, Malinda, the wife of George W. Turpin, Martha, the wife of Richard Simms Brockman, the wife of B. C. Johnson, Mary, the wife of Elisha Thurman, and Sarah, the wife of Archibald Duke.

DOLLINS.

The family of Dollins has been established in the county from early times. The first of the name was Richard, who in 1761 bought land on the head waters of Mechum's River, and a few years later purchased from the Stockton family on Virgin Spring Branch. He died in 1774. His wife's name was Elizabeth, and his children were Ann, Presley, John and William. John died in 1787. He and his wife Elizabeth had six children, one of whom was John, who died in 1823, leaving five sons and one daughter, John, Tyree, Richard, Jeremiah, William, and Susan, who was the wife of a Polson. Of this family, Jeremiah married a daughter of Nicholas Merritt, and died in 1856. His children were Tyree, Martha, the wife of William Lupton, John, Nicholas, Mary Ann, the wife of a Rogers, and Sarah, the wife of a Baber. Some of the earliest nurseries in the county were planted by members of this family, and on this account the name is will known in connection with the cultivation of fruit.

DOUGLASS.

A family of Douglass was living in the Cove neighborhood as early as 1751, two of which were James and George, probably brothers. They were among the first members of the Cove Presbyterian Church. George died in 1785.

Three brothers named Douglass resided in the north part of the county in 1761, Charles, Thomas and John. Their farms were situated on the Barboursville Road near the Orange line. Charles married a daughter of Robert and Mourning Adams, and died in 1823. His children were Robert and Charles, to whom he gave lands he owned in Kentucky, and who removed to that State, Ann, the wife of Joseph Timberlake, Judith, the wife of John Dickerson, and Sarah. Thomas died in 1830, leaving four children, James, Achilles,

Nancy and John. Achilles was appointed a magistrate in 1796, and acted a prominent part in the affairs of the county. He served as Sheriff in 1823. He married Nancy, daughter of Jason Bowcock, and died in 1844. His home the latter part of his life was on the north fork of Priddy's Creek, near the present station of Burnley's. John Douglass Jr., married Mildred Bowcock, a sister of Achilles's wife.

DOWELL.

John Dowell was one of the pioneers who broke the virgin soil of the county. He obtained a patent for four hundred acres on Priddy's Creek in 1738, and up to 1759 had received grants of more than a thousand acres in that section. He died, it is believed, sometime during the Revolutionary War. He left at least four sons, John, who died in 1794, William, who died in 1795, Ambrose, and Thomas, who died in 1815. All had large families, and from them are descended those who still bear the name in the county, besides others who removed to different parts of the West.

DUKE.

James Duke, of Henrico, was the owner of two hundred acres on Beaver Creek, in which he probably became interested through his kinsman James Burnley, both of whom were descended from the Englishman, John Burnley, before referred to. He and his wife Mary disposed of this land in 1795 to George West. Cleviers Duke, of Louisa, also descended from John Burnley, had two sons Richard and James, who were settled in Albemarle. In 1806 Richard married Maria, daughter of Thomas Walker Jr. In 1821 he purchased from M. L. Walker and John Wren the Rivanna Mills, afterwards known as the Burnt Mills, which they and G. G. Lindsay had bought from Dabney Minor in 1819. He was appointed a magistrate in 1819, served as Sheriff in 1847, and died at Morea in 1849. His children were William J., who married Emily Anderson, Lucy, who was the wife of David Wood, and with him removed to west Tennessee, where she was married secondly to John H. Bills, Mary J., the wife of William T. Smith, Mildred, the wife of Christopher, Gilmer, Sarah, the wife of Harvey Deskins, Martha, Margaret, the wife of Robert Rodes, Charles and Richard T. W. R. T. W. married Elizabeth Eskridge, of Staunton, taught school in Lewisburg, W. Va., was admitted to Albemarle bar in 1849, filled the office of Commonwealth's Attorney three times, represented the county in the House of Delegates, was a member of Congress, was Colonel on the Forty-Sixth Virginia in the civil war, and died in 1898.

James, the brother of Richard, was associated with him in the management of the Rivanna Mills. In 1832 he purchased from James McCulloch the brick mill and store located at Millington. Subsequently he established a mill on Rocky Creek, where he spent his remaining days. He was appointed to the county bench in 1838, and departed this life in 1844. His wife was Miss Biggers, of Louisa, and his children were Richard, who removed to Nelson County, Horace, who removed to Mississippi, Charlotte, the wife of Dr. William G. Carr, and Lucy, the wife of Thomas Ballard. A daughter of Richard became the wife of John Cole, and resides where her grandfather died.

Alexander Duke, of Hanover, in 1835 married Elizabeth, daughter of Alexander Garrett. For some years he was connected with Rev. Pike Powers, and afterwards with Charles Slaughter, in conducting a high school at Midway. He was the father of Mrs. Horace Jones.

DUNKUM.

Two brothers named Dunkum lived on the Carter's Bridge Road south of Charlottesville, in the early part of the century, and both were efficient and prosperous farmers. William, who resided nearer town at a place lately occupied by Lord Pelham-Clinton, and now by Mr. Harbottle, began his purchases of land in 1803, and continued it until his plantation comprised nearly a thousand acres. In 1837 he conveyed to Lewis Teel, Robert Gentry and Jeremiah A. Goodman the land on which stood the Piney Grove Baptist Church. He died in 1846. His wife was Frances Gentry, and his children were Mary Ann, the wife of Lewis Sowell, William L., Chesley, James T., Frances, the wife of Jesse L. Fry, Elizabeth, the wife of Philip Edge, Martha, the wife of John H. Barksdale, Susan, the wife of J. Ralls Abell, and Elijah, who married Elizabeth, daughter of Benjamin Ficklin, and built the large brick house on Ridge Street long occupied by the late Dr. R. B. Dice.

John Dunkum lived about a mile south of his brother, where he settled in 1807. His lands were in extent but little short of those of William. He died in 1855. He married Elizabeth, daughter of Marshall Durrett, and his children were James, Martha, the wife of William Pitts, Mary, the wife of Chester Ballard, Elizabeth, Jane, and Sarah Ann, the first wife of Philip Edge.

DURRETT.

The name of Durrett was connected with the territory of Albemarle, while it was yet a part of Hanover. In 1737 Bartholomew Durrett patented nearly three hundred acres on Priddy's Creek, and the next year Richard patented three hundred in the same section. A genealogical chart of the Terrells in the possession of Gen. W. H. H. Terrell, of Indianapolis, states that Abigail, daughter of Henry Terrell and Ann Chiles, of Caroline, was married to Colonel Durrett, of Albemarle. If this refers to Colonel Richard, she must have been a first wife. According to the records, the name of Richard's wife was Sarah. He passed his days on Priddy's Creek, and died in 1784. His children were Richard, Elizabeth, the wife of Jacob Watts. Ann, the wife of Robert Sanford, Frances, the wife of Frederick William Wills, Agatha, the wife of William Flint, Mildred, the wife of a Williams, the wife of Stephen K. Smith, and the wife of a Burrus.

Richard the younger, James Douglass and others bought parts of a large tract of land on Priddy's Creek, which had belonged to Roger Dixon. Dixon in 1766 had encumbered it with a deed of trust for the benefit of James Harford, an English merchant; and when the purchasers bought, they perhaps regarded themselves safe under the acts of the Legislature barring the debt of British creditors. But Harford brought suit against the claimants in the United States Court, and about 1809 recovered judgment, so that they were obliged to pay again for their shares. Durrett's share amounted to five hundred and fifty acres. In 1772 he began purchasing the tract adjoining Earlysville, on which he resided the remainder of his life. He died in 1820. His wife was Elizabeth, daughter of Isaac Davis, and his children John D., Isaac W., Thomas, Davis, Robert D., Mildred, the wife of James Simms, Susan, the wife of Thomas Garth, Elizabeth, the wife of James Watts, Sarah, the wife of John Early, and Frances, the wife of Archibald Buckner. John D. married Frances Davis, and his children were Matilda, the wife of William Catterton, Thomas, who married Emily Wood, Frances, Elizabeth, the wife of Daniel P. Key, Sarah, Isaac, and Richard W., who married Lucy Twyman. Thomas married Frances Simms, and his son Thomas married Mary, daughter of James Early, and was the father of Dr. James T., and Frank. Robert D. married Elizabeth Price.

Two brothers of this name became residents of the Batesville district the latter part of the last century. They came from Caroline, and were no doubt of the same stock with those just mentioned, though it seems impossible now to trace the relationship. Marshall Durrett in 1783 purchased from Robert Terrell nearly four hundred acres on the head waters of Mechum's River, where he was living at the time; and as the land he bought was part of that entered by Henry Terrell, of Caroline, the Abigail Terrell already alluded to may have been his first wife. In 1803 he purchased from Robert Bolling in the North Garden, whither he removed and resided until his death in 1834. He was appointed a magistrate in 1796, and served as Sheriff in 1819, succeeding Charles Wingfield Jr., who at the time of his death had occupied the office but a month. Marshall's wife was Dorothy, daughter of John Digges, of Nelson, and his children Sarah, the wife of Robert Field, Richard, Rice, Marcus, Silas, Benjamin, Paul, Ann, the wife of William Morris, and afterwards of John D. Rodes, Elizabeth, the wife of John Dunkum, and John. Marcus succeeded his father in the home in North

Garden. He was also a magistrate, one of the last set appointed under the old Constitution. He married Sarah Ann, daughter of H. Carter Moore, and died in 1878.

James Durrett, the brother of Marshall, in 1790 purchased land of John Epperson, where he resided until death in 1822. His place was the same afterwards owned by C. W. Purcell, of Richmond, Alton Park. He married Nancy Digges, a sister of his brother's wife, and his children were Frances, the wife of Richard Richardson, Sarah, the wife of Horsley Goodman, William, Mildred, the wife of William Bumgardner, Elizabeth, the wife of William McClunn, Nancy, the wife of Colston Heiskell, who removed to Philadelphia, James, who married Susan Goodman, John, who married Mary Diggs, and Richard, who married Elizabeth, daughter of William Piper. Many of the descendants of these brothers removed to Kentucky and Missouri.

DYER.

Samuel Dyer appeared before the Albemarle Circuit Court in October, 1835, to apply for a pension as a Revolutionary soldier. He then stated that he was born October 8th, 1756, and was in his eightieth year. His first purchase of land was made in 1787 from Thomas Staples, consisting of five hundred acres, and extending from Hudson's Creek to Totier, in all likelihood embracing his home, Plain Dealing, where he lived and died. His store, a well known place of business in those days, was situated at the junction of the roads from Staunton and Charlottesville to Scott's Landing. He was so successful in his mercantile pursuits, that he soon became the owner of more than twenty-two hundred acres. He established extensive milling operations at Glendower. He was much employed in public business, being appointed on account of his integrity and sound judgment largely to superintend matters of general concern in his section of the county. He finished his earthly course in 1840, aged eighty-four, and his venerable partner, whose name was Celia Bickley, died the same year.

Their family consisted of eleven children. William H.

who was appointed a magistrate in 1824, Ann, the wife of George Robertson, Elizabeth, the wife of George M. Payne, John, Thomas, Mary Jane, the wife of George A. Nicholson, Martha, the wife of Joseph S. Watkins, Samuel, Francis B., Robert and Sarah. During the decade of 1830 most of the children emigrated to Missouri. Francis was one who remained. For a number of years he was a prominent member of the Albemarle bar. He built the brick house and office on East Jefferson and Seventh Streets, now occupied by Major Horace Jones. Obliged by business misfortune, induced perhaps by extravagant living, to surrender this property, he removed to the house on Park Street, the present residence of Drury Wood, where he died in 1838. Many now living remember him as a man of genial disposition and great corpulence; yet withal he was captain of an artillery company (with John Eubank as orderly sergeant) which drilled annually at Old's Forge on the north fork of Hardware. He married Sarah White, of Staunton, and was the father of five children, one of whom, Celia, was the wife of William P. Staples, of Richmond.

EADES.

A family named Eades were among the early settlers in the southern part of the county. Abraham Eades patented land on Ballenger's Creek in 1751. In 1758 Joseph gave to his sons, Thomas and John, one hunded and fifty acres on Totier, and the next year Jacob sold three hundred acres on Totier to Rev. John Ramsey, rector of St. Anne's. It is likely Abraham, Joseph and Jacob were brothers. The two latter disappear from the records, and they, or their families, probably fell in with the tide of emigration that bore away such numbers to the West. Abraham, a son of Abraham, was for many years in the early part of the century, engaged in the inspection of tobacco in the Nicholas Warehouse at Warren. He died in 1828. His family were Joseph, Mildred, the wife of a Shepherd, Abraham, Susan, Charlotte, and Sarah, the wife of Richard Chandler. Shepherd Eades, a son of one of this family, married Mary, daughter of Benjamin Norvell, and died in 1848. He left a son Shepherd, and three daughters, Mary Ann, the wife of a Starke, Charlotte, the wife of a Turner, and Sarah, the wife of a Venable.

EARLY.

The name of Early is first mentioned in the records in 1790, when Joel, executor of Jeremiah Early, purchased from Charles Hammond three hundred acres on the Rivanna in the Burnt Mills neighborhood, which had formerly belonged to Walter Carr. It is probable these persons were citizens of Orange. In 1809 James Early, certainly from Orange, bought eighteen hundred and ninety-four acres on Buck Mountain Creek from the representatives of Major Henry Burke, who had been a magistrate of the county, and Major in the Eighty-Eighth Regiment, and who died in 1803. The children of James Early and his wife Elizabeth, were John, James, Joab, William, Lucy, the wife of James Simms, Theodosia, the wife of George Stevens, and Elizabeth, the wife of Thomas Chapman.

John Early in 1822 bought from the executors of Richard Durrett nearly a thousand acres lying between the Buck Mountain Road and Jacob's Run. From him the village of Earlysville derived its name, and in 1833 he gave to Thomas Lane, David Thompson and Henry Marshall the ground on which its church was built. He was twice married, first to Sarah, daughter of Richard Durrett, and secondly to Mrs. Margaret Allen Timberlake. He died 1833. His children were James T., Isaac Davis, Susan, Elizabeth, the wife of Edward Ferneyhough, Amanda, the wife of Joshua Jackson, Mildred, the wife of Richard Wingfield, Thomas, Frances, Joseph, Jeremiah A. and William. James, son of James, married Sarah Carr, and among his children were John F. Early, who some twenty years ago opened a female Seminary in the Shackelford house on High Street, and afterwards removed to Texas, Mary, the wife of Thomas Durrett, and Frances, the wife of Isaac Davis, and mother of Mrs. W. R. Burnley. Joab married Elizabeth Thompson, and his children were William T., well remembered by many as Buck

Early, and James and Nathaniel, of Greene County. William, son of James, married Sarah Graves, and his children were William L., of Madison, and Thomas J., who married Caroline, daughter of the elder Drury Wood.

EUBANK.

Families of the Eubank name have lived along the south fork of Hardware from the earliest times. They sprang from two brothers, George and John. It is believed they came from Orange County. In 1758 George bought from James Ireland three hundred acres on Beaverdam, not far from the present Soapstone Quarries. The next year John purchased from Matthew Jordan in the same vicinity. The year after the organization of the county, 1746, a John Eubank obtained a grant of nearly three hundred acres on Rocky Creek, in its northwest section; it is possible he was the same person as the one just mentioned.

John died in 1789. His wife's name was Hannah, and his children were John, James, William, Nancy, Elizabeth and Sarah, who were both married to brothers named Fortune, a family that lived in the same neighborhood, and Frances, the wife of a Gilmer. George died in 1802. He and his wife Mary had six children, John, Elizabeth, George, Frances, the wife of her cousin, John Eubank, Nancy, the wife of David Watson, and Mary, the wife of Richard Hazelrig. George also brought up two orphan children, Nelson and Sarah Key, whom he committed to the care of his daughter Frances and her husband, and for whose subsequent welfare he made special provision. His two sons, John and George, had each twelve children.

The Eubanks appear to have been quiet, industrious farmers, fairly prosperous in the worldly affairs. The family particularly marked for its energy and success was that of James, son of John. He married Mildred Melton, and had five sons and three daughters. He died in 1821, leaving a considerable estate. Two of his sons, John and George W., took advantage of the opening of the Staunton and James River Turnpike, established taverns on the road, and for many years did a large business in the entertainment of those transporting the vast amount of produce at that time passing between the Valley and Scottsville. George married his cousin, Winifred Eubank, and had eight children. He died in 1841. John married Sarah Strange, and died without children in 1854. Emigration to the West has taken many from the different branches of this family, so that comparatively few of the name remain now in the county.

EVERETT.

John Everett was the first of the name to appear in the county. At one time he lived on the waters of Moore's Creek, on the place adjoining the old Lewis place, the present Birdwood. This place he purchased from John Spencer in 1781, and in 1788 sold it, and removed to a farm near the Cross Roads, which he bought from Joseph Claybrook. His second home was what is still known in the neighborhood as the old Methodist Parsonage. Here he laid out a town about the beginning of the century, called Traveller's Grove, but it never advanced beyond the sale of three or four lots. When the prospects of the town had lost their roseate hue, the Colonel, as he was known, changed the name to Pleasant Grove, and under this designation conducted a tavern for some years. He was somewhat of a sporting character, raised fine horses, and had a training track on his place. He was twice married, first to Sarah, daughter of Tarleton Woodson, and secondly to Sarah, daughter of Samuel Dedman. In 1807 he disposed of his property, and removed to Cabell County.

Dr. Charles Everett was established in Charlottesville as one of its physicians as early as 1804, when he purchased from Tucker M. Woodson the part of Lot Fifty-Nine fronting on High Street. Two years later he bought from Reuben Burnley the two lots opposite, Seventy-Three and Seventy-Four, where he had his office and stable; this property he sold to Dr. Charles Brown in 1814. It is probable however that before the last date he had removed to Belmont near Keswick, which he made his subsequent residence during life; having bought from John Rogers six hundred and thirty-six acres in 1811. It was not till 1821 that he became owner of the place adjoining on the south, which has since been known by the name of Everettville; this tract of four hundred acres he purchased from Mr. Jefferson, whose father had obtained a patent for it in 1756. The Doctor, besides being actively engaged in the practice of his profession, devoted much attention to the public affairs of the county, and to politics. He was appointed a magistrate in 1807, and represented the county for several terms in the House of Delegates. He never married, and died in 1848, by his will emancipating his servants, and devising his estate to his nephew, Dr. Charles D. Everett. Not long before the war a person named Thom, from Mercer County, Pennsylvania, presented to the Circuit Court a certificate of his appointment as Guardian of some of the Doctor's old servants, and applied for the legacies he had left for their benefit.

FAGG.

John Fagg was a Revolutionary soldier, and in the early years of the century was a tavern keeper in Charlottesville. In 1818 he bought from William Garth a part of the old Barracks place, which he called Barrack Grove, and which is now the residence of Mrs. Garland A. Garth. There he lived until his death in 1829, at the advanced age of ninety-two years.

A son William married Nancy, daughter of John Alphin and removed to Blount County, Tennessee. From that place he sold in 1834 his wife's share of her father's estate to Jesse Lewis. John, another son, married Elizabeth, daughter of Jacob Oglesby, and was associated with his father-in-law as Inspector in Henderson's and Randolph's Tobacco Warehouses. He afterwards conducted a store in Milton, as late as 1834. It is related of him, that in the fall of 1833, when the memorable storm of star-falling occurred, he was with a number of others beyond the Valley on a hunting expedition. While the meteoric phenomenon was in progress, some of the servants, who had risen early in discharge of their duties, rushed terror-stricken into the camp to arouse the sleeping hunters. All started at once to observe the scene, some with the interest of curiosity, others in mortal dread that the day of judgment had come—all except Fagg. He clung to his blankets, involuntarily, it was believed, because of too abundant potations the night before; and when appealed to by the cries and vivid descriptions of his friends, he explained, "Oh boys, that's nothing. Why, I see that every morning when I'm at home; the fact is, you might see it too, if you weren't too lazy to get up." In 1836 he sold Barrack Grove to Garland Garth, and probably went to join his relatives in the South West.

FARISH.

William P. Farish came to Albemarle from Caroline about 1820. He is mentioned in 1823 as a manager for Charles L. Bankhead. In subsequent years he was engaged in superintending the affairs of John N. C. Stockton. In 1834 he purchased from John M. Perry six hundred acres on the south fork of the Rivanna below Hydraulic Mills, and the same year sold to William H. Meriwether the tract on which Meriwether erected the Rio Mills. He bought in 1837 from Ira Garrett the plantation south of Charlottesville, now in the possession of Rev. J. T. Randolph, on which he subsequently resided until his death. After the demise of Mr. Stockton in 1837, he was appointed the administrator of his estate, and in the years following sold off his large possessions, except Carrsbrook, which was reserved for his family. He also had the direction of the Stage lines which Stockton controlled. In 1845 the firm of Farish & Co. was formed, by which the Stage property was bought and managed for many years. The firm consisted of W. P. Farish, Dr. O. B. Brown, of Washington City, Slaughter W. Ficklin and John S. Cocke. About this time Mr. Farish entered the ministry of the Baptist Church. He died in 1869. His wife was Mellicent Laughlin, and his children Thomas L., and Ann, the wife of Rev. J. T. Randolph.

Stephen M. Farish was a brother of William P., and probably came to the county before him. He was for a time a resident of Milton, and afterwards lived in the vicinity of Earlysville. He was twice married, and his children were Susan, Andrew J. and William.

In 1823 Hazelwood Farish sold to Thomas Poindexter Jr., the stock and equipment of a Stage line running through Charlottesville.

FARRAR.

John Farrar lived in the southwest part of the county, and died in 1769. His children were Perrin, Catharine Jopling, Sarah Spencer, William, Peter, Thomas, Elizabeth and Richard. Perrin, William, Peter and Richard were all owners of land on Green and Ivy Creeks, branches of the lower Rockfish. Perrin died about 1793, leaving eight children who removed to Amherst.

Richard married Susan Shelton, of Louisa, and died in 1807. He was a ruling elder in the Cove Church. His children were Joseph, Landon, John S., Lucinda, the wife of Samuel L. Wharton, Elizabeth, the wife of George Wharton, both of whom emigrated to Davidson County, Tennessee, and Sophia, the wife of Dr. Samuel Leake, and mother of Hon. Shelton F. Leake. John S. was appointed Colonel of the Forty-Seventh Regiment in 1815. He died in 1832, and left nine children, Richard L., Matthew G., Elizabeth, Martha, Marcellus, Sarah, the wife of Alexander K. Yancey, Sophia, the wife of George W. Piper, Lavinia and Susan.

FICKLIN.

Benjamin Ficklin became a citizen of Albemarle about 1814, and it described in one place as being from Frederick County, and in another from Culpeper. Either then, or shortly after, he entered the Baptist ministry. He purchased in the western part of the county upwards of thirteen hundred acres, and his residence for twenty years, called Pleasant Green, was the place adjoining Crozet on the west, now occupied by Abraham Wayland. He was appointed to a seat on the county bench in 1819. In 1822 he proposed to sell his lands with the design of removing to Ohio or Indiana. This purpose however was abandoned, and in 1832 he removed to

Charlottesville where for a number of years he was engaged in the manufacture of tobacco.

He was noted for his uprightness and decision of character. At the time of his removal to Charlottesville, the state of things in the town, morally and religiously, was far from being unexceptionable. In a clandestine manner, most of the stores did more business on Sunday than on other days. The negroes came in in large numbers for purposes of traffic. Great quantities of liquor were sold. In the later hours of that day, the roads leading from town were lined with men and women in all stages of drunkenness, some staggering with difficulty, others lying helplessly by the wayside. Mr. Ficklin set himself vigorously to remedy these evils. He warned the merchants that every violation of the Sunday law should be visited with the highest penalty. A similar warning was given to the negroes; and by the lively application of the lash to those who neglected it, the town and roads were soon cleared of transgressors. Sabbath observance put on a new face. The comfort of worshippers, and the general order of the community, were vastly promoted. So impartial was the old man in the execution of his duty, that when one of his own wagons, sent out to sell tobacco, trespassed upon the sacred hours of reaching home, he imposed a fine upon himself. It is said, that a member of the bar remonstrated with him on what he considered his excessive zeal, and stated by way of illustration, that in the preparation of his cases he had often been obliged to work on Sunday; whereupon Mr. Ficklin at once fined him on his own confession. Altogether the whole county was laid under many obligations to his courage, efficiency, and public spirit.

His last years were overclouded by business reverses. He closed his earthly career during the war, in the last days of 1864. His wife's name was Eleanor, and his children were Slaughter W., Benjamin F., who was one of the last Stage proprietors in the country, Ellen, the wife of a Brown, Susan, the wife of J. R. Hardesty, Elizabeth, the wife of Elijah Dunkum, and Lucy, the first wife of Fontaine D. Brockman.

FIELD.

For many years before the end of the last century, and in the early part of the present, the name of Field was a familiar one in the vicinity of Batesville. The family head was Robert, who began to purchase land in that section in 1766. From small beginnings he rose gradually, till he acquired a considerable estate. He died in 1824. He was twice married, and raised a family of ten children, Mary, the wife of a Garland, Elizabeth, the wife of John Mills, Sarah, the first wife of Charles Yancey, Jane, the wife of Thomas Grayson, John, Robert, Ralph, Joseph, Susan, the wife of Nelson Moss, and Nancy, the wife of William Wood.

Three of the brothers married sisters, daughters of the elder Jesse Woods, John being united to Sarah, Ralph to Mildred, and Joseph to Elmira. Joseph died before his father, leaving two sons, William and Joseph. His widow afterwards became the wife of John Robinson. Robert led the way in emigrating first to Kentucky, and subsequently to Missouri, and was ultimately followed by most of the family; by all indeed bearing the name. John's home was east of Batesville, where Mrs. William H. Harris resides. Here he kept for many years a well known public house. In 1807 he conveyed to Marshall Durrett, James Wood, Charles Massie, Jonathan Barksdale, Oliver Cleveland, Thomas Massie, Henry Emerson, William Wood Sr., and John Wood, son of Isaac, ground for the old Mount Ed Church, on the south side of the public road, and on the top of the hill between Whitesides Creek and Captain White's. His son, bearing his name, was a druggist in Charlottesville, doing business on the public square under the firm of Field & Goss. In 1831 the father sold his place to Isaac White, and all the family joined their kindred in the West.

FITCH.

In 1759 William Daniel Fitch bought land on the east side of the South West Mountain, near Hammock's Gap, where he seems to have had his home. He died in 1814. His family consisted of twelve children, only two of whom were sons, John, who died before his father, and William D. The latter was one of the early and leading inhabitants of Milton. He maintained his interests there, until the place was completely shorn of its prestige and trade. While its flourishing days lasted, he was an Inspector of tobacco in Henderson's Warehouse, and the proprietor of a public house. About 1829 he removed to Charlottesville, and took charge of the Eagle Tavern. This property he purchased in 1833. He continued to be engaged in its management during the remainder of his life. His death occurred in 1848. He married Mary Bernard, who survived him twenty years. This worthy couple, though without children of their own, exercised the kindly care of parents over many of their nieces and nephews.

FRETWELL.

The first Fretwell appearing on the records was William, who in 1776 bought part of the Sumter land near Piney Mountain. It is conjectured his wife was a Crenshaw, as his eldest son bore that name. He died in 1822. His children were Crenshaw, John, Thomas, William, Susan, believed to have been the first wife of Elijah Garth, and the wife of Fendall Sebree. At the time of his death Thomas, William and Susan had already departed this life.

Crenshaw lived on the waters of Ivy Creek, not far from Garth's Mill. This place he and his wife Sarah sold to Dr. Charles Brown in 1822. A protracted litigation in which he was concerned, in connection with the old Draffen tract of land in the same neighborhood, was finally settled by the Court of Appeals in 1831. As no subsequent mention of him is found, it is supposed he removed from the county. John married Mildred, daughter of Thomas Garth Sr. His home was on the western side of the Garth plantation, on the Whitehall Road. He died in 1837. His children were Emily, the wife of Mortimer Gaines, Lucy, the wife of Samuel Kennerly, Susan, William G., Frances, Selina and John T. William G. married Emeline, daughter of Thomas H. Brown, and his children were John T., Susan and Lucy Elizabeth. John T., son of John, married Nannie A. ———, and his children were William G., Susan B., and Frances. Thomas lived between Free Union and the old Garrison Meeting House. He kept a store, which was known as Fretwell's Store, and which at the beginning of the century was the place for holding elections for Overseers of the Poor for the northwest district of the county. His wife was Agnes Burrus, and at the time of his father's death, she and her family were living in Kentucky.

William married Jemima Brown. He resided on the Staunton Road, above Mechum's Depot. He was deemed by his neighbors fit to be a landmark, because of his uncommon stature; in a deed of Nelson Hardin to his brother Isaac, the property is described as adjoining that of the tall William Fretwell. He died in 1807. His children were William C., who married first Mildred, daughter of Henry Burnley, of Louisa, and secondly Vienna, daughter of G. W. Kinsolving, Susan, the wife of William Brown, Judith, the wife of Benjamin H. Brown, Nancy, the wife of Augustine Stephenson, and Hudson. Hudson married Eizabeth, daughter of John Burnley, of Louisa, and sister of Nathaniel Burnley. His home was the large brick house on the Staunton Road, above Mechum's Depot, where for many years he kept a public house. He died in 1834. His children were Mary, the wife of Paul Tilman, Burlington, William, Franklin, Susan, the wife of Overton Tilman, Jurena, the wife of James H. Jarman, Brightbury, and Bernard.

Alexander Fretwell was for the first quarter of the century one of the business men of Warren. He was probably the same Alexander, who sold to Isaac Hardin in 1792 five hundred acres on the Staunton Road, adjoining the William just mentioned; from this too it may be inferred, that he also was a son of the first William. He died in 1825. He seems to have been twice married, first to Ann, daughter of William Barksdale, and secondly to Jane Hughes. His children were James B., who died in 1868 in Sumner County, Tennessee, aged eighty-three, Richard, Nancy, and three other daughters, the wives of Robert Anderson, Matthew

Martin and William Moorman. Richard married Sarah, daughter of Samuel Barksdale, and had ten children. He lived on the east side of Dudley's Mountain, at the place recently occupied by Major Berkeley. About 1840 he removed to Lewis County, West Virginia.

FRY.

Joshua Fry was born in England, and educated at the University of Oxford. Coming to this country, he was made Professor of Mathematics in William and Mary College. He was present at the organization of Albemarle County, and was appointed one of its first magistrates, its Lieutenant, and its Surveyor. For some years he was actively engaged in surveying lands in this and adjacent counties, and entered a considerable number of tracts in his own name. When the French and Indian War broke out in 1754, and a regiment was raised in Virginia on that occasion, Fry was appointed its Colonel, and Washington its Lieutenant Colonel. Fry repaired to Fort Willis, now Cumberland, Md., the rendezvous, to assume the command, but shortly after died, and was there buried. The home of Colonel Fry was the plantation just south of Carter's Bridge, which he patented in 1750, and which is now known by the name of Viewmont. There his widow lived till her death in 1773, and in 1786 the place was sold to Governor Edmund Randolph.

The wife of Colonel Fry was Mrs. Mary Micou Hill, and his children were John, Henry, Martha, the wife of John Nicholas, Clerk of the county, William, and Margaret, the wife of John Scott. John married Sarah, sister of Thomas Adams, who was once the owner of Blair Park, and had three children, Joshua, William and Tabitha. He died in 1778. Joshua married Peachy, youngest daughter of Dr. Thomas Walker. He was appointed a magistrate of the county, and represented it in the House of Delegates. Towards the end of the last century he removed to Kentucky, where he taught for a time a classical academy, and was the ancestor of a numerous posterity, the Frys, Greens, Bullits and Speeds, who have acted a prominent part in the affairs of that State. Henry served as deputy Clerk of the county, married Susan, daughter of Dr. Thomas Walker, and removed to Madison County near Rapidan Station, where he died in 1823 in his eighty-fifth year. He had nine children, one of whom, Reuben, was the father of Joseph L. Fry, for twenty years the Judge of the Wheeling Circuit; another, Henry, married Mildred, daughter of Rev. Matthew Maury, and was the father of J. Frank Fry, long a Commissioner of the Revenue of the county; and another, Wesley, was the father of Captain W. O. Fry. William, the Colonel's son, died unmarried about 1760.

GANTT.

Henry Gantt, of Prince George County, Maryland, came to Albemarle in 1813, and purchased from James Bullock, agent of Brown, Rives & Co., seven hundred and eighty-four acres, which had belonged to Robert and William Alcock, and which were situated southwest of the Cross Roads in North Garden. He made this place his residence for some years. On the fifth of December 1821, he bought a ticket of the State Lottery of Maryland, and on the thirteenth drew a prize of forty thousand dollars. He afterwards returned to his old home in Maryland, and was succeeded on the farm in North Garden by his son, Dr. John W. Gantt, to whom he and his wife Ann formally conveyed it in 1830. Here the Doctor lived and practised his profession till 1835, when he purchased from Charles A. Scott the plantation on James River, just above the mouth of Totier. On this place he passed the remainder of his days. He was appointed a magistrate in the county in 1830. In 1837 he and his wife Sarah conveyed the farm near Cross Roads to Joseph Sutherland, in whose family it has since remained. The Doctor died in 1860. His children were Henry, Philip, Albert, and Mary, the wife of Z. R. Lewis.

GARLAND.

The first of the Garland name who settled in Albemarle was James. He came from Hanover County, where he had married his wife, Mary Rice. In 1761 he bought land in the coves of the mountains southwest of the Cross Roads. He purchased first from James and John Coffey, and afterwards from Robert Nelson, till he possessed considerably more than a thousand acres. He also purchased from Samuel and William Stockton upwards of four hundred acres near the head of Mechum's River, including a mill which the Stocktons had built. He was acting as a magistrate in 1783, when the existing records begin, and was appointed Sheriff in 1791. He died in 1812. His children were Elizabeth, the wife of Thomas Garland, Edward, Rice, Robert, Clifton, Mary, the wife of James Woods, who in 1797 emigrated to Garrard County, Kentucky, and as nearly as the lines of descent in this family can be ascertained, James and Nathaniel.

Edward lived on the south side of the north fork of Hardware, near the crossing of the old Lynchburg Road. He was appointed a magistrate in 1801, and in 1808 succeeded Francis Taliaferro as Commissioner of the Revenue for St. Anne's, which office he filled until his death in 1817. His wife was Sarah, daughter of Colonel John Old, and his children Nathaniel, Mary, the wife of Nicholas Hamner, Fleming, James, Elizabeth, the wife of Joseph Sutherland, Sarah, the wife of Pleasant Sowell, and Maria, the wife of Thomas Hamner, who removed to Lewis County, West Virginia.

The home of Rice was the present farm of Bloomfield near Ivy Depot. He was appointed a magistrate in 1791, was elected to the Legislature in 1808, and served as Sheriff in 1811. He married Elizabeth, daughter of Samuel Hamner, and died in 1818. His children were William, James, Rice, Samuel, Elizabeth, the wife of Henry White, Mary Rice, the wife of Robert H. Slaughter, Burr, Maurice and Nicholas. William and James were their father's executors. The former lived for a time in Charlottesville, was the constructor of the present Lynchburg Road, and died in 1841. Rice was a lawyer, and settled in Leaksville, N. C. Samuel became a prosperous man of business in Lynchburg.

Robert was an active practitioner at the Albemarle bar,

and about 1822 removed to Nelson. Clifton was appointed a magistrate in 1806, and in 1813 contested unsuccessfully the election of Jesse W. Garth to the House of Delegates. He died unmarried in 1815.

James, as already narrated, lost his life at the Prison Barracks in 1781. His wife was Ann, daughter of John Wingfield and Mary Hudson, and his children Hudson M., James P., and Spotswood. They all removed to Amherst. Hudson was admitted to the bar, represented Amherst in the Legislature, was a captain in the war of 1812, was an intimate friend of General Jackson, and received from him an office in Washington, which he held until the administration of President Tyler. His wife was Letitia Pendleton, and he was the father of Judge James Garland, of Lynchburg, and General John, of the United States Army, who daughter was the the wife of General Longstreet. Spotswood became the first Clerk of Nelson, married a Rose, and was the father of Landon, late Chancellor of Vanderbilt University.

In 1778 Nathaniel bought land from Colonel Charles Lewis in North Garden, near Taylor's Gap. He died in 1793. His wife's name was Jane, and his children were Frances, the wife of John Woodson, Nelson, Mary, the wife of Isham Ready, Anderson, whose widow Nancy was married to Richard Bruce, and whose children removed to Lewis County, Kentucky, Elizabeth and Peter. Peter married Elizabeth, daughter of Benjamin Martin, who after her husband's decease became the wife of Daniel, son of Thomas Martin and Mary Ann White. Peter's sons were James and Goodrich.

William Garland, who was probably a brother of the first James, married Ann, daughter of Christopher Shepherd, and died comparatively young in 1777. His children were Frances, the wife of Reuben Pendleton, Mary, James, and David S. David S. resided at New Glasgow in Amherst, and in 1807 represented the district in Congress. His wife was Jane, daughter of Colonel Samuel Meredith and Jane Henry, sister of the renowned orator.

Another branch of the Garlands was resident in the county at a later date. About 1833 a mercantile firm did business

on the public square in Charlottesville under the style of
Binford and Garland. The Garland of the firm was James,
who soon after removed to Richmond. In 1835 his brother
Thomas purchased from John R. Campbell the fine low
grounds on the Rivanna, just below the mouth of Buck Island. He was appointed a magistrate in the county in 1838.
He was a man of unamiable temper and unsavory reputation.
He died in 1874. The brothers came from Goochland County.
Their mother was Elizabeth, daughter of Richard Morris,
of Green Spring, Louisa, and sister of Mrs. Dr. Frank Carr.

GARRETT.

The name of Garrett must always awaken interest in Albemarle, because of its long official connection with its affairs.
William Garrett appeared on the scene in 1764, when he purchased from Francis Jerdone, the same person who bought
the Farmington lands and sold them to George Divers, two
thousand acres along the northern base of Tom's Mountain,
in North Garden. In the course of the next ten years he
disposed of this property to different parties, but far the
greater portion of it to John Jones. Garrett as well as Jerdone belonged to Louisa. It is thought he was the grandfather of Alexander Garrett. The father of Alexander was
Henry, who in 1810 removed from Louisa to Kentucky, and
in passing through Charlottesville constituted his son his
attorney to settle up his business. He departed this life in
his new home in 1815.

Alexander came to the county as early as 1794. In 1799
he was a deputy of Samuel Murrell, who at that time was
Sheriff. A year or two after he married Elizabeth, daughter
of James Minor, who resided on the north fork of the Rivanna, near Stony Point; and from the mention of his name
among those assigned to work the roads, Mr. Garrett evidently lived for a time in the same vicinity. In 1806 he
received the appointment of deputy Clerk under John Nicholas. About that time his wife died, and in 1808 he married
Evalina, daughter of John Bolling, of North Garden. In
1815 he succeeded Mr. Nicholas as County Clerk, and in

1819 was appointed Clerk of the Circuit Court upon the resignation of John Carr, who had occupied that office since the Circuit Court superseded the District Court in 1809. Both of these offices he held until 1831, when his brother Ira was made County Clerk. Besides his official duties, he was assiduous and successful in many lines of business. He was a large dealer in real estate, owning at different times fine tracts of land in various neighborhoods of the county, Meadow Creek, Birdwood, North Garden, North Blenheim, Ivy Cottage and Greenwood. About 1815 his home was on the south side of University Street, and during the decade of 1820 he erected the large brick mansion at the foot of Second Street. In 1825 he laid out and brought into market the lots on Ridge Street, and in 1828 built Midway as a hotel, of which J. A. Xaupi was the first occupant. During his latter years, owing no doubt to the constant and long continued strain on his powers, he was afflicted with softening of the brain. He died in 1860. By his first marriage he had a daughter, Elizabeth, the first wife of V. W. Southall, and by his second, Dr. John Bolling Garret, Susan, the wife of Dr. Thomas Johnson, Eliza K., the wife of Alexander Duke, and Clarissa, the wife of Dr. Thomas J. Pretlow.

Ira Garrett, like his brother, commenced his business life by riding Sheriff. He was a deputy under Benjamin Harris in 1815, and Robert Davis in 1817. Soon after he became deputy County Clerk under his brother, and in 1831 succeeded him as principal. When the office became elective, he was chosen both to it and the Circuit Court Clerkship, term after term, as long as the people had a voice; and even when another was appointed by military authority, it was demanded by an overwhelming public sentiment that the faithful old man should act as deputy. In 1818 he bought from Jonathan B. Carr the place at the east end of Main Street, which he made his home the rest of his life. He always had a strong inclination to rural pursuits, and in 1836 purchased a plantation south of Charlottesville, afterwards the farm of W. P. Farish; but with him the lack of a close hand marred the knack of accumulation, and the project soon failed. Just before the war he bought Sunnyside, the late residence of Colonel Duke, but the outbreak of hostilities interfered with his enjoyment there. After the war however he indulged this fancy at Hobby Hill, a cottage with a few acres east of James D. Goodman's, where he and his wife, who shared in his taste for horticulture, spent a part of every summer. He died full of years in 1870. His wife was Eliza, daughter of John Watson, and his children Dr. Henry, of Southwest Virginia, John Alexander, George, Jane, the wife of Benjamin Winn, Ann, the wife of Thomas M. Smyth, Isaetta, the wife of K. Kemper, and Ellen, the wife of ―――― Watkins, who emigrated to Mississippi.

GARTH.

The first of the Garth family in Albemarle was Thomas, who in 1762 bought from Samuel Taliaferro four hundred and fifty acres on the Indian branch of Buck Island Creek. In 1770 he purchased from John Lewis, of Halifax, nearly a thousand acres on Blue Run, not far from Barboursville. The next three or four years he was employed by Mr. Jefferson to buy the Lego estate from William and James Hickman, sons of Edwin Hickman, the second Sheriff of the county. In 1779 he bought another thousand acres of the Lewis estate on Ivy Creek, and continued his purchases in that section, till he owned all the land stretching from near the Staunton Road, opposite Jesse Lewis's place, to the forks of Mechum's and Moorman's Rivers. On this tract he resided until his death. He was appointed a magistrate in 1791, and served as Sheriff in 1807. He died in 1812. His wife, it is said, was Judith Long, and his children Thomas, John, Elijah, Jesse, Garland, Ann, the wife of Richard Gaines, whose daughter Margaret was the wife of George Crank, and mother of R. G. Crank, a representative of the county in the Legislature twenty years ago, Sarah, the wife of Samuel Poindexter, who removed to Bedford County, Susan, the wife of Isaac Dalton, who emigrated to Stokes County, North Carolina, and Mildred, the wife of John Fretwell.

Thomas succeeded his father on Chestnut Ridge. He died in 1834. He married Susan, daughter of Richard Durrett, and his children were Jesse Winston, Willis, William, Elizabeth, the wife of Dr. Thomas K. Clark, and mother of Cornelia, the wife of Drury Burnley, and of Catharine, the wife of George McIntire, and Frances, the wife of James Michie. Jesse W. was deputy Sheriff, was admitted to the bar, was for six years Commonwealth's Attorney, was member of the Legislature, sold Birdwood to his brother William, and in 1818 removed to Alabama. His wife was Unity Dandridge, of the same kindred as Patrick Henry's second wife. Willis lived at the place occupied by the family of Legh R. Waddell, married a Miss Graves, and was prominent in the establishment of Mount Harmony Church. He died without children in 1851. William resided at Birdwood, built the spacious brick dwelling it contains, and by his improvements made it one of the principal country seats of the county. He married Elizabeth, daughter of George Martin and Barbara Woods. He died in 1860, leaving eleven children, J. Woods, Edgar, Lewis, George, Eugene, Georgiana, the wife of Rollin Kirk, Gabriella, the wife of James Kirk, Susan, the wife of Smith P. Bankhead, Elizabeth, the wife of William S. Bankhead, Celestine, the wife of Marshall Walker, and secondly of John Stockton, and Alice, the wife of Philip Gilchrist.

John married Ann, daughter of John Rodes, sold the land on Blue Run which was given him by his father, and near the close of the last century removed to Kentucky. Elijah received from his father a plantation of more than five hundred acres southwest of Still House Mountain, and in the early years of the century acted as deputy Sheriff. He was twice married, first to Susan Fretwell, and secondly to Catharine, widow of George Wayt. He died in 1817. His children were Littleton, Paschal, Elizabeth, the wife of a McGarvey, and Virginia, the wife of a Cross.

Jesse lived on a plantation his father gave him, lying west of the Barracks. His wife was Elizabeth, daughter of Bezaleel Brown, and his children Thomas, William T., Brightberry, Bezaleel, Mary, the wife of John H. McKennie, and Sarah, the wife of Willis C. Goodman. He died in 1836. Garland resided on the old Barracks place, where he built the large brick mansion recently occupied by the late George Carr. He married Susan Crenshaw, and his children were Dr. Garland A., Burwell, Isaac, Harriet, the wife of Isaac Davis, and Hardenia, the wife of Dr. Waller Head, who removed to Missouri. Mr. Garth was deprived of his home by business reverses, and spent his last days with one of his children in Nelson County.

GENTRY.

The different Gentry families in Albemarle seem to have sprung from the same head. Nicholas Gentry died in 1779, leaving eleven children, Moses, David, Nicholas, Mary Hinson, Robert, Benajah, Nathan, Martin, Elizabeth Haggard, Jane Timberlake, and Ann Jenkins. Moses bought land in 1778 from Samuel Gray on the old Lynchburg Road north of Garland's Store. He was a ruling elder in the Cove Church. He died in 1810. His children were Claiborne and Nicholas, who married sisters, Jane and Mary, daughters of Bezaleel Maxwell, Frances, the wife of Thomas Fitzpatrick, and Joanna, the wife of Joseph Walters. Addison, a son of Nicholas, married Lucy, a sister of Shelton F. Leake.

Prior to 1778 David and Martin were owners of land on Doyle's River, which they afterwards sold to Benajah Brown. A son of one of these brothers probably was Richard Gentry, who in 1784 married Jane, daughter of James Harris, and removed to Kentucky, and whose descendants held a reunion at Crab Orchard in August 1898. And from one of them in all likelihood came George Gentry, who died in 1818, whose home was not far from Free Union, whose wife's name was Elizabeth, and whose children were James, George, William, Frances, the wife of Nathaniel Tate, Austin, Aaron, Christopher, Martha, the wife of John Walton, Elizabeth, the wife of Edward Ballard, and Nancy, the wife of Edward Walton. The children of Christopher and his wife Sarah, were Martha, the wife of Joel Maupin, Mary, the wife of Henry Via,

Frances, the wife of Thomas Gibson, Elizabeth, the wife of James Dunn, Paschal, Henry, and Dicey, the wife of Garret White.

Benajah lived on Biscuit Run, where he commenced to purchase land in 1764. In 1817 he transferred his property to his son Robert, although his death did not occur till 1830. Martha, the wife of Elijah Dawson, son of Rev. Martin, who removed to Callaway County, Missouri, and Elizabeth, the wife of William Goodman, were daughters of Benajah. Robert married Mary, daughter of Francis Wingfield, and was the father of Albert.

Robert Gentry, believed to be the son of Nicholas, bought in 1766 from Martha, widow of Samuel Arnold, a place on the head waters of Ivy Creek, which he and his wife Judith sold in 1776 to John Woodson. Philip Joyner, whose daughter was the wife of a Robert Gentry, and who once owned the land the University stands on, devised the land to his two grandsons, Charles and Jesse Gentry. They sold, the one in 1775, and the other in 1783, and appear to have emigrated to North Carolina. Whether the Robert just mentioned was the same with the son of Nicholas, is unknown.

GILMER.

George Gilmer, immigrant, was a native of Scotland, who after a short sojourn in London, came to this country. He settled in Williamsburg, and practised his profession as a physician. His son Peachy, a fellow student of Nicholas Meriwether in William and Mary College, paid a visit to his friend in Albemarle, and fell in love with and married his sister Mary. This led to his brother George visiting the county, and ultimately marrying Lucy, daughter of Dr. Thomas Walker.

George like his father was a physician. He settled in Charlottesville, and his first residence was on Main Street, near the present store of T. T. Norman. He seems afterwards to have lived on Jefferson Street, on the south end of the lot facing the west side of the Square. He was a man of great activity and public spirit. The agitation preceding the Revolution had already begun when Dr. Gilmer came to Charlottesville, and from the first he displayed the liveliest concern in the question involved. Allusion has already been made to the prominent part he performed in the earliest movements towards independence. In 1777 he purchased from John Harvie Pen Park, which he made his home for the remainder of his life, the home of intelligence and refined hospitality graphically described by John P. Kennedy in his Life of Wirt. About the same time he purchased land on Mechunk, until he owned more than two thousand acres in that section. He was appointed a magistrate, served as Sheriff in 1787, and was a member of the House of Delegates. He died in 1796. His children were Mildred, the wife of William Wirt, George, Peachy, John, James, Lucy, the wife of Peter Minor, Harmer, Francis W., and Susan, the wife of Zachariah Shackelford.

Pen Park continued to be the home of the family during the life of Mrs. Gilmer. That part of the plantation called Rose Hill, where the children of John D. Craven now reside, was given to Mr. Wirt, and there he built a house; but having no family, he and his wife lived for the most part with her mother. The mother and daughter both died in 1800, and the next year Mr. Wirt removed to Richmond. The homestead was soon after sold to Richard Sampson, and still later to John H. Craven, whose residence there many yet remember.

George married Elizabeth, daughter of Christopher Hudson, of Mount Air. He became the owner of the Mechunk lands, which some years after were sold under deeds of trust to Dabney Minor. He died in 1836. His children were Thomas W., George Christopher, John H., Sarah, the wife of Dr. Samuel W. Tompkins, Georgiana, the wife of Colin C. Spiller, Maria, the wife of Samuel G. Adams, Ann, the wife of Peter McGee, Martha, and Lucy, the wife of Edward Pegram. Thomas W. was a lawyer, member of the Legislature, Governor of Virginia, member of Congress, Secretary of the Navy, and lamentably perished on board of the United States ship Princeton in 1844. His wife was Ann Baker, of Shepherdstown, Va. In 1826 he lived on Park Street where Drury Wood now resides, in 1831 bought from W. B. Phillips the brick house and lot at the west end of Jefferson Street, where John C. Patterson lives, and in 1836 purchased from John W. Davis the property on the hill recently occupied by John T. Antrim. G. Christopher married first Leana Lewis, of the Scottsville neighborhood, and secondly Mildred, daughter of Richard Duke. He died in 1887.

Peachy was admitted to the bar, and practised in Bedford County. He and Lucy were two of the devisees of the Farmington estate, Mrs. George Divers being their mother's sister. Peachy died in 1836. John was a physician, married Sarah Gilmer, a distant kinswoman, and lived at Edgemont, where he died in 1835. Francis adopted the profession of law, but was cut off in early life. He was a young man of fine endowments and rare culture, and gave promise of filling a distinguished position in his generation. He was a close friend of Mr. Wirt and Judge Dabney Carr, and a great favorite of Mr. Jefferson. The implicit reliance Mr. Jefferson had in his penetration and judgment, was manifested in his being entrusted with the selection of the first professors of the University. He himself was designed for the professorship of law. In his modesty, which was as great as his ability, he thrice declined the place. At length he accepted, but before entering upon its labors, was removed from the scene of all earthly activities in 1826.

GOOCH.

William Gooch, written in the early records Gouge, came to the county from Hanover. In 1751 he bought land from John Graves in the Everettsville neighborhood, which nine years after he sold to Benjamin Sneed, and it is believed, removed to Amherst. Another William, who, from being denominated Junior, is presumed to be his son, purchased land on the south fork of Hardware in 1764, but in 1770 began buying in the Ragged Mountains south of Ivy Depot, and in that vicinity fixed his residence. His dwelling stood where his son Dabney afterwards lived, and where still later W. O. English taught school. He died in 1796. He and his wife Lucy had ten children, Matthew, Philip, Dabney C., Nicholas L., William, Thomas W., Elizabeth, the wife of Nathan Dedman, Martha, the wife of William Thurmond, Susan, and Mary, the wife of William Moore. Matthew, who was admitted to the Albemarle bar in 1796, and Nicholas removed to Kentucky. Philip removed to Amherst, and to him his father transferred the land which he first bought on the Ragged Mountains, and which somehow acquired the name of Little Egypt, included the present reservoir, and was sold by his son Claiborne to the Houchens and Mayo families that still live on it. Claiborne Gooch removed to Richmond, became Adjutant General of the State, and was associated with Thomas Ritchie in publishing the Richmond Enquirer.

Dabney married Elizabeth, daughter of Rev. William Irvin, of the South Garden, and had a daughter Mary, the wife of her cousin, Dr. William F. Gooch. He died in 1844. Thomas W. married Nancy, another daughter of Mr. Irvin, and for many years kept a tavern at the D. S. He died in 1838. His children were Alonzo, Edwin, Meade, Angelina and Elizabeth, the wife of John Fray Jr. Alonzo was for some years a merchant in Charlottesville, and a magistrate of the county, and lived on the lot west of the Episcopal Church, now occupied by Capt. H. Robertson. His wife was a daughter of B. F. Porter, of Orange, and died in 1897 in Bluefield, W. Va.

Dr. William F. Gooch was a grandson of William Jr., and came to Charlottesville from Amherst about 1823. The next year he married his cousin Mary, the only child of Dabney C. For many years he practised his profession actively both in town and country. His town residence was the house now occupied by James F. Burnley on High Street. He was appointed a magistrate in 1843. Not long before the war he removed to his farm south of Ivy, where he died at an advanced age in 1881. He had two daughters, Maria, the wife of Paul H. Goodloe, and Elizabeth, the wife of W. O. English.

Another person bearing the name of Gooch belonged to the county in former times. He married Sarah, daughter of David Wood, and sister of the elder Drury. He had four sons and five daughters. Two of the sons, John and Roland, appear to have owned land on Rough Run, a branch of Moorman's River. They all removed to Lincoln County, Kentucky, probably in the closing years of the last century.

GOODMAN.

The first of the Goodman family was Charles. He is noticed as early as 1761 as having married Elizabeth, daughter of Roland Horsley. He began the purchase of land where he continued to live until his death, on the south fork of the Rivanna, west of the mouth of Ivy Creek. In the course of years he acquired considerably more than a thousand acres. His dwelling stood where Edward Wingfield now lives. He was appointed a magistrate in 1794, but apparently averse to the publicity of office soon resigned. He seems to have been a quiet, industrious man, notably upright in all his dealings. When in his will he made bequests of negroes to his children, he required a certain proportion of the value of their labor to be paid them year by year; and it is probable he did himself what he enjoined upon others. He died in 1827. His children were William, Joseph, Nathan, John, Susan, the wife of John Rogers, Roland Horsley, Jeremiah A., and Elizabeth, the wife of an Anderson. William married Elizabeth Gentry, Joseph married Nancy, daughter of Patrick Michie, Nathan married Mildred, daughter of Manoah Clarkson, and emigrated to Kentucky. John was one of the early Methodist preachers, and his wife was Frances, daughter of Thomas Dickerson. Jeremiah A. married Mary Clarkson, sister of Nathan's wife, and lived until his death in 1857 four of five miles south of Charlottesville.

Horsley Goodman married Elizabeth, daughter of David Rodes, and his children were D. Rodes, who was a deputy Surveyor of the county, Nathan C., who married Sarah, daughter of Joel Terrell, William, Horsley, who married Sarah, daughter of James Durrett, of the Batesville neighborhood, Susan, the wife of James Durrett, brother of Horsley's wife, Ann, the wife of Seth Burnley, and Lucy, the second wife of Thomas H. Brown. Horsley Sr., died the same year as his father.

GOOLSBY.

Thomas Goolsby was one of the earliest settlers within the present bounds of the county. In 1732, thirteen years before its organization, he patented twelve hundred acres on James River. In 1745 he sold more than five hundred acres to Samuel Shelton, and in the description of the deed are mentioned two tributaries of the James, called Holmans and Goolsby's Creeks. This deed is noteworthy also from a memorandum inscribed on it in 1788, showing that it had been previously recorded, but the record had been destroyed by the British in 1781. Thomas Goolsby died in 1774. He was twice married, his last wife being Lucy Bryant. His children were William, Thomas, Susan, the wife of a Childress, Ann, the wife of a Nowling, Lucy, the wife of a Saunders, and Elizabeth. William owned land on the waters of the south fork of Hardware. He died in 1819, and his children were William, Tabitha, the wife of Joseph Harlan, Tarleton, who married Mildred, daughter of Thomas Walker Jr., Sarah, the wife of a Thurmond, Susan, the wife of a Davis, Fleming, Jane, the wife of Samuel Harlan, Arthur, Mary, the wife of a Samuel Richardson, and Nancy, the wife of a Phillips.

Charles, James and John Goolsby, of Albemarle, were Revolutionary soldiers, members of the Ninth Virginia Regiment. Charles, who was a non-commissioned officer, and James were taken prisoners at Germantown; all three died in the service. They were beyond doubt sons of Thomas Sr., as William was stated to be their heir.

GORDON.

Before the middle of the last century two brothers named Gordon, natives of Scotland, were settled on opposite sides of the Rappahannock River as merchants, plying a thriving trade with the old country. James resided in Lancaster County, and John at Tappahannock in Essex. James's wife was Mary Harrison, of the Harrisons of Surry, and the wife of John was Lucy Churchill. Descendants of both became inhabitants of Albemarle. Rev. James Waddell, who preached and taught school near Gordonsville, married a daughter of James, and William F. Gordon, who acted a leading part in the affairs of the county in the first half of the present century, traced his lineage to John, or rather to both brothers at once. His father, James Gordon, was the son of John, and his mother, Elizabeth, was the daughter of James. William F. was admitted to the Albemarle bar in 1809. In 1812 he succeeded Joesph J. Monroe as Attorney of the Commonwealth, but resigned the next year, giving place to Jesse W. Garth. From 1818 to 1829 he was almost continuously a member of the House of Delegates, and in 1830 a member of the State Senate. He also represented the district in Congress. The title of General by which he was commonly known, he derived from his appointment in 1829 as Brigadier General of the Third Brigade, Second Division of the Virginia militia, and in 1840 of Major General of the Second Division. His home was at Spring Hill, at the eastern base of the South West Mountain, not far from Gordonsville. He died in 1858. His wife was Elizabeth, daughter of Reuben Lindsay, and his children, James, George, Hannah, the wife of W. J. Robertson, Reuben, William F., Charles, Dr. John C., Alexander and Mason.

In the last century there came to the county an Alexander Gordon, who seems to have been of kindred with the noble Scottish family of Gordon, of Huntly. He lived on Sowell's Branch near Carter's Bridge, where he obtained a patent for a small tract of land in 1785. He sued Humphrey Gaines for a piece of vacant land on Buck Island Creek to which they both laid claim, his counsel being Walter Leake, while Mr. Wirt appeared for Gaines. He was not an ornament to the county. He died in 1805, leaving a son, Alexander Duff Gordon, who two years after removed to Tennessee.

GOSS.

The first known settlement of the Goss family was in that part of Albemarle, which in its division in 1761 was erected into Buckingham. A James Goss was witness to a deed, conveying land on a branch of Slate River, in 1749. The head of the family now living in the county was Benjamin, who with a large household emigrated to Georgia. In process of time two of his sons, Jesse and John, returned to Virginia.

John soon became a teacher in the family of Governor James Barbour. He married Jane, daughter of James Walker, of Madison, and for a time had his residence in that county. He, as well as Jesse, entered the ministry of the Baptist Church. In 1803 he settled in Albemarle in the Priddy's Creek neighborhood, where he passed the remainder of his days, preaching for the most part to the church of that name. In 1816 he was appointed a magistrate. His death occurred in 1838, at the age of sixty-three. His children were Harriet, Sarah, the wife of Nimrod Bramham Jr., James W., John W., William, and Ebenezer, who died some years ago near Somerset in Orange.

James, when a young man, was engaged in the drug business on the public square in Charlottesville, in partnership with John Field Jr. In 1836 he took a leading part in establishing the Disciples' Church on Market Street, becoming a minister in that denomination, and publishing for a short period one of its organs, the Christian Intelligencer. He was appointed a magistrate in 1841. He was afterwards successfully employed in educational work, founding the Piedmont Female Academy near Priddy's Creek, and at the time of his death in 1870, filling the presidency of a similar institution in Hopkinsville, Ky. His wife was Jane A. Grigsby, of Rockbridge County.

John was in early life a merchant in Charlottesville in partnership with Christopher Hornsey. He married Polydora, daughter of Major John Lewis, of the Sweet Springs, and sister of Mrs. John Cochran. In 1838 he succeeded his father as magistrate, and in 1854 and 1855 represented the county in the Legislature. Since the war he occupied the offices both of Sheriff and County Clerk. He died in 1883, aged sixty-eight.

GRAYSON.

William Grayson was a native of Spotsylvania, and came to Albemarle some time before the Revolutionary War. In 1764 he bought land on the head of Mechum's River from Speaker John Robinson, who was then selling off the immense tracts in Rockfish valley, patented by his brother-in-law, John Chiswell. Having sold this property a few years after, he purchased from Gamaliel Bailey and Obadiah Martin at what was then known as the Little D. S., where the old Richard Woods Road forks with that passing through Batesville, and where his descendants have been living ever since. In 1804 he sold a small parcel at this place to William Simpson, who there establshed a tanyard that for many years went by his name, and afterwards by the name of Grayson, and that was one of the most noted landmarks in that neighborhood. Simpson in 1818 sold it to Joseph Grayson, a grandson of William. William died in 1829, having attained the remarkable age of ninety-seven years. His wife was Ann, daughter of Thomas Smith, and his children were John, Thomas, Martha, Elizabeth, the wife of Joseph Sutherland, and Susan, the wife first of Isaac Wood, and secondly of a Tomlin. Joseph Grayson married Rhoda, daughter of Daniel White, and died in 1867. His children were Thomas, who married Mary, daughter of John Jones, Ann, the wife of James H. Shelton, Frances, Elizabeth, the wife of Benjamin F. Abell, John and William.

HAMNER.

Tradition relates, that the immigrant Hamner bore the name of Nicholas, that he came from Wales and settled in Middlesex County, and that he had six or seven sons. Three of them fixed their homes in Albemarle. The first who appears on the records was William. In 1759 he bought from Thomas Fitzpatrick nearly five hundred acres on the south fork of Hardware, not far from Jumping Hill. The same year he obtained a patent for nearly two hundred acres on the north fork of Hardware, and acquired near by upwards of seven hundred more, all of which he sold in 1782 to Colonel John Old. In 1777 he purchased from Dr. James Hopkins about fifteen hundred acres on the waters of Totier. He died in 1785. He and his wife Elizabeth had eleven children, Jeremiah, Turner, Richardson, Henley, Samuel, Mildred, the wife of Jacob Moon, Elizabeth, the wife of Thomas Fitzpatrick, Mary, the wife of a Perry, Susan, the wife of Reuben Turner, Rebecca, the wife of James Turner, and the wife of David Strange. Jeremiah and Henley lived in the Biscuit Run valley, Turner at the mouth of Eppes Creek, Samuel near Jumping Hill, Jacob Moon, the Turners and Strange on Totier, though the Turners soon removed to Amherst. Jeremiah married Rebecca, daughter of Castleton Harper, and died in 1815. Most of his children emigrated to Georgia and Alabama, but his daughter Mary remained in Albemarle as the first wife of Samuel Barksdale. Samuel, who died in 1817, married, it is believed, a Morris, probably a daughter of Hugh Rice Morris, of the Totier region, and his children were William, Elizabeth, the wife of Rice Garland, Henley, Morris, Samuel, Jane, the wife of a Thomas, and Rhoda, the wife of James Nimmo. William died in 1831, and his children were John T., Jesse B., Susan, the wife of a Rice, Martha, the wife of Jacob Waltman, Austin and Samuel, who emigrated to Tennessee, and William, Morris and Samuel married sisters named Lucas, and about the beginning of the century removed to Charlotte County. The latter was the father of James G. and Thomas L., ministers in the Presbyterian Church.

The second of the brothers was Robert, who died in 1750. In 1772 his son Nicholas conveyed to William Hamner two hundred and seventy acres at the mouth of Eppes Creek, which had been devised to him by his father. In 1784 he purchased land north of Glendower, which is still the residence of his grandson. In 1794 he associated in business with Samuel Dyer at Warren, where he died soon after. His wife was Agnes, daughter of Giles Tompkins, and his children Susan, the wife of John L. Cobb, of Bedford, and mother of Nicholas Hamner Cobb, a former Chaplain of the University, and the first Episcopal Bishop of Alabama, Nicholas, who married Mary, daughter of Edward Garland, Edmund, who married Charlotte, daughter of Manoah Clarkson, James, who married Isabel Maxwell, Elizabeth, the wife of a Scruggs, of Buckingham, and Nancy, the wife of Samuel Childress.

The third of the brothers is belived to have been John, who lived in the Biscuit Run valley, and first appears as a purchaser of land in 1778. He married Mary, a daughter of Charles and Rachel Wingfield, and his children were Charles W., of Buckingham, from whom descended James and Wade Hamner, of Lynchburg, John, who married Susan Fretwell, Francis, who married Sarah Eubank, Thomas, who married Maria, daughter of Edward Garland, and removed to Lewis County, West Virginia, Mary and Susan, the wives respectively of Meekins and John B. Carr, who emigrated to Dickson County Tennessee, Elizabeth, the wife of Samuel S. Gay, and Sarah, the wife of David Gentry.

HANCOCK.

One of the original patentees of land in the county was Solomon Hancock. In 1756 he obtained the grant of four hundred acres between the Hardware and Totier Creek. Four years after he sold part of it to Giles Tompkins, and removed to Halifax County. In 1777 he sold the remainder to William Tompkins, son of Giles.

David Hancock in 1834 purchased from John R. Campbell eleven hundred acres on both sides of the Rivanna, above the mouth of Buck Island Creek. He died in 1858. His children were David, who married Janetta Thurman, Dr. Charles, who married Catharine Thurman, Gustavus, who married Lily Wimbert, and lived on James River below Howardsville, and Virginia, the wife of Dr. Francis Hancock, of Richmond. David died in 1872, Mrs. Virginia in 1884, Dr. Charles in 1885, and Gustavus 1898. All left families.

Richard J. Hancock was a native of Alabama, and came to Virginia during the civil war with the troops of Louisiana. Sojourning in Albemarle while recovering from wounds received in battle, he married Thomasia, daughter of John O.

Harris. He succeeded his father-in-law at Ellerslie, which is a part of the old Indian Camp plantation, once the estate of William Short, Washington's Minister to the Hague, and the fame of which as a stock farm he has spread abroad throughout the land.

HARDIN.

The family of Hardin occupied a position of some prominence in the county at the beginning of the century. Its head was Isaac, who, after living on different places, finally settled about 1785 on the plantation near Greenwood Depot, recently owned by Thomas C. Bowen. Here he resided until his death in 1820, at the age of eighty-four. His wife was Elizabeth, daughter of William Brown, and his children Mary, the wife of Samuel B. Smith, whose sons removed to Tennessee, Benjamin, Elizabeth, the wife of Gideon Morgan, Sarah, the wife of Nathaniel Landcraft, Nelson, Isaac B., Lucinda, the wife of William Scott, Berry M., and John. About 1808 Nelson emigrated to Mississippi Territory, and Isaac to Tennessee. Berry M. died in 1826.

For many years Benjamin was a conspicuous figure in the western part of the county. He bought in 1805 the brick house about a mile west of Ivy Depot, which was at first the nucleus, and soon the whole, of the town of Morgantown. Here he kept a tavern having the name of Albemarle Hotel until 1826. From time to time he bought up a few lots of the projected town, as their owners endeavored to realize a return from their investment; but as they lay unmarked amidst the trees and bushes of the forest, it is surmised the great mass of them quietly lapsed in his hands, totally forgotten by those who held the title. Hardin was a fancier of fine horses, and kept a number of racers. It is likely the temptations connected with such pursuits involved him in undue expense, and led to a neglect of his proper business; at all events in 1827 all his property was sold under deeds of trust. He then removed to Nelson County. In January 1899, his son, Dr. Charles W. Hardin, died near Longwood, Rockbridge County, in the eighty-fifth year of his age.

HARPER.

Castleton Harper was a deputy of Joseph Thompson, the first Sheriff of the county. His home was on the north fork of Hardware, near the mouth of Sowell's Branch. His death occurred about 1799. His children were Richard, Castleton, Henry, Rebecca, the wife of Jeremiah Hamner, Mary, the wife of Reuben White, Jemima, the wife of Edward Lyon, and Ellinda, believed to have been the wife of Thomas Staples.

Charles Harper came to Albemarle from Culpeper about 1814. In that year he bought from Thomas Wells eight hundred acres south of Ivy Depot. By continued purchases he became the owner of more than twelve hundred acres in that vicinity. In 1817 he disposed of three hundred acres, and half of the mill on Ivy Creek, to his son Joseph. He died in 1848. His wife was Lucy Smithers, and his children Joseph, Sarah, the wife of John Slaughter, Mary, the wife of William H. Glasscock, William, Charles, Gabriel, Lydia, the wife of Stephen C. Price, Robert, Lucy, the wife of Dr. M. L. Anderson, Nancy, the wife of Uriah P. Bennett, and Eliza Jane, the wife of John Wood Jr.

Joseph in 1826 sold to Benjamin Wood a tract of fifty acres, which acquired the name of Woodville, but has since been called Ivy Depot. In 1832 he sold his property, and removed to Daviess County, Missouri, where he died the same year as his father. He was twice married, first to Eliza Ann Green, and secondly to Mary Ann Miller, the widow of Robert W. Wood. His children were Twyman W., William, Mary, the wife of ——— Martin, Lucy Ann, the wife of Norborne T. Martin, a former merchant of Charlottesville, Charles and John. Gabriel married Sarah, daughter of Edmund Anderson and Jane Lewis. He was appointed a magistrate of the county in 1838. Some years before the war he removed to Appomattox County, and later to Prince Edward. When the war closed, he settled on James River below Richmond, where not long after he died.

HARRIS.

Matthew Harris in 1741 patented four hundred acres on the waters of Totier, which he afterwards sold to John Harris. It is believed he soon removed to the present territory of Nelson. He married Miss Lee, and had two sons, William and Lee. Lee married Miss Philips, and his son, William Lee Harris, who married Elizabeth, daughter of Clayton Coleman, was admitted to the Albemarle bar in 1798, but probably lived in the present bounds of Nelson.

William Harris, in all likelihood a brother of Matthew, was long one of the early and leading citizens of Albemarle. His first patent was located on Beaverdam of Hardware in 1739. He also made entries on Totier and Green Creeks, until during the next forty years he possessed more than two thousand acres. He was evidently a man of fine judgment and great energy. He established on Green Creek one of the first mills erected in that part of the county, and it has ever since been an important centre to the surrounding country. In 1746, the year after the county was organized, he was appointed one of its magistrates. He died in 1788. His wife was Mary Netherland, and his children, Matthew, Sarah, the wife of a Mosby, Elizabeth, the wife of John Digges, Catharine, the wife of a Steger, John, William, Mary, the wife of a Woodfolk, Benjamin, Ann, the wife of Hawes Coleman, and Judith, the wife of George Coleman. From this stem has sprung a greater number of families perhaps than from any other ever domiciled in the county.

Matthew married Miss Tate, and had fifteen children. Among them were Schuyler, who married Frances Blades, lived two miles north of Covesville, and died in 1803, and whose son, William B., married Elizabeth, daughter of Andrew Hart, was the father of Alfred and William Henry, was a magistrate of the county, and a ruling elder in the Cove Church, and died in 1862; Matthew, who married Miss Blades, and had a large family, of which the only one remaining is venerable Lloyd Harris, now living near Warren; Henry T., who became a member of the Albemarle bar in 1808, lived south of Covesville, married his cousin Mary, daughter of Benjamin Harris, and died in 1845, and whose daughters, Mary and Cornelia, were the wives respectively of Dr. Daniel E. Watson, and Dr. William D. Boaz; and Mary, the wife of a Barnett, and mother of Nathan J., who lived near Covesville, and was for many years Surveyor of the county.

Sarah Mosby was the grandmother of Alfred, the father of Colonel John S. Mosby, of Confederate fame. Elizabeth, the wife of John Digges, was the mother of nine children, of whom Elizabeth became the wife of Rev. Isaac Darneille, an Episcopal clergyman, Charlotte, the wife of William Moon, Dorothy, the wife of Marshall Durrett, Nancy, the wife of James Durrett, of Batesville, and Lucy, the wife of Dabney Carr, of North Garden.

John Harris was at the time of his death in 1832 the wealthiest man in the county. His home was at Viewmont, south of Carter's Bridge, which he purchased in 1803 from Tucker Moore Woodson. It is said, he added largely to his estate by his business operations during the war of 1812. He was appointed a magistrate in 1807. He was twice married, first to Frances Rowzy, and secondly to Sarah, widow of Robert Barclay. He left no children of his own, but devised a large portion of his estate to the children of his second wife, two of whom were married to the brothers, John D. and Edward H. Moon. His will was contested, and a long litigation ensued before it was finally established in 1838.

William married Miss Wagstaff, and had eight children. Among them were William B., and Frances, the wife of Lewis Nicholas. William B. married Elizabeth, daughter of Samuel Woods, and was the father of William H., who married Mary J. Wayland, lived on the old Field place near Batesville, was appointed a magistrate in 1838, and died in 1887.

Benjamin was a man of great wealth, was appointed a magistrate in 1791, and served as Sheriff in 1815. He married Mary, daughter of Samuel Woods, and had eleven children. Among them were Dr. William A., who married his cousin Elizabeth, daughter of Schuyler Harris, was a magistrate of the county, and a ruling elder in the Cove Church; and in 1837 removed to Illinois; and Colonel George W., who died in 1877, and whose children still occupy the old homestead on the old Irish Road, west of Porter's Precinct. Ann, wife of Hawes Coleman, was the grandmother of Mary, the wife of Dr. Charles D. Everett.

One of the early settlers on Doyle's River was Robert Harris. He obtained patents for nearly three thousand acres in that vicinity, his first entry having been made in 1750. His death took place in 1765. He and his wife Mourning had ten children, Christopher, Robert, Tyree, James, William, Lucy, the wife of William Shelton, Sarah, the wife of John Rodes, the wife of William Dalton, Mourning, the wife of John Jouett, and Elizabeth, the wife of William Crawford, and mother of William H. Crawford, United States Senator from Georgia, Minister to France, Secretary of the Treasury under Mr. Monroe, and a prominent candidate for the Presidency in 1824. Robert was a Captain in the Revolutionary service, and removed to Surry County, North Carolina. William died early in 1776, and Christopher in 1794.

James died in 1792. He and his wife Mary had ten children, Thomas, Joel, Nathan, James, Lucy, the wife of Thomas Grubbs, Mourning, the wife of Cornelius Maupin, Sarah, the wife of James Harrison, Susan, the wife of Nicholas Burnley, Ann, the wife of a Haden, and Jane, the wife of a Dabney. Joel was appointed a magistrate in 1801, and about 1811 Commissioner of the Revenue for Fredericksville parish, which office he held until his death in 1826. He and his wife Anna had three sons, Ira, Joel and Clifton. Ira succeeded his father in the Commissionership, as well as in the old home, the place where Jeremiah A. Early now resides, and died in 1863. He married Sarah, and his brother Clifton, Mary, daughters of Howell Lewis, of North Garden. Nathan removed to Lexington, Va., where he resided till his death. He was the father of the Hon. John T. Harris, and Rev. William A. Harris, for many years Principal of the Female Seminary in Staunton. James was appointed a magistrate in 1807. He married Mary, daughter of John and Mary McCulloch, and was associated with his brothers-in-law, Robert and James McCulloch, in conducting the mill at Millington. In 1822 he sold his property, and removed to another part of the country.

Another family of this name lived near Free Union. Its head was James, who died in 1797. He and his wife Elizabeth had six sons and five daughters. One of his sons, Blake, married Mary, daughter of John Alphin, and from another was descended Randolph Frank Harris, who was for some years the mayor of Charlottesville.

At a later date John O. Harris came to the county from Louisa. He purchased part of the old Indian Camp place, which William Short sold in 1813 to David Higginbotham. His wife was Barbara Terrell, and his daughters, Ann and Thomasia, became the wives respectively of John O. Pendleton and R. J. Hancock. Mr. Harris died in 1877, and his wife in 1882.

HARRISON.

Richard Harrison in 1789 purchased from James Overstreet, of Bedford, a tract of two hundred acres on the Martin King Road, between the waters of Buck Island and Hardware, which he sold four years later to Charles McGehee. One of the same name, and in all probability the same person, married Mary, daughter of Peter Clarkson. He resided in the Whitehall neighborhood, and was the father of a large family. His children were Elizabeth, the wife of Weatherston Shelton, Ann, the wife of John Clarkson, Mary, the wife of Charles W. Maupin, who removed to St. Louis, Peter C., Charles, John C., who married Frances Rodes, Julius C., who married Elizabeth Strange, Richard, David, James, who married Sarah Harris, and William.

In 1829 Dr. Charles Cocke and George M. Payne, as trustees of William Moon, sold Belle Grove, the seat of Old Albemarle Court House on James River, to Peyton Harrison. Mr. Harrison was a son of Randolph Harrison, of Clifton in Cumberland County, and a grand nephew of Benjamin, the signer of the Declaration of Independence. He married Jane, daughter of Judge Dabney Carr. Settling on his plantation near Scottsville, he practised law for three or four years, but abandoning that profession he entered the Presbyterian ministry. After making this change in vocation, he returned to Scottsville, and became pastor of the Presbyterian Church. Near the close of 1833 he sold Belle Grove to his brother, Carter H. Harrison. Here Carter resided till his death in 1844. He was appointed a magistrate of the county in 1835. His wife was Jeanette Fisher, and his sons were George Fisher, Henry, Edward Jacquelin, and Carter. Henry was the father of George M. Harrison, Judge of the present Court of appeals.

HART.

Andrew Hart was a Scotchman by birth, and was established as a merchant in the southern part of the county as early as 1786. His store was on Jumping Hill, at the south end of Gay's Mountain. At that time the road from Staunton to Scott's Landing passed immediately in its front, so that it was a point of public concourse. Mr. Hart was eminently successful in his business operations, and attained a high reputation for integrity and worth. Besides the management of his private interests, he was frequently engaged in public affairs, devoting much time to the execution of trusts devolved upon him by the County Court. He was for many years a ruling elder in the Cove Church, and one of its main supporters. His home was at Sunny Bank, the present residence of his great-grandson, Andrew Hart. He was twice married, first to Elizabeth, daughter of Rev. Samuel Leake, and secondly to Elizabeth Bickley, sister of the wife of Samuel Dyer. He died in 1832.

His children by the first marriage were Samuel L. and Mary, the wife of David Young. These brothers-in-law were in the early part of the century associated as merchants, and prosecuted an active business in North Garden. Samuel Hart was exceedingly popular, and a wide circle of friends availed themselves of his rare executive gifts. About 1829 he removed to Missouri. By the second marriage Mr. Hart's children were James, Andrew, John B., Francis, William D.. Eliza, the wife of William B. Harris, Margaret, the wife of

Rev. Thornton Rogers, and Celia, the wife of Dr. Jacob Snider, who removed to Mississippi.

James was twice married, first to Sophia, daughter of Schuyler Harris, and secondly to Frances Thomas, widow of Dr. Charles H. Meriwether. His home was in North Garden where H. Carter Moore afterwards lived, but he subsequently removed to Fruitland near Keswick, the present residence of his son-in-law, A. P. Fox. He died in 1874. Andrew was a Presbyterian minister, and died a few years ago at Buchanan, the place of his last pastorate. John B. was appointed a magistrate in 1824, did business in Scottsville and Mississippi successfully for a time, but at length overtaken by commercial disaster, removed to Alexandria where he died. Francis received from his father a plantation near Covesville, sold it in 1837 to Dr. Daniel E. Watson, and removed to Richmond. William D. was a man of much energy and vivacity, studied law, was a magistrate, represented the county both in the House of Delegates and State Senate, and was a Director of the Orange and Alexandria Railroad. He succeeded his father both in the old homestead and the eldership of the Cove Church. He married Elizabeth De Jarnette, and had one daughter Elizabeth, the wife of Thomas R. Dew. He departed this life in 1877.

John Hart, a brother of Andrew, settled in Richmond, where he died unmarried in 1796. He managed his affairs prosperously, and acquired considerable property. By his will he bequeathed a thousand pounds to a sister in Linlithgow, Scotland, and the residue of his estate to his brother in Albemarle.

HARVIE.

John Harvie was a native of Stirlingshire, Scotland, and at the time Albemarle was organized, was living at Belmont near Keswick, a place he bought from Matthew Graves. He was the guardian of Mr. Jefferson, and one of the earliest efforts of the great statesman's pen, was an inquiry addressed to Mr. Harvie respecting the method of his education. He died in 1767. His wife was Martha Gaines, and his children Richard, John, Daniel, who married Sarah

Taliaferro, William, who married Judith Cosby, Martha, the wife of John Moore, Margaret, the wife of John Davenport, Elizabeth, the wife of James Marks, Janet, the wife of Reuben Jordan, and Mary, the wife of David Meriwether. Some of these families resided for a time in Amherst, but all except John emigrated to Wilkes County, Georgia, in the decade of 1780.

John was a prominent man in his generation. He was one of the first lawyers in point of time who practiced at the Albemarle bar. He was a member of the House of Burgesses, and of the Continental Congress. He owned large tracts of land in the county, among them Belmont, the Barracks and Pen Park. By his influence as a Congressman, he procured the establishment of the Prison Camp at the Barracks. He made his home for some years at Belmont, but on receiving from Mr. Jefferson the appointment of Register of the Land Office he removed to Richmond, and continued in the discharge of its duties during the remainder of his life. He died at Belvidere, his country seat near Richmond, in 1807. He was a public spirited man, and did much to improve his city property, building among other houses what was afterwards known as the Gamble mansion, in the erection of which his death was caused by falling from a ladder. His wife was Margaret, daughter of Gabriel Jones, the distinguished Valley lawyer. His son Jacquelin married Mary, the only daughter of Chief Justice Marshall, and his daughter Gabrielle, a great beauty and wit, became the wife of the elder Thomas Mann Randolph in his old age, a marriage which produced a prodigious sensation at the time, and which occasioned some prudent advice on the part of Mr. Jefferson to his daughter, the wife of Mr. Randolph's son, in accordance with the wonderful practical wisdom that dwelt in the man. After the death of her husband, Gabrielle was married to Dr. John W. Brockenbrough, of Richmond and the Warm Springs.

HAYS.

Four persons named Hays came to the county from Augusta about 1870, William, James, David and John. It is likely they were brothers; James and David certainly were. William bought land from Thomas Smith on the head waters of Mechum's River. He married Charity, a sister of Rev. Benjamin Burgher, and in 1795 sold out and removed to Kentucky. James at first settled in the same vicinity, but afterwards purchased from John Mills a tract that included the present farm of Brooksville. There just before the close of the last century he laid out the town of New York, and disposed of a number of lots. For many years he kept a tavern, a well known stand in its day, which after his death was carried on by his widow. He displayed such prudent skill in the management of his affairs, that he was able to devise to his three sons a thousand acres of land. He died in 1813. His wife was Mary, daughter of Claudius Buster, who was married a second time to John Morrison. His children were James, Nathaniel, Thomas, and Elizabeth, the wife of Robert Brooks. James purchased the portions of his brothers, who seem to have removed to Monroe County. He married Margaret Yancey, a daughter probably of Colonel Charles Yancey. He gradually sold off his property, and appears to have emigrated to another part of the country about 1830.

John Hays conducted a public house in the same section, and died in 1826. David owned land near the foot of Yellow Mountain, a short distance north of Batesville. He was a farmer, a storekeeper, a ruling elder in the Lebanon Church, and for a time Colonel of the Forty-Seventh Regiment. He died about 1856. Shortly after that time, a son, David T., sold his land in that neighborhood, and removed elsewhere. William, another son as is supposed, married Mary, daughter of John Dettor, and died not long before, or during, the war.

HENDERSON.

At an early date the family of Henderson owned land near Milton, both on the north and south sides of the Rivanna. A stream which empties into the river below Milton, and which rises not far from Colle, was for many years known as Henderson's Branch. John Henderson bought the land on which Milton stands from Dr. Arthur Hopkins, who entered it in 1732. He died in 1786. It is conjectured his wife was a Bennett, as that was a given name in the family from generation to generation. His children were John, Bennett, William, Elizabeth, the wife of David Crawford, Susan, the wife of John Clark, Mary and Hannah, both married to Bullocks, and Frances, the first wife of John Thomas, of Amherst.

John Jr., was the owner, by gift from his father and father-in-law, of a large quantity of land lying below Milton, and in the Biscuit Run Valley. He was manifestly a man of influence on his own account. He was a magistrate, and filled the office of Sheriff, though in consequence of the loss of the early records the time is not known. He died in 1790, only four years after the death of his father. His wife was Frances, daughter of John Moore, and his children Bennett, Matthew, William, Mary, the wife of Hopkins Lewis, Frances, the wife of John Hines, Sarah, the wife of Micajah Clark, and Elizabeth, the wife of Peter Martin. Bennett emigrated to Jessamine County, Kentucky, about 1800, and Matthew followed him a few years later. William, who married Rebecca, daughter of John Hudson, conveyed six hundred acres on Biscuit Run to Walter Coles in 1806, when he presumably joined his kindred in the West. John Hines lived at the pillars of Hercules, now known as Millington, sold the place in 1807 to Thomas Ellis, and removed to Kentucky, where after his decease his widow became the wife of John Nicoll, of Allen County. Hopkins Lewis lived on a farm on Biscuit Run given his wife by her father, but his management of it was so intolerable, that in 1801 the court took it from his control, and in 1827 his seven children, scattered over Kentucky and Tennessee, appointed attorneys to dispose of it.

Bennett, the second son of John Sr., was a man of much consideration. He was a magistrate of the county. It was on his land Milton was built. He resided there, and in the exercise of a liberal, enterprising spirit erected a large flouring mill, and a tobacco warehouse, that during the next thirty years preserved the name of Henderson in the community. He married Elizabeth, daughter of Colonel Charles Lewis Jr., of Buck Island, and had twelve children, John, who married Ann B. Hudson, sister of his cousin William's wife, William, Sarah, the wife of John R. Kerr, James, Charles, Isham, Bennett, Hillsborough, Eliza, the wife of John H. Bullock, Frances, the wife of Thomas Hornsby, Lucy, the wife of John Wood, and Nancy Crawford, the wife of Matthew Nelson. Bennett Henderson died comparatively young in 1793, and within the next fifteen years his widow and all her children had removed to Kentucky. Their land around Milton, which was sold to Craven Peyton, came into Mr. Jefferson's hands in 1811; and in the deed to Mr. Jefferson, evidently written by his own hand in the precise language which marks all his writings, there is a full account of Bennett Hendersons family.

James P. Henderson was a grandson of Justice John Blair, of the United States Supreme Court, and one of the heirs of Blair Park. By purchasing the interest of John Blair Peachy, the other heir, in 1831, he became the sole owner. He married Margaret C., daughter of Richard Pollard, and granddaughter of Robert Rives, and had one child, Pauline, who became the wife of David M. Clarkson, of New York. He put an end to his own life at Cocke's Tavern in 1835.

HENING.

William Waller Hening, the compiler of the Statutes at Large of Virginia, was at one time a resident of Charlottesville, and a regular practitioner at its bar. He settled in the town in 1793, and seems to have come from Spotsylvania. His place of residence was first on the southern boundary of the place, near where Vandegrift's Planing Mill recently stood, and subsequently on the south side of University Street, not far from the Delavan Church. He dealt somewhat in real estate, but apparently not with much success. He was the owner of a Distillery which was once located beside the spring on the west side of the old Lynchburg Road, a little northeast of Orangedale, and with which his name was associated long after his removal from the county. This event occurred in 1805, when he went to Richmond to engage in the useful work of collecting and publishing the laws of Virginia. He was unquestionably induced to undertake this task by Mr. Jefferson, to whom it had been a matter of deep interest and great labor for many years. He was also associated with William Munford in publishing Hening & Munford's Reports. His wife was Agatha, daughter of Henry Banks. Mr. Hening continued to hold the ownership of some lots in the southern portion of the town, and of some land near Moore's Creek, which was finally closed out in 1830 by his son-in-law, Robert G. W. Spotswood. He died in Richmond in 1828.

HOPKINS.

As early as 1732, Dr. Arthur Hopkins, who resided on one of the branches of Byrd Creek in Goochland, obtained a patent for four hundred acres where Milton now stands, another in 1748 for nearly twenty-three hundred on Totier Creek, and a third in 1765 for fourteen hundred and seventeen between Hardware and Totier, which had been granted to Hardin Burnley, but forfeited for failure to pay the quit rents. He died in 1766. He and his wife Elizabeth had eight children, Samuel, John, Arthur, William, James, Lucy, the wife of George Robinson, of Pittsylvania, Mary, the wife of Joseph Cabell, and Isabel.

Samuel married Isabella Taylor, a cousin of President Madison's grandmother, and of President Taylor's grandfather, and an aunt of John Taylor, of Caroline. Their son Samuel was Lieutenant Colonel of the Tenth Virginia in the Revolution, and General in Kentucky in the war of 1812, for whom Hopkins County and Hopkinsville in that State were named. Arthur went to Kentucky, and died unmarried. William lived in Albemarle on Totier. He married Elizabeth, daughter of Jacob Moon, and died in 1820. His children were Ann, the wife of Peter Porter, who removed to Missouri, Mildred, the wife of James Thomas, Jane, the wife of Littleberry Moon, and mother of Samuel O. Moon, Mary, Margaret, Isabel, the wife of Henry Turner, and mother of the venerable William H. Turner, Elizabeth, the wife of Jesse Haden, Samuel—the last two emigrated to Kentucky—and William. William had his home in the vicinity of Scottsville, married Rebecca Estis, and died in 1832. His children were Mary, the wife of Lain B. Jones, Martha, the wife of John H. Henderson, James, and Margaret, the wife of Moses Arnold.

James, the son of Dr. Arthur, was the accomplished physician who settled in Nelson County, and as already narrated, was basely murdered in 1803.

Mary, daughter of Mary Hopkins, and Joseph Cabell, became the wife of John Breckinridge, then of Botetourt County, but subsequently United States Senator from Kentucky, and Mr. Jefferson's Attorney General. Mr. Cabell, who had bought the glebe of St. Anne's on the south fork of Totier, presented it to his daughter, and there Mr. Breckinridge made his residence from 1785 to 1793, when he removed to Kentucky. During that time he was a member of the Albemarle bar, and in 1792 in the interval between the resignation of the first John Nicholas, and the appointment of the second, as Clerk of the county, he acted as Clerk *pro tem*. His two eldest children were born in Albemarle, one of whom was the father of the Vice President.

HUDSON.

One of the earliest patentees of land in the wilds of Albemarle was Charles Hudson, of Hanover. His first entry was made in 1730 on the Hardware, below Carter's Bridge. It was for two thousand acres, and within the next three years he obtained grants for sixteen hundred more in the same locality. It embraced Mt. Air, which was one of the seats of the Hudson family for more than a hundred years. The stream entering the south side of the Hardware below Mount Air, was formerly known as Hudson's Creek. Charles Hudson also took out a patent in 1735 for two thousand acres on Ivy Creek, southwest of Ivy Depot, which he sold two years later to the elder Michael Woods. It is almost certain he never lived in Albemarle himself. He died in 1748, and the executor of his estate was his son-in-law, John Wingfield. His wife was probably a Royall, and his children were William, John, Christopher, Mary, the wife of John Wingfield, Elizabeth, the wife of Nicholas Johnson, Rebecca, the wife of Robert Wathen, Sarah, the wife of Richard Holland, and Ann, the wife of Joseph Lewis. In 1762 Mary Wingfield, still living in Hanover, conveyed to her son Charles part of five hundred acres in Albemarle given her by her father, and named Prospect, where Charles was living at the time. This Charles was the forefather of most of the Wingfields, who have since resided in the county.

John Hudson had his residence on the lower Hardware. He died in 1768. He and his wife Ann had four children, Charles, John, Christopher, and Mary, the wife of a Gaines. Charles married Jane, daughter of Colonel Charles Lewis Jr., of Buck Island. Their daughter, Martha Eppes, was the wife of Tucker Moore Woodson, who about 1804 removed to Kentucky. Charles Hudson seems not to have been prosperous in his affairs. In 1807 he exchanged with Samuel Dyer the place on Hardware where he lived, for a tract of land in Barren County, Kentucky, to which he probably removed. John, whose residence was on the Hardware, died in 1801. His children were John, who died in 1827, Charles, who died in 1837, and whose daughter Isaetta became the wife of Isaac R. Barksdale, Elizabeth, the wife of Charles A. Scott, Rebecca, the wife of William Henderson, Sarah, Mary, the wife of a Cobbs, and Ann Barber, the wife of John Henderson.

Christopher, the son of the first Charles, displayed more of the ability and thrift of his father than any other of his descendants. At the time of his death, which took place in 1825, he was the possessor of more than five thousand acres of land. He was appointed a magistrate in 1800, but four years after resigned. His home was at Mount Air. He married Sarah, daughter of David Anderson, and his children were Elizabeth, the wife of George Gilmer, and Ann, the wife of William Tompkins. His grandson, Thomas W. Gilmer, had charge of the administration of his large estate.

HUGHES.

Thomas Hughes, who came from Buckingham, and lived on James River, died in 1779. His children were William, Moses, Mary, the wife of a Jude, and Rebecca, the wife of a Ball. William was a man of some prominence. He was acting as a magistrate of the county in 1783, and served as Sheriff in 1797. He and his wife Mary had five children, Rebecca, Robert, Jane, the wife of Alexander Fretwell, Hannah, the wife of Edward Thomas, and Sarah, the wife of Samuel Irvin. He died in 1813.

Stephen Hughes was a large landholder near Charlottesville at the time the town was established. In 1764 he purchased from John Grills nearly a thousand acres on Moore's Creek, including the mouth of Biscuit Run. In June 1762 he bought from Colonel Richard Randolph, of Henrico, five hundred and fifty-eight acres lying mainly on the east side of the present Scottsville Road, and extending from the limits of the town beyond Moore's Creek; this tract, except a few acres, he sold in 1765 to Creed Childress, who the same year sold it to Nicholas Lewis. His dwelling was not far from where the old Lynchburg Road crosses Moore's Creek. He died in 1793. He was twice married, and his children were Stephen, Mary, the wife of James Mayo, Edward, Sarah, and Letitia, the wife of Francis Taliaferro. Stephen about 1810 built a mill on Moore's Creek, which occupied the site of that which now belongs to Jesse L. Maury. He disposed of it to John Wheeler, who in 1820 sold it to Reuben Maury and John M. Perry. Edward died about 1826. His wife was Elizabeth Chisholm, and his children, Nancy, Mary, Martha, Susan, Sarah, William and John. Mary became the wife of Washington Chiles, who was for many years one of the cabinet makers of the town, and lived on the south side of Main Street, east of the Perley Building.

IRVIN.

Rev. William Irvin was one of the early Presbyterian ministers of the county. He received his education in part at the school of Rev. John Todd in Louisa. He was received by the Presbytery of Hanover in 1769, and settled as pastor of the Cove and Rockfish Churches in 1771. He married Elizabeth, daughter of Joseph Holt, who served in the Revolution as First Lieutenant in the Fourth Virginia, and who purchased land from Colonel Charles Lewis on the Staunton Road west of Ivy Depot, where he resided until 1794. Mr. Irvin bought part of this land from his father-in-law, but sold it in 1783, and the same year purchased from Charles Martin a farm on the south fork of Hardware, where J. Goulet Martin now lives, and where he made his home until his death in 1809. His relation to Rockfish Church was dissolved in 1776, and he then devoted his time to preaching at the Cove, D. S., and Mountain Plains. In July 1793 his old preceptor, Rev. John Todd, met with a tragic death on his return from a meeting of Presbytery at the Cove. The road on the east side of Persimmon Mountain passed then, as it does still, along the bed of the South Hardware for a short distance; there the venerable minister was found, lying in the stream with life extinct. Whether he was smitten with an apoplectic stroke, or whether his horse took fright, and starting suddenly threw him, was not known. It is said, he was accustomed to ride a spirited horse.

Mr. Irvin had ten children, some of whom attained a degree of eminence in the world; Joseph Holt, Margaret, Elizabeth, the wife of Dabney C. Gooch, Nancy, the wife of Thomas W. Gooch, Sarah, the wife of Robert Sangster, John, William W., James, Thomas and David. Joseph was admitted to the Albemarle bar in 1796, married Elizabeth, daughter of William Cole of North Garden, and died in 1805, leaving two daughters, one of whom, Susan, was married first to Colonel Thomas Wood, and was the mother of Dr. Alfred Wood and Mrs. Jeremiah A. Early, and secondly to John Fray. John lived on the old place, was a magistrate of the county, and died in 1828, leaving a number of children, all of whom removed to Campbell and Prince Edward Counties. William became a member of the Albemarle bar, but emigrated to Lancaster, Ohio, where he was appointed a Judge of the Supreme Court, and elected to Congress in

1828. Thomas joined his brother William in Ohio, and became Judge of the Lancaster Circuit. David was also a lawyer, received the appointment of Governor of Wisconsin Territory, and afterwards settled in Texas, where he was left by the war with only the shreds of a large fortune, and where he shortly after died.

JAMESON.

The Jamesons were settled at an early day on Moorman's River, both above and below Whitehall. John Jameson took out a patent for land on the north side of that stream in 1741, and Samuel, his brother or son, on the branches of Spring Creek in 1747. In 1765 Samuel purchased the land in the old Woods Gap from Archibald Woods, who had entered it in 1756. His son Alexander sold it in 1809 to David Stephenson, of Augusta. Samuel died in 1788. He and his wife Jean had nine children, four of whom were Alexander, Thomas, John and Samuel. Samuel Jr., died about 1805. His wife's name was Margaret, and his children were Hannah, the wife of William Harris, Jane, the wife of William Maupin, Elizabeth, the wife of a Harris, Catharine, the wife of Nathan Mills, Mary, the wife of Nehemiah Birckhead, William and Samuel. Some of the sons of this family were mighty hunters, as is manifest from their frequent reports of wolf scalps to the County Court.

It is supposed that Thomas Jameson, who was a physician in busy practice in Charlottesville the early part of the century, was a scion of this stock. In 1806 he lived on the lot on which the family of J. J. Conner resides at present, and which he purchased from William G. Garner. In one of his conveyances it is described as being "on the upper street leading out to Jameson's Gap," that being evidently the name of what is now called Turk's Gap. He married Evalina, daughter of William Alcock, and sister of the second wife of John Kelly. In 1815 he sold his residence to Mr. Kelly, and it is believed emigrated to the West.

JARMAN.

The first of the Jarman name settled in the county was Thomas, who obtained a grant of land on Moorman's River in 1762. His children were Elizabeth, the wife of Zachariah Maupin, Mary, the wife of Benajah Brown, William, Martha, the wife of Daniel Maupin, Frances, the wife of John A. Michie, and James. James had his residence on the east side of the road in Brown's Cove, about a mile south of Doylesville. He was appointed a magistrate in 1819, and was frequently employed in the county business of his district. He died in 1847, and was succeeded in the homestead by his son, Miletus, who departed this life in 1874.

William established himself in 1790 near the present Mechum's Depot. He soon after built the mill at that place, which was for many years known by his name, and on the site of which one has existed ever since. In 1805 he and Brightberry Brown undertook the construction of Brown's Turnpike, beginning at a point called Camping Rock, crossing the Ridge at Brown's Gap, descending through Brown's Cove, and terminating at Mechum's Depot. A formal acceptance of it took place the next year by Commissioners appointed from both sides of the mountain. William Jarman died in 1813. He married Sarah, daughter of John Maupin, and had five sons and six daughters. In 1819 James, his eldest son, sold his half of the Turnpike to Ira Harris for one hundred dollars. His son Thomas bought the land on the summit of the Ridge at the old Woods Gap, and since his purchase the Gap has generally gone by his name. His daughter Mary became the wife of the younger William Woods, of Beaver Creek, and mother of Peter A. Woods, formerly one of the merchants of Charlottesville.

JEFFERSON.

Peter Jefferson, the father of the President, was a native of Chesterfield, and removed to the present limits of Albemarle in 1737. He entered the wilderness literally, as when he first came there were but three or four persons living in the neighborhood. His first entry was that of a thousand acres on the south side of the Rivanna, between Monticello Mountain and the Henderson land above Milton. Wishing a more eligible site for his house, he bought from his friend William Randolph, of Tuckahoe, the Shadwell tract of four hundred acres, where his distinguished son was born. He had been a magistrate and Sheriff in Goochland, and when Albemarle was formed, was one of its original magistrates, and its Lieutenant Colonel. He also represented the county in the House of Burgesses. He was employed with Colonel Joshua Fry to run the boundary line between Virginia and North Carolina, and to make the first map of Virginia ever drafted. When William Randolph died in 1747, leaving a son of tender age, he committed him to Mr. Jefferson's care, and more efficiently to discharge this trust Mr. Jefferson removed to Tuckahoe, where he resided seven years. This circumstance explains the difficulty in Mr. Waddell's mind, when in his Annals of Augusta County, he wondered how Thomas Lewis and his friends, who had gone to Mr. Jefferson's to make a map of the survey of the Northern Neck line, could ride from his house to Richmond to hear preaching on Sunday. He returned to Albemarle in 1755, and died in 1757. His wife was Jane, daughter of Isham Randolph, of Dungeness, and his children Jane, who died unmarried, Thomas, Randolph, Mary, the wife of Thomas Bolling, Martha, the wife of Dabney Carr, Lucy, the wife of Charles Lilburn Lewis, and Ann, the wife of Hastings Marks.

Thomas was born in 1743, married in 1771 Martha, daughter of John Wayles, of Charles City, and widow of Bathurst Skelton, and died July 4, 1826. He had two daughters, Martha, the wife of Governor Thomas Mann Randolph, and Mary, the wife of John W. Eppes. He was one of the largest landholders in the county, being assessed in 1820 with four thousand eight hundred and ninety-nine acres. Soon after attaining his majority, he was appointed a magistrate of the county, and at the first session of the County Court after his decease, the following memorial was entered upon its records:

"As a testimonial of respect for the memory of Thomas Jefferson, who devoted a long life to the service of his country, the principles of liberty, and the happiness of mankind; who aided conspicuously in the cause of the American Revolution; who drafted the Declaration of the principles, on which the Independence of these States was declared; who uniformly exerted his great talents to aid both the civil and religious liberties of his countrymen, and by whose practical administration of the principles he had promulgated in many stations, legislative, diplomatic and executive, in which he had acted as a public functionary, the equal rights of his countrymen were promoted, and secured at home and abroad; who, uniting to a native benevolence a cultivated philanthropy, was peculiarly endeared to his countrymen and neighbors, who were witnesses of his virtue:

Resolved therefore that this testimonial be recorded as a perpetual memorial of respect and affection of his countrymen, and of the Court of Albemarle, of which he was once a member; and

Resolved that this Court and its officers, as a testimony of public respect, will wear crape on the left arm for thirty days, and will now adjourn."

Randolph Jefferson in 1781 married Ann, daughter of Charles Lewis Jr., of Buck Island. He had his residence in Fluvanna County. He had two sons, Thomas and Isham R. Thomas was twice married, first to his cousin Mary R., daughter of Charles Lilburn Lewis, and secondly in 1858 to Mrs. Elizabeth Barker, daughter of Henry Siegfried. His children were Peter Field and Robert L. Peter Field lived in Scottsville, and by his shrewdness and frugality amassed a large fortune. He died in 1861, leaving a son bearing his own name, and a daughter, the wife of Peter Foland. Peter Field Jr., died in 1867. Robert L. married Elizabeth, daughter of Robert Moorman, lived near Porter's Precinct, and died in 1858. His children were Eldridge, who lived in the same section of the county till after the war, and Mary, the wife of Albert W. Gantt.

A story is told of Randolph, that one day he came to his brother to unburden his mind of a weighty idea that had struck him, and announced himself thus: "Tom, I'll tell you how to keep the squirrels from pillaging the corn. You see they always get on the outside row. Well then, don't plant any outside row"—which, if true, well illustrates a reflection of Miss Sarah Randolph, "It is curious to remark the unequal distribution of talent in this family, each gifted member seeming to have been made so at the expense of one of the others."

A Thomas Jefferson, who in the first days of the county was one of its deputy Surveyors, was no doubt a brother of Peter, the President's father.

JONES.

Many persons named Jones have lived in Albemarle. Orlando Jones appears at the earliest date. In 1760 he bought four hundred acres from John Scott, and fourteen years later four hundred more from Joseph Anthony, both tracts being on the waters of Totier. It was unquestionably at his place that Major Anbury, and others of the Saratoga prisoners, were quartered, while in the county; and there is as little question that it is the same place near Glendower, that was recently occupied by the late R. J. Lecky. Jones married as his second wife Elizabeth Clayton, sister of Edith, wife of Rev. Charles Clay, and daughter or niece of John Clayton, the celebrated botanist of Virginia. He died in 1793. His widow was subsequently married to William Walker, and his son, Lain, succeeded to the homestead, which then went by the name of Mount Gallant. In 1800 Lain was the bearer of a challenge from George Carter to James Lewis, and together with his principal was placed under bonds. He died in 1805, leaving three sons, Orlando, Lain B., and William. Lain B. in 1825 married Mary, daughter of Captain William Hopkins. His mode of living led to the incumbering of his estate, and in 1824 it was sold under a deed of trust to John Neilson, one of the builders of the University. When after the death of Neilson the place was sold by Andrew Leitch, his executor, it was purchased by James Jones, a gentleman of considerable wealth. He made it his residence until his death in 1838. He and his wife Margaret had six children, James, William, Ann, Sarah, Lucy, the wife of a Moseley, and Virginia. The next year the plantation was sold to John H. Coleman and Dr. Samuel W. Tompkins.

In 1762 a James Jones bought eight hundred acres from Joseph Anthony at the northeast corner of Dudley's Mountain. His home was on the old Lynchburg Road, and Jones's Still House, and Jones's Branch constantly occur in the early records as marking the lines of the road precincts. He had a son, James Jr., who lived on part of the estate. It is believed that Allen Jones, who resided in the same vicinity, was also a descendant. Allen married Nancy, daughter of John Carr. In 1821 he was desirous of removing South, and advertised his place for sale. He finally sold in 1833 to John H. Maddox, and presumably accomplished his purpose.

In 1765, John Jones, of Louisa, bought from Henry Terrell more than eight hundred acres adjoining Batesville, and including Castle Mountain. During the next eight years he purchased from William Garrett upwards of thirteen hundred in North Garden, on the north side of Tom's Mountain. He sold in 1778 a thousand and eighty-one acres of that lying east of Israel's Gap to William Cole, of Charles City, and a portion of that lying west to Robert Field in 1782. He died in 1793. His wife's name was Frances, and his son John in 1806 married Elizabeth, daughter of Daniel White. The son's home was on Beaver Creek, where his grandson, James Rea, now resides, and he died in 1868. His children were Nancy, the wife of William Woods, Mary, the wife of Thomas Grayson, Elizabeth, the wife of Bland Rea, and Sarah Jane, the wife of John M. Godwin.

Thomas Jones, who commenced his purchase of land in 1767, became the owner of more than twelve hundred acres on Blue Run, and the Orange line. The most of it was acquired from Thomas Garth, and his son John. Jones sold the larger portion of it to Francis Gray. He died in 1799.

Later appeared on the scene John R. Jones, a name well remembered by many. Perhaps no man in the county ever led a more energetic and industrious life. He was at first connected in business with his brother-in-law, Nimrod

Bramham, with whom he subsequently entered into partnership. This was dissolved in 1821, when Mr. Jones became a merchant on his own account. In 1819 he was appointed a magistrate, and was active in performing the duties of that office. He was constantly called upon to act as trustee, or administrator, in managing the affairs of others. Particularly as trustee of Edmund Anderson, he took charge of his property in this county in 1829, and sold off the remaining lots in Anderson's Addition to Charlottesville. He was the first President of the Branch of the Farmer's Bank of Virginia established in Albemarle. In 1814 he purchased the square west of the Baptist Church, and built the brick mansion which was some time his residence. In his latter years he was embarrassed by financial troubles, and died in 1868. His wife was Gilly Marshall, and his children William, the father of Rev. J. William Jones, Dr. James L., Gen. John M., who fell in 1864 at Spotsylvania C. H., Thomas, Mary, the wife of James M. Daniel, Ariadne, the wife of T. T. Hill, Georgiana and Gilly.

Still later Dr. Basil Jones, the father of James D. and Major Horace, was for a time a citizen of Charlottesville.

JOUETT.

Among the earliest entries on the Court records of Albemarle in 1745, is a notice of the death of Matthew Jouett, and the appointment of John Moore as his executor. It can scarcely be doubted that John Jouett, who was for many years a prominent citizen of Charlottesville, was a son of this Matthew. In 1773 John purchased from John Moore one hundred acres adjoining the town on the east and north, and at that time most likely erected the Swan Tavern, of famous memory. Three years later he bought from the same gentleman three hundred acres south of the town, including the mill now owned by Hartman. In 1790 he laid out High Street, with the row of lots on either side, and by an act of the Legislature they were vested in trustees to sell at auction, after giving three weeks' notice in the Virginia Gazette. He kept the Swan until his death in 1802. In the Central Gazette of October 8th, 1824, there appeared an earnest appeal to the citizens of Charlottesville to erect a stone over his grave, but the voice died away unheeded, and the grave is now unknown. At the time of his death, and for many years after, no public place of burial in the town existed. According to the custom of that day, he was most probably buried in the yard in the rear of his house, and his remains lie somewhere in the square on which the old Town Hall is situated His wife was Mourning, daughter of Robert Harris, of Brown's Cove, and his children Matthew, John, Robert, Margaret, the wife of Nathan Crawford, Mary, the wife of Thomas Allen, Frances, the wife of Menan Mills, Elizabeth, the wife of Clifton Rodes, Charles, and Susan, the wife of Thomas C. Fletcher.

Matthew was a Captain in the Revolutionary army, and fell in the battle of Brandywine. John succeeded his father in conducting the Swan, but shortly after removed to Bath County, Kentucky. His wife was Sarah Robards, a sister of the first husband of President Jackson's wife. Robert was also a Captain in the war of the Revolution, and afterwards a member of the Albemarle bar. He owned and resided on the lot on the Square where the Saunders House now stands. He died in 1796, leaving a daughter Alice, who became the wife of James W. Bouldin, of Charlotte County. She and her husband in 1818 conveyed this lot, and the square on High Street on which Dr. Hugh Nelson lives, to John Winn. Charles Jouett removed to the West. In the latter part of 1804 he was in Detroit, but whether he settled there is not known. His father devised to him the tract of land south of Charlottesville, and in 1813 he and his wife Susan conveyed it to William D. Meriwether. This explains why the mill was known as Meriwether's for many years. Most of the daughters removed with their husbands to Kentucky.

The general tradition about Charlottesville has always been, that it was John Jouett Sr. who performed the exploit of outstripping Tarleton, and apprising Mr. Jefferson and the Legislature of his approach in 1781. It was supposed that the appeal for a monument to be raised to his memory already alluded to, was based upon the recognition of the splendid act, by which he honored the town of his residence, and conferred one of the greatest benefits on the State and country; but unfortunately the file of papers which contained the appeal, was consumed in 1895 by the fire at the University where it was deposited. It has recently been learned from Thomas M. Green, of Kentucky, that the descendants of the family residing in that State, claim that the bold and opportune ride from Louisa C. H. was made by John Jouett Jr., that the Legislature of Virginia presented him with a sword in commemoration of the deed, and that the sword still remains in the family as a testimonial of the fact. If the sword was given by the Legislature, the act, or resolution, directing the presentation ought to appear in its proceedings; but Hening's Statutes for the period have been searched for it in vain. As the father and son bore the same name, might it not be that the achievement belonged to the father, and the sword of acknowledgment descended by gift or inheritance to the son?

KELLY.

John Kelly was already engaged in business in Charlottesville under the firm of John Kelly & Co. in 1795. He had previously been a citizen of Lancaster County, Virginia, and from that county was accompanied by his first wife, Sarah Norris, the daughter of his uncle. She died a few years after, and in 1802 he married Mary, daughter of William Alcock. For many years he transacted business as a merchant with great success. About the beginning of the century, he received into partnership his nephew, Opie Norris, of Lancaster, who married his daughter Cynthia. His other daughter, Eliza, became the wife of Dr. John C. Ragland. In 1803 he purchased from Hudson Martin Lot No. Three, on the west corner of Fifth Street and the Square, where his store was located. In 1814 he bought from John Nicholas, who then resigned the County Clerkship, four hundred forty acres, extending from near the western boundary of the town across Preston Heights to Meadow Creek. In 1816 he gave to Mrs. Norris Lot No. Four, running from Jefferson Street to the old People's Bank, which he had acquired in 1809 from Edward Butler, and to Mrs. Ragland the north half of Lot Fifty-Nine, and Lot Sixty, at present occupied by the family of J. J. Conner, and Dr. Joseph Norris. In 1821 he contemplated removing to another part of the country, and advertised for sale his land west of the town; and in 1824 he sold to Rev. John D. Paxton thirty-three acres on the north side of University Street, reaching from Harris's Warehouse to the Junction. In 1828 he purchased from Rice Wood the property on Park Street, where he built the large brick in which he resided till his death, and which his widow occupied till her death during the war. Mr. Kelly was often employed in the general affairs of the town, discharging many responsibilities as administrator, trustee, and offices of a similar kind. He was a man of earnest piety, assisting in the founding of the South Plains Presbyterian Church, in which he was a ruling elder, and in the erection of the old Presbyterian house of worship in town. He died in Staunton in 1830, on his way to or from the Virginia Springs.

His son-in-law, Dr. Ragland, died in 1821. He was exceedingly popular both as a man, and as a physician. His death was greatly lamented, and his remains were followed by a large concourse of friends and Masons to the family burying ground in Louisa. Four or five physicians at once settled in Charlottesville, to fill the gap occasioned by his decease. His widow was some years after married to Talbott Bragg, and subsequently removed with him and her children to Missouri.

Opie Norris, his other son-in-law, was an enterprising and prosperous man. He was concerned in many other engagements, in addition to his stated business as a merchant. For many years he was one of the town trustees, sometimes acting as their president. In 1819 he was appointed a magistrate of the county, and filled the office with much diligence. He was Secretary and Treasurer of the Rivanna and Rockfish Gap Turnpike Co., and awarded the contracts for the construction of that road. At one time he owned the Swan, and half of the Eagle Tavern. With Dr. Charles Everett he was largely interested in the real estate of Anderson's Addition to the town. He departed this life in 1839.

KERR.

James Kerr, an emigrant from Scotland, came to the county about 1762, and soon after bought a small place at the head of Ivy Creek. He subsequently leased the present Birdwood plantation, in 1773 purchased it from the trustees of John Dabney, and made it his residence for twenty-seven years. During this time he became a man of no little note and consideration in the community. When the records made a second beginning in 1783, he was one of the acting magistrates, and frequently participated in the deliberations of the County Court. He was appointed Sheriff in 1793. He was a ruling elder in the D. S. Church. In 1800 he sold the Birdwood place to Hore Brouse Trist, and bought from Michael Woods, son of Colonel John, a farm on Mechum's River, not far above the Depot of that name. From increasing age, or because of the distance from the county seat, he took no further part in the public business. In 1808 he sold his property to James Kinsolving Sr., and removed to Kentucky. After the death of Sarah, his first wife, he married Susan, widow of David Rodes. This union was a brief one, as Mrs. Kerr died in 1798. She left a will, which for want of proof was not recorded; and it was not till 1826 that it was sent to Georgetown, Ky., to procure the depositions of William Rodes, and Milton and Rodes Burch, to prove the handwriting of David Kerr, a deceased witness to the document.

The children of James Kerr, as far as known, were James, John Rice, David, Mary, the wife of Samuel Burch, and Elizabeth, the wife of Joseph J. Monroe, a brother of the President. James seems to have been a young man of tact and sprightliness, but of prodigal life. He once owned the lots on which the Farish House, and the old Presbyterian Church, now stand. He died in Richmond in 1788, leaving a short will written in a light, sceptical tone; and when it was presented for probate, until his father gave his consent, his brother magistrates declined admitting it to record. John Rice was admitted to the Albemarle bar, but appears not to have practised. In 1807 he was appointed a magistrate, and with his father served as an elder in the D. S. Church. He married Sarah, daughter of Bennett Henderson, and lived for a time on the south side of the Staunton Road, where it crosses Ivy Creek, on land that belonged to his brother-in-law, Samuel Burch. He accompanied, or followed, his father to Kentucky, and there entered the Presbyterian ministry. A son named for Andrew Hart lived near Memphis, Tenn., and was Moderator of the Southern General Assembly, when it convened in that city in 1868. David Kerr married Dorothy, daughter of the elder Clifton Rodes, and by many years preceded the rest of his family in removing to Kentucky.

KEY.

John Key was one of the pioneers who fixed their abodes within the present limits of the county. He made his first entry of land in 1732, and up to 1741 had obtained patents for nearly twelve hundred acres on the west side of the South West Mountain. His home was where William W. Minor now resides. His children were Martin, John, and Mary, the wife of a Dalton. Martin succeeded to the home and estate of his father, and by repeated purchases became the owner of all the land reaching from Edgemont, the place of the late Henry Magruder, down to the bend of the river on the farm of the late R. F. Omohundro. He died in 1791. He and his wife Ann had twelve children, Thomas, John, Martin, Tandy, Joshua, William Bibb, Henry, Jesse, James, Walter, Elizabeth, the wife of James Daniel, and Martha, the wife of John White. Each of the sons was comfortably provided for by their father's will, though intimations are there given that the habits of some unfitted them for the proper management of their affairs.

Within the first score of years in the present century, the members of this household were for the most part scattered over the South and West. Thomas removed to South Carolina, where he invented some contrivance for the more effective action of water wheels. The families of John, James and Martha emigrated to Kentucky and Tennessee, and that of Elizabeth, to North Carolina. Tandy lived for many years in the southern part of the county near Covesville, but is said to have removed eventually to Fluvanna County. Jesse P., a son of Tandy, married Sarah, daughter of the younger William Woods, of Beaver Creek, and lived for some time near Mechum's Depot. William Bibb married Mourning, daughter of Christopher Clark, and went to Elbert County, Georgia. Henry settled in Bedford County, and Jesse died in Richmond in 1826. Walter appears to have been the only one who spent his whole life in the county, and his death occurred in 1834. John, Tandy, and Joshua were all magistrates of the county, and Walter was appointed to the office, but declined to accept. John served as Sheriff in 1795, and Tandy in 1809. John was an Ensign in the Eighth Virginia, and Henry a soldier in the army of the Revolution.

KINKEAD.

The Kinkeads were early settlers in the western part of the county. As far as can be made out, there were three brothers of the name, David, Joseph and James. In 1746 David patented nearly eight hundred acres on the north fork of Rockfish, and the next year four hundred more on Stockton's Creek. By entry and purchase together, the family connection became owners of not far from three thousand acres in that vicinity. Joseph, James and John, probably the son of Joseph, appear as subscribers to the call of Rev. Samuel Black in 1747. The homes of Joseph and James were situated about half a mile west of Immanuel Church, on the place now owned by Rev. Dabney Davis. An old graveyard, a few hundred yards south of Mr. Davis's house, is still known in the neighborhood as the Kinkead burying ground; a broken down wall, and a few rough stones, are all that mark the spot. James died in 1762, leaving three sons, Thomas, John and James, and probably two more, Matthew and Andrew, and a daughter, the wife of Ninian Clyde. Joseph died in 1774. His children were Jean, the wife of Hugh Alexander, John, and Ruth, the wife of Andrew Grier.

Hugh Alexander had a mill, which at one time was a noted centre in that section; roads were made to it from every quarter. It was built on Stockton's Creek, not far from the foot of the hill west of Hillsboro. In subsequent years it was known as Keye's, and still later as Humphrey's Mill. It is supposed Andrew Grier was one of the early merchants of that vicinity. He was the owner of nearly six hundred acres adjoining Yellow Mountain, which, likely in liquidation of his debts, he conveyed in 1766 to Jeremiah Parker and Richard Warden, merchants of Philadelphia. In the course of years part of this land passed into the hands of John Lobban Jr., and part into the hands of Dr. Peter B. Bowen. A grandson of Joseph Kinkead married a daughter of Adam Dean, another early settler on Stockton's Creek, and in December 1898, there died in Greenbrier County, Adam Dean Kinkead, doubtless their son, at the age of ninety-two. All of the kindred bearing the name, seem to have removed from the county before the close of the last century. Its latest appearance on the records occurs in 1784, when Jean, the widow of James, sold to Abner Wood a parcel of land in what is known as the Piper and Patrick neighborhood. She was at that time a resident of Rockbridge County. In the Black call the name is spelled Kincaid.

KINSOLVING.

In 1788 James Kinsolving began to purchase land near Mechum's River Depot. The name was variously written in the early records, Consolver, Kingsolaver, Kinsolving. At that date a Martin Kinsolving lived near the Burnt Mills. James Kinsolving was successful in his business pursuits, and at the time of his death in 1829 owned upwards of fourteen hundred acres on both sides of Mechum's River. His home was near the Depot, and bore the name of Temple Hill. He and his wife Elizabeth were the parents of twelve children, George W., Diana, Mary, Ann, Elizabeth, Jefferson, Lucy, Jane, Madison, Napoleon, James, Martha, and Amanda. None bearing this name have for years been resident in the county, but it has attained a high distinction in the annals of the Episcopal Church.

George W. married Nancy, daughter of Jonathan Barksdale. For some time previous to 1822 he was the proprietor of the Central Hotel in Charlottesville, but in that year he retired to his farm near Mechum's Depot. In 1830 he was appointed Colonel of the Forty-Seventh Regiment. He was an earnest Episcopalian, and a vestryman in the North Garden Church. He died in 1856, leaving one son and seven daughters. The tendency in the family to remarkable names was especially apparent in his household. His son, Ovid Alexander, became an Episcopal clergyman, and passed his ministerial life mainly near Leesburg and Danville, Va. Three of his sons entered the Episcopal ministry, George Herbert, Bishop of Western Texas, Arthur Barksdale, a prominent rector in Brooklyn, N. Y., and Lucien Lee, recently consecrated Bishop of Brazil. The names of the seven daughters were selected with a view to having V as the initial, and A as the final letter—Virginia, the wife of William A. Abney, Vienna, the wife of William C. Fretwell, Veturia, the wife of Thomas Clark, Volusia, Verona, Verbelina, and Vermelia.

Diana was the wife of Clifton Garland Jr., and a grandson of hers was Rev. Howard McQuary, who, because of his extreme views on Evolution, was but a few years ago deposed from the Episcopal ministry by the Bishop of Northern Ohio. Mary was the wife of James W. Leigh, Ann, the wife of William B. Wood, and removed to Washington County, Illinois, Elizabeth, the wife of William M. Brander, and Martha, the wife of Reuben Wood. Lucy Jane was twice married, first to Achilles Barksdale, and secondly to Valentine Head. Madison married America, daughter of Philip Watts, James married Margaret, daughter of Andrew Brown, of North Garden, and made his home for many years near the Cross Roads. He became a Baptist minister, was Treasurer of the County School Commissioners, and about 1835 emigrated to western Kentucky. Most of the children of this family finally removed to Kentucky, or Mississippi.

LEAKE.

The Leakes have been domiciled in the county since its formation. Walter Leake Jr., patented land on the south fork of Hardware in 1746, and John on Green Creek in 1748.

It is believed these two were brothers. Data for accurately tracing the early relations of this family are wanting, but it is probable that John Leake and his wife Ann were the parents of Samuel and Mask. Samuel was one of the first Presbyterian ministers, who were natives of Virginia. In 1770 he was installed pastor of the Cove and D. S. Churches, and his home was four or five miles northeast of Covesville. He died young in 1775. He and his wife Elizabeth had three children, Elizabeth, the first wife of Andrew Hart, Sarah, the wife of Rev. James Robinson, one of Mr. Leake's successors in the Cove pastorate, and Mary. His widow died in 1799.

Mask Leake lived in the same section of the county, not far from the South Garden Thoroughfare. He was a ruling elder in the Cove Church, and frequently represented it in the Presbytery of Hanover. He died in 1813. His wife was Patience Morris, and his children William, Walter, Austin, Samuel, and Lucy, the wife of John Buster. William succeeded his father at the homestead, and died in 1833. He and his wife Caroline had five children, Elizabeth, the wife of an Anderson, Samuel, Walter, William M., and Josiah. Walter, son of Mask, was deputy Surveyor of the county in 1784, and was admitted to the Albemarle bar in 1793. It is believed he was the Walter Leake who emigrated to Mississippi, and rose to prominence in the legal and political affairs of that State. He was elected United States Senator in 1817, and resigning soon after was appointed to the State bench. He died in Hinds County in 1825. Austin was also a member of the Albemarle bar, and died before his father, leaving two sons, Joseph and Philip Jefferson. Samuel, son of Mask, was a physician, and practised in the southern part of the county, and also in Nelson. His wife was Sophia, a daughter of Richard Farrar, and his children William, Philip, Samuel, Shelton F., Eliza, and Lucy, the wife of Addison Gentry, who at one time conducted a school for young ladies near Hillsboro. The career of Shelton F. is well known, not only in the county, but in the State. His natural gifts were unusually brilliant. He settled in Charlottesville, was admitted to the bar in 1838, easily attained a place in its front rank, was a member of the House of Delegates, was Lieutenant Governor of the State, and for a term represented the district in Congress. He married Rebecca Gray, and departed this life in 1884. Samuel in 1836 married M. A. Boyd of the Cove neighborhood, and finished his course a few years ago near Hillsboro, where the son William now resides.

LEVY.

In 1836 Uriah P. Levy, Commodore of the United States Navy, became a citizen of Albemarle by the purchase of Monticello. He bought the place from James T. Barclay. It is commonly understood, that it was owing to his exalted estimation of Mr. Jefferson's political wisdom and conduct he was led to become the possessor of his home, and thereby to identify his name with that of the President. He died in 1862, and having no family of his own, and cherishing the desire to make the place a permanent memorial of the great statesman, the Commodore devised Monticello to the United States as a Hospital for the worn-out tars of the Navy; and that arrangement failing, to the State of Virginia, to be used as a sort of naval school. By the decisions of the courts, both dispositions were declared invalid. During the Civil War the property was confiscated. It was placed for the time in the hands of care-takers, who took no care of it further than to extort as large gratuities as possible from those who still resorted to it from admiration of its former presiding genius. The whole establishment was greatly injured, and the monument in its burial place, by the chipping of relic hunters, was literally reduced to a shapeless block. When public affairs resumed their usual course, the Commodore's nephew, Jefferson M. Levy, of New York, purchased the interests of the other heirs, and devoted himself to the improvement of the estate. Congress also handsomely enclosed the cemetery, and erected a noble shaft to Jefferson's memory. Filled with the spirit of his distinguished kinsman, Mr. Levy has been at much pains and expense to restore things to the same condition in which Mr. Jefferson left them; and appreciating the sentiment which impels multitudes to visit it as a place of pilgrimage, he allows them entire freedom in repairing to the spot, and surveying its interesting scenes.

LEWIS.

Three families named Lewis, apparently not related, have lived in Albemarle. The first of the name entering lands within its present limits was Charles, of Goochland, who in 1731 obtained a patent for twelve hundred acres on both sides of the Rivanna, at the mouth of Buck Island. He also entered nearly three thousand acres in the Rich Cove. As nearly as can be ascertained, this Charles was the son of John Lewis and Isabel Warner. In 1717 he married Mary Howell, and his children were John, Charles, Elizabeth, the wife of William Kennon, James, Mary, Howell and Ann. His home was the place that has since borne the name of Monteagle. To his son, Charles, he transferred his land on Buck Island in 1766, the son reconveying it to his father and mother, and the survivor, for life. Charles Jr., purchased, chiefly from his cousin Robert Lewis, more than eighteen acres on the north fork of the Hardware, including what is now Red Hill Depot, which he gave to his son, Isham. He died in 1782. His wife was Mary, daughter of Isham Randolph, of Dungeness, and sister of Peter Jefferson's wife, and his children were Charles Lilburn, Isham, Mary, the wife first of Colonel Charles Lewis, of North Garden, and secondly of Charles Wingfield Jr., Jane, the wife of Charles Hudson, Elizabeth, the wife of Bennett Henderson, Ann, the wife of Randolph Jefferson, Frances, the second wife of John Thomas, and Mildred, the wife of Edward Moore. Isham Lewis died unmarried in 1790, leaving his estate to his two nephews, John Lewis Moore and Charles Lewis Thomas. Charles Lilburn married Lucy Jefferson, sister of the President, and his children were Randolph, Isham, Lilburn, Jane, the wife of Craven Peyton, Mary R., the wife of Thomas Jefferson, Jr., Lucy, the wife of Washington Griffin, Martha and Ann M. Randolph lived on his plantation, Buck Island, on the north side of the Rivanna, but in 1805 sold it to David Michie, and moved to Goochland. Lilburn also lived on the north side of the river, and in 1806 disposed of his place to Hugh Nelson. His wife was Jane Woodson, by whom he had five children, among them Mary H., the wife of Charles Palmer, and mother of Dr. William Palmer, the compiler of the Calendar of the State Papers of Virginia. All the daughters of Charles Lilburn Lewis except Jane and Mary, emigrated to Livingston County, Kentucky.

Robert Lewis, a nephew of the first Charles above mentioned, lived at Belvoir, on the east side of the South West Mountain. He was the son of John Lewis and Frances Fielding, and a brother of Fielding, Washington's brother-in-law. He married Jane, daughter of Nicholas Meriwether, the large landholder, and he was himself one of the largest landholders in the county. In 1736 he entered upwards of four thousand acres in North Garden, and in 1740 nearly sixty-five hundred near Ivy Depot. He died in 1765. His children were John, Nicholas, Robert, Charles, William, Jane, the wife of Thomas Meriwether, Mary, the wife first of Samuel Cobb, and secondly of Waddy Thomson, Mildred, the wife of Major John Lewis, Ann, the wife of another John Lewis—both of these gentlemen of Spotsylvania and kinsmen —Elizabeth, the wife of William Barrett, and Sarah, the wife of Dr. Waller Lewis, of Spotsylvania, son of Zachary Lewis, and brother of Mildred's husband. John, the eldest son, received the main portion of his estate in Gloucester.

Nicholas lived at the Farm, adjoining Charlottesville on the east, a gift from his grandfather, Nicholas Meriwether. He was a public spirited man, a Captain in the Revolution, a magistrate, Surveyor and Sheriff of the county, possessed of a sound judgment and kindly spirit, appealed to on all occasions to compose the strifes of the neighborhood, the trusted friend of Mr. Jefferson, and the adviser of his family during his long absences from home. He married Mary, eldest daughter of Dr. Thomas Walker, and died in 1808. His children were Nicholas M., Thomas W., Robert Warner, Jane, the wife of Hudson Martin, Elizabeth the wife of William D. Meriwether, Mildred, the wife of David Wood, Mary, the wife of

Isaac Miller, and Margaret, the wife of Charles L. Thomas. Nicholas married his cousin, Mildred Hornsby, of Kentucky, and doubtless emigrated to that State. Robert married Elizabeth Wood, and removed from the county. Thomas W. lived at Locust Grove, the northern part of his father's farm. He was appointed a magistrate in 1791, and died in 1807. In his will he directed that the families of his servants should not be separated, and expressed the wish that circumstances had permitted their emancipation, as according to his view all men were born free and equal. He married Elizabeth, daughter of Nicholas Meriwether, and sister of his brother-in-law, William D., and his children were Nicholas H., Margaret, the wife of James Clark, Mary, the wife first of James Leitch, and secondly of David Anderson, Lydia, the wife of Samuel O. Minor, Thomas, Charles, Elizabeth, the wife of John C. Wells, Alice, the wife first of George D. Meriwether, and secondly of John W. Davis, Jane, the wife first of Walker Meriwether, and secondly of Dr. Richard Anderson, and Robert W., of Castalia. By far the greater number of this family emigrated in 1837 to Pike County, Missouri. In 1804 Mary removed with her husband, Isaac Miller, to Louisville, Ky.

Robert, son of Robert, married a Miss Fauntleroy, and removed to Halifax County. Charles lived in the North Garden, where James G. White now resides. He was one of the first to offer his services at the outbreak of the Revolutionary War. He was Captain of the first volunteer company raised in Albemarle, Lieutenant Colonel of the first regiment formed, and afterwards Colonel of the Fourteenth Virginia. He died in 1779, while in command of the Guards at the Barracks near Charlottesville. His wife was Mary, daughter of Charles Lewis Jr., of Buck Island, and his children Howell, Charles Warner, who died young, Mary R., the wife of Edward Carter, Jane, the wife of John Carr, Sarah, the wife of Benjamin Brown, Ann, the wife of Matthew Brown, and Susan, the wife of Joel Franklin. Mrs. Lewis was married the second time to Charles Wingfield Jr., and died in 1807. Howell lived at the old homestead, and died in 1845. His wife was Mary, daughter of Thomas Carr, and his children Thomas Fielding, Howell, of Mechunk, Mary, the wife of Clifton Harris, and Sarah, the wife of Ira Harris.

William Lewis, son of Robert, lived at Locust Hill, near Ivy Depot. He was a Lieutenant in the Revolutionary army. He died in 1780. His wife was Lucy, daughter of Thomas Meriwether, and his children, Meriwether, Reuben and Jane, the wife of Edmund Anderson. Meriwether was the famous explorer of the Rocky Mountains, and the Pacific Coast, and while acting as Governor of Missouri Territory, died by his own hand near Nashville, Tenn., in 1809. Reuben studied medicine, lived on a part of his father's place, married his cousin Mildred Dabney, and died without children in 1844. Mrs. Lucy Lewis was married the second time to Colonel John Marks, and with him removed to Wilkes County, Georgia, in 1787. On the death of Colonel Marks, she returned to Locust Hill, where she departed this life in 1836. By her last marriage she had one son, John Hastings, who died in Baltimore, and one daughter, Mary, who became the wife of William Moore, and lived in Georgia.

The second family of this name sprang from David Lewis, who, with his brother-in-law, Joel Terrell, in 1734 entered three thousand acres just west of the University. The next year his brother, Abraham Lewis entered eight hundred acres, including the land the University now occupies. These brothers belonged to Hanover County. Abraham never lived in Albemarle, but David at once settled on the hinder part of the present Birdwood farm, so that when the county was organized, his residence was a well known place in the country. He was an active man, a captain in the militia, one of the early magistrates, and bore his part in clearing the roads, and executing other works of public convenience. He died in 1779, at the great age of ninety-four. He was married three times, his first wife being a sister of Joel Terrell, and his third, Mary McGrath, widow of Dr. Hart, of Philadelphia. By the first marriage he had eight children, and by the third three, William Terrell, Susan, the wife of Alexander Mackey, who lived for a time on Ivy Creek, near the crossing of the Whitehall Road, Hannah, the wife of James Hickman, probably the son of Edwin Hickman, second Sheriff of the county, Sarah, the wife of Abraham Musick, who lived in the Mechum's Depot vicinity, where his son Ephraim also lived, and thence emigrated to Kentucky, David, John, Joel, Ann, the wife first of Joel Terrell Jr., and secondly of Stephen Willis, Elizabeth, the wife of John Martin, James, and Miriam, the wife of Gabriel Madison.

William Terrell Lewis kept a tavern on the Staunton Road, about three miles west of Charlottesville, called at first Terrell's and subsequently Lewis's Ordinary. He married Sarah Martin, and had eleven children. All the family emigrated to North Carolina, and later he himself went to Nashville, where he died in 1802. Three of his sons, Micajah, Joel and James, were in the battle of Kings Mountain, and Micajah was killed at Guilford C. H. A great, great granddaughter, Mrs. Patty L. Collins, has in these last days been in the Dead Letter Office at Washington, where she is held in high repute for her marvellous skill in deciphering bad chirography. David Jr., was a man of great enterprise and ability. He owned numerous parcels of land in the Mechum's Depot section, and carried on a brisk mercantile business in that vicinity. He also removed to North Carolina just before the Revolution. Though twice married, he seems to have left no sons, as in the final settlement of his affairs in Albemarle in 1794, his legatees all bore other names. John was twice married, first to Sarah Taliaferro, and secondly to Susan Clarkson, no doubt a sister of Peter Clarkson. He had twelve children, among whom were Taliaferro, a brave soldier of the Revolution, Charles C., whose descendant, William T., a resident of Louisville, Miss., compiled a history of the family, Jesse P., and David Jackson, who was a man of commanding presence, measuring six feet, four inches, was a soldier in the Whiskey Insurrection of 1794, an active magistrate of the county, and the father of eleven children, lived north of the Rivanna, on the Hydraulic Road, and in 1818 removed to Breckinridge County, Kentucky.

Jesse Pitman was also a soldier of the Revolution. His

wife was Nancy, daughter of Manoah Clarkson. His home was on the Staunton Road, above the University. He died in 1849, and with him the name of old David Lewis's line in the county passed away, as he left only daughters. These were Jane, the wife of Nelson Barksdale, Mary, the wife first of Julius Clarkson, and secondly of John H. Craven, Elizabeth, the wife of Reuben Maury, Sophia, the wife of Michael Johnson, and Sarah, the wife of Alexander St. C. Heiskell.

James Lewis, son of David Sr., was in his day a figure of great prominence in the county. He was a gallant soldier of the Revolution, a magistrate, a contractor, a large landholder, the owner and keeper for some years of the old Stone Tavern in Charlottesville, the agent of President Monroe, and much employed both by the Courts and his fellow citizens in the appraisement and division of estates. His first residence was doubtless the homestead, the home of old David. He married Lucy, daughter of John Thomas, by whom he had eleven children. In 1818 he emigrated to Franklin County, Tennessee. In 1826 he returned on a visit to Albemarle, and married the second time, Mary, daughter of Peter Marks, and at last finished his course in Tennessee at the advanced age of ninety-three.

The head of the third family of the name was John, who was one of the earliest settlers in the county. He entered land on Totier Creek in 1741. When the location of the old courthouse was fixed, he obtained a license to conduct an ordinary at the place. He seems to have married a daughter of Samuel Shelton, and had two sons, and a daughter, Jane, who became the wife of Richard Davenport, and removed to Georgia. John, the elder son, died in 1804, and left three children, Sarah, John Waddy, who died in 1824, and Elizabeth. Owen, the other son, died in 1805, and his children were William, John, Hardin P., Howell, Robert, Nicholas, Daniel P., Zachariah, and Sarah, who was the wife of Jacob Tilman, and removed to Tennessee. Most of the sons were considerable land owners in the southern part of the county, particularly on the lower Hardware. Some of them also transacted a lucrative business in transporting freight on James River, and the canal. Hardin P. emigrated to Alabama. In 1821 Robert in a quarrel fatally stabbed Thompson Noel, a tavern keeper in Scottsville, and fled the country. It is said he went to Memphis, Tenn., and in course of time acquired a large fortune. A great granddaughter of the first John Lewis was the first wife of the late Christopher Gilmer, and a great grandson, Zachariah, recently died in Nelson County, immediately above the mouth of Rockfish River. A similarity of names suggests a relationship between this family and that first mentioned.

LINDSAY.

Reuben Lindsay came to Albemarle from Westmoreland about 1776. In that year he purchased from John Clark seven hundred and fifty acres on the east side of the South West Mountain, where he made his home. During the ensuing twenty years he had purchased upwards of two thousand acres. He was already a magistrate at the close of the Revolutionary War, frequently sat on the County bench, and was otherwise often engaged in the duties of that office. He departed this life in 1831. He was twice married, first to Sarah, daughter of Dr. Thomas Walker, by whom he had no children, and secondly to Miss Tidwell. By the last marriage he had three daughters, Sarah, the wife of James Lindsay, his nephew, whose home was at the Meadows, a short distance southwest of Gordonsville, and whose daughter became the wife of John M. Patton Jr., Elizabeth, the wife of General William F. Gordon, and Maria, the wife of M. L. Walker, son of Captain Thomas Walker Jr.

Another nephew bearing his own name, Reuben, lived on the Rivanna, near the mouth of Limestone. His wife was Mary Goodman, and his children were Susan, the wife of John G. Gray, Mary, the wife of Albert G. Watkins, Ann, the wife of Stephen F. Sampson, James, William and Reuben. He died in 1837, and his wife in 1841. His son Reuben was a physician, practised his profession with much success at Scottsville, and died in 1881.

LYNCH.

Charles Lynch, it is said, was a native of Ireland. Taking offence while a mere youth at some ill-treatment, he determined to quit home and country, and with this purpose took passage on a vessel bound for America. As the ship was leaving her moorings, he repented the step, and leaping into the sea, struck out for land. He was however rescued by the sailors from his perilous position, and after the usual voyage of those days, safely reached the shores of the new world. Coming to Virginia, and exerting the energy and perseverance that belonged to his nature, he soon began a successful career. He commenced entering land within the present county in 1733, and in the next seventeen years had obtained patents for sixty-five hundred acres in different sections, on Hardware, on the Rivanna, on Moore's Creek, and on the waters of Mechum's, not far from the Blue Ridge. He established his home on the Rivanna, on the place now known as Pen Park. The ripple in the river at that point was beyond question Lynch's Ferry, or Ford, which is often mentioned in the early records. He was one of the original magistrates of Albemarle, and had previously been one in Goochland. He served as Sheriff in 1749, and was a representative of the county in the House of Burgesses. His last entry of land was made in 1750, and embraced sixteen hundred acres on the James, opposite Lynchburg. To this land he removed at that time, but did not long survive the change. He died in 1753.

His wife was Sarah, daughter of Christopher and Penelope Clark. She joined the Friends about the time of their removal from Lynch's Ferry on the Rivanna to Lynch's Ferry on the James. A Quaker Meeting House called South River, was built in 1754 on her land on Lynch's Creek, a branch of the Blackwater, three or four miles south of Lynchburg. Her children were Charles, John, Christopher, and Sarah, the wife of Micajah Terrell. John was the founder of Lynchburg. Charles was the clerk of South River Meeting till the beginning of the political ferment prior to the Revolution, when the warmth of his patriotism surmounted the pacific principles he had espoused, and he became a Colonel in the Revolutionary army. His busy promptitude in dealing with outlaws and violent Tories during those disturbed times, gave rise to Lynch Law. Mrs. Lynch was married the second time to John Ward, of Bedford. Besides the imprints of this family about Lynchburg, they have left their memorial in the names of this county, Lynch's River, and Lynch's Creek, a tributary of the Rockfish.

MCGEHEE.

James McGehee obtained a patent for four hundred acres of land on Little Mechunk in 1747. In 1768 William McGehee patented nearly two hundred acres on Henderson's Branch, and near the Secretary's Road, a description, which indicates that the place was not far from Colle, especially as in 1774 it came into Mr. Jefferson's hands. William was probably a son of James, and it was he who gave the name to the ford at Milton, that passage of the river being known in early times as McGehee's Ford. The family seems subsequently to have been settled near the present Woodridge, as the forks of the roads at that place went for a long period by the name of McGehee's Old Field. William died in 1815. He and his wife Elizabeth had eight children, William, Elizabeth, Joseph, Nancy, the wife of William Adcock, Sarah, the wife of William Campbell, Mary, the wife of James Martin, Lively and Charles. After the death of the father, most of the family removed, some to Franklin County, Virginia, and some to Kentucky.

Whether Francis McGee was related to this family, is not known. He appears early in the century as having married Martha, daughter of Peter Marks. He purchased the interests of some of the Marks heirs in Lots Seventeen and Eighteen in Charlottesville, on which the old Stone House stood, and exchanged them with James Lewis for the place on Moore's Creek, which has long been the home of the Teels. In 1817 he bought from Dabney and Thomas Shelton the farm between Ivy and Mechum's Depot, which is still owned by his descendants. For some years he conducted the old Hardin Tavern on the Staunton Road. He died in 1846. His children were Ann, Peter, Mary, the wife of James Lobban, Martha, the wife of John J. Woods, Lewis and Joanna. Lewis died in 1858. Peter in his youth was a merchant at Hillsboro, and subsequently County Surveyor. He died on his farm south of Ivy Depot in 1888.

MCKENNIE.

Clement P. McKennie deserves commemoration among the people of Albemarle for being the publisher of the first newspaper ever issued in the county. On the twenty-ninth of January 1820, appeared the first number of the Central Gazette. He and his brother, J. H. McKennie, were associated in the enterprise. It is said the office of publication stood on the northwest corner of Jefferson and Third Streets. By the withdrawal of J. H. McKennie at the close of the first year, his brother became the sole publisher. The paper was issued weekly until about 1828, when on account of the appearance of the Virginia Advocate, it was discontinued. About 1834 Mr. McKennie purchased from the heirs of W. G. Garner the property adjoining the University, where he established the book store so long conducted by himself and his son Marcellus. In 1822 he married Henrietta, daughter of Matthew Rodes, and departed this life in 1856. In 1821 J. H. McKennie married Mary, daughter of Jesse Garth, and soon after removed to Nelson County.

MACON.

Thomas Macon came to the county from New Kent in 1833. In that year he purchased from John Price Sampson Tufton, a plantation, which contained a thousand and forty acres, had once belonged to Mr. Jefferson, and which has since been the home of the Macon family. Mr. Macon was an earnest member of the Episcopal Church. On account of his intelligence and high character, he was soon appointed a magistrate of the county, in which office he served until his decease. He died in 1851.

MAGRUDER.

John B. Magruder came to Albemarle from Maryland in the early years of the century. With him from the same

State came George Jones, the father of Robert S., Jesse and Thomas. They were friends, both good men, and local preachers of the Methodist Church. They settled in the eastern part of the county, on the borders of Fluvanna. Mr. Magruder died in 1812. He and his wife Sarah had nine children, Sarah, the wife of John Timberlake, Mildred, the wife of Gideon A. Strange, Elizabeth, the first wife of Dr. Basil Jones, James, Horatio, Benjamin H., William, Hilary and John B.

The family were largely engaged in the improvements of the Rivanna Navigation Company. Besides founding the Union Mills in Fluvanna, John B. Magruder and John Timberlake in 1829 bought the Shadwell Mills from the Jefferson estate, and in addition to the grist mills already existing, established cotton and woolen factories, which continued in operation until swept away by the disasters of the war. In 1833 they purchased from a family named Schofield, of Montgomery County, Pennsylvania, a large body of timber land in the Buck Island section, which had lain in its virgin state from time immemorial. James Magruder after the war purchased Frascati, the former home of Judge Philip Barbour near Gordonsville, where he resided until his death. Benjamin H. was admitted a member of the Albemarle bar in 1829, and lived for some years in Scottsville. He subsequently bought Glenmore, opposite Milton, which he made his home until his death in 1885. Both before and since the war he represented the county in the Legislature. He was twice married, first to a daughter of James Minor, of Sunning Hill, Louisa, and secondly to Evalina, daughter of Opie Norris. Mildred and her husband, Gideon A. Strange, were the parents of Sarah, the wife of William Stockton, a brother of John N. C. Stockton, who emigrated to Florida, John B., Colonel of the Nineteenth Virginia in the late war, and Mary, the wife of John W. Chewning.

Mary, the sister of John B. Magruder Sr., was the wife of Thomas D. Boyd. At the beginning of the century he conducted a public house at the junction of the Three Notched and River Roads, the locality still known as Boyd's Tavern.

He had six children, John H., who went to Richmond, Charity, the wife of James Thrift, of Montomery County, Maryland, James M., Elizabeth, the wife of Thomas A. Woodson, Mary, the wife of Bartley Herndon, of Shenandoah County, and Thomas J. The last was admitted to the Albemarle bar in 1829, and removed to Wytheville, where he recently died at an advanced age.

Allan B. Magruder, a nephew of John B., and brother of General John Bankhead, became a member of the Albemarle bar in 1838. He resided in Charlottesville in the house at the rear of the late Thomas Wood's until a short time before the war, when he removed to Washington City, and subsequently to Frederick County, Virginia. His daughter Janet became the wife of Major Robert H. Poore, who fell in the battle of Gettysburg, and his daughter Julia, by the productions of her pen, has attained quite a position of note in the literary world.

MARKS.

An Englishman named Marks married Elizabeth Hastings, and emigrated to Virginia. They had five sons and a daughter, Peter, John, James, Hastings, Thomas, and Sarah, who in 1782 became the wife of James Winston, of Louisa. The children were all settled in Albemarle prior to the Revolution. Peter probably lived in Charlottesville, as his business operations were mainly connected with the real estate of the town. He was Escheator for the county, and during the Revolution superintended several inquisitions, for the confiscation of property of those who took sides with the British. In 1791 he bought from Mr. Monroe the square on which the Stone House stood, and from Dr. Gilmer part of Lot Thirty-Two, on which stands the store of T. T. Norman. His death occurred in 1795, and gave rise to complications in his affairs that were not fully straightened for many years; in fact, the part of lot Thirty-Two was not finally disposed of till 1830. His wife was Joanna Sydnor, and his children Sarah, the wife of Joshua Nicholas, Martha, the wife of Francis McGee, Mary, the second wife of James Lewis, Sophia, the wife of Russell Brown, Elizabeth, the wife of John W. Hinde, Nancy, the wife of Temple Gwathmey, a nephew of George Rogers Clark, Hastings and Peter. The most of the children removed to Kentucky. The only one who spent her entire life in the county, was Mrs. McGee. Her sister Mary seems to have made her home with her, but in 1826 James Lewis returned from Tennessee, and took her back as his wife.

John Marks was a Captain in the Revolutionary War, and for this service received a grant of four thousand acres of land on Brush Creek, Brush County, Ohio. After the death of William Lewis, he married his widow, Lucy. He was a magistrate of the county, and was appointed Sheriff in 1785. During his incumbency of the office, he removed with the Gilmer emigration to Georgia, where he died shortly after. James was also a magistrate. He lived on a farm consisting of eight hundred acres near Keswick Depot, and likely including it. He emigrated to Georgia, and when taking this step sold his plantation to John Harvie, whose sister Elizabeth was his wife. Hastings owned a place in the Ragged Mountains, not far from the D. S. In 1785 he married Ann Scott, sister of Mr. Jefferson, and removed to the tidewater district of the State. The kind and considerate disposition of the President, who at the time was Minister to France, was shown in the letters he addressed to each of the parties, on the occasion of this union.

MARTIN.

The name of Martin has belonged to a number of families in the county. The year it was organized, 1745, Captain Joseph Martin, as he was called in the patents, obtained grants of more than fourteen hundred acres on Priddy's Creek, and eight hundred on Piney Run. His will disposing of land in Essex County, it is surmised he came from that part of the State. He and his wife Ann had eleven children, Brice, William, Joseph, John, George, Sarah, the wife of John Burrus, Mary, the wife of a Hammock, Susan, Martha, Ann, and Olive, the wife probably of Ambrose Edwards. The Captain died in 1761.

James Martin owned at an early date a considerable tract of land that now belongs to the Grayson family, near the present site of Miller School. In 1759 he gave two hundred acres to each of his six sons, Stephen, John, James, Obadiah, William and David. These sons, or the most of them, it is believed, emigrated to North Carolina, about the time of the Revolution. It is possible the John just mentioned was the John Martin who lived in the western part of the North Garden. His place was formerly known as the Pocket Plantation. He was a prosperous man, and became the owner of upwards of fifteen hundred acres. He died in 1812. His wife's name was Elizabeth, believed to have been a Wheeler, and his children were Benjamin, Sarah, the wife of John Watson, Mary, the wife of William Wood, Susan, the wife of Hickerson Jacob, and Clarissa. Benjamin succeeded to his father's place, and died in 1821. His wife's name was Catharine, and his children were Ann, the wife of Augustine Woodson, Lindsay, John, Caroline, the wife of Joshua W. Abell, Julia, the wife of Micajah Wheeler, Benjamin, Emily, the wife of Richard Abell, James, Elizabeth, the wife first of Peter Garland, and secondly of Daniel Martin, and Jane, the wife of Samuel M. Powell.

A John Martin in 1762 purchased from Joseph Thomas upwards of six hundred acres in the southern part of the county, on Ballenger's Creek. He died in 1810. He married Ann, daughter of James Tooley, and his children were Sarah, the wife of James Wood, Ann, the wife of John Dawson, Dabney, James, Celia, Alice, Simeon, Massey and Lindsay.

Thomas Martin was already settled on the south fork of Hardware in 1764, where his descendants have been resident ever since. He seems not to have been a patentee, and when he purchased does not appear. He died in 1792. He and his wife Mary had ten children, Abraham, George, Thomas, Charles, John, Pleasant, Letitia, the wife of Richard Moore, Mildred, the wife of an Oglesby, Ann, the wife of a Blain, and Mary, the wife of Benjamin Dawson. Pleasant removed to Amherst. John married Elizabeth, daughter of David Lewis, was a Captain in the Revolutionary army, had charge of the troops that in 1780 guarded as far as Frederick, Md., the British prisoners, on their removal from the Barracks, and of those stationed in Charlottesville at the time of the Tarleton Raid, and in 1786 emigrated to Fayette County, Kentucky. Charles lived on the place where J. Goulet Martin now resides, and sold it in 1783 to Rev. William Irvin. His wife's name was Patty, and he had two daughters, Elizabeth and Martha, who became the wives of brothers, Thomas and James Cobbs, of Halifax County; and selling the remainder of his land the next year, he probably followed them to that county. George married Barbara, daughter of Samuel Woods, and died in 1799. His children were Malinda, the wife of Lewis Teel, Samuel W., and Elizabeth, the wife of William Garth. Samuel W. married Sarah, daughter of Garrett White, and died in 1857. His children were Garrett W., George, Thomas, John A., Samuel W., Jeremiah, and Eleanora, the wife of Jesse L. Heiskell.

Hudson Martin was a Second Lieutenant in the Ninth Virginia, during the Revolution. For a number of years he was deputy Clerk of the county, and subsequently a magistrate. He married Jane, the eldest daughter of Nicholas Lewis. Near the beginning of the century he removed to Amherst, in the vicinity of Faber's Mills, where his descendants still live. In 1834 Captain John Thomas testified before the County Court in behalf of his heirs, to the fact of his having served in the Revolutionary army. A son John M. Martin became a member of the Albemarle bar in 1809. Another son, Hudson, married Mildred, daughter of Dabney Minor, and at one time lived in Arkansas.

In the early years of the century, a Thomas Martin married Mary Ann, daughter of Daniel White. His home was west of Batesville, north of the place now occupied by William H. Turner Jr. He died in 1827. His children were Ann, the wife of John L. White, Azariah, Diana, the wife of James Lobban, Thomas, Mary, the wife of William Stone, Charles, Elizabeth, Daniel, Henry, Barbara, the wife of John Lobban, and Lucy, the wife of William H. Garland.

MASSIE.

The Massie family was a numerous one which in early times migrated from New Kent, and was widely scattered over Albemarle, Nelson and Amherst. The first of the name that settled in Albemarle was Charles. His home was in the southwest part of the county on the waters of Lynch's Creek, on what was known as the Wakefield Entry. The plantation, Spring Valley, became noted from the perfection of its Albemarle Pippins, and though now held by other hands, it is still designated by the Massie name. Charles Massie commenced the purchase of this place in 1768. He died in 1817. His children were Thomas, Charles, John, Elizabeth, the wife of a Smith, and Mary, the wife first of Robert Ware, and secondly of William Lobban. His son Charles succeeded to the place, and died in 1830. His wife's name was Nancy, and his children were Hardin, Nathaniel, Charles G., Sarah, the wife of a Ragland, Elizabeth, the wife of a Bailey, and Nancy.

Hardin was a physician, who came to Charlottesville in 1824, and for many years practised in partnership with Dr. Charles Carter. He was largely interested in the real estate of the town. He lived on Fourth Street next to the old Baptist Church, the site of which he sold to that congregation. He was himself an earnest member of that Church, and for a time acted as its Clerk. He never married, and died in 1848. Nathaniel was for a considerable period of his life a successful merchant in Waynesboro, but as his years increased, he returned to the old homestead on the borders of Nelson, where he died in 1871. He was twice married, first to Susan, daughter of Michael Woods, son of Colonel John, and secondly to Elizabeth, daughter of Matthew Rodes. His children by the first marriage were James, Professor in the Virginia Military Institute, N. Hardin, of Charlottesville, Susan, the wife cf Robert B. Moon, and Hetty, the wife of William Patrick; and of those by the second marriage were Rodes and Edwin. Charles G. died in 1857.

An Edmund Massie lived in the county the same time with the first Charles. His home was in the vicinity of

Brown's Cove. He died in 1782. He and his wife Judith had several children, of whom the only one mentioned was Thomas. It may be he was the Thomas Massie, who in 1792 rented from the representatives of Hugh Moss a large tract of land on the Rivanna, in the Buck Island neighborhood. In that neighborhood he died in 1799, leaving six children, Martha, the wife of Hugh Pettit, Nancy, the wife of Reuben Mansfield, Susan, James, Thomas and John.

MAUPIN.

Two brothers, Daniel and Gabriel Maupin, came to the county just before the middle of the last century. From the name it may be inferred they were of French extraction. The idea has been entertained that they were French soldiers, who crossed the ocean with Lafayette at the time of the Revolution; but Daniel obtained a patent for land on Moorman's River in 1748, twenty-seven years before that event. The name however was represented in the Revolutionary army, Daniel, William and Cornelius appearing on the pension list; these in all probability were brothers, sons of John Maupin, and grandsons of Daniel. Daniel entered more than fifteen hundred acres in the Whitehall neighborhood. He died in 1788. He and his wife Margaret had seven sons and three daughters, Thomas, Gabriel, Daniel, John, Margaret, the wife of Robert Miller, William, Zachariah, Jesse, Jane, the wife of Samuel Rea, and Mary, the wife of Matthew Mullins.

Gabriel died in 1794. He seems to have lived in the vicinity of Free Union. His wife's name was Marah, and Thomas, Bland, Daniel and Gabriel were names of his sons. The truth is, the families of this stock were generally so numerous, containing hardly ever less than ten, and sometimes thirteen children, and the same names were so often repeated in the different households, that it would be well nigh impossible at this date to make out an accurate statement of their lines of descent. They frequently intermarried among themselves, and with the Harrises, Jarmans and Vias, and their descendants are widely scattered over the West, particularly in Kentucky and Missouri. They seem to have been in their generations an industrious, quiet, unambitious people. They have usually been attached to the Methodist Church, a Daniel Maupin being an original trustee of Austin's or Bingham's, Meeting House, and another Daniel and his wife Hannah in 1834 giving the ground for Mount Moriah near Whitehall, which indeed for many years commonly went by the name of Maupin's Meeting House.

Dr. Socrates Maupin, who was Professor of Chemistry first in Hampden-Sidney College, and afterwards in the University of Virginia, was one of this family. He died from injuries in consequence of a runaway accident in Lynchburg, in 1871. He was the son of Chapman W. Maupin, who was third in descent from the first Daniel, was appointed a magistrate of the county in 1835, and died in 1861. Addison, another son of Chapman W., had his residence before the war on Carr's Hill, adjoining the University. J. Addison Maupin, of Richmond, author of the Maupin bill of recent notoriety, was Addison's son.

MAURY.

In the last century Rev. James Maury was the rector of Fredericksville parish. His parents, Matthew Maury and Mary Ann Fontaine, were Huguenot exiles, and were residents of King William. Instead of occupying the glebe, he resided on his own farm, which lay on the borders of Albemarle and Louisa. He attained great notoriety as suitor in the famous case under the Two Penny Act, in which Patrick Henry first displayed his marvellous powers of eloquence. In addition to his clerical duties, he taught on his plantation a classical school in which Mr. Jefferson was one of his pupils. In 1767 he purchased nearly seven hundred acres southwest of Ivy Depot from the executors of old Michael Woods, which his son Matthew sold in 1797 to Rev. William Woods and Richard Woods. He married Mary Walker, a cousin it is said of Dr. Thomas Walker, and died in 1769. His children were Matthew, James, Ann, Mary, Walker, Catharine, the wife of James Barrett, Elizabeth, the wife of James Lewis, of Spotsylvania, Abraham, Fontaine, Benjamin and Richard. James was appointed by Washington in 1789 Consul to Liverpool, which office he continued to fill till 1837. Richard, who married Diana, daughter of Major John Minor, of Spotsylvania, and removed to Franklin, Tenn., was the father of Commodore Matthew F. Maury, and the grandfather of General Dabney Maury, of the Confederate army.

Matthew was an Episcopal minister, and succeeded his father both at the homestead, and in the parish. He also taught school. He married Elizabeth, daughter of Dr. Thomas Walker, and died in 1808. His children were Matthew, Thomas Walker, Francis, Mary Ann, the wife of William Michie, Mildred, the wife of Henry Fry Jr., Reuben, Elizabeth, Catharine, the wife of Francis Lightfoot, and John. Thomas W. was a member of the Albemarle bar, was appointed a magistrate in 1816, married Elizabeth, daughter of Julius Clarkson, and granddaughter of Jesse Lewis, taught school in the small brick at the east end of Main Street, and afterwards at his own place above the University, now occupied by Samuel Emerson, and died in 1842. Reuben married Elizabeth, daughter of Jesse Lewis, and died in 1869. His son, Jesse L., succeeded to the home of his father, and still lives in a green old age, a link between the present and the past. Mildred was the mother of J. Frank Fry, long the Commissioner of the Revenue for St. Anne's. James S. Maury, son of the Consul, lived at one time on a place near the north end of Dudley's Mountain, and in 1833 sold it to Jesse L. John, son of Rev. Matthew, also once lived in the same vicinity.

MAYO.

The Mayos have had a name and place in Albemarle from the beginning. Colonel William Mayo, the County Surveyor of Goochland, obtained a patent for eight hundred acres on the branches of Rockfish, near the Blue Mountains, in 1738. The patent of Dr. William Cabell for forty-eight hundred acres on both sides of the Fluvanna, obtained the same year, adjoined this entry of Mayo. Among the first deeds recorded in Albemarle, is one from Ann Mayo, conveying this land to Robert Barnett in 1748.

In 1749 Philip Mayo, of Henrico, entered four hundred acres on the branches of Hardware, situated in the limestone belt, and long known as the Limestone Survey. In 1752 he sold it to Peter Jefferson, Joshua Fry, Arthur Hopkins, Thomas Meriwether, Daniel Scott, and William Stith, President of William and Mary College. It is presumed that in making this purchase, these gentleman had in mind some project for utilizing the mineral it contained.

The original record of the deed having been destroyed, it was restored in 1802. As late as 1830 these separate interests were not all united, as in that year Governor Gilmer, as executor of Christopher Hudson, sold to George Gilmer, his father, one-sixth of the tract.

James Mayo died in 1777, leaving eleven sons and two daughters. The most of them no doubt lived in Goochland. One of them, Thomas, who belonged to that county, bought in 1779 from Thomas Collins four hundred acres on Edge Creek, the small branch of Moore's Creek that runs on the east side of the Teel place. Four years later Thomas sold part of this tract to his brother, Richard George Mayo. If Richard George ever lived on it, he removed elsewhere, as in 1809 his brother Joseph, as his attorney, sold it to another brother, James. James died in 1821, in his eighty-third year. His wife was Mary, daughter of Stephen Hughes, and his children John W., Stephen, Claudius, James E., Catharine, the wife of William Thompson, and Nancy, the wife of John Harris.

MERIWETHER.

The progenitor of the Meriwethers was Nicholas, an emigrant from Wales, who died in 1678. He had three sons, Francis, who married Mary Bathurst, and from whom descended Governor George W. Smith, who perished in the burning of the Richmond theatre in 1811, David and Nicholas. Nicholas was the large landholder. Besides obtaining grants of extensive tracts in several of the counties of eastern Virginia, he entered in one body seventeen thousand, nine hundred and fifty-two acres on the east side of the South West Mountain in Albemarle. He also entered in 1735 one thousand and twenty acres on the Rivanna, extending from Moore's Creek to Meadow Creek. This was the place on which he lived, and which he devised to his grandson, Nicholas Lewis. He died in 1744, and it is said he and his grandson, Richard Meriwether, son of William, were buried on the east side of the Rivanna, most probably on the summit of the hill north of Mrs. Crockford's residence, on the parcel of land which Richard purchased from Thomas Graves. His wife was Elizabeth Crawford, and his children Jane, the wife of Robert Lewis, Thomas, Nicholas, William, David, Elizabeth, the wife of Thomas Bray, Ann, the wife of Thomas Johnson, the colleague of Patrick Henry from Louisa in the House of Burgesses, and the grandfather of the eminent lawyer, Chapman Johnson, Sarah, the wife of William Littlepage, and Mary, the wife of John Aylett.

Nicholas received from his father a share of the lands east of the South West Mountain, of which Castle Hill was the seat. He married Mildred Thornton, and died in 1739, leaving one child, Mildred. About 1741 his widow became the wife of Dr. Thomas Walker, and in due time Mildred his daughter, became the wife of John Syme, of Hanover, the half-brother of Patrick Henry. In 1741 and 1746 there were entered in the daughter Mildred's name, two tracts of sixteen hundred, and nineteen hundred acres, lying near the gorge of the South Hardware between Gay's and Fan's Mountains, and extending up the road towards Batesville; and for many years her lines frequently figure in the descriptions of lands sold in that neighborhood. Both tracts were sold by Mildred's son, John Syme Jr., to President William Nelson, but the deed was never recorded. President Nelson devised them to his son Robert, who sold the sixteen hundred tract to James Powell Cocke, and the other in parcels to different purchasers. A chancery suit instituted againt the children of John Syme Jr., then living in Nelson County, to make title to these lands, was decided in 1809; and a considerable part of Deed Book Sixteen is occupied with the deeds of these parties to the vendees.

David Meriwether married Ann Holmes, and had six sons and two daughters. Thomas, the eldest, married Elizabeth Thornton, and his children were Nicholas, Francis, David, Mary, the wife of Peachy R. Gilmer, Elizabeth, the wife of Thomas Johnson, Sarah, the wife of Michael Anderson, Ann, the wife of Richard Anderson, and mother of David Anderson, of Milton and Pantops, Lucy, the wife of William Lewis, and afterwards of John Marks, Mildred, the wife of John Gilmer, and Jane, the wife of Samuel Dabney, mother of Mildred, Reuben Lewis's wife, and grandmother of Rev. Robert Lewis Dabney, the eminent theologian. Nicholas, the eldest of this family, married Margaret, daughter of Rev. William Douglass, a native of Scotland, rector of the parish of St. James, Northam, Goochland, who added teaching to his ministerial duties, and was the preceptor of Presidents Monroe and Jefferson, and who spent his last days at his plantation of Ducking Hole, Louisa. The children of Nicholas and Margaret Douglass Meriwether were William Douglass, Thomas, Nicholas H., Charles, Francis T., and Elizabeth, the wife of Thomas W. Lewis. Mrs. Margaret D. Meriwether was married the second time to Chiles Terrell.

William Douglass lived at Clover Fields, on the east side of the South West Mountain. He was a man of fine sense and great wealth. He was a magistrate of the county for fifty years, and the only one of the whole body of magistrates that filled the office of Sheriff twice in 1801 and 1828. His wife was Elizabeth, daughter of Nicholas Lewis, and through her he inherited the part of the Farm nearest Charlottesville, which in 1825 he sold to John A. G. Davis, who built on it the brick house, the present residence of Mrs. Thomas Farish. He died in 1845. His children were William H., Charles J., Mary, the wife of Peter Meriwether, Margaret D., the wife first of Dr. Francis Meriwether, and secondly of Francis K. Nelson, and Thomas W. William H., a man of incessant activity, was admitted to the bar, built the first mill at Rio, and a bridge across the Rivanna at the Woolen Mills, sold his land in 1835 to George L. Craven, and went to Texas. He was twice married, first to Francis Poindexter, and secondly to Kate W. Meriwether, who after his death was married to Dr. Prior, of Memphis, Tenn. Charles J. received from his father Mooresbrook, the present residence of Mr. Newman, but being impoverished by the war, he and his wife Louisa Miller, a sister of President Tyler's first wife, passed their remaining days under the hospitable roof of Mrs. Harper and her son, Warner Wood, at Farmington. Thomas W. was a physician, succeeded to the homestead, was a ruling elder in South Plains Church, and died in 1863. His wife was Ann, daughter of Hugh Nelson, and his children William D., also a physician, Mildred, the wife of George Macon, Ann, the wife of Frederick W. Page, Eliza, the wife of N. H. Massie, and Charlotte, the second wife of T. J. Randolph Jr.

Thomas, second son of Nicholas and Margaret D. Meriwether, married Ann, daughter of Garrett Minor, of Louisa. They had four children, among whom was Peter N., who resided at Cismont, married first his cousin Mary, as already noted, and secondly, Mrs. Frances Tapp, and died in 1851.

Nicholas H., third son of Nicholas and Margaret, married Rebecca Terrell. They had six children, among whom were Dr. Charles H., who married first Ann E. Anderson, and secondly Frances E. Thomas, lived at the present station of Arrowhead, and died in 1843, Ann T., the wife of Nicholas H. Lewis, and mother of Lydia L., the wife of Peter, son of Dr. Frank Carr, and Walker G., who married first his cousin Elizabeth Meriwether, and secondly his cousin Jane W. Lewis.

Charles, fourth son of Nicholas and Margaret, studied medicine in Scotland, and while visiting his Douglass kin in that country, married a young lady named Lydia Laurie. On his return he settled in Tennessee. Lydia Laurie died, and he married twice afterwards; but her sweet-sounding name has ever since been a favorite in all branches of the connection.

Francis T., fifth son of Nicholas and Margaret, married Catharine Davis, and had six children. Among them were

Elizabeth, the wife of her cousin Walker G., George D., who married his cousin Alice Lewis, and Dr. Francis, who married his cousin Margaret D., and whose daughter, Mary W., was the first wife of T. J. Randolph Jr.

Of all this numerous family, there is not one now living in Albemarle who bears the name. Their descendants however are scattered in every part of the West and South.

MICHIE.

The first Michie who settled in the county was John, who bought land near the Horse Shoe of the Rivanna from John Henry, father of the great orator. When the purchase was made does not appear, but he sold to Hezekiah Rice, and repurchased from him in 1763. He died in 1777. His children were John, who died before his father, Robert, James, Patrick, William, Sarah, the wife of Christopher Wood, and Mary, the wife also of a Wood. Robert and his sisters seem to have lived in Louisa.

Patrick had his home southwest of Earlysville, between the Buck Mountain Road and the south fork of the Rivanna. He died in 1799. His wife's name was Frances, and his children were Nancy, the wife of Joseph Goodman, James, Elizabeth, the wife of Thomas Maupin, Sarah, the wife of William G. Martin, Martha, the wife of Richard Davis, Susan, the wife of William Michie, Mary, the wife of John Maupin, and David.

William became a large landholder in the same section. He purchased in 1793 from Lewis Webb, of New Kent, two thousand and ninety acres in one tract. On the Buck Mountain Road he established the public House, which has since been known as Michie's Old Tavern. He was appointed a magistrate in 1791, served as Sheriff in 1803, and died in 1811. He was twice married; one of his wives, it is believed, being Ann, daughter of David Mills. His children by the first marriage were John A., and Mary, the wife of John Mullins, and by the second William, David and Lucy, the wife of Benjamin Richards.

John A. was appointed a magistrate of the county in 1807. His wife was Frances, daughter of Thomas Jarman. He died in 1827. His children were Frances J., Ann, Sarah, Elizabeth, the wife of Bezaleel G. Brown, Theodosia, the wife of Edmund Brown, John E., James, William, Robert J., Jonathan, Mary and Martha. Of these James attained a prominent position in the affairs of the county. He was a successful business man, was appointed a magistrate in 1816, and served as Sheriff in 1843. He was an earnest Episcopalian, and displayed his zeal in active efforts to rebuild the ruins of the old Buck Mountain Church. His home was on the north fork of the Rivanna, south of Piney Mountain. He died in 1850. His wife was Frances, daughter of Thomas Garth Jr., and his children Mary Elizabeth, the wife of William T. Early, Virginia, Susan, Adeline, Dr. J. Augustus, Thomas, Theresa, the wife of Lucian Michie, Alexander H., and Henry Clay. Jonathan married a sister of Thomas J. Michie, of Staunton, and his children were John P., Margaret, the wife of Dr. Theodore Michie, Frances, the wife of Dr. R. N. Hewitt, of Campbell County, Thomas, Chapman and Franklin.

William Michie, son of William, married, it is believed, Susan, daughter of his uncle Patrick. His children were Dr. James W., David and Frances. His brother David was a man of great enterprise and thrift. In early life he was a merchant first in the Michie Tavern neighborhood, and afterwards at Milton. He invested in real estate in different parts of the county, purchasing in 1805 from Randolph Lewis his plantation Buck Island on the north side of the Rivanna, which he seems to have made his home till 1837. In that year he bought the brick house on the northeast corner of Market and Seventh Streets in Charlottesville, where he resided until his death in 1850. He left no children, and his large estate was divided among his numerous relatives, under the direction of George Carr, as administrator.

James Michie Jr., or Beau Jim, as he was commonly called, was the son of a William Michie. His residence was at Longwood, west of Earlysville. His death occurred in 1847. He married Eliza Graves, of Rockingham, and his children were Dr. Theodore, Octavius, Joseph P., Lucian, Oran,

Claudius N., Eugene, Catharine, the wife of William A. Rogers, Cornelia and Virginia.

MILLS.

In early times three large entries of lands were made within the county by persons named Mills. Between 1737 and 1759 Matthew Mills obtained grants for seventeen hundred acres on the south side of Mechum's River, east of the Miller School. After his death it was divided among three sons, Matthew, Charles and Menan. In 1782 Matthew, who at the time was living in Guilford County, North Carolina, sold his share to William Leigh, who came to take possession of it from Caswell County, North Carolina. The same year Charles and his wife Mary, who were residents of Buckingham, sold five hundred and sixty-seven acres to Richard Woods, the same land that descended to his son Richard, that after his death was sold to James Michie, and that is still in the possession of his son, Thomas Michie. The other portion, five hundred and sixty-seven acres, fell to Menan, who lived on it till 1800. He then bought from the executors of Micajah Chiles the old Joel Terrell property in Charlottesville, the square on which the present City Hall stands. He married Frances, daughter of John Jouett. He was not a prosperous man, and in 1811 all his possessions were sold under deeds of trust, his share of his father's estate being purchased by Daniel White, and now owned by his grandson, Samuel G. White. Menan Mills removed elsewhere, probably to Kentucky, leaving four children, John, Frances and Margaret, who were placed under the guardianship of Micajah Woods, and William, who was placed under that of Clifton Rodes.

Charles Mills between 1744 and 1756 took out patents for three thousand acres along the foot of Buck's Elbow, between Crozet and Whitehall. It is probable Charles was a brother of the elder Matthew, as both belonged to Hanover, and some of their patents were taken out the same day. Charles's land was inherited by his son Nicholas, who lived in Hanover, and who, after selling a portion of it, conveyed the remainder in 1786 to his sons, Joseph and William Mills, and his son-in-law, James Burnley, of Louisa. In 1790 Joseph sold his share to William, who lived in Spotsylvania, and in 1793 William sold to John Burnley, the son of James.

The third series of entries was made by David Mills. They ran from 1738 to 1755, and amounted to more than eleven thousand acres. They were located south of Earlysville, on Buck Mountain and Beaverdam Creeks, and in the Brown's Cove district. David Mills died in 1764. He and his wife Lucy had eight children, Zachariah, David, Wyatt, Joseph, Ann, the wife of William Michie, Elizabeth, the wife of William Doswell, of Nottoway, Mary, the wife of William S. Lane, and Lucy, the wife of Philip White, of Hanover. David sold out to his brother Wyatt in 1786, and emigrated to South Carolina. Wyatt died in 1808. He and his wife Sarah had four children, Elizabeth, the wife of James Beazley, Wilson, John S., and Sophia, the wife of Fontaine Richards. Joseph Mills Jr., probably the son of Joseph, taught school in the Buck Mountain neighborhood, was admitted to the bar in 1823, and soon after removed to Harrisonburg.

A John Mills—whether related to any of those before mentioned, is not known—in 1782 married Elizabeth, daughter of Robert Field, and was owner of the land which is now known as Brooksville. In 1795 he sold it to James Hays, and probably left the county.

MINOR.

John Minor, of Topping Castle, Caroline County, was the patentee of land on the north fork of the Rivanna as early as 1735. Of the eleven children of himself and his wife, Sarah, daughter of Thomas Carr, three have been represented in Albemarle. His son James, came to the county from Spotsylvania not far from 1770, and lived on the land entered by his father east of the Burnt Mills, which he beyond all question first built. He was a man of energy and industry, and a public spirited magistrate, but died in 1791, at the age of forty-five. His wife was Mary Carr, and his children Dabney, James, John, Sarah, the wife of William Wardlaw, Mary, the wife of Richard H. Allen, Nancy, the wife of Dr. Thomas Yancey, and Elizabeth, the wife of Alexander Garrett. Dabney resembled his father in capacity for business, became a large landholder in this and other counties, and for a number of years served as a magistrate. He resided at first at the home of his father, but subsequently purchased Carrsbrook, and there spent his last years. He died in 1824, about fifty years of age. He was twice married, first to Eliza Johnson, a niece of William Wirt, and secondly to Martha J., daughter of Richard Terrell, and granddaughter of Mr. Jefferson's sister, Martha. By the first marriage his children were Mildred, the wife of Hudson Martin, Catharine, the wife of E. W. Reinhart, Sarah, the wife of James Tompkins, and William W., of Gale Hill, and by the second Lucy J., the wife of Robert N. Trice. James lived at Brookhill, on the south fork of the Rivanna. His wife was Catharine Tompkins, and his children Dabney, John, James, Elizabeth, the wife of Samuel Moore, Ann, the wife of Rev. Albert Holladay, missionary to Persia, and President-Elect of Hampden-Sidney College, Catharine, the wife of Rev. Luther Emerson, and Martha, the wife of Lafayette Harris. He departed this life in 1848. John was a physician, and married Jane Bell, a Scotch lady, who was a resident of Lynchburg. He resided at Gale Hill, which at his death in 1841 he devised to his nephew, William W. Minor.

Another son of John Minor, of Topping Castle, was Garrett, of Louisa, who married Mary O. Terrell. Their son Peter came to the county early in the century, and married Lucy, daughter of Dr. George Gilmer, of Pen Park. In 1809 he purchased from Jesse and John Key the present farm of Ridgeway, and in 1811 was appointed Treasurer of the Rivanna Navigation Company. He was for many years Secretary of the County Agricultural Society, in the great objects of which he was deeply interested. To his wife George Divers at his death in 1830 left one-third of his estate. He died in 1835, and his children were Hugh, Franklin, Peter C., George, John S., James E., Martha, the wife of Robert Grattan, Lucy, the wife of Dr. Charles Minor, and Mary, the wife of R. W. N. Noland. Hugh married first a Fry, and secondly Mary Ann, daughter of J. Boucher Carr, and lived at Ridgeway; but exchanging it with his brother Franklin for the Rigory, he resided there until his death in 1858. Franklin married Lucy Ann, daughter of Dr. John Gilmer, of Edgemont, and established a classical school at the Rigory, but afterwards removed it to Ridgeway, where it attained a wide-spread reputation. He died in 1867, but owing to ill health, and the interruption of the war, the school had been relinquished some years before. Samuel O., another son, of Garrett, married Lydia Laurie, daughter of Thomas W. Lewis, of Locust Grove. In 1817 he bought from Martin Dawson upwards of six hundred acres on the north side of the Rivanna, below Milton. He afterwards lived and conducted a school at the Farm. Dr. James H. Minor, of Music Hall, and Elizabeth, the wife of Andrew Brown, were his children.

Another son of John Minor, of Topping Castle, was Major John, whose son Launcelot, of Minor's Folly in Louisa, married Mary O. Tompkins. Several of their children resided in Albemarle. Lucian was admitted to the bar in 1830, practised for a time in Charlottesville, and subsequetnly became Professor of Law in William and Mary. John B., after practising law for a brief period in Buchanan on James River, settled in Charlottesville, erected at his home the house at Northwood, the present residence of Charles Benson, and in 1845 entered upon his distinguished career as Professor of Law in the University of Virginia, where he died in 1896. Dr. Charles, who married Lucy, daughter of Peter Minor, taught a classical school at Brookhill, and afterwards lived until his death in 1862 at Land's End, near Stony Point. George W. Trueheart, a son of Ann Minor, daughter of Launcelot, and wife of Overton Trueheart, was for a time a member of the Albemarle bar.

MONROE.

President James Monroe was for many years a citizen of Albemarle. Being a great admirer as well as a special favorite of Mr. Jefferson, he was attracted to the county by his influence. His first purchase of real estate was made from George Nicholas in 1790. He then bought from him Lots Seventeen and Eighteen in Charlottesville, with the Stone

House which Nicholas had erected thereon. That was his first residence. At the same time he purchased the farm on which the University stands. In the conveyance of his town property to Peter Marks in September 1790 it is recited that he sold to him "the pine plank and materials deposited thereon, except that which was planed, and the walnut plank," and reserved in the house "room for his furniture and family, until his houses were ready to receive them on his farm." This farm he also bought from George Nicholas, who, having purchased more than two thousand acres in different parts of the county, sold them, and removed without making conveyances for any of them; and it was not until nearly twenty years after his death, that James Morrison, his executor, gave title to the heirs of his vendees. For the land he sold Mr. Monroe, no deed was ever made, or at least was ever recorded; on account of Mr. Monroe's celebrity, and the property having changed hands several times, perhaps it was deemed unnecessary. The house Mr. Monroe was getting ready on his farm, was part of that now occupied by Professor Thornton, situated on what is still called Monroe Hill.

But he did not reside there long. In 1793 he purchased on the east side of Carter's Mountain, where he was a still closer neighbor to Mr. Jefferson. Part of this land he bought from Mr. Jefferson, and part from William C. Carter. His home was Ash Lawn, now owned by Rev. John E. Massey. Here he lived till the termination of his presidency, when all his lands in the county, amounting to between four and five thousand acres, were sold, or transferred to the United States Bank, in payment of his debts. Like Mr. Jefferson, he was so completely absorbed in his public engagements, and so frequently and long absent from home, that his private affairs suffered from neglect. When a man's mind is accustomed to dwell upon the broad expanse of a nation's interests, it is not unnatural perhaps that he should insensibly contract a sort of sublime indifference to the petty range of his mere personal concerns. As already stated, Mr. Monroe never did get a deed for his University land, and that which he bought from William C. Carter in 1793, was not conveyed to him till 1827. He was appointed a magistrate in 1798, and the latter half of the next year he sat regularly on the bench. His wife was Elizabeth, daughter of a Lawrence Kortright, a captain in the British army, and his children Eliza and Maria. Eliza was married to George Hay, United States Attorney for the district of Virginia, at his home in the county in 1808, and Maria to Samuel L. Governeur, of New York, in Washington, while he was President. At the expiration of his second term, he removed to Oak Hill, a farm he had purchased in Loudoun.

The President had an elder brother, Andrew, who, it is believed, in 1781 purchased a farm near Batesville, where he resided for four years. In 1816 he was living on a farm which the President purchased on Limestone, below Milton. He died in 1828. A son, Augustine G., was admitted to the Albemarle bar in 1815. Another son, James, born in the county, was an officer in the United States army, acted as the President's private secretary, married a daughter of James Douglass, an adopted son of Rev. William Douglass, of Ducking Hole, Louisa, and settled in New York City, where he was active in political affairs, and where he was appointed to perform his last public service as a member of the Peace Convention in 1861.

Joseph Jones Monroe, another brother of the President, became a member of the Albemarle bar, married Elizabeth, daughter of James Kerr, was appointed Commonwealth's Attorney in 1811 as successor to Judge Dabney Carr, and the next year gave place to William F. Gordon. In 1812 his daughter Harriet was married in Charlottesville to Edward Blair Cabell, and removed to Keytesville, Mo. He himself subsequently removed to Missouri, where he died in Franklin County in 1824.

MOON.

The genealogy of the Moons is somewhat difficult to trace. It seems however that two brothers, Jacob and William, settled in the county in early times. In 1750 Jacob purchased land from Thomas Fitzpatrick in the gorge of the south fork of Hardware. He also entered a small tract in the same vicinity. He sold out in 1777, and removed to Bedford County.

William bought a thousand acres from Hardin Burnley on the lower Hardware. When this purchase was made is not known, but the fact is stated in a conveyance of part of the land made by Moon to John Lewis in 1760. He died in 1800. His wife's name was Elizabeth, and his children were William, Richard, Littlebury, Jacob, Judith, the wife of Charles Moorman, Susan, the wife of Thomas Tilman, Martha, the wife of William Viers, who removed to Mason County, Kentucky, Elizabeth, the wife of Henry A. Bryant, Lucy, the wife of John Steele, and Sarah, the wife of Robert Moorman.

William married Charlotte, daughter of John Digges and Elizabeth Harris, of Nelson County. Their children were John Digges, Robert, Richard, Elizabeth, the wife of John Steele, Edward H., and Mildred, the wife of Nathaniel Anderson. He was at one time the owner of Belle Grove, the plantation above Scottsville on which the old courthouse stood. In 1819 he was appointed a magistrate of the county, and died in 1833. John D., who was called Senior to distinguish him from a cousin of the same name, marrie Mary E. Barclay, step-daughter of John Harris, and his home was at Mount Air. He became a magistrate in 1835, and died in 1869. His children were Robert B., who was appointed a magistrate in 1846, served as County Surveyor, married Mary, daughter of Nathaniel Massie, and died in 1891, Sarah, William F., who married Marietta Appling, and removed to Tennessee, and whose son, Judge John A. Moon represents the Chattanooga district in Congress, Ann, J. Schuyler, James N., Mary and J. Luther. Richard lived for a time in Tennessee, and as a mark of distinction bore the addition of T. to his name. Edward H. married Ann Maria Barclay, another step-daughter of John Harris, and lived at Viewmont, the old Fry homestead. He died in 1853. His children were Thomas B., Oriana, the wife of Dr. John

S. Andrews, Charlotte, Isaac A., Sarah, Mary and Edmonia. Richard, son of the first William, died in 1819. His wife's name was Winifred, and his children were Thomas, Richard, who lived on Briery Creek, and hence had the affix of B. to distinguish him from Richard T., William, Nathaniel, who married his cousin Roxana Moon, and removed to Upshur County, Elizabeth, the wife of Jeremiah Cleveland, Sarah, the wife of William Cleveland, Lucy, Fleming, Jacob, Martha and Samuel W. William married Elizabeth Hamner, and his children were John, William, Roxana, the wife of Henry Boatright, Archer, Martha, Elizabeth, Judith, Sarah, Pleasant, and Mildred, the wife of Thomas Garland. Jacob married Elizabeth Darneille, and his children were John D. Jr., Isaac D., Elizabeth, Mary, the wife of Thomas N. Trice, Charlotte, Anna, and Martha Louisa.

Littlebury married Sarah, daughter of Thomas Staples, and died in 1827. His children were Maria, the wife of Samuel O. Moon, son of Littlebury Moon, of Buckingham County, and Jane Hopkins, Martha, the wife of Littlebury Moon, a brother of Samuel O., Mary, the wife of William H. Turner, and Mildred, the wife of Rev. Thomas J. Deyerle.

Jacob, son of the first William, married Mildred Hamner, and died in 1811. His children were Samuel, Schuyler, Mary, Roxana, the wife of Nathaniel Moon, Susan, Turner, and Elizabeth, the wife of William Hopkins.

It is said the early Moons, like the Lewises of the same part of the county, were largely engaged in the business of transportation on James River, and after its construction, on the canal.

MOORE.

John Moore was appointed the executor of Matthew Jouett in 1745, the same year the county of Albemarle was organized. It is likely his first wife was Matthew Jouett's daughter. He was evidently a man of means and fine business capacity. At different times he owned more than five thousand acres in the county, including Lot No. Three, on which the first court at the new county seat was held, several of the outlots around Charlottesville, a thousand acres on Meadow Creek, and more than thirteen hundred east of the South West Mountain, on part of which stood his home, subsequently the home of Reuben Lindsay. From the fact that it was through his land east of the town the road to the river was made, it is surmised the name of Moore's was given to the ford, which crossed just below the site of the Free Bridge. He was a large landholder also in Louisa, to which county he removed after selling his residence in Albemarle. He died in 1785. He appears to have been joined in matrimony the second time with Martha, daughter of the elder John Harvie. His children were John, Edward, James, Matthew, Frances, the wife of John Henderson Jr., and Elizabeth, the wife first of Tucker Woodson, and secondly of Major Joseph Crockett. It is thought that William Moore, who married Mary, daughter of Colonel John Marks and Mrs. Lucy Lewis, and lived in Georgia, was also his son by the last marriage.

John was one of his father's executors, and probably lived in Louisa. Matthew received from his father a farm on the borders of Louisa, which he and his wife Letitia sold in 1774 to Rev. Matthew Maury, and removed South. Edward occupied a position of considerable prominence, but unfortunate habits seem to have ruined both him and his estate. He was a magistrate, and in the decade of 1790 represented the county in the House of Delegates. His plantation of five hundred acres, which he bought from John Harvie, lay on the Gordonsville Road below Keswick, and in 1805 was sold under deed of trust to William D. Meriwether. Overwhelmed with debt, stripped of his property, and declared insane in 1807, he was by order of Court placed in the Asylum, where he died the next year. His wife was Mildred, daughter of Colonel Charles Lewis Jr., of Buck Island. His son, John Lewis, was left by his uncle Isham Lewis, a thousand acres of land on Blue Run, on the Barboursville Road, which he sold in 1807 to James Barbour. A daughter Ann is mentioned, to whom her brother John Lewis was appointed guardian, and a son Charles, who was bound as apprentice for four years to William Watson.

Another family named Moore resided in the county, the descendants of which still remain in considerable numbers, though bearing different names. Contrary to the usual course of emigration, three brothers, Richard, William and Stephen, came to Albemarle from Person County, North Carolina, sometime before the Revolutionary War; yet it is said by relatives now living in North Carolina, that the family first emgirated thither from Albemarle. Richard lived on the head waters of the south fork of Hardware, not far from the Cove. He was twice married, first to Letitia Martin, and secondly to Keturah, daughter of William Austin, and died in 1809. He had twelve children, the most of whom, it is believed, removed to Tennessee. William lived at first near Richard, but afterwards in the North Garden, on the place recently owned by the late Garrett White. He married Mary, daughter of William Gooch, and died in 1818. His son, Dyer, was a captain in the war of 1812, and removed to Tennessee, where he married Mary, daughter of James Lewis. Stephen was a man of industry and sound judgment, acquired a large estate, and died in 1833. His home was in North Garden, the same place recently occupied by his grandson, William Durrett. His wife, it is said, was a Miss Royster, and his children Sarah, the wife of Marcus Durrett, Caroline, the wife of John White, and Eliza, the wife of Henry Carter Moore, a kinsman also from North Carolina. H. Carter Moore resided where Anderson Rothwell now lives, and died in 1867. The only son in his large family, Shepherd, died without children in 1871.

MOORMAN.

Charles Moorman came from the Isle of Wight, England, and in 1744 was living in Louisa, not far from the Green Spring. He was a leading Quaker, and at that time he and his son Thomas were overseers of the Friends' Meeting House on Camp Creek, in Louisa. As early as 1735 they were both patentees of land within the present bounds of Albemarle. Charles entered four hundred acres "at the forks of the Rivanna, near the Blue Mountains"—the junction of Mechum's and Moorman's Rivers—and the entry of Thomas comprehended the present Carrsbrook, and was described as "including the Indian Grave low grounds." Seven years later Thomas entered a larger tract further up the Moorman's and thus gave his name to that stream. Charles also purchased land on Totier Creek, where two of his sons, Thomas and Robert, afterwards lived. He himself appears never to have resided in the county. He married Mary, daughter of Abraham Venable, whose home was on Byrd Creek in Goochland, and his children were Thomas, Charles, Robert, Achilles, James, Judith, the wife of Christopher Anthony, Elizabeth, the wife of Christopher Johnson, Agnes, the wife of John Venable, and Mary, the wife of a Taylor.

Thomas Moorman was married twice, first to Rachel, daughter of Christopher Clark, and secondly to Elizabeth, daughter of Robert and Mourning Adams. He died in 1787, and left one son, Robert, who died in 1813, whose widow, Dorothy, became the wife of John T. Holman, and whose children were Dorothy, the wife of James L. Neville, Mary, the wife of Eli Tutwiler, Elizabeth Ann, the wife of Robert L. Jefferson, and Robert J. Charles married Judith, daughter of William Moon. Robert married Sarah, another daughter of William Moon, and had eight children, of whom Mary was the wife of William Roper, and Elizabeth the wife of Benjamin Johnson, of Locust Hill on James River; these last were the parents of Janet, the wife of Austin M. Appling, Sarah, the wife of John Darneille, Louisiana, the wife of Edwin H. Gooch, and Dorothy, the wife of William A. Turner. Robert Moorman sold his land on Totier Creek to John Harris in 1792, and with the view of emigrating to South Carolina, appointed John Hudson and William Roper his attorneys in fact. Achilles married Mary, daughter of Robert and Mourning Adams, and removed to Bedford County. The land on Mechunk, which came to the wives of Thomas and Achilles from their father, Robert Adams, was purchased by Dr. George Gilmer, of Pen Park.

MORRIS.

Two persons named Morris obtained patents for land in 1743, Hugh on the lower Hardware, and Jacob on Totier

Creek. They were, as their names indicate, of Welsh origin, and the strong probability is they were brothers. Jacob's daughter Ann became the wife of Jacob Kinney, subsequently a citizen of Staunton. Kinney owned the Stone Tavern in Warren, and Lots Seven and Eight in Charlottesville. His widow and daughter, Mrs. Matilda Stribling, sold the property in Warren to William Brown in 1812, and the lots to Twyman Wayt in 1815. It may be stated, that the Kinney family were residents of Albemarle at an early date. In 1779 the father, William Kinney, bought a tract of land on the lower Hardware from William Moon Sr., which his heirs, Chesley, Jacob, William and Nancy Whitesides, then of Amherst, sold in 1795 to William Moon Jr.

Hugh Morris, sometime previous to 1769, purchased land in the North Garden, contiguous to the Cross Roads. An Episcopal Church was built on this land, on the hill south of the village, and in the conveyance of the land to his son in 1772, Hugh recites that he never gave the land the church occupied, but invests his son with power to act as it seemed best. He died in 1774. His son, Hugh Rice Morris, resided on the land in North Garden, and died in 1820. It is said he was an Episcopal clergyman. In the notice of his death it was stated, that he was present at the first court held in the county, and witnessed the proceedings attending its organization. About 1817 he built the mill below the Cross Roads, now known as Kidd's Mill. His wife's name was Ann, and his children Henry, Samuel, Rice, William, Tandy and Elizabeth. Rice removed to Augusta County, but returned to Albemarle, and resided in the neighborhood of Scottsville; his daughter Sarah became the wife of Robert Dyer. Tandy was a physician, and practised in the vicinity of Warren. William married Ann, daughter of Marshall Durrett, bought from Howell Lewis the farm, with the large brick house, on which Stephen Carpenter now resides, and died in 1832. His son William married Helen, daughter of James Alexander, and removed to Mississippi. Henry continued to live near the Cross Roads. The old church, a wooden structure, becoming dilapidated by the ravages of time, he gave the ground in the village, on which the brick edifice was erected. He departed this life in 1859.

NEILSON.

John Neilson, a native of Ireland, a carpenter by trade, was attracted to Albemarle by the erection of the University buildings. While engaged in this work, he prospered in his affairs. He bought from Joseph Bishop several acres between Vinegar Hill and the Whitehall Road, and built one or two of the brick houses in Random Row. He also built the large brick near the forks of the Lynchburg Road, which afterwards became the property of Professor Blaetterman, in which his wife for a time conducted a seminary for young ladies, and which is now owned by G. L. Bruffey. He purchased the Refuge, the old Jones plantation in the southern part of the county, where Major Anbury, the Revolutionary prisoner, indited a number of his letters. He died in 1827, devising his property to his family still residing in Ireland. Andrew Leitch, as his executor, carried out the provisions of his will.

NELSON.

Solomon Nelson in 1759 bought from John Grills two hundred acres on Moore's Creek, and built the first mill that occupied the site of that now owned by Hartman. This tract he sold in 1764 to John Moore, and bought from Edward Carter a parcel of land in the Ragged Mountains, not far from Batesville. He sold this place in 1773, and no doubt removed from the county.

The large tracts in North and South Garden, patented in the name of Mildred Meriwether, were sold by her and her husband, John Syme, to President William Nelson, of Yorktown, and by him devised to his son Robert. Robert and his wife Susan sold them in course of time to different parties. In reference to these interests in North and South Garden, Samuel Murrell acted as Mr. Nelson's agent. He was also the owner of a tract of upwards of two thousand acres on Mechunk, which was patented by Thomas Darsie in 1733, descended to his son Thomas, and by him sold in 1748 to

James Power. How, or when, it came into the hands of Robert Nelson, is not known, but in 1778 he sold it to John Clark.

Hugh Nelson, son of Governor Thomas, and grandson of President William, became a citizen of Albemarle in 1802. In that year he was admitted a member of its bar. He married Eliza, daughter of Francis Kinloch, of South Carolina, and Mildred, only daughter of John Walker, eldest son of Dr. Thomas Walker. His home was at Belvoir, on the east side of the South West Mountain. In 1803 he purchased from Lilburn Lewis his plantation of nearly nine hundred acres on the north side of the Rivanna, which in 1815 he sold to John R. Campbell, and which is now in part the property of David Hancock's heirs. He represented the county in the House of Delegates, of which he was Speaker, and was a member of Congress from 1811 to 1823, when he resigned to accept the appointment of Minister to Spain. In 1819 he became a magistrate of the county. He died in 1836. His children were Francis K., Mildred, the wife of Thomas Nelson, of Clark, Ann, the wife of Dr. Thomas Meriwether, Dr. Thomas, of Elk Hill, Rev. Cleland K., Keating, and Dr. Robert W., who still lives to represent the name in Albemarle.

NICHOLAS.

The first patentee of land on James River within the present county was George Nicholas, of Williamsburg. He made the entry—the third in the county—of twenty-six hundred acres in 1729. This was Dr. George Nicholas, the immigrant, as the same land descended to his eldest son, Robert Carter Nicholas, Treasurer of the colony. Robert Carter never lived in Albemarle. John, Dr. George's second son, became its Clerk in 1750, and continued to hold the office till 1792. In that year he resigned, and spent the remainder of his life in the southern part of the county, or in Buckingham. His wife was Martha, daughter of Colonel Joshua Fry, and his children John, Robert, George, Joshua, Elizabeth, and another daughter, the wife of a Scott. John succeeded his father as Clerk. He was an extensive dealer in the real estate of the county. He purchased a large plantation near Ivy Depot, on which he lived for some years, and which he sold to Dabney and Thomas Gooch. He became the owner of all the land surrounding Charlottesville on the south and west, extending from the Scottsville Road to Meadow Creek. His last residence was at Hor de Ville, where James D. Goodman now lives. In 1815 he resigned his office, and removed to Buckingham. His wife was Louisa Howe Carter, of Williamsburg. His brother Joshua, who was for a time his deputy, married Sarah, daughter of Peter Marks, and removed to Charlotte County.

Three of Robert Carter Nicholas's sons, George, Wilson Cary and Lewis, were residents of Albemarle. George was Captain, Major and Colonel in the Revolutionary army. After the war he practised law in Charlottesville, and in 1788 was a member of the House of Delegates, and of the Convention to ratify the United States Constitution. He owned the square on which Lipscomb's Stable stands, and built as his residence the stone house, which was long known as the Stone Tavern. He purchased about two thousand acres of land in the county, part of it that on which the University stands, part on Moore's Creek, and part in the western section on Ivy Creek and Lickinghole. He married Mary, sister of General Samuel Smith, of Baltimore. In 1790 he removed to Kentucky, was active in its formation as a State, and was its first Attorney General. At the time of his removal, he sold most of his lands to Samuel Beale, of James City, but died in 1799 before they were transferred; and this act was not accomplished till 1818, when James Morrison, his executor, conveyed them to Beale's heirs.

Wilson Cary was also a soldier of the Revolution, the commander of Washington's Life Guards. He filled the offices of magistrate of the county, member of the Legislature, United States Senator, and Governor of Virginia. His home was on his plantation on James River, including Warren, which he laid out as a town in 1794. His desire for acquiring the broad acres amounted to a passion. Besides his possessions in the southern part of the county, he owned about two thousand acres at the Barracks, more than a thousand on both sides of the Rivanna, including Carrsbrook, and tens of thousands of acres in Bedford and Botetourt, and on the Ohio River. He was in consequence greatly oppressed with burdensome debts, which no doubt contributed to the shortening of his days. Being advised to travel on account of ill health, he set out for the North, but unable to continue his journey, he returned on his way home as far as Tufton, then the residence of his son-in-law, Colonel T. J. Randolph, where he died in 1820. His wife was Margaret, sister of his brother George's wife, and his children Mary, the wife of John Patterson, Cary Ann, the wife of John Smith, and mother of Margaret, Robert Hill Carter's wife, Robert C., Wilson C., Margaret, Jane, the wife of T. J. Randolph, John S., Sarah, and Sidney, the wife of Dabney Carr, Minister to Constantinople.

Lewis had his home at Alta Vista, a fine plantation west of Green Mountain. He became involved in his brother Wilson's embarrassments, and was thereby seriously broken in fortune. He married Frances, daughter of William Harris, and his children were John S., Wilson C., Robert, Cary Ann, the wife of Rev. Charles Wingfield, and Sarah, the wife of John H. Coleman. John S. and Wilson C. were appointed magistrates of the county in 1838.

OLD.

John Old came to Albemarle from Lancaster County, Pennsylvania, in 1769, and engaged with John Wilkinson in establishing a forge for the manufacture of iron. This was erected in the gorge of the south fork of Hardware, a short distance south of Garland's Store. In 1782 he bought from William Hamner nine hundred acres on the north fork of Hardware, at the crossing of the old Lynchburg Road, and there built another forge. This was a widely known point in its day. Mr. Jefferson mentions it in his Notes. The road to it was spoken of as the road to Old's Forge oftener perhaps than as the Lynchburg Road. This property he sold in 1793 to Henry Weaver and his brother James. He died in 1809. He and his wife Sarah had a son John, and a daughter Sarah, the wife of Edward Garland. John married in 1785 Elizabeth, daughter of Benjamin Dod Wheeler, and died in 1812. His children were Nancy, the wife of Thomas Eubank, who removed to Monroe County, Kentucky, Elizabeth, the wife of Reuben Eubank, Ann, the wife of Joseph F. Wingfield, Thomas J., George W., and probably Abijah. Thomas and George removed to Campbell County. Abijah married Sarah Fretwell, lived in the neighborhood of Old's Forge, and died in 1840. His children were James A., John, William, Martha, Mary, the wife of John D. Douglass, and Sarah, the wife of Samuel Norvell. The most of the last family removed to Missouri.

James Old, brother of the first John, came to Albemarle several years after his brother. He had been a Revolutionary soldier, was in the unfortunate expedition against Quebec, and fought in the battle of Long Island. His home was on Black Walnut Branch, between Mount Olivet Church and Garland's Store. He built the mill two miles east of Red Hill Depot about 1804. He died unmarried in 1821, devising the mill to George M. Woods and James Old Walters.

OLDHAM.

James Oldham was one of the contractors for erecting the buildings of the University. This work most probably allured him to the county, and its profits induced him to settle in it. In 1828 he purchased from the trustees of Benjamin Hardin the land on the Staunton Road, immediately east of Mechum's River Depot. There he kept for some years a house of public entertainment. He seems to have been of an irascible temper. In such a state of mind he shot Archelaus Robertson, the son of a neighbor about Christmas 1834. As the grand jury declined to indict him, there must have been but slight injury, and likely some provocation. His wife was Mary, daughter of Henry Gambell. He died in 1843.

PAGE.

In former times several Pages lived in Albemarle. In 1770 Robert Page purchased from Hezekiah Inman four hundred acres on Taylor's Creek, near the border of what is now Nelson. His children were James, William, Robert, George, Samuel, Nicholas, Jane, the wife of Burgess Griffin, Mary, the wife of Sherrard Griffin, and Elizabeth, the wife of Peter Davis, of Hanover. All of these emigrated to Adair County, Kentucky, except William, and Nicholas, who died in 1817. In 1829 Nicholas M. Page, son of the younger Robert, returned to Albemarle, where for some years he prosecuted business as a merchant in Batesville, and achieved the notable task of administering the great estate of Samuel Miller. He was a magistrate under the old regime, having been appointed in 1841. He still lives, a venerable memorial of a former generation. A William Page was the owner of land below Milton, and of Lot Forty in Charlottesville, in the early part of the century. When he sold the lot in 1815, he was described as a citizen of Nelson. He may have been the William mentioned above.

Dr. Mann Page, son of Major Carter Page, of Cumberland, came to the county about 1815. In that year he was united in marriage to Jane Frances, daughter of Francis Walker. His home was at Turkey Hill, a part of the Castle Hill place, which his wife inherited from her father. Dr. Page was appointed a magistrate of the county in 1824, and died in 1850. His children were Maria, Ella, Jane, Charlotte, William, Francis W., Carter H., Frederick W., Mann, Thomas W., and Dr. R. Channing, of New York.

PATRICK.

John Patrick, of Augusta, bought nearly a thousand acres in the western part of the county, most, if not all, being a portion of the immense Chiswell patent. His purchase commenced in 1765. Two years after he conveyed three hundred acres to his son Charles; the remainder he appears to have sold to other persons. Charles died in 1797. His children were John, Charles, Mary, the wife of Joseph Burgher,

Rachel, the wife of Thomas Smith, Martha, the wife of Joel Smith, and Margaret. Charles married Dorcas, daughter of Samuel Black, and removed to Fayette County, Kentucky. John succeeded to his father's place, and died in 1832. He was twice married, and his children were John M., Mary Susan, the wife of Thomas O. Carr, and ——— the wife of James Lobban. The old homestead is still in the possession of one of the descendants, Sarah A. Patrick, who became the wife of James W. Timberlake.

PERRY.

George Perry was the owner of nearly five hundred acres on Shepherd's Creek, a tributary of the lower Hardware, just before the Revolutionary War. It is likely he was the father of John M. Perry, the most noted of the name resident in Albemarle. Countenance is given to the view by the fact, that John M. first appears in the same section of the county, purchasing in 1804 from Henry Wood a parcel of land on Buck Island, which two years later he sold to Martin Railey. About the same time a brother, Reuben, bought from Whitaker Carter his interest in his father's lands in Kentucky, and in all probability removed to that State. George Perry, who owned a tract of more than three hundred acres on Moore's Creek, and in 1817 sold it to Nelson Barksdale, was perhaps another brother.

John M. in 1814 purchased from John Nicholas, the County Clerk, a tract of land including that on which the University stands, and three years after sold that part of it to Alexander Garrett, as Proctor of the Central University. In 1818 he bought from James Scott the Hydraulic Mills, and from David J. Lewis a large plantation in the same neighborhood. At the same time he was busily engaged as a contractor in the erection of buildings. He constructed a number of the edifices connected with the University, and built as his own residence the brick house near by, known as Montebello. He also built the mansion of Judge Philip Barbour on his place Frascati, not far from Gordonsville. He was appointed a magistrate in 1816, and for some years took an active part in the business of the county. In 1829 he began selling off his property, in 1834 disposing of the Hydraulic Mills to Nathaniel Burnley and Rice Wood, and his land in that vicinity to William P. Farish. A year or two later he removed to Missouri, and subsequently to Mississippi, where he soon after died. His wife's name was Frances ——— and his children were Ann, the wife of Samuel Campbell, Elizabeth, the wife of George W. Spooner, who was associated with him in his work at the University, and Calvin L., who was admitted to the bar in 1828, and married Mary Tuft, a sister of Professor Bonnycastle's wife.

PEYTON.

John Peyton, son of Craven Peyton, of Loudoun County, was an officer in the Revolutionary army, and during the war was sent to Fluvanna County to purchase supplies. Three nephews, sons of his brother Valentine, joined him there, Craven, Robert and John. The nephews settled in Milton, and Robert and John died unmarried at an early age. Craven, inheriting the property of his brothers, and likely that of his uncle, who also died unmarried, became the possessor of a large estate. He purchased from the family of Bennett Henderson more than eleven hundred acres surrounding Milton, which in 1811 he sold to Mr. Jefferson. He also acquired from his father-in-law nearly a thousand acres on both sides of the Rivanna, including the old Lewis homestead of Monteagle, which he made his home. He married Jane Jefferson, daughter of Charles Lilburn Lewis and his wife Lucy, a sister of Mr. Jefferson. He died in 1837. His children were Margaret, the second wife of Isham R. Jefferson, Valentine, Lucy, the wife of James W. Eskridge, Mary, the wife of William C. Eskridge, and Charles Lewis. The family removing to other places, most of them to the Valley, the estate passed into other hands. Charles Lewis settled at Richlands, Greenbrier County, where he died a few years ago, and his son, Rev. Charles W. Peyton is preaching as a Presbyterian minister in Texas.

Bernard Peyton, a merchant of Richmond, about 1850 bought Farmington from John Coles Carter, when he removed to Missouri. He made it his home, and died there suddenly in 1854. He was the father of Major Green Peyton, Proctor of the University, and a second cousin of Craven before mentioned, and of John Howe Peyton, the distinguished lawyer of Staunton.

Another family of the name was settled in the county. Henry Peyton became the owner of Park Hill, the old Drury Wood place near Stony Point, where he resided until his death. His wife was a sister of William P. Farish, and his sons were William, Benjamin, George L., Dr. E. O., Bernard and Eugene, all of whom exhibited a marked degree of enterprise, some in conducting lines of Stages, and some in hotel keeping. They removed for the most part to West Virginia.

PHILLIPS.

In 1746 Joseph Phillips obtained a grant of land on Buck Mountain Creek, and removing to North Carolina in 1778, sold it to John Phillips, who by further purchases acquired a considerable landed estate. From 1750 to 1760 Leonard Phillips patented nearly a thousand acres in the southern part of the county on Ivy and Green Creeks, portions of which he sold to George Blain, and to Peter and William Farrar.

William B. Phillips came to the county at the time the University buildings were projected, and was engaged in the work of their construction. He was afterwards active in his dealings in real estate, both in town and country. In 1823 he bought Lots Thirteen and Seventy-Seven, and built upon them the brick houses, the former of which he sold to Governor Gilmer in 1831, and the latter to Dr. James A. Leitch. He purchased in 1833 from Eli Alexander nearly five hundred acres of the Colle estate, and built thereon the large brick mansion, which was subsequently the residence of Dr. George M. Bowen, and more recently of Hamilton Potts. His busy career terminated in Charlottesville in 1861.

PILSON.

It is probable the Pilson family originally belonged to Augusta County. In 1760 Richard of that name purchased from Jean Kinkead two hundred and twenty-four acres lying at the foot of the Blue Ridge. He appears to have died not long after, and the property descended to his son Samuel. In 1778 Samuel was living in Augusta, and in that year sold the land to William Pilson. William sold it to Nathaniel Harlow in 1783, and five years later it was the first purchase of John Dettor of York County, Pennsylvania. It is likely that Samuel and William were brothers, and that Mary Pilson, who became the wife of William Wallace in 1771, was their sister.

John Pilson next appears, and was the son of Samuel. He was a man of sterling character, sincere piety, and the strictest integrity. He carried on the mercantile business in partnership with his cousin William Wallace until the death of William in 1809, and then conducted it alone for many years. The store stood on the old Staunton Road on the north side of the branch, opposite the house now owned by Rev. Dabney Davis. He invested the earnings of his business in the old Hardin property, which in 1837 he sold to Thomas C. Bowen. He was appointed a magistrate in 1824, and served for a time as ruling elder in the Mountain Plains Church. He never married, but was once engaged to his cousin Polly Wallace. Their union being opposed by friends because of relationship, they quietly acquiesced, but withal still loved and lived in each other's eyes until her death in 1845; and to her memory he remained constant until his own death, which occurred ten years later. A nephew, Matthew Pilson, from Augusta County, was for some years an assistant in the store. After John's death he returned to Augusta, where he died not long ago at an advanced age.

PIPER.

John Piper first purchased land in Albemarle in 1779. He then bought from Alexander Henderson four hundred acres on Lickinghole, which he sold to John Buster in 1792. In the meantime, in 1783, he bought from Charles Wingfield a place between Batesville and the Nelson line, which he made his home. When the records begin again in 1783, he was an acting magistrate of the county. In 1815 he conveyed nearly five hundred acres of his land to his son. His wife's name was Ann, and his children William and Elizabeth, the wife of Garrett White, of North Garden. William, who succeeded to the homestead, died in 1835. He and his wife Elizabeth had eleven children, Mary Ann, Garrett W., William, Nancy, the wife of Robert Field, Marshall, Willis, Jeremiah, Elizabeth, the wife of Richard M. Durrett, Richard, Frances and John. Some years after the death of the father, the place was sold to William H. Turner, and those of the family still living removed to Missouri.

PRICE.

Edmund Price owned land for a short time in the neighborhood of Scott's Landing prior to 1770. John Price married Elizabeth, daughter of Benjamin Brown, of Brown's Cove, and in 1777 seems to have been a resident of Augusta County.

Richard Price was one of the earliest inhabitants of Milton, and there spent his life. He died in 1827. He was twice married. His children by his first wife were Jane, the wife of John Watson, Isabel, the wife of Edmund Read, and Lucy, the wife of John Burks, and mother of Lucy Jane, the wife of Lilburn R. Railey. His second wife, Frances, had a daughter, Sarah, who became the wife of Robert C. Scott, of Lynchburg.

In the early years of the century, John Price lived in the northeast part of the county. His wife was Sarah, daughter of Abraham Munday, and his children John, Henry, Matilda, the wife of William Marshall, Amanda, the wife of Nimrod Herring, Louisa, the wife of Thomas Harlow, Harriet, the wife of Thomas Salmon, Daniel and Nimrod.

Henry Price about 1823 came to Charlottesville from Mecklenburg County. He was a native of Stockport, England, and a tailor by trade. He owned at one time the house on the corner of the west side of the Square and High Street, and the house in the rear of the late Thomas Wood's. The latter he sold in 1829 to Dr. Frank Carr. He died in 1835. The next year his widow Nancy bought the lot on Park Street, north of Thomas Wood's, and built the brick house, which in comparatively recent years was enlarged by

R. R. Prentis. He had a daughter Rebecca, who became the wife of Christopher Hornsey, and a son Henry, who lately acquired some notoriety, by exploiting a patent for an immense tract of land in the disputed zone between Venezuela and British Guiana.

Stephen C. Price in 1826 married Lydia Ann, daughter of Charles Harper. He lived on a farm on the south side of the old Richard Woods Road, southwest of Ivy Depot. He acted for a time as Treasurer of the County School Commissioners. He died in 1845. His children were Lucy, the wife of Jesse L. Maury, Charles H., Daniel, Robert, Elizabeth, and Sarah, the wife of James E. Pride.

QUARLES.

Roger Quarles in 1741 obtained a grant of four hundred acres on both sides of Priddy's Creek, which William Quarles, who was no doubt Roger's son, and who was described as of Orange County, sold to Richard Durrett in 1763. Whether any of the family ever lived on the land, is not known; it was however sufficiently recognized by the public, to give the name of Quarles's Creek to a branch of Priddy's Creek passing through it, and crossing the Barboursville Road.

In 1767 James Quarles, of King William, purchased from John Walker a plantation called Rock Hall, and containing nearly nine hundred acres, originally a part of the large Meriwether grant. He sold it in 1776 to Cornelius Ruddell, who two years after sold it to John Hunton, of Augusta. It remained in the Hunton family many years. Charles B. Hunton, a son of John, being appointed a magistrate in 1791, serving as Sheriff in 1813, and dying in 1818. James Quarles in 1778 bought from John Clark nearly thirteen hundred acres on Mechunk, which four years later he sold to Francis Kinloch, of South Carolina. He was appointed a magistrate, and was occupying the office of Sheriff in 1783, when the records again begin. He had a daughter Ann, who in 1785 became the wife of Henry Washington, of King George. Washington died in 1788, leaving two children, Frances Maria, and Ann Catharine, and in 1791 his widow was married to John Tinsley. Whether Quarles continued to reside in Albemarle till his death, or removed elsewhere, does not appear.

A tract of seventeen hundred acres lying on the waters of Buck Island and Hardware, was purchased from Duncan McLaughlin by a company consisting of Benjamin Fitzpatrick, Robert Wright, Robert French, and John Quarles of Louisa. In connection with the final disposition of this land, it appeared that John Quarles had six children, two of whom were Albert G., and Garrett Minor. Garrett became a member of the Albemarle bar in 1813. Albert G. married Mary, daughter of Dabney Minor, and his children were Matilda, Lucy, Henry, and Albert, who removed with their parents to Kentucky.

RAILEY.

Martin Railey came to Albemarle from Chesterfield in 1806. He lived on Buck Island, on a farm he purchased from John M. Perry. He died in 1814. His wife was Elizabeth Mayo, and his children Daniel M., John M., Lilburn R., and Catharine, the wife of Anderson Shiflett. Daniel succeeded to the homestead, Woodbourne, married Lucy Jane, daughter of John Watson, of Milton, was appointed a magistrate in 1830, and not long after sold his place, and removed to Southwest Virginia. His descendants continued still further West, and some are now living in Missouri. John married Mary, daughter of William Watson. He died early about 1833. After his death his widow built the brick house on the north end of Second Street, now the residence of Mrs. J. W. Lipop. He had four children, all of whom removed from the county. Lilburn R. was educated at Washington College in Lexington, married Lucy Jane Burks, niece of John Watson, was a ruling elder in the Presbyterian Church, and was appointed a magistrate of the county in 1838. His home was on his farm near the Hydraulic Mills, recently owned by William Nuttycomb. After the war he resided in Charlottesville. He died in 1893.

RAMSAY.

Rev. John Ramsay was the rector of St. Anne's parish, lived in the southern part of the county, and died in 1770.

In 1772 John Ramsay, of Augusta, purchased from Archibald Woods nearly four hundred acres on Stockton's Creek, and five years later sold them to Alexander Ramsay, in all probability a brother. In 1774 William, another brother as is supposed, bought from Adam Dean in the same vicinity more than four hundred acres, and ten years after from Alexander all that belonged to him.

William married Margaret, daughter of Andrew Wallace, and granddaughter of old Michael Woods. His home was on the place where James M. Bowen resided. He first built the mill on the place, which in early times went by the name of Ramsay's Mill. The old dwelling still stands near the head of the mill pond. He died in 1825. He had three sons, Andrew, John and William. In 1814 Andrew was living on a farm on the Staunton Road, adjoining the lands of G. W. Kinsolving, William Fretwell and John Dettor. His children were Thomas, Higginbotham, Margaret, William Albert, Mary J., and Andrew W. John married Mary, daughter of Samuel Black. His home was where Dr. John R. Baylor lived. His children were William, Jane, the wife of John G. Lobban, Catharine, Joseph T., Mary, the wife of James C. Rothwell, and Dorcas. William, son of William, succeeded to the home of his father, and died in 1832. His children were Jane, the wife of Jarrett Harris, William S., Margaret, the wife of Meredith Martin, and Mary, the wife of Jeremiah Wayland. All the descendants of these families, bearing the name, removed to different parts of the West.

RANDOLPH.

William Randolph, of Tuckahoe, was the first of the name to enter land within the present limits of Albemarle. In 1735 he was granted twenty-four hundred acres "on the north side of the Rivanna near the mountains, a little below Mountain Falls." On the organization of the county, he was appointed its Clerk. At his death his land passed to his son, Thomas Mann Randolph, of Tuckahoe. Neither William nor Thomas ever resided in the county, but soon after the marriage of Thomas Mann's son, bearing the same name, with Martha Jefferson, and his own second marriage with

Gabriella, daughter of John Harvie, the land was transferred by the father to the son. The latter then made Edgehill his home. He engaged with much activity in public affairs. He was appointed a magistrate in 1794, elected to Congress in 1801, and chosen Governor of Virginia in 1819. He displayed a lively zeal in promoting the interests of agriculture in the county. He died in 1828. His children were Ann, the wife of Charles L. Bankhead, Thomas J., Ellen, the wife of Joseph Coolidge, of Boston, Cornelia, Virginia, the wife of Nicholas P. Trist, Dr. Benjamin F., and George Wythe.

The home of Charles L. Bankhead was Carlton. He was twice married. His children by his first wife were John W., who recently died in Missouri, Ellen Monroe, the wife of John Coles Carter, and Thomas Mann, who settled in Arkansas. His second wife was Mary Carthrae, a granddaughter of General Samuel H. Lewis, of Rockingham. He died about 1833, leaving one son, Charles L., by the last marriage. The stalwart and venerable figure of Colonel Thomas J. is familiar to many still living. For many years he took a leading part in all matters pertaining to the welfare of the county. He was a magistrate, a member of the Legislature, a devoted member of the County Agricultural Society, and President of the Farmers' Bank. He married Jane, daughter of Governor W. C. Nicholas. Benjamin F. was a physician, and lived at the south end of Carter's Mountain. He married Sarah, daughter of Robert H. Carter. In addition to his professional labors, he was appointed a magistrate in 1846, and for several terms was a member of the State Senate. George W. was admitted to the Albemarle bar in 1840, and a few years after removed to Richmond. In the days of the Confederacy, he was its last Secretary of War.

Colonel Richard Randolph, of Henrico, owned land in Albemarle. In 1760 he obtained a grant of two hundred and forty acres on Moore's Creek. At some time he purchased twelve hundred acres adjoining the tract just mentioned from some one, perhaps from William Taylor, who seems to have entered it in 1737. To Dr. Thomas Walker, as trustee of the county, he sold a thousand acres of this land, on which in 1762, Charlottesville, the new court house, was established. He also entered nearly fifteen hundred acres in the southern part of the county on Green Creek. He probably never resided on this land, but managed it through the agency of overseers.

Governor Edmund Randolph was also a landholder in Albemarle. In 1786 he purchased from John Fry twenty-five hundred acres on Green Mountain, including the Viewmont estate. For some years he sought relaxation from his professional and official cares in looking after this property. In 1793 he petitioned for the right to erect a mill on Hardware, where Colonel Fry had had one before. He sold this land to William C. Carter in 1798.

In 1805 Dr. Thomas Eston Randolph brought from Johnson Rowe the land opposite Milton, on which is situated the estate of Glenmore. His wife was Jane Cary, sister of Governor Thomas Mann Randolph. He was appointed a magistrate of the county in 1807. In 1813 he sold Glenmore to Louis H. Girardin, the continuator of Burk's History of Virginia, and purchased a plantation further down the river on Carroll's Creek, called Ashton. This place he sold in 1826 to Joel W. Brown, and removed to Campbell County. His daughter, Elizabeth, became the wife of Francis Eppes Jr., the grandson of Mr. Jefferson.

In the decade of 1840, John T. Randolph came to the county from the Valley, and married Ann, daughter of William P. Farish. In 1862 he entered the Baptist ministry.

REA.

The name of Rea is found in the county at the time of its formation. In 1747 Fergus Rea bought a portion of the Chiswell patent on Rockfish. About the same time John Rea was the owner of land on the Rivanna near Martin King's Ford, the present Union Mills. Whether these persons were related to those hereafter mentioned, does not appear.

Andrew, Thomas and Samuel Rea were considerably interested in real estate during a period extending from 1744 to 1788. At the first of these dates, Andrew entered a small tract on the south side of the Rivanna, a short distance above the mouth of Ivy Creek, and at the time was the owner of land adjoining. Beyond doubt he gave name to the ford so called, though it should be written Rea, not Ray; in the patent it is written Reay. Thomas owned land on the head waters of Mechum's near Round Mountain, and subsequently purchased in the vicinity of Rea's Ford, and on Meadow Creek, not far from the old Poor House. Samuel also had a place near Rea's Ford, and in 1788 bought on Beaver Creek between Crozet and Whitehall. All three were married, the name of Andrew's wife being Mary, that of Thomas's Ursula, and that of Samuel's Jane, daughter of Daniel Maupin and his wife, Margaret Via. These persons, it is likely, were brothers. Samuel's children were Daniel, Andrew, Thomas, Robert, and Margaret, the wife of Ezekiel McCauley. Robert married Elizabeth, daughter of Daniel Maupin and his wife, Mary Elizabeth Dabney, lived in the Beaver Creek neighborhood, and died in 1831. In a report of Bernard Brown of persons listed to work on the roads near the foot of Buck's Elbow in 1792, Andrew and Thomas Rea are mentioned; and in an order of Court on the same subject made in 1823, occur the names of Robert, Thomas and Bland.

Thomas, the third son of Samuel, lived beneath Buck's Elbow, and died in 1850. His wife was Ann, daughter of Bland Ballard, and his children Daniel, Jane, the wife of Garland Maury, Bland, Jemima, the wife of Richard Beckett, Ann, the wife of John Bales, Samuel, and Margaret, the wife of George Wolfe. Bland married Sarah Alexander, and secondly Elizabeth, daughter of Colonel John Jones. In his youth he was associated with Benjamin Ficklin in the manufacture of tobacco, but afterwards settled as a farmer near the old homestead, and died in 1868. His children were John A., Joseph, William, James, Mary, the wife of Bernard Tilman, and Maria, the wife of Oscar Lipscomb.

RIVES.

In the latter part of the last century, Robert Rives, who married Margaret, daughter of Colonel William Cabell, transacted an extensive business at Warminster, Nelson County. In the enterprising spirit which inspired his undertakings, he established a branch house in Milton, soon after the founding of that town, under the firm of Brown, Rives & Co. The partners were James Brown, of Richmond, Robert Rives, and Robert Burton. He also became the owner of large and valuable tracts of land in Albemarle. For the Boiling Spring plantation, which he bought from John Patterson, of Baltimore, in 1818, he gave sixty thousand dollars, the largest sum perhaps ever paid for any farm in this region. His sons, William C., George, Henry, Robert and Alexander, all resided in Albemarle.

William C. in 1819 married Judith, daughter of Francis Walker, who inherited Castle Hill as her portion of her father's estate. About the same time he became a member of the Albemarle bar. His career in public is a matter of history. He did service in the Legislature, in the United States Senate, and as Minister to France. He was regarded as one of the most finished orators of his day. After his retirement he was occupied in writing a history of the Life and Times of James Madison. He died in 1868. George married Mary Eliza, daughter of Robert Carter. His home was at Sherwood, on the north side of the Hardware, below Carter's Bridge. He married a second time Maria, daughter of Professor George Tucker, and died in 1874. Henry received from his father a plantation on Green Mountain in 1827. Robert married Elizabeth Pennill, and resided at the old Nicholas place near Warren. He died in 1867. Alexander was admitted to the bar in 1829, and made his home for many years at Carleton, which he purchased in 1833 from the trustees of Charles L. Bankhead. He was a member of both houses of the Legislature, and of Congress, and soon after the war was appointed Judge of the United States Court for the western District of Virginia. He was twice married, first to Isabel Wydown, and secondly to Sarah Watson, of Louisa, and died in 1885.

Paulina, a daughter of Robert Rives, was the wife of Richard Pollard, who lived in the southern part of the county. Their children were Margaret, the wife of James P. Henderson, Virginia, Rosalie, James R., Lucy, Richard, Edward A., and Henry Rives. Edward and Henry were both journalists. Besides his editorial labors on the Richmond Examiner, Edward published a number of works, and died in Lynchburg in 1772. On account of an article which appeared in the Southern Opinion, of which he was one of the editors, Henry was shot by James Grant in Richmond in November 1868, and his remains were brought for interment in the family burying ground in Albemarle.

RODES.

The first of the Rodes name to settle in Albemarle was John, and his coming occurred in 1749. In that year he bought from James Armor four hundred acres on the north fork of Rockfish, and in the conveyance was described as of St. Martin's parish, Louisa. He also purchased land on Moorman's River. He died in 1775. His wife was Mary Crawford, and he left five daughters and four sons, David, Clifton, Charles and John.

David came to the county in 1756, and lived on the north side of Moorman's River. Besides managing his plantation, he conducted a store. He was appointed a magistrate, and served as Sheriff, probably in 1776 and 1777. He was twice married, first as is believed to Mary, daughter of Matthew Mills, and secondly to Susan, daughter of Nelson Anderson. He died in 1794, and his widow became the wife of James Kerr. His children, all of whom were born of the first marriage, were John, Matthew, Charles, Mary, the wife of Robert Douglass, Elizabeth. the wife of Horsley Goodman, Nancy, the wife of William Dulaney, Ann, the wife of James Ballard, Lucy, the wife of Joseph Twyman, Martha, the wife of Joel Yancey, and Mildred, the wife of William Walden. The Douglass, Yancey, Walden, and probably Dulaney, families removed to Kentucky. John died unmarried in 1823. Matthew succeeded to his father's place. He was appointed a magistrate in 1816. By becoming security, he was involved in financial difficulties, and his property was sold to pay his debts; it was however redeemed by his son David. He died in 1834. His wife was Nancy Blackwell. and his children David, Mary, Robert, Henrietta, the wife of Clement P. McKennie, Gilly, the wife of Robert Guy, Ann, the wife of Daniel Fishburne, Elizabeth, the second wife of Nathaniel Massie, Mildred and Judith. David about 1816 was deputy Clerk of the county, and afterwards removed to Lynchburg. In 1822 he married Martha, daughter of Joel Yancey, of Bedford. General Robert E. Rodes, of the Confederate army, who fell at Winchester in 1864, was his son. Robert succeeded to the homestead, was twice married, first to Margaret, daughter of Richard Duke, and secondly to Hardenia Williams, of Nelson, and died in 1874.

Clifton first lived at the foot of Buck's Elbow, on a place he bought in 1769 from Matthew Mullins, and afterward sold to Cornelius Maupin. In 1773 he purchased from William Lewis a plantation near Ivy Depot, which he made his home until 1788, when he sold it to George Nicholas, and not long after removed to Kentucky. He was a magistrate of the county, and served as Sheriff in 1783. His wife was Sarah Waller, and three of his children were married in Albemarle, John to Jean Stapleton, daughter of Thomas Burch, Dorothy to David Kerr, and Mary to Joseph Burch, brother of John's wife, and grandfather of Rev. Dr. J. J. Bullock, and the wife of Vice-President Breckinridge.

Charles resided where his father first bought, on the waters of Rockfish. The land now lies in Nelson County. From his family the Methodist Church in that vicinity is commonly spoken of as Rodes's Church. He died in 1798. Mrs. McClunn, who resides near Batesville, is his granddaughter, and William Rodes, who lives at Brooksville, his great grandson.

John lived on the south side of Moorman's River, and died in 1810. His wife was Sarah, daughter of Robert Harris, and his children Robert, Tyree, Clifton, John, Charles, Mary, Ann, the wife of John Garth, Henrietta, the wife of Rev. Bernis Brown, and Sarah, the wife first of William Davenport, and secondly of Micajah Woods. Robert was a Captain in the Revolutionary army, and made prisoner at the capture of Charleston, S. C. He married Eliza Dulaney, and removed to Madison County, Kentucky. Tyree emigrated to Giles County, Tennessee. Clifton lived near Ivy Depot on a farm, which was given him by his father, and which he sold in 1810 to George Pickett, of Richmond. In 1807 he was appointed a magistrate of the county. He married Elizabeth, daughter of John Jouett, and was the administrator of the Jouett estate. After the sale of his property he removed to Kentucky. John succeeded to the paternal estate south of Moorman's River. He was also appointed a magistrate in 1807, and served as Sheriff in 1832. He died in 1839. His wife was Francina, daughter of Bernard Brown, and his children Sidney, wife of Powhatan Jones, of Buckingham, Ryland, John D., William, Sarah, wife of Samuel C. Woods, who emigrated to Missouri, Tyree, Virginia, the wife of W. C. Smith, Jacintha, the wife of J. Smith, Frances, the wife of Garland Brown, and Lucy Ann, the wife of James Payne. Ryland married Sarah Woods, and lived and died in Nelson. John D. married Mrs. Ann Durrett Morris, and died without children. William married E. C. Yancey, of Rockingham, and lived on the old home place, which after his death in 1822 devolved on his sons Thomas and John William. Tyree removed to Tennessee.

ROGERS.

In 1748 John Rogers, of King William, obtained grants of four hundred acres on Naked Creek, and of four hundred on Buck Mountain Creek. At the same time his son George was granted four hundred acres on Piney Run. John further patented upwards of six hundred more on Naked Creek in 1761. Neither of them however ever lived in the county. John died about 1768.

Giles, a son of John, came to the county anterior to 1765. He purchased the interest of his brother George in 1775. His home was on the waters of Buck Mountain Creek. He died in 1794. His wife was Ann, daughter of John Lewis, of Spotsylvania, and his children Achilles, Parmenas, Ann, the wife of Robert Davis, Lucy, the wife of Jonathan Barksdale, Frances, the wife of Samuel Twyman, and Rachel. Achilles married his cousin Mary George, lived on Ivy Creek, near the crossing of the Whitehall Road, and died about 1820. Parmenas succeeded to the home of his father, was appointed a magistrate in 1807, became Sheriff in 1834, and died in 1836. He was twice married, first to a Miss Baber, and secondly to Elizabeth Ferguson. He had a large family, William, Joseph, Ralph, James B., George, Parmenas, Permelia, Giles, Frances, Orville, Catharine, Thomas, Jonathan, Elizabeth, the wife of Nathan Barksdale, and Ann. James B. was a physician, lived west of Earlysville, married Margaret, daughter of David Wood and Mildred Lewis, was the father of Martha, the wife of her cousin, Dr. Alfred Wood, and Dr. W. G. Rogers, of Charlottesville, and died in 1863. Frances is the sole member of this numerous household still living in Albemarle.

Byrd, another son of John, was for a time a resident of the county. He was twice married to sisters, Mary and Martha Trice, and had by his first two sons, John and Philip, and by the second one, George. He emigrated to Kentucky about the beginning of the century, and died shortly after. George accompanied his father to the West. Philip spent his youth in Albemarle, contracted roving habits, owned an interest at one time in the Red Sweet Springs, and died in Louisville, Ky. John, familiarly known in his day as Farmer John, passed his life on his plantation in the county, near Keswick Depot. He and his son-in-law, Richard Sampson, were regarded as occupying the front rank among the sagacious and successful planters of the State. About 1820 the Albemarle Agricultural Society awarded to John Rogers the premium for having the best tilled farm in the county. He died in 1838. His wife was Susan, daughter of Charles Goodman, and his children John, Thornton, Mary, the wife of Richard Sampson, and Janetta, the wife of J. Price Sampson. John married Agnes, sister of Stephen Sampson, succeeded to the homestead, and died in 1841. Thornton resided at Keswick, a part of his father's place, on which for some years he conducted a classical school, and which gave name of the neighboring Depot. A few years before his death he entered the Presbyterian ministry. His wife was Margaret, daughter of Andrew Hart, and his children Adeline, the wife of Rev. E. L. Cochran, Susan, the wife of

Rev. Joseph Baxter, Dr. A. Hamilton Oscar, William A., Julia, the wife of Keating Nelson, Celia, the wife of Rev. James M. Wilson, and John. He departed this life in 1834.

In the decade of 1790, a John Rogers, whose wife's name was Mary, came from Stafford, and bought land in the neighborhood of Earlysville; nothing further is known of him. Some years later another John Rogers came from Lancaster County, and lived on the east side of the South West Mountain. To distinguish him from Farmer John, the syllabel Lan. was affixed to his name, while to Farmer John's was appended the letter M. He died in 1851.

SAMPSON.

Richard Sampson was the descendant of a family that settled in Goochland, in the early part of the eighteenth century. He became a citizen of Albemarle in 1804. In that year he purchased from Thomas M. Randolph, trustee of Dr. William Bache, Benjamin Franklin's grandson, the plantation Franklin, containing six hundred acres. In 1812 he bought from Francis Gilmer the Pen Park place, containing four hundred. The latter he sold to John H. Craven in 1819, and the former to John H. Craven and N. H. Lewis in 1821. He returned to Goochland, and resided near Dover Mills until his death in 1862, at the great age of ninety-two. His wife was Mary, daughter of John Rogers. Rev. Francis S. Sampson, who studied at Keswick with his uncle Thornton Rogers, was one of the early students of the University, and was Professor in the Union Theological Seminary, was his son.

John Price Sampson, Richard's brother, married Janetta, another daughter of John Rogers. He lived for some years on part of the Rogers place near Keswick, and for a time kept a public house at Everettsville. In 1829 he bought Tufton from the Jefferson estate, which he sold in 1833 to Thomas Macon, of New Kent. The next year he purchased Colle from Eli Alexander. Not long after he removed to the old Meredith place near New Glasgow, Amherst, where he died in 1842. His children were Edward, Thornton, Margaret, the wife of Micajah Clark, Elizabeth, and the wife of a Mantaprise.

Stephen Sampson was a son of Robert, brother of Richard and Price. He was twice married, first to Ann, daughter of Reuben Lindsay, and secondly to Sarah, daughter of Joseph Campbell. His home was on the old Campbell place on Mechunk, where he died a few years ago.

SCHENK.

Cornelius Schenk was one of the early merchants of Charlottesville. Coming to the place soon after the Revolutionary War, he carried on the business of general merchandising in partnership with Peter Lott, until the death of Lott in 1803. He was also a partner with Isaac Miller and Daniel Culp in other enterprises, particularly in establishing a tannery in the southern part of the town, which in later years was owned by John Pollock. He first lived not far from Ira Garrett's old home, but in 1792 bought the lots just west of the Episcopal Church, and there resided until his death in 1810. He purchased from the Woodsons the land north and northwest of the town, and from the fact that a tributary of Meadow Creek flowed through it, arose the name of Schenk's Branch, which remains to this day. For many years he was active in performing useful public services in town and county, but for some reason he declined in standing and influence, pecuniary troubles overtook him, and all his property was sold to clear off the liens with which it was encumbered.

His wife was Rebecca Winston, of Hanover, who survived him a little more than a year, and his children Peter Lott, Eleanor Winston, Mary, John W., and Richard F. Dr. Frank Carr, whose mother was a Winston, became the guardian of the younger children. Peter Lott lived on the northwest corner of Market and Fourth Streets, and owned the square on which the house stood; and though he died in 1815, his interests in the property was not finally disposed of, till commissioners appointed by the Court conveyed it to Dr. Hardin Massie and John Cochran in 1828. The others members of the family removed from the county, and all trace of them seems lost to the memory of the oldest inhabitants.

SCOTT.

Edward Scott in 1732 obtained a patent for five hundred and fifty acres "on the north side of the Fluvanna, at a place called Totier." When the county was organized in 1745, Samuel Scott gave bond for erecting the public buildings on the land of his brother Daniel. These were both sons of Edward, who it is likely was dead at the latter date, as the County Court, at its first adjournment, appointed its next meeting to be held at Mrs. Scott's plantation. The same date John Scott, who is subsequently mentioned as of Cumberland County, patented four hundred acres on Totier Creek. Whether he was also a son of Edward, does not appear, but the strong probability is that he was. Ann Scott, the wife of George Nicholas, of Dinwiddie, a brother, of Robert Carter Nicholas, was also a member of this family. Samuel, the contractor, died in 1801.

In 1764 John Scott purchased seventeen hundred and fifty acres on Totier from David Meriwether, the patentee. His wife was Margaret, daughter of Colonel Joshua Fry. He died in 1798, and his wife in 1811. His children were Edward, John, Charles Alexander, Daniel and Frances. Daniel lived on his farm on Green Mountain, and died in 1851. He never married, and for want of other objects of affection, he surrounded himself with great numbers of wild geese. His fascination over these winged coursers of the air was so remarkable that in their flights to and fro they made his plantation their stopping place. and some that remained the year round, he carefully nurtured and jealously protected. John married Elizabeth, daughter of John Bolling, of North Garden, and died before his father, leaving a son John. This John inherited the land about Scottsville, and was the founder of that town in 1818. He married Susan B. Woods, and his children were Elizabeth, Pocahontas and Mary.

Charles Alexander married Elizabeth, daughter of John Hudson. He was appointed a magistrate of the county in 1801. His children were Edward, William, Samuel, Charles A., John, and Martha, the wife of William M. Woods. Edward settled in Powhatan, and married Elizabeth and Mary, daughters of his cousin John. William married Elizabeth Powell, of Amherst, and lived in Buckingham. Samuel became a physician, practised in Albemarle and Amherst, and recently died near Howardsville at an advanced age. His wife was Ann, daughter of Landon Davies, of Amherst, and his children Elizabeth, the wife of Charles Scott, son of her uncle William, and Landon, who married Louisa, daughter of Dr. Charles D. Everett. Charles A. purchased from his cousin John the plantation on James River, on the upper side of Totier, which in 1835 he sold to Dr. John W. Gantt. He subsequently lived on the farm of his uncle Daniel on Green Mountain. He was twice married, first to Ann ———, and secondly to Pocahontas, daughter of his cousin John. His house was burned to the ground by the soldiers of Sheridan in the spring of 1865; and being out on his farm at the time, and suddenly hearing of the calamity, he fell dead on the spot. His brother John made his home in Fluvanna.

SHELTON.

Samuel Shelton was settled in the county from the beginning. In 1745 he purchased five hundred and fifty acres of the twelve hundred acre tract on James River, granted to Thomas Goolsby in 1732; the endorsement on the conveyance of this land made in 1788, expressly mentions the destruction of the records by the British in 1781. Samuel Shelton died in 1793. His wife's name was Judith, and his children were Clough, Joseph, Samuel, David, Elizabeth, the wife of John Tindall, and the wife of John Lewis, who lived near Scott's Landing. Clough was a Captain in the Revolutionary army, and was taken prisoner at the surrender of Charleston. He died about 1833. His children were Nelson, Maria, the wife of Robert Anderson, Cicely, the wife of a Walker, and William A. Samuel in the early part of the century was engaged in business in Warren. In partnership with William Walker and John Staples, under the style of Samuel Shelton & Co., he conducted a large mill and distillery at that place. In 1810 he purchased from Governor W. C. Nicholas the Boiling Spring plantation, which he soon after sold to John Patterson, the Governor's son-in-law. He died in 1826.

A William Shelton, who died in 1789, lived on Mechum's River, not far from the present Depot. His wife's name was Elizabeth, and his children were John, Gideon and Thomas. In 1794 Thomas, his wife Mary, and his mother Elizabeth, conveyed what seemed to be Thomas's portion of the estate to Tarleton Woodson, and likely removed from the county. The relation of this family with others of the name cannot be ascertained.

In 1749 William Shelton, of St. David's parish, King and Queen, purchased land on Byrd Creek, in what is now Fluvanna County. His wife's name was Patience, and he had a daughter Sarah, who was the wife of Augustine Shepherd. It is thought he was also the father of Henry and William. Henry lived in the northeast part of the county, on the Barboursville Road. He died in 1799. It is said his wife was a Long, a sister of the wife of Thomas Garth Sr., and his children were Susan, the wife of Thomas Smith, Ann, the wife of Jacob Powers, who removed to Harrison County, Kentucky, Jane, the wife of Jeremiah White, Martha, the wife of Samuel Mansfield, Mourning, the wife of John White, Ann. the wife of Achilles Barksdale, Thomas L., Mildred, William and Austin. Austin settled on Mechum's River, above the Depot, and died unmarried in 1806. He was succeeded by his brother Thomas L., who also purchased in 1812 from the trustees of Menan Mills his mill, and the tract belonging to it, which he bought in 1789 from John Black. Thomas L. died in 1859. He married Susan, daughter of James Ballard, and his children were Martha, the wife of Martin Baker, Stapleton, Austin G., Dr. Thomas W., who recently died in Augusta County, Mary, the wife of David Jefferies, James H., and Lucy, the wife of George C. Omohundro.

William, son of William, owned land on both sides of Mechums' near the Depot. His home was on the north side of the Staunton Road, on the place now owned by Charles H. Price. He died in 1815. He was twice married, first to

Lucy, daughter of Robert Harris, and secondly to Sarah ———. His children were William Harris, Mourning, the wife of Archibald Woods, Elizabeth, the wife of Richard Mobbery, Dabney, Sarah, Lucy, the wife of Elliott Brown, Agnes, Weatherston and Thomas. The first three emigrated to Kentucky. Dabney and Thomas, who sold their part of the estate in 1817 to Francis McGee, were living at the time in Augusta County. Weatherston, who married Elizabeth, daughter of Richard Harrison, sold the same year to Benjamin Hardin the interests of himself and his deceased sisters, Sarah and Agnes, and removed to Mason County, Virginia.

SIMMS.

William Simms lived in the northeast part of the county, on the waters of Priddy's Creek and Blue Run. The first mention of his name occurs in 1779, when he bought land in that neighborhood from Josiah Bush. He was Captain of a militia company in the war of the Revolution. He built one of the first mills on Priddy's Creeks, and for many years it was a noted point in that vicinity. He died in 1797. He and his wife Agatha had nine daughters and two sons, Mary, the wife of John During, Elizabeth, the wife of John McCann, Lucy, the wife of John Dalton, Joanna, the wife of James Ownsley, Ann, the wife of Samuel Brockman, Nancy, the wife of Ambrose Brockman, Agatha, the wife of William Catterton, Frances, the wife of Richard Flint, Rosamond, the wife of Joseph Williams, Richard and John. James Simms, who lived in the same section, was probably a brother of William, certainly the guardian of his younger children. He was twice married, first to Mildred, daughter of Richard Durrett, and secondly to Lucy, daughter of James Early. He had two sons, Richard D. and Isaac.

Richard D. married Elizabeth, daughter of David Clarkson and his children were Eliza, the wife of Edward Wingfield, Jane, the wife of Tandy Brockman, Cornelia the wife of Rev. Robert Watts, and Lucy Ann, the wife of James D. Watts, and William J. His home was near the mouth of Priddy's Creek, and he died in 1862. Isaac lived in the Buck

Mountain District, and died in 1836. His wife was Nancy Catterton, and his children Mary, the wife of William Blackwell, Eliza, the wife of Logan Maupin, Permelia, the wife of Samuel Crawford, of the Valley, Agnes, the wife of John D. Carr, Julia and Richard D.

John Sims lived in the Buck Mountain neighborhood, and died in 1798. His wife's name was Mary, and his children John, Francis, Nathaniel, and a daughter, who was the wife of Ison Walton.

SMITH.

Joseph Smith in 1734 joined with Edwin Hickman, Thomas Graves, and Jonathan Clark in entering thirty-two hundred and seventy-seven acres on the north side of the Rivanna, where it was crossed by the South West Mountain. In the partition of the tract, the portion of Smith coincided with the Pantops plantation. He devised it to his sons, John, Larkin, Philip and Thomas. In the interval from 1746 to 1765, they sold their shares, and eventually they all came in to the possession of Mr. Jefferson. What became of the brothers, is not known. It is probable Larkin died in the county in 1763, and Larkin Smith, doubtless a son of his, or of one of his brothers, was a Captain in the Fourth Dragoons in the Revolutionary army.

About 1766, William, John and Charles Smith, of Hanover, purchased land on the head waters of Mechum's and Rockfish. They were probably brothers. Charles settled on Taylor's Creek, and William and John on Whitesides, where they both bought from Morans, William from Nicholas, and John from John Moran. Charles died in 1771, William in 1801, and John in 1808. The name of John's wife was Elizabeth, and his children were Thomas, William, Mary, the wife of Francis Montgomery, Nancy, the wife of David Burgher, Joel, Martha, Elizabeth, the wife of Robert Page, and Charles. Joel married Martha, daughter of Charles Patrick, and his children were Mary, the wife of John Massie, John P., Elizabeth, the wife of John Wallace, Harriet and Thomas J. All this family except Mrs. Wallace and her husband, removed to Kentucky. Charles lived at the foot of Armor's Mountain on the border of Nelson, and died in 1842. His wife was Mary Bailey, and his children William, Joel, Robert P., Frances and Jane.

In 1769 Thomas Smith, purchased a part of the Chiswell patent on the head waters of Mechum's. He died in 1783. His children were Thomas, John, Ann, the wife of William Grayson, Sarah, the wife of Nathan Crawford, Lawrence, Mary, the wife of (David?) Buster, Susan, and another daughter (Ursula?), the wife of a Ray. His son Thomas died in 1791. His wife's name was Susan, and his children were Nancy, the wife of James Lobban, Bolling, who removed to Lincoln County, Missouri, Elizabeth, the wife of Nicholas Merritt, Mary, Martha and Sebanah. The children of Nicholas and Elizabeth Merritt were Rhoda, the wife of Thomas Grayson, Thomas, Susan, the wife of Robert Haislip, Sarah, the wife of Andrew Black, Markwood, Rosanna, the wife of James Black, James and Retta, the wife of Jeremiah Dollins.

SOUTHALL.

Valentine Wood Southall, during a long and busy career, was one of the most prominent men of the county. He was the son of Stephen Southall and Martha Wood, and the grandson of Valentine Wood and Lucy Henry, a sister of the renowned orator. In early life he was engaged in business in Washington City, but afterwards studied law, and was admitted to the Albemarle bar in 1813. By his thoroughness and impressive elocution he soon attained a place in the front ranks of the profession. In 1829 he was appointed Commonwealth's Attorney, and held the office till it became elective under the Constitution of 1850. He was a member of the Convention that formed that Constitution, and also of that of 1861, acting as the President of the latter during the sickness of its presiding officer. Though devoted to his legal duties, he took an active part in politics, and for a number of terms was a member of the House of Delegates, and also its Speaker. He died suddenly in the latter part of 1861. He was twice married, first to Mary, the daughter of Alexander Garrett, and secondly to Martha, daughter of

James P. Cocke. The home of his early married life was on the northwest corner of High and Fourth Street, the present residence of Dr. W. G. Rogers, but about 1829 he removed to the brick mansion near the corner of Jefferson and Second, which he built.

SOWELL.

Thomas Sowell made one of the earliest entries of land within the bounds of Albemarle. In 1734 he obtained a grant of five hundred and fifty acres west of the southern end of Carter's Mountain. His name still distinguishes Sowell's Branch, a stream which passes through the land into the north fork of Hardware. He died in 1763. His wife's name was Martha, and his children were John, William, Joseph and Thomas. Thomas died unmarried three years after his father. The name of John's wife was also Martha, and his children were Thomas, Benjamin, Edmund, Elijah, Elisha, and Keziah, the wife of William Perry. Elisha Sowell married Elizabeth Gilliam in 1808. In 1834 Lewis and Nimrod, sons of one of the brothers above mentioned, purchased from William Garland the lot on University Street east of R. F. Harris's Warehouse, where for many years they conducted the wheelwright business. Lewis married Mary Ann, daughter of William Dunkum, and his children were William, Mary, the wife of Albert Gentry, and Benjamin. Pleasant, another descendant of the family, married Sarah, daughter of Edward Garland.

STAPLES.

Thomas Staples during 1783 and the next year took out patents for more than eight hundred acres on Hudson and Totier Creeks, and for one hundred and fifty in North Garden. He purchased more than four hundred more on Totier. Before the close of the century he sold most of this land to Samuel Dyer, much of it lying contiguous to Glendower. It is believed his wife was Ellinda, daughter of Castleton Harper, and his children Thomas, Beverly, and Sarah, the wife of Littlebury Moon. Thomas was for years a leading merchant in Scottsville, and died in 1868. His wife was Ann, daughter of William Tompkins, and his children Sarah, the wife of D. P. Powers, Martha, the wife of John S. Martin, Olivia, the wife of ——— Spencer, Phaniel, the wife of W. D. Davis, Susan, Catharine, Marietta, Silas, William T., and John. Beverly died in 1865. He married Judith White, and his children were William G., Elmira, Maria, the wife of ——— Chambers, Ann, the wife of John Tyler, Minerva, the wife of Alfred Flippin, Addison, and Emily, the wife of Madison Porter.

STEVENSON.

Andrew Stevenson, born in Culpeper in 1785, was the son of Rev. James Stevenson, rector of St. Marks, Culpeper, and St. George's, Fredericksburg, and his wife, Frances A. Littlepage. He was a lawyer by profession, member of Congress, Minister to England, and Rector of the University of Virginia. In 1816 he married Sarah, daughter of John Coles. The next year he purchased upwards of seven hundred acres on Totier Creek from William Watkins, a descendant of William Battersby, one of the original lawyers of the county. A stream passing through the place went for many years by the name of Stevenson's Creek. This plantation he sold to Tucker Coles in 1833, and in 1836 he bought Blenheim, the old seat of the Carters, which he made his home till his death in 1857. He was buried in the Coles cemetery at Enniscorthy. He married a second time, and his widow after his death resided in Washington City. His son, John W., was admitted to the Albemarle bar in 1834, settled in Covington, Ky., was elected Governor of that State in 1867, and represented it in the United States Senate in 1871.

STOCKTON.

Among the earliest settlers in the western part of the county, who came as is said under the leadership of Michael Woods, was a family named Stockton. Though their name has entirely disappeared, they have in a number of ways left their mark behind. They consisted of several branches. They erected perhaps the first mill in that section of the county. The north fork of Mechum's River still bears the name of Stockton's Creek, the south fork in early times was called Stockton's Mill Creek, and the first name by which Israel's

Gap was known was Stockton's Thoroughfare. The famous abbreviation of D. S. is also ascribed to the head of the family. One story recites that Michael Woods and Davis Stockton landed at Williamsburg, and came to the wilds of Goochland together, that arriving at D. S., they advanced in different directions, Woods continuing straight forward to Woods's Gap, and Stockton bearing to the left along the foot of the mountains towards Batesville, and that as a memorial of the place were they separated, Stockton carved his initials on a tree. While their landing on the eastern shores of Virginia is contrary to all the best established traditions, there may be truth in the rest of the narration. Both were patentees of land, and they may have gone from the foot of the Ridge to Williamsburg on business; on their return, the separation would naturally have taken place at the point mentioned, as Woods's home lay at the mouth of Wood's Gap, and the Stocktons were settled along Mechum's River, the south fork as well as the north.

As already intimated, the head of the family was Davis Stockton. His first entry of four hundred acres on Ivy Creek was made in 1739, and in 1741 he patented eight hundred more on both forks of Mechum's. Altogether the family connection obtained grants of nearly four thousand acres in that section. Davis died in 1760. His widow Martha seems afterwards to have been married to Samuel Arnold, who lived on Ivy Creek. Davis's children were Richard, Samuel, William and Thomas. Samuel and William had a mill on the south fork of Mechum's, not far from Batesville, the same no doubt their father built, which in 1767 they sold to James Garland. Prior to 1780 Samuel emigrated to Rutherford County, North Carolina, and was probably accompanied by William. Richard lived in the fork of Mechum's, near the old Black place; in fact, that place was a part of his land, he and his wife Agnes having sold four hundred acres to Rev. Samuel Black in 1751. He died in 1775, leaving five sons, Richard, Thomas, John, Robert and Davis. The name of John appears among the subscribers to the Albemarle Declaration of Independence, made in 1779.

Previous to 1791 Richard and Robert removed to Henry County. Richard became Clerk of the Strawberry Baptist Association, and Robert entered the Baptist ministry, and subsequently went to Kentucky, where he died about 1837. Thomas, probably the son of Davis, died in 1783. He and his wife Rachel had six sons and two daughters, some of whom were still in the county as late as 1805.

In later years John N. C. Stockton came to the county from Pennsylvania. He was a proprietor of the Stage lines running in Virginia, and made Charlottesville his headquarters. He became a large landholder in the neighborhood. In 1830 he purchased from Andrew Leitch the old Stage lot on the corner of Market and Seventh Streets, in 1832 Carrsbrook from Alexander Garrett, as executor of Dabney Minor, and in 1835 Retreat from Jonathan B. Carr. He was also the owner of Camp Holly, on the Barboursville Road. He married Emily Bernard, a niece of William D. Fitch. In 1837 he came to an untimely end, by drowning in Mobile Bay. William P. Farish became the administrator of his estate, and ultimately one of his successors in the ownership of the Stage lines. William Stockton, brother of John N. C., married Sarah, daughter of Gideon Strange and Mildred Magruder, and emigrated to Florida.

SUDDARTH.

William and James Suddarth were early settlers in the county. The were undoubtedly brothers. They and their descendants were located on the south fork of Hardware, between the Cross Roads and Covesville. Previous to 1750, William bought from Abraham Venable three hundred acres of a tract of fifteen hundred which Venable had patented in 1735 in that vicinity. In the year first named, William exchanged two hundred acres with James, for the same quantity which James had purchased from the same tract. William seems to have died before 1768, as at that time Lawrence Suddarth, apparently his son and representative, conveyed to James the other hundred acres of William's purchase from Venable. Lawrence was a resident of Amherst, but subsequently settled in Albemarle, on Green Creek. His wife's name was Martha, and he died in 1815.

James died in 1800, and left at least three children, William, James, and Mildred, the wife of John Turner. These brothers lived near where the present Lynchburg Road crosses the south fork of Hardware, a mill known as Suddarth's Mill having conspicuously marked that locality for many years. In 1830 William was assessed with more than thirteen hundred acres of land. He died in 1832. It is said his wife was Martha Sumter, and his children were William H., James. Sarah, the wife of Robert Porterfield, Martha, the wife of Richard Littleford, Richard P., who married Martha Morris, and whose daughter Sarah was the wife of Henry Darrow, Nancy, the wife of George Paris, Elizabeth, the wife of John W. Dettor, and Mildred, the wife of William Page. His brother James married Jane, daughter of John Randolph. He died about 1850, and his children were James, Randolph, William T., Mary, the wife of David Hicks, Patience, the wife of Rice Oaks, Thomas, John and Benjamin.

SUMTER.

The first mention of the Sumter name occurs in 1763, when William Sumter bought from Thomas Land one hundred acres on Priddy's Creek, which had been patented in 1739 by Major John Henry, the orator's father, and which Land had purchased from his son, William Henry. Sumter's next purchase was made in 1770 on the north fork of the Rivanna, at the south end of Piney Mountain. This land was conveyed by John Poindexter, who obtained the grant of it in 1738, and from whom the mountain was originally called Poindexter's Mountain, and the creek running through it (no doubt Herring's Creek at present), Poindexter's Creek. William Sumter continued his purchases, till he owned between six and seven hundred acres. In 1776 he and his wife Judith sold off all his property. One of the sales was made to John Sumter, probably a brother, and the land John then bought he and his wife Catharine conveyed in 1779 to Charles Bush. In all probability they sold to go elsewhere.

No intimation appears as to the place of their removal; but as their kinsman, General Thomas Sumter, had already attained a distinguished name, it is almost certain they emigrated to South Carolina, the theatre of his gallant achievements. A well founded tradition exists, that General Sumter was born in Albemarle, and in the section referred to as the home of William and John. It rests particularly on the testimony of Dr. Charles Brown, who was born just after the Revolution. The Doctor was familiarly acquainted with a sister of the General, Mrs. Martha Suddarth, the wife of William Suddarth, who lived and died in the county. Mrs. Suddarth was well known in her day throughout the community, because of her intelligence and skill as a nurse. Mr. Jefferson, in one of his letters to his daughter, Mrs. Eppes, when in declining health, recommended her to seek the advice of Mrs. Suddarth, as one whose experience and judgment were worthy of the highest regard. It may be that she and her eminent brother were children of one of the couples mentioned above.

SUTHERLAND.

In 1774 Joseph Sutherland bought from Gamaliel Bailey nearly three hundred acres a short distance east of the Miller School. This place he sold three years after to Thomas Harlow, and purchased in the South Garden, near the gorge of the south fork of Hardware. He died in 1801. His first wife's name was Judith, and he married again Elizabeth, daughter of William Grayson. His children were Joseph, and Susan, the wife of Christopher Myers. Joseph married Elizabeth, daughter of Edward Garland, and in 1817 bought from him part of the old James Garland place about two miles southwest of the Cross Roads, which in those days went by the name of the Head of the Creek plantation. He died in 1818, leaving four sons, Clifton G., Joseph, William and Edward. Clifton married Mary Ammonett, lived at the Cross Roads, had a large family, and died in 1868. Joseph in 1837 purchased from Dr. John W. Gantt the place adjoining the Cross Roads on the southwest, where he lived until his death in 1866. His wife was Elizabeth, daughter of Richard G. Anderson. William married Lucy, daughter of Roland H. Bates, and lived on the Head of the Creek Plantation, where he recently departed this life. Edward lived on the Batesville Road, west of the Cross Roads. He married Ann Shepherd, who after his death became the wife of John P. Mann.

TAYLOR.

William Taylor in 1737 obtained a grant of twelve hundred acres on Moore's Creek, which is believed to include the land whereon Charlottesville is situated. He also patented the same quantity on the north fork of Hardware in 1741. It must have been a part of this tract, nearly eight hundred acres, which James Taylor, most probably a son, sold to James Buchanan in 1765. The same year James sold to James Buchanan part of a patent of his own, which was located on Hardware and Murphy's Run in 1750, and on which he was then living. Nothing further is known of these persons, except that Nancy, a daughter, of James, was the wife of John Eaves.

During 1760 and some years after, Benjamin Taylor became the owner by patent and purchase of more than seven hundred acres on Broadaxe Creek and Mechum's River. Part of this land he sold in 1772 to Micajah Chiles. He died in 1809. His wife's name was Mary, and he had three sons, Fleming, Winston and Benjamin. In 1811 the widow, being about to remove to Georgia, appointed George M. Woods her attorney, to transact any of her unfinished business. Her sons may probably have preceded her to that State; but though none of the family remain, they have left behind a memorial of their name in the passage through the mountain near their old place, which is still known as Taylor's Gap.

At a much later period, J. C. R. Taylor came to the county from Jefferson. He married Martha J., daughter of Colonel T. J. Randolph, and resided at Lego. He died in 1875.

TERRELL.

In 1734 Joel Terrell, of Hanover, and his brother-in-law, David Lewis, patented three thousand acres north and west of what is now called Lewis's Mountain, sixteen hundred belonging to Joel. He died about 1758, devising the land to his sons, William and Joel, though all eventually came into the possession of Joel. Joel became a dealer in real estate in many parts of the county, and owned considerable property in and around Charlottesville. His home was in town, on the corner of Market and Fifth Streets, where the City Hall now stands, and where he resided till his death in 1773. He married his cousin Ann, daughter of David Lewis. After his decease she became the wife of Stephen Willis, and removed to Rutherford County, North Carolina, where she died at the great age of more than a hundred years. Her husband's large estate was sold off in subsequent years by his executors, herself, William Terrell, and James Kerr.

Henry Terrell, of Caroline, in 1737 entered seventeen hundred and fifty acres on the south fork of Mechum's and Whitesides Creek, including the site of Batesville. He died prior to 1764. The land descended to his sons, Henry and Thomas. In the year last named, Henry, who lived in Caroline, sold to Solomon Israel twenty acres near Stockton's Thoroughfare, which in time took the name of the new purchaser as Israel's Gap. The next year he closed out the remainder of his share to John Jones, of Louisa. Thomas and his wife Rebecca sold his share in 1768 to Reuben Terrel, of Orange. In 1770 Robert Terrell, of Orange, bought from Thomas McCulloch upwards of three hundred acres in the same vicinity, which in 1783 he and his wife Mary Lacy sold to Marshall Durrett. Reuben died in 1776. His wife's name was Mildred, and his children were Mary, the wife of John Wood, son of Isaac, and John. His widow became the wife of Jesse Wood, to whom the step-son sold the larger part of his father's land. John Terrell married Lucy, daughter of David Burgher, and died without children in 1857. By his will he manumitted his negroes, and directed his executors, Reuben Wood, his nephew (to whom he devised his land) and John B. Spiece, to send them to Liberia.

John Terrell, who it is believed was a brother of Reuben

and Robert, and a son of Edmund Terrell and Margaret Willis, purchased in 1799 from Robert Carter more than twelve hundred acres in the Biscuit Run Valley. In the first years of the century, Terrell's Shop was a familiar waymark on the road from Charlottesville to Carter's Bridge. He and his wife Rebecca sold his property in Albemarle, and about 1806 removed to Greenup County, Kentucky. His mother died in 1812, and his sisters were Nancy, the wife of Thomas Henderson, Jane, the wife of Joseph Bishop, Frances, the wife of Charles C. Lacy, and Lucy.

Chiles Terrell lived at Music Hall, on the east side of the South West Mountain. In 1783 he married Margaret Douglass, the widow of Nicholas Meriwether. During the war of the Revolution, he was regarded as leaning strongly to the Tory side. In 1777 the County Court refused to allow a deed to him from David Meriwether to go to record, because of their suspicion that he had not taken the oath of allegiance to the States. He was the acting executor of Micajah Chiles. His son, James Hunter Terrell, who succeeded him at Music Hall, married Susan Vibert, and died in 1856.

The family of Captain William Terrell, of Louisa, resided in Albemarle. In 1825 his widow, Martha, purchased from Dr. Frank Carr Hors de Ville, the place near the Chesapeake and Ohio Depot now occupied by James D. Goodman. She died in 1830. Her children were Richmond, the father of Mrs. William W. Minor, Eleanor, Rebecca, Nancy, Emily, the wife of Daniel F. Carr, Lucy, Mary, Martha, the wife of Samuel H. Royall, Dorothy and Malvina. These ladies, because of their eminent culture and accomplishments, were known in the community as the Nine Muses.

Joel Terrell, who was the son of Christopher, came to the county about 1828. In that year he bought from Dabney Minor's executors a part of the Carrsbrook estate, where he lived until his death in 1851. He married Lucy Marshall, a sister of the wives of Nimrod Bramham and John R. Jones. His children were Sarah, the wife of Nathan C. Goodman, Agnes, the wife of Charles Wright, Eliza, the wife of Stapleton C. Shelton, Mary, the third wife of Fontaine D.

Brockman, Albert, George, Lucy, Almira, Clementia, the wife of Nelson Elsom, Virginia, the wife of Peter V. Phillips, Harriet, and Hardenia, the wife of William Beck.

THOMAS.

Michael Thomas in 1745 and 1748 patented six hundred acres on Hog Creek and Rockfish River. He seems however to have resided on James River. At the resumption of the records in 1783, he was active as a magistrate of the county, and was appointed Sheriff in 1789. He was greatly harrassed by suits brought against him as incumbent of that office, owing to the maladministration of his deputies, Edward Moore and Menan Mills. Perhaps these annoyances incited the old gentleman to seek the balmy consolations of matrimony a second time. At all events he entered into those bonds with Elizabeth Staton in 1792; and in writing to the Clerk for a license, he stated that he was unable to visit the county seat himself, but sent his son Ralph, and his grandson John Carroll, to act in his behalf. He died in 1802. His children appear to have been Michael, Joseph, Jesse, Ralph, Edward, James, and a daughter, who was the wife of a Carroll. The future of the family is unkown, except that Joseph died in 1797, and Michael in 1826.

John Thomas came to the county from Amherst. He was twice married, first to Frances, daughter of the elder John Henderson, and secondly to Frances, daughter of Charles Lewis Jr., of Buck Island. He lived for a time on a tract of land which he received from his second father-in-law on Ivy Creek, and which he sold in 1788 to Robert Draffen, and afterwards on the land of his son Charles L. Thomas near Red Hill. He died in 1847. His children by the first marriage were Warner, Norborne K., James, Elizabeth, the wife of a Wood, and Lucy, the wife of James Lewis; those by the second were Charles L., John L., Virginia, and Margaret, the wife first of Julius Clarkson, and secondly of Robert Cashmere. In the early part of the century, Warner, Norborne and John L. did business in Richmond as commission merchants, under the firm of N. K. Thomas & Co.

About 1815 they purchased the Cole land on the north side of Tom's Mountain, a thousand and twenty-eight acres; three hundred they sold to Stephen Moore, and the remainder was assigned to John L. Thomas, when he retired from the firm in 1818.

By the will of his uncle Isham Lewis, who died in 1790, Charles L. Thomas became the owner of more than eighteen hundred acres on the north fork of Hardware, where Red Hill Depot now stands. His home was where the family of John B. Townley now reside. Before his death in 1815, he leased the eastern part of the place to his brother John L. during the lives of his parents, for their support, and that of his sisters. His wife was Margaret, the youngest daughter of Nicholas Lewis, of the Farm, and his children were Mary Walker, the wife of Alexander Clayton, Nicholas L., Charles, Robert Warner, Frances Elizabeth, the wife first of Dr. Charles H. Meriwether, and secondly of James Hart, and John J. The western part of the place was divided among the children, who in 1830, and some years following, sold their portions, and emigrated to Montgomery County, Tennessee. John L. passed his life on the place leased him by his brother. He was appointed a magistrate in 1838, and died unmarried in 1846.

THOMPSON.

Joseph Thompson was one of the original magistrates of the county, and its first Sheriff. He resided in the bounds of Fluvanna, not far from Palmyra. He died in 1765. His wife's name was Sarah, and his children were Roger, George, Leonard, John, and Frances, the wife of a Woodson. The family was well represented in the Revolutionary army. Roger was a Captain in the Second Virginia, and John, First Lieutenant in Seventh, while George and Leonard were Lieutenants in the State militia. In 1737 Roger Thompson Jr., patented nearly three hundred acres on Foster's Creek in the Stony Point neighborhood; it is probable he was the same as Captain Roger. The same year John Thompson entered more than five hundred acres on the south fork of the

Rivanna, and in 1759 one hundred and twenty more a short distance above on Moorman's. It is believed he was the brother of Roger, and the father, or more likely the grandfather, of Roger and Nathaniel, who lived on or near the land which he entered. The last mentioned Roger died in 1838. He married —————— and his children were William, Nicholas, Nathaniel, Mary, the wife of Richard Franklin, Elizabeth, the wife of a Ballard, Sarah, the wife of Samuel Ward, and Susan, the wife of William Ward. His son Nathaniel married Temperance, daughter of William Crenshaw, gave the land on which Wesley Chapel was built, and died about 1835. Nathaniel Sr. married Lucy, daughter of Bernard Brown, and died in 1874. His children were Edmund I., who died in 1868, Bernard, and Mary, the wife of James E. Chapman.

In 1766 Waddy Thompson, of Louisa, came to the county, and married Mary, daughter of Robert Lewis, and widow of Samuel Cobb. He had previously married Elizabeth, daughter of Nelson Anderson, of Hanover. His children by the first marriage were Nelson, Anderson, David, who removed to Woodford County, Kentucky, Waddy, who removed to Rockingham, Susan, the second wife of David Rodes, and afterwards of James Kerr, and Lucy. Nelson received from his father two hundred and fifty acres southwest of Still House Mountain, which he sold in 1794 to Thomas Garth Sr. He then bought on Beaverdam of Hardware, where he died in 1798. The children by the second marriage were Ann, the wife first of John Slaughter, and secondly of Philip Grafton, Mary, the wife of James Poindexter, Susan, the wife of Jesse Davenport, Mildred, the wife of James Scott, and Judith, the wife of William Poindexter. John Slaughter was Surveyor of the county, and died in 1797. His children were Mary L., Waddy T., and Robert L. Waddy T. married Frances Ballard, and in 1823 was living in New York, where he was Postmaster, and owner of the tanyard, the most lasting monument of the place, which he bought from Nathaniel Landcraft, and sold to James Lobban. Waddy Thompson died in 1801, and his wife in 1813. All their children appear to have removed from the county except Susan and her husband. For a time he kept the Swan Tavern. He died in 1822, and she in 1847.

THURMAN.

The names of Thurman and Thurmond in the early records were interchangeable. John Thurman began to purchase land on Cove Creek in 1761. William on Green Creek in 1774, and Richard and Philip on Buck Mountain Creek and Doyle's River in 1776. Those of the name in the Buck Mountain region, seem to have disposed of their property, and removed from the county about 1790.

Previous to the latter date Benjamin Thurman was settled on the west side of the South West Mountain, near Hammock's Gap, which is now generally called after this family Thurman's Gap. Benjamin married Nancy, daughter of Gideon Carr, and his children were Fendall C., Susan, the wife of John Rothwell, Sarah, the wife of Austin Sandridge, Mary, the wife of John Gentry, Ann, the wife of Micajah W. Carr, Elisha and Lucy. Fendall married Ann Royster, of Goochland, sold his land to his brother Elisha, and in 1827 emigrated to west Tennessee. He was the father of Edward Thurman, Jannetta, the wife of David Hancock, and Catharine, the wife of Dr. Charles Hancock. Elisha married Mary Dickerson, and his children were Fendall D., William, Ann, the wife of James Wheeler, Mary, the wife of John Carr, Thomas Lindsay, Caroline, the wife of William H. Peyton, Benjamin and Theodore.

TIMBERLAKE.

John Timberlake was the first clerk of Fluvanna County. He died in 1820, at the age of eighty-nine. His sons, Walker, John and Horace, lived in Albemarle. Walker was a Methodist minister, and withal an active man of business. He resided for a time at Glenmore, and subesquently at Bellair, below Carter's Bridge. He died in 1864. His children were Gideon, Clark, John W., William, Ann, the wife of B. C. Flannagan, Elizabeth, the wife of John H. Timberlake,

Sarah, the wife of H. H. Gary, Mary, the wife of Abraham Shepherd, and Christiana. Gideon, who lived on the east side of Dudley's Mountain where it abuts on the north fork of Hardware, and Clark married respectively Lucy and Letitia, daughters of Nathan C. Goodman. John was admitted to the Albemarle bar in 1812, and was associated with James and John B. Magruder in the purchase of the Shadwell Mills, and a large tract of timber land in the Buck Island section. He died in 1862. His wife was Sarah, daughter of John B. Magruder, and his children were Wilhelmina, Edward J., Ann, the wife of Dr. John C. Hughes, and Henry. Horace had two sons, John H. and Horace. John H. was appointed a magistrate of the county, lived at Greenwood Depot and Brownsville, built at the former place a large edifice in which Rev. William Dinwiddie conducted a flourishing school before the war, and died in 1881. His wife was his cousin Elizabeth, daughter of Walker, and his children were Virgilia, the wife of Rev. Paul Whitehead, John H., who was killed in 1876 by a fall from his horse above Mechum's Depot, and James W., who married Sarah Patrick, and lives on the old Patrick place west of Batesville. Horace lived in the Buck Island neighborhood.

A brother of the first John Timberlake was Lewis, one of whose daughters was the wife of Warner Minor, an original hotel keeper at the University. Another daughter, Louisa, while visiting in her sister's family, became the wife of William Wertenbaker.

Another brother of the first John was James, a purser in the United States Navy. He married Peggy O'Neal, daughter of an Irish hotel keeper in Washington City, a woman of great beauty and brilliant natural gifts. After Timberlake's death, she became the wife of John H. Eaton, General Jackson's Secretary of War, and by her elevation to the cabinet circle occasioned such violent social disturbances as eventually produced the disruption of that body.

TOMPKINS.

Giles Tompkins was the first of the name that appeared in the county. He purchased land on Totier Creek in 1765.

He died in 1795, leaving at least three children, William, Elizabeth and Sarah. William lived in the same neighborhood on an estate called Whitehall. He died in 1824. His wife's name was Elizabeth, and his children were John, William, Elizabeth, the wife of Peter White, Catharine, the wife of James Minor, Samuel W., Ann, the wife of Thomas Staples, Edmund, Robert and James. Samuel was a physician, and practised in the vicinity of Earlysville, and afterwards near Scottsville. He married Sarah, daughter of George Gilmer, and his children were Elizabeth, the wife of J. Schuyler Moon, Jane, George, Junius, Samuel, Martha, Charles, Lucy and Catharine. James married Sarah, daughter of Dabney Minor, and his children were William D., James E., and Eliza, the wife of John L. Coleman. William D. and James E. were for many years well known commission merchants in Richmond. Jomes E. married Frances, daughter of John H. Coleman.

TOOLEY.

In 1741 James Tooley obtained a patent for four hundred acres on Totier Creek, and two years later John took out one for two hundred and fifty in the same vicinity. They were most probably brothers. John died in 1750, and James in 1781. The name of James's wife was Judith, and his children were John, James, Sarah, the wife of Edmund New, Ann, the wife of John Martin, Charles, William, Arthur, Elizabeth, Mary, the wife of John Gilliam, and Judith, the wife of Archelaus Gilliam. William died about 1830. His children were Mary, William, John, Charles, Nancy, Elizabeth, the wife of James Gentry, and Arthur. In 1815 John, the son of William, married Mary Gilmore, and his children were James and Joshua. The most of this family seem to have removed to Monroe County, Kentucky. Totier was sometimes called Tooley's' Creek, and it is so designated on some of the maps of Virginia. At the beginning of the century, an eminence on the old Irish Road, where it was intersected by a road from Cocke's Mill, went by the name of Tooley's Hill.

TURNER.

Terisha Turner was granted one hundred and thirty-six acres on the south branches of Hardware in 1760, and this tract he and his wife Sarah sold to Peter Cheatham in 1777. At that time he was described as a citizen of Amherst. He was also the owner of several hundred acres on Green Creek, which in 1790 he sold for the most part to Benjamin Harris.

In 1788 Charles Turner bought from Solomon Ballou nearly two hundred acres lying to the northwest of Ivy Depot. He died in 1789. His wife's name was Mary Ann, and his children were Robert, George, Reuben, William, Matthew, Keziah, Mary and Judith. George in 1791 married Ann, daughter of Gabriel and Ann Maupin. A number of the children in 1815 sold their land to Charles Harper, and removed to Pendleton County, Kentucky. The small mountain at the foot of which their land lay is still known as Turner's Mountain.

James Turner, described as belonging to Amherst, was a considerable land owner on the lower Hardware. His wife was Rebecca, daughter of William Hamner. He sold his property in the county before the end of the last century, part to Samuel Dyer, and much the larger part to Pleasant Dawson.

TWYMAN.

George and William Twyman, in all likelihood brothers, were citizens of Culpeper. George began to purchase land in Albemarle on the Buck Mountain Road near Earlysville in 1765. In 1791 and 1804 he divided nearly six hundred acres between his sons, George and Joseph. He died in 1822, at the age of eighty-nine. His wife's name was Mary, and his children were George, Joseph, Samuel, Sarah, the wife of a Sanford, William, Abraham, Elizabeth, the wife of William J. Wood, Agatha, the wife of Robert Dearing, Ruth, the wife of David Watts, and James. A number of this family removed to Kentucky, and as none of them bearing the name now reside in the county, it is probable they all emigrated to the West.

William in 1770 bought more than five hundred acres on

the head waters of Mechum's, which he sold in 1778 to William Wood and Francis Weathered. In 1771 he purchased from Jacob Snead three hundred acres on Ivy Creek, at the crossing of the Whitehall Road. This place he sold two years after to George Wayt. From the fact that the eldest son of Wayt was named Twyman, his wife was no doubt a daughter of William. William Twyman, whose wife's name was Winifred, appears never to have left Albemarle.

WADDELL.

Rev. James Waddell, the blind preacher, resided on the borders of Albemarle and Louisa, the latter part of his life. His first home in Virginia was in Lancaster County, where he married Mary, daughter of James Gordon. To avoid the troubles incident to the exposed state of that part of the country during the Revolution, he removed to Augusta County, where he took charge of the Tinkling Spring Church, and where he purchased from James P. Cocke, Springhill, the old Patton place. When the war ended, he fixed his residence on his place called Hopewell, about a mile southwest of Gordonsville. There he died in 1805, and there his remains lay till 1871, when by the permission of friends they were transferred to the yard of the Presbyterian Church at Rapidan, which was called by his name. His children were Nathaniel, James G., Elizabeth, the wife of Rev. William Calhoun, Janetta, the wife of Dr. Archibald Alexander, Ann, Dr. Addison, Sarah and Littleton. James G. became a member of the Albemarle bar in 1800, but for the most of his life pursued the calling of a teacher. He married first Mary T., daughter of Reuben Lindsay, and secondly his cousin Lucy, daughter of John Gordon. His home was at Springhill, on the west side of the Gordonsville Road opposite the residence of his father. In 1823 he sold his place to William T. Davis, and removed to Waynesboro. The most of the family became residents of the Valley.

WALKER.

Thomas Walker was born in King and Queen in 1715, was a student of William and Mary, and about 1741 married

Mildred, the daughter of Nicholas Meriwether. Through her he came into the possession of Castle Hill. By profession he was a physician, but possessed too bold and energetic a nature to be contented with the ordinary routine of a country doctor. In his younger years he occupied with signal efficiency a number of public positions. It is believed that notwithstanding the claims in behalf of Finley and Daniel Boone, he led the first expedition that ever traversed the mountains, and stood upon the famous hunting grounds of Kentucky. In 1748, and again in 1750, he visited Southwest Virginia and Kentucky, and to this day has left his memorial in the former region, in the names of Walker's Mountain and Walker's Creek on the confines of Giles and Pulaski Counties, and in the latter, in the name of Cumberland which he gave to the mountains, gap and river so called, in commemoration of the Duke of Cumberland, who had recently crushed the rebellion of 1745 on the field of Culloden. He was Commissary of the Virginia troops under Braddock, and was at that general's defeat in 1755. More than once he was appointed to treat with the Indians in New York and Pennsylvania, and in 1778 was one of the Commission selected to fix the boundary between Virginia and North Carolina. Without any change of residence, he successively represented the counties of Hanover, Louisa and Albemarle in the House of Burgesses, and in 1763 was the trustee of Albemarle to sell and convey the lots and outlots of Charlottesville, the new county seat. He died in 1794. His children were Mary, the wife of Nicholas Lewis, John, Susan, the wife of Henry Fry, Thomas, Lucy, the wife of Dr. George Gilmer, Elizabeth, the wife of Rev. Matthew Maury, Mildred, the wife of Joseph Hornsby, who removed to Shelby County, Kentucky, Sarah, the wife of Reuben Lindsay, Martha, the wife of George Divers, Reuben, Francis, and Peachy, the wife of Joshua Fry.

John lived at Belvoir, the old home of Robert Lewis, was aide to Washington in the Revolution, member of the House of Burgesses, United States Senator to fill the vacancy occasioned by the death of William Grayson, for many years Commonwealth's Attorney for the county, and died in 1809. He married Elizabeth, daughter of Bernard Moore, and granddaughter of Governor Spotswood, and his only child Mildred became the wife of Francis Kinloch, of South Carolina.

Thomas was a Captain in the Ninth Virginia Regiment of the Revolutionary army, and died in 1798. His home was on the plantation of Indian Fields. His wife was Margaret Hoops, and his children M. L., Elizabeth, the wife of Robert Michie, Maria, the wife of Richard Duke, Jane, the wife of William Rice, of Halifax, Mildred, the wife of Tarleton Goolsby, John, Thomas and Martha.

Francis succeeded his father at Castle Hill, was a magistrate of the county, Colonel of the Eighty-Eighth Regiment, member of the House of Delegates, and Representative in Congress, and died in 1806. He married Jane Byrd, daughter of General Hugh Nelson, and granddaughter of President William Nelson, and his children were Jane Frances, the wife of Dr. Mann Page, and Judith, the wife of William C. Rives.

WALLACE.

Three brothers named Wallace came to Virginia with Michael Woods as his sons-in-law about 1734, Peter, Andrew and William. Peter married Martha Woods, and settled in Rockbridge County. He was the father of Adam and Andrew Wallace, who displayed great gallantry in the battle of Guilford C. H., the latter yielding up his life on that field. The other brother remained in Albemarle. Andrew Wallace married Margaret Woods. His home was near Ivy Depot, on part of the Charles Hudson entry, where Charles Harper afterwards resided. He died in 1785. His children were Michael, Samuel, Elizabeth, the wife of William Briscoe, Mary, the wife of Alexander Henderson, Hannah, Susan, the wife of Thomas Collins, Margaret, the wife of William Ramsay, and Jean, the wife of a Wilson. All these families except the Ramsays emigrated to the West, some probably to western Virginia, but most of them to Kentucky.

William Wallace married Hannah Woods. His home was

on land at the foot of the Blue Ridge near Greenwood Depot, which he bought from Andrew Woods, and on which some of his descendants still reside. His children were Michael, John, Jean, the wife of Robert Poage, William, Sarah, Hannah and Josiah. Michael lived on Lickinghole, was Captain of a military company during the Revolution, and a ruling elder in Mountain Plains Church, with his wife Ann sold his place to George Conner in 1786, and emigrated to Kentucky. John lived near Greenwood, with his wife Mary sold out to his brother William, and in 1780 removed to Washington County Virginia. Josiah lived at Mechum's Depot, with his wife Hannah sold his plantation to Edward Broadus in 1796, and removed to Kentucky.

William continued in Albemarle, and resided at the old home near Greenwood. He died in 1809. His wife was Mary Pilson, and his children William, Richard, Hannah, the wife of John Lobban, Samuel, Mary, Michael, Elizabeth and John. William was associated with John Pilson in the mercantile business, but died young and unmarried in 1812. His business was continued by his brother Richard, who died unmarried in 1832. Michael lived at the old homestead, married Lavinia Lobban, was a ruling elder in Mountain Plains Church, and died in 1845. His children were Samuel, who emigrated to Texas, Mary, William, Martha, the wife of Peter Le Neve, Michael W., Lavinia, the wife of Dr. A. Hamilton Rogers, J. Hervey, Sarah, the wife of Thomas L. Courtney, John R. and Charles. John married Elizabeth, daughter of Joel Smith, and lived in Nelson. His children were Jesse, Samuel, William W., Mary, the wife of William Smith, and John Pilson.

WATSON.

William Watson came from Charles City County, and resided on land east of North Garden Depot, which in 1762 he purchased from John Leake and William and Joseph Fitzpatrick. He died in 1784. His children were John P., Richard P., Joseph and Nancy, the wife of Thomas Cobbs. John P. died in 1812, and his widow Martha, to whom he devised his estate, became the wife of John Brown in 1816. Richard also died in 1812. His wife was Ann Anderson, and his children William, Lucinda and Ann, the wives respectively of Wilson Gregory and Francis Staples, both of Henrico. Richard's widow was subsequently married to Dr. C. Lewis Carr. The lands of this family have passed into other hands, though their name is still remembered in the neighborhood.

Another William Watson married, Susan, daughter of David Watts, and in 1767 received from his father-in-law a portion of his estate on the west side of the South West Mountain, not far from Stony Point. His children were John, Matthew, Elizabeth, Sarah, Lucy, the wife of Thomas Johnson, Mildred, Ann and Mary. John succeeded to his father's place. In 1804 he bought from Thomas Wells nearly five hundred acres of the Carter land south of Charlottesville, part of which was sold in 1818 by Matthew and his wife Lucy to William Dunkum, and part in 1836 by John and his wife Mary to Samuel Mitchell, of North Carolina. There being for many years simultaneously three John Watsons in the county, this John was described as of the Little Mountain.

William Watson, son of Little Mountain John, had for a long period charge of the county jail. He was a saddler by trade, and in the early years of the century was associated in business with Edward Stone, who removed to Davidson County, Tennessee. They owned the north end of the lot on the west side of the Square. In 1819 Watson bought from Edmund Anderson the lot on the west side of Park Street, where he built the brick house which was long the residence of the late Thomas Wood. He was Jailor from 1811 to 1828, and again from 1832 to 1841, when during the imprisonment of Joseph E. Semmes, he was succeeded by his son, James A. Watson. He married Elizabeth, daughter of Samuel Barksdale, and his children were James Albert, who married Mary, daughter of Anderson Brown, and Mildred, the wife of a Jones. He died in 1853, and his son James A. in 1857.

In 1779 John Watson purchased land in the northwestern

part of the county on Rocky Creek. He was succeeded by his son John, who was distinguished as John Watson, of High Top. The latter died in 1833.

About 1790 John Watson, known as of Milton, came to the county from Amherst. He was the son of James Watson, formerly of James City County. He settled in Milton, and was closely identified with its interests from its foundation. He was appointed a magistrate in 1800, and served as Sheriff in 1825. In 1813 he purchased from Brown, Rives & Co. Forest Hill, a plantation on the south side of the Rivanna below Milton, containing upwards of a thousand acres. He made this his residence until his death in 1841. His wife was Jane, daughter of Richard Price, and his children Eliza, the wife of Ira Garrett, James Richard, John W. C., Isabella, the wife of Charles B. Shaw, Matthew P., Egbert R., and Ellen, the wife of John C. Sinton. J. Richard married Ann, daughter of James Clark, was a merchant in Charlottesville, and a hotel keeper at the University, and died at Forest Hill in 1867. John W. C. was admitted to the Albemarle bar in 1830, married Catharine, sister of professor John A. G. Davis, and removed to Holly Springs, Miss. He represented that State in the Confederate Senate during the war. Matthew P. married Eliza, daughter of Opie Norris, and removed to Southwest Virginia. Egbert spent his life in Charlottesville, as one of the leading lawyers at its bar, and Judge of the Circuit Court at the close of the war. He was thrice married, first to Mary, daughter of Opie Norris, secondly to Jane Creigh, of Greenbrier, and thirdly to Elizabeth, daughter of Isaac White. He died in 1887. Dr. Daniel E. Watson, a kinsman of this family, came to the county from Amherst, and in 1837 bought from Francis B. Hart the plantation in the Rich Cove, on which he resided till his death in 1882. He was appointed a magistrate in 1838. He married Mary, daughter of Henry T. Harris.

Joseph Watson, an immigrant from Ireland, in 1832 bought from Andrew Leitch, agent of the Dinsmore estate, Orange Dale, where he lived until his death several years ago. His wife was Ellen Leitch, a sister of Samuel Leitch Jr.

WATTS.

Jacob Watts became the owner of more than eleven hundred acres on the north side of the Rivanna, near Piney Mountain. He was one of the early Methodist ministers of the county. He died in 1821, at the age of ninety years. His wife was Elizabeth, daughter of the first Richard Durrett, and his children William, John, Elijah, Fielding, Mildred, the wife of a Bruce, Mary, the wife of Hezekiah Rodes, Frances, the wife of Joseph Edmondson, Nancy, the wife of Henry Austin, and Agnes, the wife of John Huckstep. The children of Elijah were Sarah, the wife of Kenza Stone, who removed to Bourbon County, Kentucky, Mildred, the wife of James Dickerson, Elizabeth, the wife of John O. Padgett, Nancy, the wife of Wiley Dickerson, and Frances, the wife of James Malone.

David Watts, possibly a brother of Jacob, lived on the west side of the South West Mountain, south of Stony Point. He died in 1767. His children were John, David, Nathan, and Susan, the wife of William Watson. David lived in the same neighborhood, and died in 1817. His wife's name was Sarah, and his children were Charles, who married Elizabeth Buckner, John, Philip, David, who married Ruth, daughter of George Twyman, Susan, the wife of Carver Thomas, Mary the wife of William Breedlove, Mildred, the wife of Richard Breedlove, Frances and Nancy. Philip married a daughter of John Brown, and lived west of Mechum's Depot. His daughter America was the wife of Madison Kinsolving.

WAYT.

George Wayt in 1773 purchased from William Twyman the plantation on Ivy Creek, on the north side of the Whitehall Road, which long continued in the possession of the family. It is believed his wife Catharine was the daughter of Twyman. It is said that after his death, she became the wife of Elijah Garth. His children were Twyman, Tabitha, the wife of a Kennerly, of Augusta, Catharine, the wife of

Paschal Garth, who removed to Todd County, Kentucky, Frances, Sarah, Judith and Elizabeth. Twyman was for many years associated in business with his brother-in-law, John Winn, under the firm of Wayt & Winn. He was also Mr. Winn's successor as Postmaster of the town. His home was on the northeast corner of Jefferson and Second Streets, the square on which it stood having been bought by him in 1815 from the executors of Jacob Kinney. He married Mary Johnson, of Fluvanna, and his children were Charles, John, James M., Mary, the wife of Dr. J. W. Poindexter, and Twymonia, the wife of Peter A. Woods. He died in 1861.

WERTENBAKER.

Christian Wertenbaker was of German extraction. His first home was in Columbia, Fluvanna County, but he removed to Milton, when that town was established. Subsequently he became a citizen of Charlottesville, and in 1814 purchased from his brother-in-law, Joshua Grady, the farm on the old Barracks Road, east of Ivy Creek, where he spent the remainder of his days. He died in 1833. He married Mary, daughter of Joshua Grady, and his children were William, Edward, Thomas Jefferson, Elizabeth, the wife of John Walker, who removed to Pickaway County, Ohio, Susan, the wife of Patrick Martin, and Sarah Ann, the wife of David Vandegrift.

William in his youth acted as deptuy Clerk and deputy Sheriff of the county, and was admitted to the bar in 1824. Soon after he was chosen Librarian of the University, and continued to be connected with the affairs of that institution until his death in 1882. He possessed a marvellously accurate recollection of all the students who had during his time frequented its halls, and no figure associated with its scenes dwelt more famliiarly in their memory than his. He retained much of the manners of the old school, and the offer of his snuffbox was one of the acts of his stately courtesy to the last. For many years he was ruling elder in the Presbyterian Church of Charlottesville. His wife was Louisa, daughter of Lewis Timberlake, of Caroline.

WHEELER.

Benjamin Wheeler was one of the early patentees of land within the present limits of Albemarle. In 1734 he obtained the grant of six hundred acres on Mechunk, and in 1740 two hundred on Moore's Creek. He conveyed three hundred acres of his Mechunk land to Giles Allegre in 1748, and the remainder in 1768 to his grandson Benjamin Burgher. In 1764 he conveyed his land on Moore's Creek to his son-in-law, Micajah Spradling. His children were Benjamin, Micajah, and the wives of Micajah Spradling and Manus Burgher. Micajah married Susan, daughter of John Woodson, and died about 1832. His children were John, Robert, who married Frances, daughter of Callum Bailey, ——— the wife of John Woodson, and Mary, the wife of Tucker Page.

Benjamin Dod Wheeler was contemporaneous with the first Benjamin; whether he was the son of that name, is not known. He became the owner of more than eight hundred acres on the upper waters of Moore's Creek, the greater portion of which he and his wife Ann sold to George Nicholas in 1788. He appears then to have removed from the county. A daughter Elizabeth became the wife of John Old Jr., in 1785.

Micajah Wheeler, probably a brother of the first Benjamin, also bought land on Moore's Creek. He died in 1809. His wife's name was Sarah, and his children were Joshua, John, Micajah, Benjamin, Joel, Elizabeth, Sarah, the wife of Obadiah Britt, and Ann, the wife of Hezekiah Collins. John in 1814 purchased from Stephen Hughes the mill now known as Maury's, which he and his wife Ann sold in 1820 to John M. Perry and Reuben Maury. Micajah married Mary Emerson, bought in 1800 a parcel of land on Mechum's, west of Batesville, which in 1815 he sold to Ralph Field, and died in 1836. Benjamin also died in 1836. His children were Sarah, Susan, the wife of a Holson, Mary, the wife of Overton Lowry, Mildred, the wife of a Wood, and a son, who was the father of Bennett and Joel. Joshua died in 1838. His wife's name was Mary and his children were John D., who died in 1844, Micajah, who married Julia, daughter of Benjamin Martin, and died in 1841, Joshua N., who married Rebecca Pollock, and died in 1858, Sarah, the wife of John Bailey, Eliza, the wife of Goodrich Garland, Matilda, the wife of James Garland, Elizabeth, the wife of John Martin, and James.

WHITE.

John White, a native of Scotland, bought land from the Brockmans and Dowells on the west side of the South West Mountain, beginning his purchases in 1772. He married Mourning, daughter of Henry Shelton, and died without children in 1807. By his will he emancipated forty-seven negroes, and made provisions for their removal to a free State, John Walker and Chiles Terrell being appointed his executors. Jeremiah, doubtless a brother, married Jane Shelton, a sister of his wife.

Conyers White came to the county from Orange in 1776, and purchased more than fifteen hundred acres on Buck Mountain Creek. He was succeeded by his son Crenshaw, who married Sarah Austin, sold his property about 1825, and emigrated to Missouri.

In 1779 Daniel White bought from William Wood the plantation on which he was living at the time, lying southwest of Batesville. This place he subsequently sold to Benjamin Ficklin. In 1812 he purchased from the trustee of Menan Mills the farm at the bend of Mechum's River on Broadaxe, which has been in the possession of the family ever since. He died in 1818. His wife's name was Elizabeth, and his children were Mary, the wife of Thomas Martin, Elizabeth, the wife of John Jones, Margaret, the wife of Thomas Jackson, Nancy, the wife of Overton Garland, John, Henry, William, who died in New Orleans in 1817, Rhoda, the wife of Joseph Grayson, and Felicia. Henry succeeded his father at the home place. He was appointed a magistrate in 1830, and died in 1850. He married Elizabeth, daughter of Rice Garland, and his children were Samuel G., and Elizabeth, the wife of Edward C. Hamner.

Near the close of the last century Garrett White came to the county from Madison, and established his home in the

North Garden, southwest of the Cross Roads. By his sagacity and industry he acquired a large estate, becoming the owner of more than two thousand acres in the North and South Gardens. He was appointed a magistrate in 1806, and served as Sheriff in 1830. He died in 1843. He married Elizabeth, daughter of John Piper, and his children were John, Jeremiah, who died young and unmarried, and Sarah, the wife of Samuel W. Martin. John displayed the energy and thrift of his father. He died in 1866. His wife was Caroline, daughter of Stephen Moore, and his children were Garrett, John S., Jeremiah, Frances, the wife of Alfred Carpenter, Mary, the wife of Nicholas M. Page, and Sarah, the wife of Samuel G. White.

WILKINSON.

John Wilkinson deserves mention as one who early sought to develop the natural resources of the county. He came, it is likely, from Baltimore, in 1768 and at first with Nathaniel Giles and John Lee Webster, and afterwards with John Old, made several purchases of land supposed to contain iron ore. In pursuance of the same end, he took patents in 1770 for large tracts of land in the Ragged Mountains, and along the Hardware River. Ore was mined on Cook's Mountain, on Applebury Mountain near the Cove, and on the north fork of Hardware, and furnaces were built on both the north and south forks of that stream. The business was not attended with success. Litigation arose, and the lands of Wilkinson having been mortgaged to carry on the enterprise, were sold by order of Court in 1796. Nothing is known of his subsequent life He seems however to have lived in the southern part of the county, and died in 1813.

WINGFIELD.

The first appearance of the Wingfield name in Albemarle occurred in 1762. At that time Mary, the wife of John Wingfield, and daughter of Charles Hudson, conveyed to her son Charles a part of five hundred acres named Prospect, on which he was then living, and which she had received from her father. This place was manifestly situated in the Biscuit Run Valley, near the north fork of Hardware, a locality for a long period largely occupied by the Wingfield family. In 1772 Charles bought from David Glenn upwards of three hundred acres on the head waters of Mechum's, which in 1783 he sold to John Piper. He died in 1803. His wife's name was Rachel, and his children were John, Charles, William, Christopher, Joseph, Francis, Mary, the wife of John Hamner, Ann, the wife of John Harrison, Sarah, the wife of a Martin, Jemima, the wife of Samuel Barksdale, and Elizabeth, the wife of Henley Hamner.

John died in 1814. His wife's name was Robina, and his children were John, Robert, Matthew, Rebecca, the wife of a Gilham, Mary and Martha. John married Ann, daughter of John Buster, lived west of Batesville, and died in 1859. His children were Richard, Edward, Robert, John, and Mildred, the wife of a Herndon. Robert, his brother, died in 1825, and his children were Thomas F., Mary Ann, and John M. Matthew married Martha, another daughter of John Buster, and his children were Ann and Martha.

Charles, long known as Charles Wingfield Jr., was apponited a magistrate in 1794, and served as Sheriff in 1819, but died in one month after entering upon the office. His home was at Bellair, on the Hardware. In 1783 he married Mary, daughter of Charles Lewis Jr., of Buck Island, and widow of Colonel Charles Lewis, of North Garden, but had no children. In his will he mentions generally the relations of his wife, as well as his own. There is a tradition in the family that he was an Episcopal minister, but no other evidence of the fact can be found.

Christopher lived on the Plum Orchard branch of Biscuit Run. He died in 1821. His wife's name was Elizabeth, and his children were John H., Lucy, the wife of Allen Dawson, Ann Eliza, the wife of James Rosson, Charles, who married Margaret Rosson, and after whose death the widow became the wife of William Summerson, who many remember as the aged page of the County Court, and William. John H. and William removed to Nelson County.

Francis lived in the Biscuit Run valley, at the foot of Carter's Mountain. His children were Mary, the wife of Robert Gentry, Thomas, Francis, Charles M., Ann, the wife of Littleton Chick, and John. John removed to Hanover. His children were Alonzo, Chastain, Henrietta, Agnes, Elizabeth and Charles.

Other members of the family who came to the county besides Charles, were Edward and Reuben. Edward died in 1806. His wife was Nancy Hazelrig, and his children Joseph F., John, Mary, the wife of Larkin Hudson, Amanda, the wife of Rice Bailey, Sarah, the wife of William Stewardson, Edward W. G., Robina, the wife of James Martin, and Matthew. The children of Reuben, who died in 1842, were Sarah, Mary R., Lucetta, John O., Anderson and Edward.

Charles Wingfield, no doubt of the same stem, but of a different branch, came to the county from Hanover in the early part of the century, married Cary Ann, daughter of Lewis Nicholas, became a Baptist minister, and died in 1864. His children were Frances, the wife of Waddy Roberts, Mary, the wife of John A. Mosby, Sarah, the wife of John Morris, Maria, the wife of Robert Thornton, Julia, the wife of John P. Roberts, Edmonia, John, George and Dr. Charles L.

WINN.

John Winn came from Fluvanna, and settled in Charlottesville in the early part of the century. As the partner of Twyman Wayt, he was for a long time one of the principal merchants of the town, and its Postmaster. He also dealt considerably in real estate. In 1813 he purchased from John Carr his seat at Belmont, where he resided until his death in 1835. His wife was Miss Johnson, a sister of Mrs. Wayt, and of Michael Johnson, who married Sophia, daughter of Jesse Lewis, and whose home was about a mile south of Jesse L. Maury's residence. His children were Benjamin, John J., William, Thomas, Elizabeth, the wife of George R. King, of Louisiana, Mary, the wife of John A. Gretter, Martha, the wife of David Gretter—these gentlemen were brothers from North Carolina—and Sarah, the wife of John Y.

Barrett, who was a partner of George M. McIntire in the drug business, and eventually removed to Amherst. Benjamin married Mary J., daughter of Ira Garrett, and removed to Amherst, near Pedlar Mills. John J. married Alice, daughter of Rice W. Wood, and lived the latter part of his life in Hillsboro, where he died in 1885.

WOOD.

Henry Wood, the first Clerk of Goochland, was one of the earliest patentees of land within the present limits of Albemarle. In 1734 and 1739 he was granted twenty-six hundred and fifty acres on Buck Island, part at its mouth, and part where the late Christopher Gilmer lived, called the Upper Plantation. His son Valentine became a resident of the county, and was appointed one of its magistrates in 1746. When his father died in 1757, he returned to Goochland, and succeeded him in the Clerk's office. After his death his family again fixed their residence in Albemarle. His wife was Lucy Henry, a sister of the great orator, and his children Henry, Martha, the wife of Stephen Southall, Mary, the wife of Judge Peter Johnston, and mother of General Joseph E. Johnston, Lucy, the second wife of Edward Carter, John H., William and Jane. Their land in Albemarle was sold, the largest portion, nearly twelve hundred acres, to John R. Campbell in 1815, when the family transferred their residence to Fluvanna. Mrs. Lucy Wood died there about 1826. John H. was the only son who married. His wife was Elizabeth, daughter of Charles Spencer. A son, Valentine, died in infancy in 1822, and a daughter, Mary, survived him, Richard Duke being appointed her guardian in 1827.

Josiah Wood in 1741 patented four hundred acres on Buck Mountain Creek. In 1769 he bought land on the west side of the South West Mountain, which in 1787 he and his wife Mary sold to Claiborne Rothwell. He also purchased a tract of more than fifteen hundred acres which lay at the junction of the Buck Mountain and Hydraulic Mills Roads, which had been apparently entered by Major John Henry, father of the orator, and which in later times came into the possession of Nelson Barksdale and George Crank. This land in 1792 he divided between his sons David and John. John in 1801 was succeeded by Horsley Goodman as Major of the Second Battalion of the Eighty-Eighth Regiment, sold his land to John Clarkson, and probably removed from the county. David in 1781 married Mildred, daughter of Colonel Nicholas Lewis, of the Farm. His home was on Buck Mountain Creek, not far from Webb's Mountain. He was appointed a magistrate in 1801, and died in 1816. His children were Thomas W., Nicholas L., Robert W., William L., John W., David, Maria, the wife of James Clarkson, who removed to Kanawha, and Margaret, the wife of Dr. James B. Rogers. Thomas lived adjacent to his father's place, was appointed Colonel of the Eighty-Eighth Regiment in 1814, and a magistrate in 1816, and died in 1831. His wife was Susan, daughter of Joseph H. Irvin, who after his death was married to John Fray. His children were Dr. Alfred, Mildred, the wife of Jeremiah A. Early, and Mary Ann. Nicholas lived near his brother, married Nancy ———, and removed to Tipton County, Tennessee. Robert married Mary Ann Miller, lived south of Ivy Depot, and afterwards on the north side of Moorman's River, and died in 1839. William married Pamela, daughter of John Dickerson, and emigrated to Missouri. John married Amelia Harris, and removed to Richmond. David died young.

The name of Wood in the vicinity of Batesville was represented by a number of different families, and it is somewhat difficult to trace their respective lines. William Wood first appears, who about 1760 bought land from John Leake and others on the head waters of Mechum's. He seems to have had five sons, John, William, Isaac, Abner and Jesse. In 1801 he purchased from the trustees of Edward Broadus the old Josiah Wallace place, which included Mechum's Depot. He died in 1808. His son John in 1813 sold the Wallace place to George Price, of Orange, who two years later sold it to James Kinsolving. The name of John's wife was Elizabeth, and she was probably the daughter of Jeremiah Yancey. William dealt quite actively in real estate.

It was he who in 1779 sold to Daniel White the plantation near Mount Ed Church, on which the latter resided for more than thirty years. He was much concerned in military matters, was for many years Captain of his neighborhood company of militia, and was appointed Major of the Second Battalion of the Forty-Seventh Regiment. He died in 1820. He was probably twice married, first to Martha, daughter of David Glenn, and secondly to Elizabeth ———. His children were Rice, Jesse, Elizabeth, the wife of John Brown, David, Nancy, the wife of Joseph Watson, William, Milton, John and Clifton. Rice, whose wife's name was Elizabeth, daughter of David Burgher, and perhaps others of this family emigrated to Missouri. Isaac seems to have lived in the fork of Mechum's, east of Yellow Mountain. He married Susan, daughter of Captain William Grayson. His son John was the owner of eleven hundred acres near Batesville. John in 1788 married Mary, daughter of Reuben Terrell, and died in 1843. His children were Mildred, the wife of Henry Pemberton, Sarah, the wife of Hudson Barksdale, Elmira, the wife of William G. Barksdale, Mary, the wife of Lewis Poates, Lucy, the wife of Elijah Brown, Reuben, Isaac, John T., James M., Susan, Jerome B., Richard and William L. Abner and his wife Mary sold their property in 1795, and apparently removed from the county. Jesse married Mildred, the widow of Reuben Terrell, and died in 1824. His children were William, Mildred, the wife of Ralph Field, Sarah, the wife of John Field, Elmira, the wife of Joseph Field, and afterwards of John Robinson, Jesse and Richard. William married Nancy, daughter of Robert Field, and died in 1833. His children were Nancy, the wife of John Dollins, William, Mary, Elizabeth, the wife of a Stone and Edward. Jesse Jr. died in 1829. His children were Thomas G., Mildred, Jane, and Richard Walker. His wife, whose name was Lucy Wood, was subsequently married to Hudson Oaks.

A John Wood, who lived in the same section, and died about 1792, married Eleanor, daughter of Solomon Israel. His children were Solomon, William J., Sarah, Mary Ann, the wife of Reuben Woody, Susan, the wife of Jonathan

Bolling, Elizabeth, the wife of John Clack, and Mildred, the wife of Reuben Mitchell. Many of this family removed to Barren County, Kentucky. A William Wood also lived in the same section. His wife's name was Mildred, and his children were Jesse, who was distinguished by the affix of Cull—whether because he came from Culpeper, or for another reason, is not known—and Mildred, the wife of Jechonias Yancey.

In 1774 David Wood came from Louisa, and purchased land from David Watts, on the west side of the South West Mountain. In that section he established his home. He died in 1813. His wife was a Watson of the Green Spring family, and his children Martha, the wife of Nathaniel Thomason, Elizabeth, the wife of Micajah Carr, Mary, the wife of John Sandridge, who emigrated to Green County, Kentucky, Drury, Lucy, the wife of Elisha D. Gilliam, who removed to Christian County, Kentucky, Henrietta, the wife of James Jeffries, Nancy, the wife of Meekins Carr, James, Sarah, the wife of a Gooch, who emigrated to Lincoln County, Kentucky, and Ann, the wife of Barnett Smith. Drury resided at Park Hill, opposite the bend of the north fork of the Rivanna, near Stony Point. As a man of business he was judicious and energetic, and acquired a large estate. He died in 1841. He married Malinda, daughter of John Carr, and his children were Sarah, the wife of Nathaniel Burnley, James, who married Frances, daughter of Hancock Allen, David, who married Lucy, daughter of Richard Duke, William, George, Fendall—these five brothers emigrated to West Tennessee—Rice W., Thomas, Drury, Mary, the wife of Robert Durrett, Martha, the wife of James D. Allen, and Caroline, the wife of Thomas J. Early. Rice was admitted to the bar in 1821, and represented the county in the House of Delegates. He died in 1831, on the threshold of a promising career. His wife was Sarah Donahoe, of Staunton, and his children Cornelia, the wife of George D. Brent, Alice, the wife of John J. Winn, Mary and Antoinette. Thomas was admitted to the bar in 1830—at the time of his death its oldest member—and was also a member of the Legislature. He was twice married, first to Mary Morton, of Prince Edward, and secondly to Mrs. Sturdivant, of Washington City. He died without children in 1895. Drury also became a member of the bar in 1842.

In 1779 William Wood came from Maryland, and bought land on the west fork of Priddy's Creek. He was the ancestor of nearly all the families of the name who have resided in the northern part of the county. About the same period there came from the same State, and settled in the same neighborhood, Thomas Wills and John Turner, and a few years later Michael Catterton, Samuel Wills, John Ward and John Elliott.

WOODS.

The first Woods who settled in Albemarle was Michael, who was born in the north of Ireland in 1684, and with his wife Mary Campbell, and most of his children, came to this country sometime in the decade of 1720. Landing on the banks of the Delaware, he spent some years in Lancaster County, Pennsylvania, thence ascended the Valley of Virginia, and crossed the Blue Ridge by Woods's Gap in 1734. In 1737 he entered more than thirteen hundred acres on Mechum's River and Lickinghole, and the same day purchased two thousand acres patented two years before by Charles Hudson, and situated on the head waters of Ivy Creek. It is believed he was the first settler in western Albemarle, and perhaps anywhere along the east foot of the Blue Ridge in Virginia. His home was near the mouth of Woods's Gap. He died in 1762, and was interred in the family burying ground about a hundred yards from the dwelling. His tombstone was standing just after the Civil War, when it was broken to pieces and disappeared; but a fragment discovered a few years ago indicated the year of his birth. His will is on record, in which are mentioned three sons and three daughters, Archibald, John, William, Sarah, the wife of Joseph Lapsley, of Rockbridge, Hannah, the wife of William Wallace, and Margaret, the wife of Andrew Wallace.

Archibald, whose wife's name was Isabella, was one of his father's executors, and in 1767 joined with John, his co-executor, in conveying nearly seven hundred acres of the land on Ivy Creek to Rev. James Maury. In 1771 he purchased land on Catawba Creek in Botetourt County, now Roanoke, and removed thither about that time. He died in 1783. His children were James, who removed to Fayette County, Kentucky, John, Archibald, Andrew and Joseph. Joseph died in Roanoke about 1840, devising half of his property to the Presbytery of Montgomery. The descendants of John are still citizens of that county, his grandsons John W. being the present Judge of Roanoke City, and James P. its present Mayor.

John lived on Mechum's River, not far above the Depot of that name. In 1745 he was sent as a Commissioner to prosecute before the Presbytery of Donegal in Pennsylvania, a call which the churches of Rockfish and Mountain Plains had given to Rev. John Hindman. He is the only one of the original family, the dates of whose life are certainly known. He was born February 19th, 1712, and died October 14th, 1791. He married Susanna, daughter of Rev. James Anderson, whom he knew as a child in Pennsylvania, and whom years later he returned to woo as his wife. His children were Michael, James, Susan, Mary, Luta and Ann. Michael lived on his father's place on Mechum's till about 1801, when he removed to a farm in Nelson on the south fork of Rockfish, recently occupied by Charles Harris. His wife was Esther Carothers, of Rockbridge, and his children were William M., Mary, the wife of Hugh Barclay, Susan, the wife of Nathaniel Massie, John, James and Samuel. William M. was twice married, first to Louisa, daughter of William S. Dabney Sr., and secondly to Martha, daughter of Charles A. Scott. He left eight children, who removed to Mississippi. His brothers, John, James, and Samuel, who married Sarah, daughter of John Rodes, emigrated to Marion County, Missouri. James (1748-1823) was an officer in the Revolutionary army, married Mary, daughter of James Garland, of North Garden, and removed to Garrard County, Kentucky, where he had a family of twelve children. Susan became the wife of Daniel Miller, who removed to Kentucky, and from whom descended General John Miller, who fell at Perryville on the Federal side, Mary, the wife of John Reid, Luta, of Samuel Reid and Ann, of James Reid and afterwards the second wife of her cousin William Woods. William, no doubt the oldest of the family and born in 1706, succeeded his father at Mountain Plains, the old homestead. He seems to have been unfortunate in his business affairs. Twice he mortgaged his property, first to Thomas Walker, and then to a number of Valley men, among whom were his brother-in-law, John Bowyer, and his nephew, Samuel McDowell. At length in 1774 he made sale of it to Thomas Adams, of Augusta. At that time he was living in Fincastle County. His wife was Susanna, a sister of his brother-in-law, William Wallace, and his children, Adam, Michael, Peter, John, Andrew, Archibald, William, Sarah, the wife of a Shirkey, Susan, and Mary, the wife of George Davidson. All the children except William emigrated to Kentucky, and from there some went to Tennessee, and some to Missouri. Adam, Peter and Andrew became Baptist preachers. Archibald is mentioned in Hening's Statutes as a trustee of the towns of Boonesboro and Milford, Ky., and in that State he died in 1838, at the age of eighty-nine. William remained in Albemarle. He lived on Beaver Creek, about a mile north of Crozet; on this account, as there were two other William Woodses contemporaneous, he was commonly known as Beaver Creek Billy. In many respects he was a remarkable man, in his sphere somewhat of a born ruler, of fine sense, and great decision. Many amusing stories have been told of his management of men and things, particularly of his fostering care over Mountain Plains Church. He died in 1836, ninety-two years of age. He was married three times, first to his cousin Sarah Wallace, next to his cousin Ann Reid, and thirdly to Mrs. Nancy Richardson. He had one son, William, who married Mary, daughter of William Jarman, and died in 1829. Their children were James, who lived on Beaver Creek, married Ann Jones, of Bedford, and died in 1868, William, who lived near Crozet, married Nancy, the daughter of John Jones, and died in 1850, Peter A., who was a merchant in Charlottesville and Richmond, married Twymonia Wayt, and afterwards Mrs. Mary Poage Bourland, of Augusta, and died in 1870, Thomas D., who married Miss Hagan, lived near Pedlar Mills in Amherst, and died in 1894, and Sarah J., the wife of Jesse P. Key.

According to credible evidence, Michael Woods and his wife Mary Campbell had two sons and two daughters in addition to those just mentioned, Michael, Andrew, Magdalen and Martha. Michael lived southwest of Ivy Depot till 1773, when with his wife Ann he removed to a plantation in Botetourt, on the south side of James River, a few miles below Buchanan. He died in 1777, leaving eleven children, among whom were Samuel, from whom descended Rev. Neander M. Woods, of Memphis, and Rev. William H. Woods, of Baltimore, and William. William remained in Albemarle, and became a Baptist minister, on which account he was known as Baptist Billy. His home was also southwest of Ivy. He represented the county in the House of Delegates in 1799, and in 1810 removed to Livingston County, Kentucky, where he died in 1819. His wife was Joanna, daughter of Christopher Shepherd, and his children Micajah, David, Mary, John, and Susan, the wife of Henry Williams. Micajah resided in Albemarle, was appointed a magistrate in 1816, served as Sheriff in 1836, and while filling that office died at his country seat near Ivy in 1837. He was twice married, first to Lucy Walker, and secondly to Sarah, daughter of John Rodes, and widow of William Davenport. His children by the first marriage were Martha, the wife of John Wilson, Mary, the wife of James Garth, Elizabeth, the wife of John Humphreys, and Henry, who died young, and by the second William S., who died unmarried, and Dr. John R., still pleasantly remembered in the community.

Andrew lived at the foot of the Blue Ridge near Greenwood Depot, a few hundred yards south of the brick mansion, long the home of Michael Wallace's family. He owned nearly five hundred acres in that vicinity, and nearly nine hundred at the foot of Armor's Mountain. He sold his property in 1765, and removed to Botetourt. He was one of the first magistrates of that county, and was appointed its Sheriff in 1777. His home was about nine miles south of Buchanan, not far from the Mill Creek Church. He died in 1781. His wife was Martha, daughter of Robert Poage, of Augusta, and his children James, who lived and died in Montgomery County, on the north fork of Roanoke, and whose descendants removed to Nashville, Tenn., Robert, Andrew, Archibald, who all removed to the vicinity of Wheeling in Ohio County, Elizabeth, the wife of David Cloyd, of Rockbridge, Rebecca, the wife of Isaac Kelly, of Bedford, Mary, the wife of James Poage, who removed to Mason County, Kentucky, and then to Ripley, Ohio, and Martha, the wife of Henry Walker, of Botetourt. Archibald married his cousin Ann, daughter of Thomas Poage, of Augusta, represented Ohio County in the House of Delegates, and the Constitutional Convention of 1788, and when he died in 1846, had been for many years the senior magistrate of that county. The writer of these notes is his grandson.

Magdalen Woods was married successively to John McDowell, Benjamin Burden Jr., and John Bowyer. She is said to have lived to the age of one hundred and four years. Her children were Samuel, James, and Sarah McDowell, the latter the wife of George Moffet, and Martha Burden, the wife of Benjamin Hawkins. Martha Woods was the wife of Peter Wallace.

Another branch of the Woodses, though beyond question of the same stock, came to the county a few years later. James, Samuel and Richard Woods were most probably brothers. James first appears in 1749, when he patented two hundred acres on Stockton's Creek. He lived on the north fork of Rockfish, and at his house the District Committee met in 1775 to devise measures in furtherance of the Revolution. Samuel lived in the same section. He was one of the original purchasers of lots in Charlottesville. He died in 1784. His children were Barbara, the wife of George Martin, Margaret, the wife of Richard Netherland, who removed to Sullivan County, Tennessee, John B., Mary, the wife of Benjamin Harris, Jane, the wife of Joseph Montgomery, and Elizabeth, the wife of William B. Harris. Richard lived north of Taylor's Gap, on the road from D. S. to Rockfish Gap by way of the Miller School, a road which he is said to have laid out, and which is still called by his name. He dealt largely in real estate both in Charlottesville and the county. He was twice married, first to Margaret ———, and secondly to Eliza Ann, a sister of Colonel John Stuart, of Greenbrier. His children were William, George Matthews, Richard, and Elizabeth, the wife of James Brooks. He died in 1801. William succeeded his father at the homestead near Taylor's Gap. He was the County Surveyor from 1796 to 1828, whence he was generally known as Surveyor Billy. He was appointed a magistrate in 1816, succeeded Micajah Woods in the Sheriffalty, and was a ruling elder in Mountain Plains Church. He and his brother George gave much attention to improving the breed of horses, bringing to the county a number of sires from the stud of John Randolph of Roanoke. His wife was Elizabeth, daughter of Jacob Warwick, of Bath, but he died without children in 1850. George lived on the opposite side of the road from his brother, filled for many years the office of Commissioner of the Revenue for St. Anne's, and died in 1847. He married Jane, daughter of Sampson Matthews, of Bath, and his children were John, Sampson L., William Andrew J., Warwick, George, Mary, the wife of Tilloston Janney, and Martha, the wife of Dr. Day. The daughters and their husbands removed to Lewis County. Richard was deputy Surveyor under his brother, and died unmarried in 1822. His place was near the Miller School, and is now in the possession of Thomas G. Michie.

WOODSON.

In 1769 Tucker Woodson became the deputy Clerk of Albemarle. He was the son of Tucker Woodson, of Goochland, and his wife Sarah Hughes. He married Elizabeth, daughter of John Moore, and his home was on the land just north and west of Charlottesville, given to his wife by her father. He died in 1779; and in 1782 his widow became the wife of Major Joseph Crockett, an officer of the Revolutionary army, who soon after removed to Kentucky. Tucker Woodson left two sons, Tucker Moore and Samuel Hughes. Tucker M. about the beginning of the century purchased a considerable amount of real estate in town and county, among other places the plantation of Viewmont, which in 1803 he sold to Captain John Harris. The next year he removed to Kentucky. His wife was Martha Eppes, daughter of Charles Hudson. Samuel had emigrated to Kentucky some years before. He received from his mother her land adjoining Charlottesville, and part of it he sold to Charles Jouett in 1799, and the remainder to Alexander Garrett in 1808. He became Clerk of Jessamine County, Kentucky, and in 1821 represented his district in Congress.

In 1769 John Woodson, of Goochland, most probably a half-brother of Tucker, bought land on the head waters of Ivy Creek. He departed this life in 1779. His wife's name was Elizabeth, and his children were Tarleton, Susan, the wife of Micajah Wheeler, and Sarah, the wife of John Everett. Tarleton is believed to have married Annis, daughter of Augustine Shepherd, and his children were Tarleton, Augustine and Prior. Prior married Josephine Abell, and was the father of John, who recently died on or near the same land his ancestor had purchased more than a century and a quarter before.

In later years, about 1835, Thomas Woodson came to Charlottesville from Goochland. He was for many years one of the teachers of the town, and a ruling elder in the Presbyterian Church. He died in 1862. He was twice married, first to a sister of James C. Halsall, a member of the Albemarle bar, and secondly to Clarissa, daughter of D. Ferrell Carr. His daughter Mary became the wife of Charles C. Preston, of Southwest Virginia.

YANCEY.

Jeremiah Yancey was the first of the name who settled in Albemarle. He purchased land on Moorman's River in 1765, and during the next few years patented several small tracts on Buck's Elbow. He died in 1789. His wife's name was Margaret, and his children were Robert, Charles, Mary, the wife of David Rodes, Elizabeth, the wife of John Wood, Jechonias and Joel. Jechonias married Mildred, a sister of Jesse Wood, Cull, was appointed a magistrate in 1807, and died in 1820. His children were Jeremiah, a soldier in the United States army, who died in 1828, William, Charles, David, Martha and Joel. Joel, the brother of Jechonias, married Martha, daughter, of David Rodes, and in 1811 removed to Barren County, Kentucky.

Charles Yancey, who was a prominent man in the early part of the century, was the son of Robert Yancey, of Buckingham. An energetic man of business, he conducted a tavern, store, mill and distillery at what was afterwards May's, and still later Cocke's, Tavern. This was originally the location of the postoffice called Yancey's Mills, and though transferred to the more important centre of Hillsboro, the old name is retained. Mr. Yancey was appointed a magistrate in 1796, became Colonel of the Forty-Seventh Regiment in 1806, and served as Sheriff in 1821. He was twice married, first to Sarah, daughter of Robert Field, and secondly to Jane Alexander. His children by the first marriage were Jeremiah, Joel, Charles and Robert, and by the second Jechonias, Sarah, the wife of J. W. Ralls, Alexander K. and Jane. Jeremiah married Sarah, daughter of Claiborne Rothwell. He and his brother Joel built the mill on Lickinghole near Crozet about 1820, and sold it in 1822 to Philip S. Pleasants. Alexander K. married Sarah, daughter of Col. John S. Farrar, transacted business as a merchant in Hillsboro, and died in 1889.

YERGAIN.

John Yergain came to the county in the latter part of the last century, probably from Tidewater Virginia. He was a resident of Charlottesville in 1796, and in that year obtained a license for keeping an ordinary. He subsequently bought one of the houses that are situated to the east of the Farish House, and there for many years kept a store, chiefly for the sale of liquor. He never married, and lived alone.

Hard and parsimonious, he hoarded his earnings, and was reputed to be rich; and this impression was strengthened by his mode of living, and the jealous care he took in his latter years to barricade his door against all who approached. A report prevailed that he had a large amount of specie buried in his cellar. Altogether from his peculiar habits, his solitary life, and the rumors of his hidden wealth, he was an object of great curiosity in the community. He died in 1837. The reports of his concealed treasure were verified after his death, but its amount fell far short of the general supposition. A relative named William Lee appeared from New Kent, and administered on his estate.

HEBREWS.

The people destined to be "wandering among the nations," have been represented in Albemarle from the earliest times. In 1757 Michael Israel patented eighty acres in North Garden near Stockton's Thoroughfare, which he and his wife Sarah sold in 1770 to William Williams, of Goochland. It will be seen he was one of the Border Rangers. In 1772 he purchased more than three hundred acres on Mechum's River in the same section, which he sold in 1779. Solomon Israel, a brother or son, bought in the same neighborhood in 1764. Eleanor, a daughter of Solomon, was the wife of John Wood, and in 1783 Solomon gave his land to his grandson, Solomon Wood. Whether the Israels died in the county, or removed elsewhere, is not known, but their name has been left as a permanent memorial. The conspicuous pass through the mountains between North Garden and Batesville, is no longer Stockton's Thoroughfare, but Israel's Gap.

Isaiah Isaacs died in Charlottesville in 1806, leaving six children, Frances, Isaiah, Henrietta, David, Martha and Hays. They for the most part removed to Richmond. David remained in Charlottesville, was one of its merchants in the decade of 1820, was the owner of a number of lots on Main Street, and died in 1837. One of his sisters was a milliner of the place at the same date. Jacob and Raphael were also Jewish mechants in Charlottesville at that period, and besides their business there, they at the same time conducted stores at Stony Point and Port Republic.

ITALIANS AND FRENCH

In early times a number of persons came to the county from Italy and France. They were induced to this step by the influence of Mr. Jefferson, who in his comprehensive views of things sought to promote in this country the cultivation of the vine. Foremost among them was Dr. Philip Mazzei. He settled here in 1774, and to be a neighbor of Mr. Jefferson fixed his residence at Colle. He was warmly interested in the American cause during the Revolution, and to promote its interests went back to Europe in 1779. He visited this country again in 1785, presumably to dispose of his property, but soon returned permanently to his former home, where he died in 1816.

About the same time came the family of Gianniny, descendants of which are still living in the county. In 1784 Anthony Gianniny bought land on Buck Island Creek. In 1792 he petitioned for liberty to build a mill on that stream. One of the same name, no doubt a son, became a Baptist minister, and was licensed to celebrate the rites of matrimony in 1807. A Nicholas Gianniny was one of his sureties.

Peter Plumard de Rieux bought a hundred and fifty acres south of Milton, which in 1790 he sold to Anthony Mullins, and which afterwards became a part of Mr. Monroe's estate. He then purchased a house and one hundred and thirty acres on the west side of Charlottesville, which in 1795 he conveyed to Colonel Thomas Bell to pay his debts. His daughter Sarah was bound in 1801 to Mrs. Samuel Taliaferro. Claude de La Cour died in the county in 1789. His will written in French is on record. In 1809 Charles Elvy Bezet was the owner of a parcel of ground west of Charlottesville, extending from the Staunton to the Barracks Road. There appear also the names of De Prado, Colecassieu, La Porte and Modena. In 1820 Francis Modena, who was a carriage maker by trade, became the owner of Lot Forty on Main

Street, which he and his wife Mary subsequently sold to Dabney Minor.

In later times D'Alphonse came to the county as Instructor in Gymnastics at the University. He purchased the tract of land which is still known to the older citizens as D'Alphonse's Garden. It lies in the southwest angle of the intersection of the Whitehall Road and the Southern Railroad. During his residence he was popular among the students. When the war broke out, he went North and joined the Federal army. He came back to Charlottesville with Sheridan as a Captain of cavalry. When hostilities were past he returned, proposing to occupy his old place at the University; but the countenances of students and people were turned to him so coldly, that he shook off the dust of his feet, and quit Virginia in disgust.

Another distinguished foreigner was connected with Albemarle. Thaddeus Kosciusko, the illustrious Pole, who performed so gallant a part in the war of the Revolution, made his will while in this country. On returning to Europe, he left it with Mr. Jefferson, whom he had appointed his executor. When Mr. Jefferson heard of his death in 1817, he had it recorded in the office of the Albemarle Circuit Court, where the original document remained on file until May, 1875. At that time, in response to a resolution of the General Assembly, the Court ordered it to be transmitted to the Secretary of the Commonwealth, to be deposited for preservation in the State Library.

APPENDIX, No. 1.

The original of the following Call was found by Mr. Nicholas Black in looking over the papers of his uncle, the late Thomas Black. It was published in the Charlottesville *Chronicle* of March 21st, 1879.

IVY CREEK, MARCH 29, 1747.

Whereas it is agreed or proposed that ye Inhabitants of Ivy Creek and ye Mountain Plain Congregation joyn together with ye Congregation of Rockfish, to call and invite ye Reverend Samuel Black, now Residing in ye bounds of ye Reverend John Craig's Congregation, to be our Minister and Pastor to administer ye ordinances of ye Gospel among us: All ye, whose names are hereunto affixed, do promise and oblige ourselves to pay yearly and every year ye several sums annexed to our names, for ye outward support and Incouragement of ye said Mr. Samuel Black during his abode and continuance among us, for ye one half of his Labor in ye Administration of Gospel Ordinances to us in an orderly way, according to ye Rules and Practice of our Orthodox Reformed Presbyterian Church: as Witness our hands.

	£	s.	d.		£	s.	d.
Michael Woods	1	10		Samuel Jameson	1	00	
William Woods	1	10		John Lockhart		15	
Archibald Woods	1	5		Hendry Burch		10	
William Wallace	1	5		Thomas Alexander		10	
Andrew Wallace		15		Patrick Woods		8	2
John Woods Sr.		15		John McCulloch		10	
John Greer		10		William Ogans		12	6
Thomas Lockhart		10		William Chamberlain		5	
Peter Hairston		8		Thomas Craig		5	
Adam Gaudylock		10		John Thompson		5	
Michael Woods Jr.		10		John Corban		6	2
William McCord		10		Hendry Carr		5	2½
John Gamble		10		James Weir		12	2
Davis Stockton	1	00		Robert McNeilly		6	2
Hugh Dobbins		10		John Dicky		6	1
David Lewis		5		William Morris		6	1
James Gamble		5		John Kincaid		5	
Charles Lambert		5		John Woods Jr.		5	
John Monday		5		John Jameson		10	
Thomas Evins		5		Benjamin Wheeler		5	
Thomas Wright		5		W. Bucknall		5	
William Little		10	2½	John Burrisse		5	
Nathan Woods		10	3	Robert Stewart		5	2

HISTORY OF ALBEMARLE

	£	s.	d.		£	s.	d.
James Kincaid		10	5	William Whiteside		10	
Andrew McWilliams		10	2½	William Bustard		6	
George Dawson		5	2½	Thomas Whiteside		10	
Joseph Kincaid	1	00		Matthew Mullins		5	
John McCord	1	00		Richard Stockton		12	
Archibald Woods		10					

APPENDIX. No. 2.

Albemarle Company of Militia, lately in actual service for the defence and protection of the frontier against the Indians, September, 1758. Hening's Statutes, VII, 203.

James Nevill, Captain
John Woods, Lieut.
William Woods, Lieut.
William Woods, Ensign
David Martin, Ensign
Andrew Greer, Sergeant
Charles Wakefield, Sergeant
William Martin, Sergeant
Samuel Stockton
Thomas Jameson
Hugh Alexander
Robert Poage
John Wallace
Adam Gaudylock
Michael Woods Jr.
Bartholomew Ramsay
Henry Randolph
William Stockton
Michael Israel
James Kinkead
Thomas Harbet
Henry Brenton
Joshua Woods
Alexander Jameson
Daniel Maupin
John Maupin
William Maupin
Matthew Mullins

Samuel Woods
William Whiteside
David Gass
Abraham Howard
Thomas Grubbs
John Cowan
George Breckinridge
William Poage
William Wakefield
William Cartie
Charles Hughes
Langdon Depriest
Aaron Hughes
John Depriest
James Glenn
James Robertson
Charles Crawford
John Biggs
John McAnally
Robert McWhorter
Richard Pryor
James Martin
Michael Morrison
James Morrison
Adam Lackie
Alexander McMulen
Lawrence Smith
Matthias Hughes

APPENDIX. No. 3.

Extracts from memoranda connected with the Revolution, found among the papers of Dr. George Gilmer.

The following volunteers in the Independent Companies of Albemarle County bound themselves to the ensuing Resolves by subscribing thereto:

1. Should they fail or fly back, they should be held unworthy of the rights of freemen, and as inimical to the cause of America.

2. Any one elected as Captain, Lieutenant, or Ensign, and refusing to serve, shall pay, the first £25, the second £15, and the third £10, for the use of the Company.

3. To obey the officers by themselves elected, muster four times a year, provide gun, shot-pouch and powder horn, and appear on duty in hunting shirt.

*Charles Lewis, Captain	Shadrach Battles
*George Gilmer, Lieut.	J. S. Logan
*John Marks, Lieut.	J. S. Lisle
John Harvie, Ensign	William Flint
William Simms, Sergeant	Roger Shackelford
*William Wood, Sergeant	John Dickerson
*William T. Lewis, Sergeant	Edward Hughes
*John Martin, Sergeant	Stephen Hughes
*Fred Wm. Wills, Corporal	J. S. Dudley
*Thomas Martin Jr., Corporal	J. S. Stephenson
Patrick Napier, Corporal	John Coles
*David Allen, Corporal	*Charles L. Lewis
*John Lowry, Drummer	*James Quarles
*Edward Garland	Isaac Davis
*John Henderson	Spencer Norvell
*Isaac Wood	*Reuben Lindsay
*Falvy Frazier	Robert Martin Jr.
Samuel Carr	*William Johnson
John Watkins	James Lewis
Micajah Defoe	Edward Carter
John Wood	Turner Richardson
David Dalton	George Thompson

Those marked with an asterisk, marched to Williamsburg, May 2nd, 1775, to demand satisfaction of Lord Dunmore for the removal of the powder.

The following marched to Williamsburg, July 11th, 1775 under Lieut. George Gilmer.

Matthew Jouett	William Wood
Richard Harper	William Lewis
William Flint	William Henderson
Isham Lewis	Thomas Strachan
Richard Harvie	John Martin, Sergeant
Erasmus Ball	Isaac Davis
Bennett Henderson	Nelson Thompson

HISTORY OF ALBEMARLE 365

Charles L. Lewis
Hastings Marks
Thomas Mitchell
Hudson Martin
John Wood
Micajah Chiles

Micajah Lewis
Richard Durrett
Bernard Mills
John Henderson
John Wood
Thomas Walker

Thomas Martin, Corporal

A Declaration of Independence, signed by citizens of Albemarle, April 21st, 1779, the original of which is preserved in the rooms of the Virginia Historical Society in Richmond.

George Gilmer
James Quarles
William Lewis
Richard Anderson
Peter Marks
James Bridgett
John Fielder
George Norvell
Nathaniel Haggard
Henry Mullins
Tucker Woodson
Isaac Davis
Samuel Taliaferro
John Day
Micajah Chiles
Richard Harper
William Barton
John Greer
Thomas Jefferson
John Harvie
John Coles
James Marks
John Harris
John Jouett
Nicholas Lewis
Benjamin Harris
Samuel Dedman
James Hopkins
C. Simms
James Kerr
William Hays
Edward Butler
R. Davenport Jr.
William Irvin, V. D. M.
Jason Bowcock

James Reid
Benjamin Lacy
William Tandy Sr.
John Reid
William Hopkins
Clough Shelton
Samuel Woodson
Thomas Overton
Thomas Martin Jr.
John Wilkinson
Benjamin Dod Wheeler
Peter Jackson
Henry Heard
John Jouett Jr.
Isaac Davis Jr.
Philip Mazzei
George Saunders
Richard Gaines
William Briscoe
William Carroll
Robert Sharp Sr.
Robert Sharp Jr.
Joseph Lamb
John Bailey
Roland Horsley
Richard Harvie
Alexander McKinzie
Robert Thompson Jr.
John Kirby
John Black
William Pilson
Robert Pilson
James Epperson
John Lott
Richard Sharp

366 HISTORY OF ALBEMARLE

Henry Shelton
James Minor
Anderson Bryan
John Fitzpatrick
John Stockton
Josiah Wood
William Flannagan
Peter Ferguson
Nathaniel McAllister
John Henderson Sr.
John Lewis Sr.
W. Langford
Peter Burrus
John Tandy
Richard Goodall
Spencer Norvell
Orlando Jones
Stat. Morris
William Michie
Thomas Craig
John McCulloch
Charles L. Lewis
William Johnson
Zachariah Mills
John Thomas
Castleton Harper Sr.
John Newcomb
Samuel Bing
Richard Carter
John Wingfield
Henry Hooper
Nicholas Hamner
Joseph Terrell
Daniel Goolsby
Richard Davenport
Charles Tucker
William Hitchcock
Henry Copeland
Richard Goolsby
Hiram Gaines
John Prince
Castleton Harper Jr.
Daniel Coleman
William Wingfield
William Leake
Martin Haggard

Robert Burrus
Henry Randolph
William McGhee
Samuel Karr
Samuel McCord
Joseph Holt
William L. Bing
Benjamin Jordan
John Henderson Jr.
William Barksdale
Thomas Thorp
James Wm. Crossthwait
R. Dixon
T. Marshall
Daniel Coleman
William Wingfield
Christopher Wingfield
William Leake
Martin Haggard
Peter Ballou
Thomas West
William Anderson
Joseph Neilson
William Colvard
William Fossett
Edward Moore
Charles Lewis Jr.
David G. Mosby
Isham Lewis
Henry Ford
William Sandridge
William Chenault
Thomas Musick
Samuel Huckstep
Jacob Oglesby
John Wood
Thomas Collins
Arthur Graham
Thomas Morgan
Charles Hudson
William Jeffers
Richard Scott
Bernis Brown
William Statham
Stephen Hughes Jr.
Horsley Goodman

HISTORY OF ALBEMARLE   367

Peter Ballou
Thomas Fentress
James McManus
Samuel Rea
Abraham Eades
John Fentress
William Sorrow
William Fry
Charles Goodman
Michael Wallace
Randolph Jefferson
John Hall
David Allen
Charles Kerr
Benjamin Henderson
Samuel Bowcock
David Morris
John Wallace
Matthew Maury
Mask Leake
Robert Cobbs
Thomas Gooch

William Shelton
Littlebury Sullivan
William Karr
William Ramsay
David Nimmo
William Reynolds
Richard Watson
Shadrach Reynolds
Daniel Reynolds
Francis Browning
William Rannald
Abraham Gollan
William Cleveland
James Bird
William Ballard
Thomas Jameson
George Mann
Daniel Miller
Francis Hodge
Francis Taliaferro
John Kirby
James Woods

APPENDIX, No. 4.
ALBEMARLE SOLDIERS OF THE REVOLUTION
OFFICERS.

David Anderson, Ensign, 9th Va.
Nathaniel Anderson, Lieut, 3rd Va.
John Beck, Ensign, 9th Va.
Samuel Bell, Ensign, Grayson's Reg.
Thomas Bell, Captain, Gist's Reg.
Bezaleel Brown, Captain, State troops at Yorktown.
Henry Burke, Captain, State militia.
John Burke, Captain, State militia.
May Button, Captain, State militia.
Peter Davie, Quartermaster, 14th Va.
Samuel Eddins, Captain, 1st Cont. Artillery.
Edward Garland, Captain, 14th Va.
Peter Garland, Captain, 6th Va.
Nathaniel Garland, Lieut., State militia.
William Gooch, Lieut., State militia.
William Grayson, Captain, State militia.
John Hargis, Ensign, 13th Va.
Benjamin Harris, Captain, State militia.

Robert Harris, Captain, State militia.
Reuben Hawkins, Captain, State militia.
William Henderson, Captain, 9th Va.
Reuben Herndon, Lieut., 7th Va.
Joseph Holt, Lieut., 4th Va.
Samuel Hopkins, Lt. Col., 10th Va., captured at Charleston, S. C.
Charles Hudson, Quartermaster, 14th Va.
John Hudson, Captain, State militia.
Isaac Israel, Captain, 8th Va.
John Jameson, Lt. Col., Dragoons.
Matthew Jouett, Captain.
Robert Jouett, Captain, 7th Va.
John Key, Ensign, 8th Va.
Mask Leake, Captain, State militia.
Charles Lewis, Colonel, 14th Va.
Nicholas Lewis, Captain, State militia.
William Lewis, Lieut., Cont. Line.
Reuben Lindsay, Col., State militia.
Richard Lindsay, Col. Gen., Lawson's Brigade.
Bernard Lipscomb, Captain, State militia.
Col. Mallory.
John Marks, Captain, 14th Va.
Hudson Martin, Lieut., 9th Va.
John Martin, Captain, State militia.
Abraham Maury, Adjutant, 14th Va.
David Meriwether, 14th Va., captured at Charleston.
James Meriwether, Adj., State militia.
Thomas Meriwether, Major, State militia.
Peter Minor, Captain, 5th Va.
Archelaus Moon, Lieut., 14th Va.
Jacob Moon, Paymaster, 14th Va.
George Nicholas, Lt. Col., 11th Va.
John Nicholas, Lieut., 9th Va.
Wilson C. Nicholas, Com., Washington's Guards.
Lipscomb Norvell, Lieut., 5th Va.
John Piper, Lieut., State militia.
James Quarles, Captain, State militia.
Robert Rodes, Captain captured at Charleston.
Clough Shelton, Captain, 10th Va., captured at Charleston.
William Simms, Captain, 6th Va.
Larkin Smith, Captain, 4th Dragoons.
George Thompson, Lieut., State militia.
John Thompson, Lieut., 7th Va.
Leonard Thompson, Lieut., State militia.
Roger Thompson, Captain, 2nd Va.
Thomas Walker Jr., Captain, 9th Va.

Captain Warr, probably Marr.
Daniel White, Captain, State militia.
Tarleton Woodson, Sergeant, State militia.

PRIVATES.

John Burton, disabled and pensioned.
John Buster, died 1820, served against Indians, and in Revolution.
Nathan Clausby, Grenadier, 1st Partisan Legion.
James Craddock, died in the service.
Charles Davis, 1st Light Dragoons, wounded and pensioned.
David Epperson, died in the service.
John Fagg Sr., died 1829, aged 92.
Simpson Foster, died in the service.
John Gillaspy, 9th Va., killed at Germantown.
Charles Goolsby, Corporal, 9th Va., captured at Germantown, and died in the service.
James Goolsby, 9th Va., captured at Germantown, and died in the service.
John Goolsby, 9th Va., died in the service.
John Greening, 2nd Va.
William Hardin, killed at Ninety-Six.
Bartlett Hawkins, pensioned.
Ambrose Howard, 9th Va.
Richard Marshall, pensioned by Act of Assembly.
Peter Massie, 5th Va.
Thomas Mitchell, Sergeant, Cont. army, died in the service.
James Old, died 1821, in battles of Quebec and Long Island.
William Smith, died 1823, aged 95, served against Indians, and in Revolution.
John Snead, in Cont. army.
Kenneth Southerlin, State militia.
Daniel Tilman, died 1820, served at 16 against Indians, and in Revolution.
Applying for pensions under Act of Congress passed in 1818.

ENLISTED IN ALBEMARLE

William Bailey, in Capt. Thomas Walker's Co., 9th Va., in battles of Brunswick and Saratoga, discharged in Pa.
Joseph Brockman, in Capt. Lindman's Co., Col. Davies's Reg., in no battle, discharged at Powhatan.
William Eastin, in Capt. Reuben Taylor's Co., Col. Moses Hazen's Reg., in battles of Staten Island, Brandywine and Germantown, discharged at Morristown, N. J.
Nehemiah Greening, in Capt. Stribling's Co., Buford's Reg., at Fort

Motte, Ninety-Six and Eutaw Springs, discharged at Salisbury, N. C.
Edward Hughes, in Capt. John Mark's Co., 1st Va., in battles of Brandywine, Germantown and Guilford C. H.
Thomas Johnson, in Capt. Roger Thompson's Co., 2nd Va., in no battles, discharged at Long Island, Holston River.
John Jones, in Capt. Winston's Co., Col. Charles Lewis's Reg., in battles of Brandywine, Germantown, and Monmouth, discharged at Middlebrook, N. J.
Sabrit King, in Capt. Robert Jouett's Co., 7th Va., in battle of Monmouth.
Martin Mooney, in Capt. Fontaine's Co., 14th Va., and Capt. Wm. Lewis's Co., Col. Cleveland's Reg., in battles of Long Bridge, King's Mountain and Ninety-Six.
Richard Mooney, in Capt. John Mark's Co., 1st Va., in battles of Guilford C. H., Camden, Ninety-Six and Eutaw Springs, discharged at Salisbury, N. C.
Samuel Munday, in Capt. Wm. Simm's Co., Col. Green's Reg., at Guilford C. H., Camden, Ninety-Six and Eutaw Springs, discharged at Salisbury, N. C.

Enlisted in other places, but residents of Albemarle after the war.

Humphrey Beckett, in Frederick County, Capt. Porterfield's Co., 11th Va., in battles of Somerset, Amboy and Monmouth, discharged in Frederick.
Thomas Burton, in Hanover County, Capt. Hurd's Co., Buford's Reg., in no battle, discharged in Fluvanna.
Youen Carden, in Cumberland County, under Lt. Benj. Garrett, Capt. Baylor's Cavalry, and twenty months under Col. Washington, discharged at Charleston, S. C.
John Grinstead, in Hanover County, Capt. Woodson's Co., Col. Posey's Reg., at Savannah and Yorktown, discharged in Cumberland County.
Sabrit Hoy, in Culpeper County, Capt. Harrison's Co., 2nd Va., at Cowpens, Guilford C. H., Camden, Ninety-Six and Eutaw Springs, discharged at Salisbury, N. C.
William Kirby, in Hanover County, Capt. Stribling's Co., Buford's Reg., at Guilford C. H., Camden, Ninety-Six, and Eutaw Springs, discharged at Salisbury, N. C.
Isaac Milliway, at Dover, Del., Capt. McCannon's Co., Col. Vaughan's Reg., at Guilford C. H., Camden, Eutaw Springs, where he was severely wounded, discharged at Dover.
George Norvell, in Capt. Richard C. Anderson's Co., 5th Va., at Brandywine, Germantown and Yorktown, discharged at West Point.

Joseph Shepherd, at Fredericksburg, in Capt. John Wallace's Co., 3rd Va.
Cephas Shickett, in Capt. John Stuart's Co., 1st Maryland, at Brandywine and Germantown, discharged at Annapolis.
John Wm. Shube, in Philadelphia, in Pulaski's Corps, at Savannah, Camden, Mount Scoota, and James Island, discharged at Smithfield, Va.
John Smith, in Pennsylvania Artillery, Capt. Proctor, at Trenton, with Gen. Clark down the Ohio in 1781, and one year with Gen. Harmar, discharged at Fort Pitt.
William Turner, in Capt. Francis Taylor's Co., 2nd Va., at Germantown and Stony Point.
John Williams, in Brunswick County, Capt. John Overton's Co., 10th Va., at Guilford C. H., Eutaw Springs, and Yorktown, discharged at Williamsburg.

PRIVATES IN STATE MILITIA.

Samuel Barksdale
Micajah Bowen
William Boyd
Gideon Carr
Meekins Carr
John Collins
Major Dowell
James Dunn
George Gentry
James Gentry
Sharod Going
John Hall
Nathan Hall
George Hardin
William Harris
Richard Hill
Charles Huckstep
Richard Johnson

William Jordan
Adam Keblinger
Samuel McCord
Cornelius Maupin
Daniel Maupin
William Maupin
Jonathan Munday, at Yorktown
Ephriam Seamonds
Richard Snow, at Yorktown
Richard Spinner
John Spradling
David Strange, at Yorktown
John Taylor
Nathaniel Thacker
Absalom Thomas
John Thomas
Roger Thompson, at Yorktown
Micajah Wheeler
John Wood.

HISTORY OF ALBEMARLE

APPENDIX. No. 5.
MILITARY ORGANIZATION OF THE COUNTY.

It may be of interest to many to be informed in regard to the military force of the county, the bodies of which it was composed, and their officers, during the period extending from 1794 to 1802.

Forty-Seventh Regiment, South of the Three Notched Road.
Colonels.
Wilson C. Nicholas   Samuel Murrell

1ST BATTALION.
Majors.
Samuel Murrell   James Lewis

1ST COMPANY.

Captain	*Lieut.*	*Ensign.*
Benj. Lacy	Thos. Hamner	Mart. Davenport
Edward Garland	Mart. Davenport	Edward Garland
Joseph Wingfield	Charles Lacy	Stephen Lacy
		Joseph Wingfield
		Francis Wingfield

2ND COMPANY.

Cornelius Schenk	Christopher Wingfield	R. H. Allen
	Thomas Carr Jr.	Thomas Carr Jr.
	John T. Hawkins	Charles Jouett
		Thomas Wells Jr.

3RD COMPANY.

William Leake	Walter Leake	Walter Coles
Walter Leake	George Wharton	George Wharton
		Edward Thomas
		Samuel Leake

4TH COMPANY.

William Tompkins	Clifton Garland	John Scott Jr.
William Hopkins	Samuel Hopkins	Samuel Hopkins
John Staples	Charles A. Scott	Turner Monn
	William Moon Jr.	William Moon Jr.
		William Hamner

LIGHT INFANTRY.

Samuel Shelton	Lewis Nicholas	James Ming
Richard Pollard	William Davenport	Joseph Bishop
John S. Farrar	John S. Farrar	Joseph Coleman
	Walter Lacy	N. A. Thompson

HISTORY OF ALBEMARLE 373

CAVALRY.

Samuel Carr	Thomas Divers	George Gilmer
		Cornet
		Dabney Minor

2ND BATTALION.
Majors.
John Jordon   Edward Garland

1ST COMPANY.

Captain	*Lieut.*	*Ensign.*
George Martin	William Wharton	Schuyler Harris
William Wharton	Abraham Martin	Bez. Maxwell Jr.
	James Watson	Thomas Key

2ND COMPANY.

Menan Mills	Francis Montgomery	John Piper
William Wood Jr.	William Wood Jr.	Clifton Rodes
	John Field	Jesse Wood Jr.

3RD COMPANY.

James Brooks	Rice Garland	Michael Woods
Charles Yancey	Michael Woods	Charles Yancey
	Jechonias Yancey	Ephriam Musick

4TH COMPANY.

James Lewis	Tarleton Woodson	Richard Harrison
Micajah Woods	Benj. Buster	Micajah Woods
		Tipton Lewis

LIGHT INFANTRY.

Howell Lewis	Robert Garland	John R. Kerr
Robert Garland	William Woods	William Woods
		John Gilliam
		John P. Watson

LIGHT HORSE.

Clifton Garland	John Clarkson	Weatherston Shelton
Charles Hudson	Walter Coles	Cornet

Eighty-Eighth Regiment, North of the Three Notched Road.
Colonels.
Thomas Bell   Francis Walker

1ST BATTALION
Majors.
Robert Jouett   James Simms
Francis Walker   Robert Warner Lewis

1st Company.

Captain	Lieut.	Ensign.
James Simms	Achilles Douglass	Samuel Brockman
Achilles Douglass	Samuel Brockman	William Simms Jr.
Samuel Brockman	Ambrose Brockman	Ambrose Brockman
	John Douglass	John Douglass
		William Smith

2nd Company.

Joshua Key	Micajah Carr	Drury Wood
Micajah Carr	Drury Wood	George Gilmer
Drury Wood	John Sandridge	John Sandridge
		Thomas Travillian

3rd Company.

Wm. D. Meriwether	Charles B. Hunton	John Rogers
Charles B. Hunton	James B. Lindsay	James G. Waddell
James B. Lindsay	Thomas Hunton	Thomas Hunton
		Matthew Maury

4th Company.

Edward Moore	William Crenshaw	John Henderson
David Anderson	John Henderson	David Anderson
	Kemp Catlett	Kemp Catlett
		George W. Catlett

LIGHT INFANTRY.

Francis Walker	David Clarkson	Thomas Walker Jr.
David Clarkson	William Wirt	Robert W. Lewis
Nimrod Bramham	Nimrod Bramham	Ludlow Bramham
	Madison Breedlove	Madison Breedlove
	George Martin	George Martin
		Reuben Herndon

RIFLEMEN.

Thomas S. Buster	Reuben Lewis	Gerland Brown

2nd Battalion.

Majors.

Henry Burke   John Wood   Horsley Goodman

1st Company.

Captain	Lieut.	Ensign.
Wyatt Mills	Thomas Fretwell	Parmenas Rogers
Parmenas Rogers	Parmenas Rogers	Matthew P. Walton
	Edmund Davis	

2nd Company.

John Wood	David Wood	David Michie
David Wood	John Crenshaw	Joseph Edmondson
	Thomas Wood	

3RD COMPANY.

William Jarman	Brightberry Brown	John Rodes Jr.
Brightberry Brown	John Rodes Jr.	Robert T. Brown
		James Harris
		Charles Brown

4TH COMPANY.

Horsley Goodman	Thomas Garth Jr.	Joseph Goodman
Thomas Garth Jr.	Joseph Goodman	John A. Michie
		Alexander Garrett

LIGHT INFANTRY.

Matthew Rodes	Elijah Garth	Nathan Harris
Elijah Garth	Swanny Ferguson	Swanny Ferguson
	William Thompson	William Thompson
		James Ballard

LIGHT HORSE.

Thos. M. Randolph   Peter Carr   William Love, Cornet
Robert Jouett, Col. Artillery, 2nd Division

Subsequent Colonels.

FORTY-SEVENTH.

Colonels
Charles Yancey, 1806
John S. Farrar, 1815
William Woods, S. 1817
Joseph Coffman, 1828
George W. Kinsolving, 1830
David Hays, 1832
William H. Brown, 1839
John H. Timberlake, 1860.

Lieut. Colonels.
John Coles
George W. Kinsolving
Michael Johnson
John R. Jones

EIGHTY-EIGHTH.

Colonels
Nimrod Bramham, 1806
Thomas W. Woods, 1814
David Carr, 1828
James O. Carr, 1829
John J. Bowcock, 1839

Lieut. Colonels.
Jesse W. Garth
Isaac Simms
David Carr
Thomas Durrett

APPENDIX. No. 6.
LIST OF COUNTY OFFICERS.
Magistrates.
1745.

Joshua Fry   Charles Lynch
Peter Jefferson   Joseph Thompson

William Cabell, M. D.
Allen Howard
James Daniel

Thomas Ballou
Edwin Hickman

1746.

Isaac Bates
Charles Lewis Jr.
Edmund Gray
Samuel Jordan
Valentine Wood

David Lewis
John Reid
James Nevell
William Harris
John Anthony

Date of Appointment Unknown.

John Hunter
John Cobb
John Cannon
Robert Lewis
Nicholas Meriwether
John Lewis
Hudson Martin

Isaac Davis
Jesse Burton
Roger Thompson
Thomas Napier
Thomas Jefferson
William Leigh

Acting in 1783.

Nicholas Lewis
George Gilmer
Clifton Rodes
James Kerr
James Quarles
James Garland
John Key
John Henderson
James Minor
Michael Thomas

John Marks
James Marks
Bennett Henderson
Joshua Fry
David Rodes
Reuben Lindsay
John Piper
William Hughes
Henry Burke

1791.

Bezaleel Brown
Bernard Brown
William Clark
Thomas W. Lewis
George Divers
Thomas Garth
William Michie
Rice Garland

Tandy Key
William D. Meriwether
Wilson C. Nicholas
Samuel Murrell
James Simms
Thomas Bell
Charles B. Hunton
Benjamin Harris

1794.

Charles Goodman
Samuel Black
Robert Davis
Charles Wingfield Jr.
Edward Moore
William Wardlaw

Joshua Key
Francis Walker
Benjamin Brown
Thomas M. Randolph
Thomas C. Fletcher

1795.
Garland Carr

1796.
Achilles Douglass   Charles Yancey
Marshall Durrett

1798.
James Monroe

1800.
John Watson   Howell Lewis
Christopher Hudson

1801.
David Wood   Peter Carr
William Walker   Charles A. Scott
David Anderson   Walter Coles
Edward Garland   Joel Harris
Nimrod Bramham   Isaac Miller

1806.
Dabney Minor   Garrett White
Martin Dawson   James Lewis
Samuel Carr   John Staples
Clifton Garland

1807.
John R. Kerr   Clifton Rodes
John Harris   Jechonias Yancey
James Harris   Parmenas Rogers
James Old   David J. Lewis
John Rodes Jr.   John A. Michie
Charles Everett

1816.
Matthew Rodes   Thomas W. Wood
Micajah Woods   Francis Carr
John Goss   John Irvin
William Woods, S.   James Clark
Thomas W. Maury   Charles Brown
William A. Harris   Joseph Coffman
John M. Perry   James Michie
Thos. Eston Randolph

1819.
Hugh Nelson   Allen Dawson
William Moon   Thomas H. Brown
Opie Norris   Charles Cocke
Isaac Curd   Robert Brooks

Benjamin Ficklin
James Jarman
Richard Duke
Achilles Broadhead

Edmund Davis
John Pilson
John B. Hart

Henry White
Lewis Teel
Gilly M. Lewis
John Morris

William A. Bibb

Chapman W. Maupin
John S. Cocke
Bezaleel Brown
Ira B. Brown
Carter H. Harrison

James Duke
James D. Watts
John J. Bowcock
Lilburn R. Railey
Nimrod Bramham Jr.
John S. Nicholas

John L. Thomas
Daniel E. Watson
William H. Harris

George W. Spooner
Robert H. Carter
Franklin Minor
Francis K. Nelson

John Cochran
John H. Timberlake
Alexander P. Abell
Matthew Blair

John R. Jones
William H. Dyer
Thomas J. Randolph

1824.

John T. Holman
Mann Page

1830.

William B. Harris
Daniel M. Railey
John W. Gantt
James Harris

1832.

James R. Watson

1835.

Charles Wingfield
John Coles Carter
John D. Moon
William S. Dabney
John A. G. Davis

1838.

W. C. Nicholas
Thomas Macon
Thomas Garland
Gabriel S. Harper
William C. Adams
William D. Hart

1838.

M. L. Anderson
John W. Goss
M. L. Walker

1841.

Nicholas M. Page
John Tyler
Alonzo Gooch
James W. Goss

1843.

Thomas C. Bowen
Thomas R. Dunn
William F. Gooch
D. J. Hartsook

HISTORY OF ALBEMARLE 379

1846.
Benj. F. Randolph   Austin M. Appling
Robert B. Moon   Marcus Durrett
John E. Roberts   James E. Chapman

The following were recommended, but not appointed, as the new Constitution, about to go into effect, made the office elective.

1850.
Stokes Tunstall   James C. Carter
James Durrett   Paul H. Goodloe
William W. Minor   James L. Dunn
Samuel G. Burnley   R. W. N. Noland
Edwin B. Brown   John T. Randolph
Carter H. Page

ATTORNEYS FOR THE COMMONWEALTH.

1745.	Edmund Gray	1829.	Valentine W. Southall
1746.	Gideon Marr	1852.	William J. Robertson
1783.	John Walker	1858.	R. T. W. Duke
1801.	Dabney Carr	1865.	Egbert R. Watson
1811.	Joseph F. Monroe	1866.	R. T. W. Duke
1812.	William F. Gordon	1869.	William F. Worthington
1813.	Jesse W. Garth	1870.	R. T. W. Duke
1818.	Jonathan Boucher Carr	1870.	Micajah Woods

SHERIFFS.

1745.	Joseph Thompson	1807.	Thomas Garth
1747.	Edwin Hickman	1809.	Tandy Key
1749.	Charles Lynch	1811.	Rice Garland
1751.	James Daniel	1813.	Charles B. Hunton
1753.	Samuel Jordan	1815.	Benjamin Harris
1755.	John Reid	1817.	Robert Davis
1757.	John Hunter	1819.	Charles Wingfield Jr.
	Nicholas Lewis	1819.	Marshall Durrett
	David Rodes	1821.	Charles Yancey
	John Henderson	1823.	Achilles Douglass
1781.	James Quarles	1825.	John Watson
1783.	Clifton Rodes	1828.	William D. Meriwether
1785.	John Marks	1830.	Garrett White
1787.	George Gilmer	1832.	John Rodes
1789.	Michael Thomas	1834.	Parmenas Rogers
1791.	James Garland	1836.	Micajah Woods
1793.	James Kerr	1837.	William Woods, S.
1795.	John Key	1839.	Francis Carr
1797.	William Hughes	1841.	Charles Brown
1799.	Samuel Murrell	1843.	James Michie

380   HISTORY OF ALBEMARLE

1801. William D. Meriwether   1845. Benjamin Ficklin
1803. William Michie   1847. Richard Duke
1805. Bezaleel Brown   1849. Thomas H. Brown
                                 1851. Charles Cocke

JAILORS.

1792. George Bruce   1851. Washington Chiles
1801. Thomas Wells   1855. William C. Walstrum
1806. Triplett T. Estes   1856. Orange S. Peterson
1810. Elijah Garth   1859. Allen Bacon
1811. William Watson   1870. William C. Walstrum
1828. Joel W. Brown   1875. Allen Bacon
1832. William Watson   1879. William G. Wright
1841. James A. Watson   1885. John G. Martin
1849. William Summerson

ATTORNEYS OF THE ALBEMARLE BAR.

1745.

Edmund Gray   Clement Read
Gideon Marr   Thomas Prestwood
James Meredith   Obadiah Marriott
William Battersby   John Harvie

1783.

John Walker   Robert Jouett
Thomas Miller   John Allen
W. Sidney Crawford   William McDowell
George Nicholas   John Carr
John Breckinridge

1791.

John Rice Kerr   John Shackelford
Robert Ware Peacock   Joseph J. Monroe
William Waller Hening   David Bullock
Peter Carr   Alexander Stuart
Walter Leake   Richard Bruce

1794.

William Wirt   James Barbour Jr.
James McCampbell   William Cabell
Fleming Payne

1796.

Joseph Holt Irvin   Dabney Carr
Austin Leake   Reuben Thornton
Matthew Gooch   Samuel L. Crawford
Jesse Wharton

1798.

Charles Jouett   George Poindexter

Philip Gooch
William Lee Harris
David Michie

1800.

James G. Waddell
Joseph Ferguson
Frederick Harris
Richard C. Johnson
Robert Michie
David Watson
Benjamin Brown
William Buckner
Francis Johnson
Patrick Rose

Robert Anderson
Thomas T. Jones
Thomas R. Whitlock
John S. Wood
Clifton Garland

Henry White
John M. Martin
William Taylor
Jonathan B. Carr
James Forbes
John Timberlake

Archibald Austin
Valentine W. Southall
Briscoe G. Baldwin

George Booker
John L. Marye
Charles Downing

Augustine G. Monroe
Francis B. Dyer

William H. Meriwether
Joseph M. White
James Barbour
James H. Simison

William Aylett
Thomas Clark

William W. Irvin
William Clark
Isaac A. Coles
Thomas W. Maury
Hugh Nelson
Philip P. Barbour
Hudson M. Garland
Peachy R. Gilmer
Edward C. Stanard
William White

1806.

Robert Mallory
Robert Garland
James Garland
Henry T. Harris

1809.

William F. Gordon
James Crawford
Jesse Winston Garth
John S. Barbour
John N. Nicholas

1813.

Garrett M. Quarles
Walter L. Fontaine
Richard H. Field

1815.

William Kinney
Thomas Clark

1817.

Rice Garland Jr.
Edward J. Magruder

1820.

John Ormond
David Irvin
William C. Rives
George Carr

Chapman Johnson
Rice W. Wood
Grandison Moseley
Franklin Stanard
John Wilson
Thomas W. Gilmer
George M. Payne
Daniel G. Morrell
Edgar Macon

John B. Spiece
Joseph Mills Jr.
William McCord Jr.
Thomas C. Gordon
George Robertson
Thomas G. Garth
William Kingsley
William R. Mills
William Wertenbaker

1825.

Chesley Kinney
Peyton Harrison
Hugh P. Taylor
Robert S. Brooke
Thomas J. Michie
Alexander Clayton
Nicholas P. Trist
Eston Stanard
Alexander Rives

Calvin L. Perry
Thomas J. Boyd
James W. Saunders
Robert H. Carter
Daniel Perrow
Benjamin H. Magruder
Wilson M. Cary
Nathaniel Wolfe

1830.

John W. C. Watson
Lucian Minor
William B. Napton
Egbert R. Watson
Thomas Wood
William D. Hart
John Forbes Sr.
John T. Craig
Alexander Moseley
Hugh A. Garland
Peachy R. Grattan
William Tompkins

Sterling Claiborne
James P. Henderson
Burwell Garth
John C. R. Taylor
John H. Gilmer
William H. Brockenbrough
John W. Stevenson
William M. Randolph
James L. Carr
John B. Minor
Thomas L. Preston

1835.

James L. Gordon
Hudson S. Garland
John Hill
Franklin Minor
William W. Minor
Benj. W. Darneille
Peter Carr

William O. Maupin
Hiram W. Dawson
Shelton F. Leake
James C. Halsall
Angus R. Blakey
Allen B. Magruder

1840.

Thomas T. Hill
George W. Randolph
Stephen O. Southall

William J. Robertson
R. W. N. Noland
Paul H. Goodloe

HISTORY OF ALBEMARLE 383

George W. Trueheart
Smith P. Bankhead
Eugene Davis

1845.

J. D. Imboden
Clayton C. Harris
Francis W. Rives
William C. Rives Jr.
Reuben L. Gordon
William J. Shelton
Robert W. Poore
John L. Cochran

R. T. W. Duke
William F. Gordon Jr.
James D. Jones

John B. Gilmer
John S. Mosby
William H. Crank
John B. Peyton

R. R. Prentis
Joel Miller
Thomas S. Martin

John B. Moon
Howe Y. Peyton
George Perkins
Louis T. Hanckel
Bennett Taylor
W. E. Bibb
Jefferson R. Taylor
W. O. Fry

Thomas N. Page
W. H. Boaz
Walter D. Dabney

James Blakey
Samuel B. Woods
James L. Gordon

William M. Lile
C. D. Shackelford

Drury Wood
Thomas T. Tutwiler
John R. Tucker

Alexander H. Michie
William M. Wade
Roger A. Pryor
N. H. Massie
St. George Tucker
William T. McCarty
James C. Southall

1850.

S. V. Southall
Burwell W. Snead
William M. Morris

1855.

Isaac A. Moon
George P. Hughes
M. L. Randolph

1859.
Charles Wood
1865.

Micajah Woods
Camm Patterson
James G. Field

1870.

T. L. Michie
J. W. Fitz
J. R. Wingfield
J. M. McBryde
Robert Sampson
R. T. W. Duke Jr.
Shelton F. Leake Jr.

1875.

Robert H. Wood
Frank Gilmer
George W. Morris

1880.

Z. J. Blakey
J. Samuel McCue
Daniel Harmon

1885.

F. A. Massie

APPENDIX. No. 7.

Representatives of Albemarle in the House of Delegates, and Legislature.

Year	Representatives	Senate
1748.	Charles Lynch	
1755.	Peter Jefferson	
1756.	Peter Jefferson, Allen Howard	
1757.	John Nicholas, William Cabell	
1758.	John Nicholas, William Cabell	
1759.	Allen Howard, William Cabell Jr.	
1761.	Allen Howard, William Cabell Jr.	
1765.	John Harvie	
1767.	Thomas Walker, Edward Carter	
1768.	Thomas Walker, Edward Carter	
1769.	Thomas Walker, Edward Carter	
1770.	Thomas Walker, Thomas Jefferson	
1771.	Thomas Walker, Thomas Jefferson	
1772.	Thomas Jefferson, John Walker	
1773.	Thomas Jefferson, John Walker	
1774.	Thomas Jefferson, John Walker	
1775.	Thomas Jefferson, John Walker	SENATE.
1777.	Thomas Jefferson, Charles Lewis	William Cabell
1779.	Thomas Jefferson, George Gilmer	William Cabell
1785.	W. C. Nicholas, Edward Carter	Joseph Cabell
1786.	W. C. Nicholas, Joshua Fry	Nicholas Cabell
1788.	George Nicholas, Edward Carter	Nicholas Cabell
1793.	William Clark, Edward Moore	Nicholas Cabell
1795.	W. C. Nicholas, Edward Moore	Nicholas Cabell
1796.	W. C. Nicholas, Edward Moore	Nicholas Cabell
1797.	W. C. Nicholas, Joseph J. Monroe	Nicholas Cabell
1798.	W. C. Nicholas, Francis Walker	Nicholas Cabell
1800.	W. C. Nicholas, Francis Walker	Nicholas Cabell
1805.	Walter Leake, W. W. Hening	Charles Yancey
1806.	W. W. Hening, Joel Yancey	William B. Hare
1808.	Hugh Nelson, Peter Carr	William B. Hare
1809.	Hugh Nelson, Rice Garland	William B. Hare
1811.	James Monroe, Tucker Coles	Joseph C. Cabell
1812.	Nimrod Bramham	
1814.	Charles Everett, Jesse W. Garth	Joseph C. Cabell
1816.	Thomas W. Maury, Charles Yancey	Joseph C. Cabell
1818.	Dabney Minor, Jesse W. Garth	Joseph C. Cabell
1819.	Samuel Carr, William F. Gordon	Joseph C. Cabell
1820.	William F. Gordon, Charles Everett	Joseph C. Cabell
1821.	Charles Everett, Charles Cocke	Joseph C. Cabell
1822.	William F. Gordon, William C. Rives	Joseph C. Cabell
1824.	William F. Gordon, T. M. Randolph	Joseph C. Cabell
1825.	William F. Gordon, Rice W. Wood	Joseph C. Cabell

HISTORY OF ALBEMARLE 385

1826.	William F. Gordon, Rice W. Wood	Joseph C. Cabell
1827.	William F. Gordon, Charles Cocke	Joseph C. Cabell
1828.	William F. Gordon, Charles Cocke	Joseph C. Cabell
1829.	William F. Gordon, Hugh Nelson	Joseph C. Cabell
1830.	Thomas W. Gilmer, Rice W. Wood	William F. Gordon
1831.	Thomas W. Gilmer, Rice W. Wood	Charles Cocke
1832.	Rice W. Wood, Thomas J. Randolph	Charles Cocke
1833.	Thomas J. Randolph, T. W. Gilmer	Charles Cocke
1835.	Thomas J. Randolph, Alexander Rives	Charles Cocke
1837.	Thomas J. Randolph, Alexander Rives	Samuel Carr
1839.	Thomas W. Gilmer, V. W. Southall	Samuel Carr
1840.	Thomas W. Gilmer, V. W. Southall	Charles Cocke
1841.	V. W. Southall, Isaac A. Coles	Charles Cocke
1842.	V. W. Southall, Isaac A. Coles	Charles Cocke
1843.	T. J. Randolph, Shelton F. Leake	Charles Cocke
1844.	V. W. Southall, Bezaleel Brown	John Thompson Jr.
1845.	V. W. Southall, Bezaleel Brown	John Thompson Jr.
1846.	V. W. Southall, Bezaleel Brown	John Thompson Jr.
1847.	Bezaleel Brown, William D. Hart	John Thompson Jr.
1848.	William D. Hart, Egbert R. Watson	John Thompson Jr.
1849.	William D. Hart, Egbert R. Watson	John Thompson Jr.
1851.	John J. Bowcock, Charles Carter	John Thompson Jr.
1853.	Alexander Rives	Egbert R. Watson
1854.	John W. Goss, James W. Mason	Benj. F. Randolph
1855.	John W. Goss	Benj. F. Randolph
1856.	Thomas Wood, William T. Early	Benj. F. Randolph
1857.	Thomas Wood, William T. Early	Benj. F. Randolph
1858.	John J. Bowcock, Benj. H. Magruder	Alexander Rives
1859.	John J. Bowcock, Benj. H. Magruder	Alexander Rives
1860.	Benj. H. Magruder, William Garth	Alexander Rives
1863.	Benj. H. Magruder, Franklin Minor	William D. Hart
1864.	Benj. H. Magruder, William A. Branch	William D. Hart
1865.	Benj. H. Magruder, William A. Branch	William D. Hart
1866.	John Wood Jr., William A. Turner	James Galt
1867.	John Wood Jr., William A. Turner	James Galt
1868.	John Wood Jr., William A. Turner	James Galt
1870–1.	S. V. Southall, J. C. Hill, J. D. Jones	Robert C. Beazley
1872–3.	J. C. Hill, G. B. Stephens, J. A. Early	Robert C. Beazley
1874–5.	Benj. H. Magruder, John E. Massey, Richard G. Crank	Robert C. Beazley
1876–7.	John E. Massey, Richard G. Crank, Thomas M. Dunn	Robert C. Beazley
1878–9.	Richard G. Crank, T. L. Michie, J. Massie Smith	John E. Massey
1880–1.	R. T. W. Duke, T. L. Michie	Everett T. Early
1882–3.	Thomas M. Dunn, John B. Moon	J. R. Wingfield

APPENDIX, No. 8.
EMIGRANTS FROM ALBEMARLE TO OTHER STATES.

NORTH CAROLINA.

Samuel Bell, Orange Co.
Alexander Montgomery, Orange Co.
John Wright, Orange Co.
John Campbell, Orange Co.
Obadiah Martin, Orange Co.
Josiah and Martha (Daniel) Brown, Orange Co.
James Glenn, Surry Co.
William Burrus, Surry Co.
David Nowlin, Surry Co.
Samuel and John Boyd, Surry Co.
Robert Harris, Surry Co.
Thomas Burrus, Surry Co.
William Bruce, Surry Co.
Davis and Elizabeth Durrett, Surry Co.
Samuel and William Stockton, Rutherford Co.
Ann (Lewis) Willis, Rutherford Co.
David Lewis Jr., Rutherford Co.
Eli and Daniel Melton, Rutherford Co.
William and Mary (Melton) Jones, Rutherford Co.
William T. Lewis, Wilkes Co.
John Hamman, Wilkes Co.
Robert Ayres, Wilkes Co.
Richard Blalock, Cumberland Co.
John Geer, Johnson Co.
John Graves, Rowan Co.
Henry Tilley
Thomas Carlton
Joseph Phillips
Churchill Jackson, Burks Co.
Matthew Mills, Guilford Co.
Jesse Gentry, Washington Co.
David and Susan Dalton, Stokes Co.
Micajah and Elizabeth Allen, Stokes Co.
Rice Garland Jr., Leaskesville.
Nancy (Daniel) Graves, Caswell Co.
Samuel Daniel, Granville Co.
Thomas D. Burch, Wake Co.
James K. Burch, Wake Co.
David S. Napier, Walker Co.

GEORGIA.

John Thornton, Augusta Co.
James and John Marks, Wilkes Co.

Richard and Daniel Harvie, Wilkes Co.
William and Judith (Cosby) Harvie, Wilkes Co.
John and Margaret (Harvie) Davenport, Wilkes Co.
David and Mary (Harvie) Meriwether, Wilkes Co.
Richard and Jane (Lewis) Davenport, Wilkes Co.
John and Mary (Davidson) Forlaw, Washington Co.
Fleming Jordan, Oglethorpe Co.
Thomas Kennerly
William Spears
Mary Taylor
William B. and Mourning (Clark) Key, Elbert Co.
John Hamner, Wilkes Co.
Jeremiah Hamner, Greene Co.

KENTUCKY.

John and Elizabeth (Lewis) Martin, Fayette Co.
John and Mary (Cabell) Breckinridge, Fayette Co.
Vincent and Mary (Rozell) Stephens, Fayette Co.
John T. and Lucy Hawkins, Fayette Co.
Charles and Dorcas (Black) Patrick, Fayette Co.
Samuel Hughes Woodson, Jessamine Co.
Nathan Dedman, Jessamine Co.
Michael and Ann Wallace, Madison Co.
William Briscoe, Madison Co.
Thomas Collins, Madison Co.
Evan and Lucy (Coleman) Watson, Madison Co.
Daniel and Frances Maupin, Madison Co.
Robert Rodes, Madison Co.
Richard and Jane (Harris) Gentry, Madison Co.
Josiah and Nancy (Mullins) Gentry, Madison Co.
Austin Gentry, Madison Co.
Edward and Elizabeth (Gentry) Ballard, Madison Co.
Bernard Franklin, Madison Co.
Henry and Elizabeth (Ewell) Carr, Madison Co.
James Goodman, Madison Co.
John Mansfield, Madison Co.
Charles Atkisson, Madison Co.
Samuel Wallace, Madison Co.
Thomas and Nancy Kindred, Madison Co.
William Kindred, Madison Co.
Ephriam and Winifred Musick, Madison Co.
Archibald and Mourning (Shelton) Woods, Madison Co.
Richard and Elizabeth (Shelton) Mobbery, Madison Co.
Joshua Morris, Shelby Co.
William and Charity (Burgher) Hays, Shelby Co.
Joseph Hornsby, Shelby Co.

Elizabeth (Lewis) Henderson's family, Shelby Co.
Flint H. Goodridge, Shelby Co.
Barzillai Brown, Shelby Co.
Nathaniel Haggard, Clark Co.
Dabney and Lucy Haggard, Clark Co.
Robert Grimes, Clark Co.
Hastings Marks, Clark Co.
John W. and Elizabeth (Marks) Hinde, Clark Co.
James and Benajah Gentry, Clark Co.
Charles and Jane (Lewis) Hudson, Barren Co.
Hardin Davis, Barren Co.
Joel and Martha (Rodes) Yancey, Barren Co.
Walter Crenshaw, Barren Co.
Elizabeth W. Watts, Barren Co.
Elijah and Benjamin Davis, Barren Co.
Jonathan and Susan (Wood) Bolling, Barren Co.
William J. and Elizabeth Wood, Barren Co.
John and Elizabeth (Wood) Clack, Barren Co.
Bennett H. Henderson, Barren Co.
Clifton and Elizabeth (Jouett) Rodes, Barren Co.
David and Elizabeth (Crenshaw) Watts, Barren Co.
Samuel and Susan Murrell, Barren Co.
James and Martha (Humphreys) Foster, Barren Co.
Cornelius and Sarah Gilliam, Barren Co.
James and Mary (Garland) Woods, Garrard Co.
Thomas Rothwell, Garrard Co.
George and Jane (Newcomb) Naylor, Garrard Co.
Asa and Elizabeth (Naylor) Storms, Garrard Co.
Pleasant Sandridge, Green Co.
John and Mary (Wood) Sandridge, Green Co.
Peter A. and Lucinda Hall, Green Co.
Garnett and Harriet (Smith) Ingram, Green Co.
Thomas J. Smith, Green Co.
Burton W. Carr, Green Co.
James and Susan Page, Adair Co.
Robert and Maria Page, Adair Co.
Samuel and Mary (Smith) Page, Adair Co.
Sherod and Mary (Page) Griffin, Adair Co.
Burgess and Jane (Page) Griffin, Adair Co.
John P. and Elizabeth Smith, Adair Co.
John and Mary (Smith) Massie, Adair Co.
John and Rebecca Terrell, Greenup Co.
Henry Gaines, Greenup Co.
John and Sarah Garth, Scott Co.
John Herndon, Scott Co.
William Kerr, Scott Co.

Joseph and Mary (Rodes) Burch, Scott Co.
John and Rachel Sharp, Henry Co.
Isaac and Susan (Fitz) Sharp, Henry Co.
John and Frances (Sharp) Kelly, Henry Co.
James and Catharine (Goodridge) Burton, Henry Co.
William Clarkson, Bourbon Co.
Kenza and Sarah (Watts) Stone, Bourbon Co.
James Stone, Bourbon Co.
Elizabeth and Moses Brockman, Boone Co.
John Rogers, Boone Co.
Elijah Lucas, Boone Co.
William Dollins, Boone Co.
Isaac Wood, Hardin Co.
John Davidson, Hardin Co.
Reuben and George Turner, Pendleton Co.
Isaac and Mary (Lewis) Miller, Jefferson Co.
Temple and Ann (Marks) Gwathmey, Jefferson Co.
Richard and Harriet (Beale) Maupin, Jefferson Co.
Nathaniel G. Carr, Jefferson Co.
Robert and Mary (Rodes) Douglass, Jefferson Co.
Moses J. and Matilda Moore, Jefferson Co.
Henry and George Garrett, Montgomery Co.
John and Martha (Key) White, Montgomery Co.
Elisha D. and Lucy (Wood) Gilliam, Christian Co.
Mildred Flint, Christian Co.
Tandy Brockman, Christian Co.
Jesse Grady, Christian Co.
Samuel Hopkins, Christian Co.
Dr. Alfred Wood's family, Christian Co.
William and Martha (Moon) Vires, Mason Co.
Giles and Janet (Boyd) Allegre, Mason Co.
John B. Wheeler, Mason Co.
Charles McGehee, Mason Co.
John Jouett, Bath Co.
Abraham and Mildred (Burrus) Jones, Bath Co.
Thomas Burrus, Allen Co.
John and Frances (Henderson) Hines, Allen Co.
William T. Henderson, Allen Co.
Nicholas Burgher, Estill Co.
William and Arthur Tooley, Monroe Co.
James and Elizabeth (Tooley) Gentry, Monroe Co.
Thomas and Nancy (Old) Eubank, Monroe Co.
David and Dorothy (Rodes) Kerr, Warren Co.
Joseph Burgher, Warren Co.
William Wood Jr., Warren Co.
Josiah and Jane Huntsman, Lincoln Co.

Sarah (Wood) Gooch, Lincoln Co.
Fontaine Reynolds, Lincoln Co.
Robert and Agatha (Twyman) Dearing, Franklin Co.
Travis and Elizabeth (Carver) Brown, Franklin Co.
Joseph M. White, Franklin Co.
Moses and Ann (Dedman) Clack, Fleming Co.
Samuel Burch's family, Fleming Co.
James and Lucy Fitzpatrick, Casey Co.
George and Mary Fitzpatrick, Pulaski Co.
James W. and Mary (Kinsolving) Leigh, Caldwell Co.
James and Margaret (Brown) Kinsolving, Caldwell Co.
Matthew Gooch, Caldwell Co.
John Thomas, Cumberland Co.
Jesse and Elizabeth (Hopkins) Haden, Cumberland Co.
John and Ann (Bailey) Gilliam, Logan Co.
John N. Hopkins, Logan Co.
Bennett D. Ballard, Todd Co.
Paschal and Catharine (Wayt) Garth, Todd Co.
Wilson Munday, Todd Co.
Thomas Kimbrough, Todd Co.
Thomas and Lucy (Carver) Broadhead, Todd Co.
Thomas and Margaret Gay, Washington Co.
Reuben and Jane Dowell, Wayne Co.
Rodes Garth, Wayne Co.
John and Mary Burks, Grant Co.
William and Joanna (Shepherd) Woods, Livingston Co.
David Woods, Livingston Co.
Henry and Susan (Woods) Williams, Livingston Co.
Ann M. and Martha C. Lewis, Livingston Co.
Washington and Lucy (Lewis) Griffin, Livingston Co.
William Jones, Livingston Co.
William Carver, Livingston Co.
William and Nancy Cunningham, Trigg Co.
William and Mildred (Rodes) Walden, Trigg Co.
David J. and Martha Lewis, Breckinridge Co.
Jacob and Ann (Shelton) Powers, Harrison Co.
Anderson Garland's family, Lewis Co.
Reuben and Lucy Clarkson, Meade Co.
David Thomson, Woodford Co.
Goodloe and Mary (Crenshaw) Carter, Woodford Co.
David and Ruth (Twyman) Watts, Woodford Co.
Joshua and Peachy (Walker) Fry, Boyle Co.
John and Ann (Rodes) Garth
Thomas Upton
George and Mary (Smith) Nicholas
Clifton and Sarah (Waller) Rodes

HISTORY OF ALBEMARLE 391

Josiah and Hannah Wallace
Tucker M. and Marie E. (Hudson) Woodson
James Kerr
John Rice and Sarah (Henderson) Kerr
John Smith
Robert L. Slaughter
Robert Brooks
Nathan and Mildred (Clarkson) Goodman
Anselm Clarkson
Nicholas L. Gooch
John and Sarah McWilliams

TENNESSEE.

John Jameson, Bedford Co.
Bland Maupin, Bedford Co.
Richard Moon Jr., Bledsoe Co.
William and Nancy (Alphin) Fagg, Blount Co.
Jane (Alphin) Owen, Blount Co.
Samuel and Lucinda (Farrar) Wharton, Davidson Co.
George and Elizabeth (Farrar) Wharton, Davidson Co.
Jacob and Sarah (Lewis) Tilman, Davidson Co.
Henry Kirby, Davidson Co.
Samuel and Austin Hamner, Davidson Co.
Edward Stone, Davidson Co.
Nathan and Mary Blain, Fayette Co.
William N. and Mary (Bates) Oliver, Fayette Co.
James and Lucy (Thomas) Lewis, Franklin Co.
James Woods, Franklin Co.
Dyer and Mary (Lewis) Moore, Franklin Co.
Lawrence T. Catlett, Franklin Co.
Tyree Rodes, Giles Co.
John Shiflett, Hawkins Co.
James and Frances (Allen) Wood, Hardeman Co.
David and Lucy (Duke) Wood, Hardeman Co.
William, George and Fendall Wood, Hardeman Co.
Robert and Mary (Wood) Durrett, Hardeman Co.
James D. and Martha (Wood) Allen, Hardeman Co.
Fendall and Ann (Royster) Thurman, Hardeman Co.
Gideon Carr, Dickson Co.
Meekins and Mary (Hamner) Carr, Dickson Co.
John B. and Susan (Hamner) Carr, Dickson Co.
Aaron Gentry, Knox Co.
Elijah and Sarah Dowell, Knox Co.
Peter Ogg, Knox Co.
James S. and Frances (Harris) Blades, Madison Co.
Isaac B. Hardin, Maury Co.

John H. and Calvin M. Smith, Maury Co.
Nathan Harris, Monroe Co.
Dr. Charles Meriwether, Montgomery Co.
Alexander and Mary W. (Thomas) Clayton, Montgomery Co.
Nicholas L. and Ellen Thomas, Montgomery Co.
Charles L. and Margaret Thomas, Montgomery Co.
John J. and Lucy (Quarles) Thomas, Montgomery Co.
Frances (Thomas) Hart, Montgomery Co.
Nathaniel Anderson, Memphis
John and Elizabeth (Burrus) Davis, Overton Co.
Gideon and Elizabeth (Hardin) Morgan, Roane Co.
Lewis C. Anthony, Rutherford Co.
Strother and John Winn Key, Sumner Co.
Robert McClary, Sumner Co.
John Davidson, Sumner Co.
Thomas Jones, Sumner Co.
Alexander Duff Gordon, Sumner Co.
Reuben D. and Robert T. Brown, Sumner Co.
Micajah Clark, Sumner Co.
Roland and Nancy Horsley, Sumner Co.
William and Lucy Nimmo, Sumner Co.
Thomas Meadow, Sumner Co.
William and Elizabeth Smith, Sumner Co.
Abraham Martin, Sumner Co.
Taverner and Mary (Edwards) Head, Sumner Co.
Nicholas L. and Ann Wood, Tipton Co.
Thomas G. Watkins, Washington Co.
Randolph and Elizabeth Turner, White Co.
Thomas Carr, Wilson Co.
John R. and Margaret (McKesson) Campbell, Nashville
George and Elizabeth (Buster) Moore
Dr. Lachlan McLean
Andrew McWilliams

MISSOURI.

Samuel L. Hart, Callaway Co.
Samuel and Robert Dyer, Callaway Co.
Thomas McCulloch, Howard Co.
D. Douglass, Howard Co.
Thomas Fitzpatrick, Washington Co.
Joseph T. Monroe, Franklin Co.
Edward Blair and Harriet (Monroe) Cabell, Chariton Co.
John A. and James Woods, Marion Co.
Samuel and Sarah E. (Rodes) Woods, Marion Co.
Joel R. Maupin, Marion Co.
Jonathan A. J. Bishop, Marion Co.
Rice and Elizabeth Wood, Saline Co.

John and Adeline Piper, Saline Co.
Robert and Nancy Field, Saline Co.
John A. and Elizabeth (Durrett) Dunkum, Saline Co.
Benjamin and T. (Pemberton) Durrett, Saline Co.
Henry and Elmira Keister, Saline Co.
Eli and Nancy Keister, Saline Co.
Samuel Keister, Saline Co.
Isaac and Elizabeh (Keister) Stone, Boone Co.
George and Mary Glenn, Monroe Co.
Elizabeth (Meriwether) Lewis, Lincoln Co.
N. H. and Ann (Meriwether) Lewis, Lincoln Co.
James and Margaret (Lewis) Clark, Lincoln Co.
Thomas and Emeline (Weimer) Lewis, Lincoln Co.
Charles and Mary (Quarles) Lewis, Lincoln Co.
Elizabeth (Lewis) Wells, Lincoln Co.
John W. and Alice (Lewis) Davis, Lincoln Co.
Jonathan B. and Barbara (Carr) Carr, Lincoln Co.
Achilles and Mary (Carr) Broadhead, Lincoln Co.
Peter and Lydia L. (Lewis) Carr, Lincoln Co.
John and Julia (Thurmond) Damron, Lincoln Co.
Bolling and Mildred Smith, Lincoln Co.
Elijah and Martha (Gentry) Dawson, Callaway Co.
William Adams, Jackson Co.
Pleasant Adams, Clay Co.
Dawson Adams, Ray Co.
Joseph Harper, Daviess Co.
Nathaniel and Langdon Bacon, St. Louis
Charles W. and Mary (Harrison) Maupin, St. Louis
Colin Johnson
John M. and Frances Perry
Talbot and Eliza (Kelly) Bragg
William L. Wood
Crenshaw and Sarah (Austin White
John Duggins

ALABAMA.

Jesse Winston Garth
Pleasant F. Boyd
Nimrod and Martha (Hamner) Hendricks, Tuscaloosa
Nathaniel Ragland, Madison Co.
Joab Watson, Madison Co.
Jeremiah Gilliam, Limestone Co.
John Hudson, Limestone Co.
John N. Rose, Mobile
Richard McLeod, Mobile
Hardin P. Lewis

MISSISSIPPI.

John and Nancy Dawson
Nelson Hardin
William and Burr Garland
John W. C. and Catharine (Davis) Watson, Holly Springs
William M. Woods's family
William and Helen (Alexander) Morris

LOUISIANA.

Joseph Brand, New Orleans
William White, New Orleans
Gideon Fitz, St. Landry

FLORIDA.

William H. Brockenbrough
Charles Downing
William and Sarah (Strange) Stockton

ARKANSAS.

Walter T. Dabney

OHIO.

James and Mary (Woods) Garth
William and Elizabeth (Davis) Irvin, Lancaster
Thomas Irvin, Lancaster
Martin and Mildred Dawson, Gallia Co.
Andrew J. Humphreys, Logan Co.
John Wiant, Champaign Co.
John and Sarah Garrison, Preble Co.
Joseph and Agnes (Garrison) Waggoner, Preble Co.
John and Frances (Garrison) Trent, Preble Co.
Christopher and Jacob Bartley, Pickaway Co.
Peter West, Pickaway Co.
Daniel and Elizabeth Pence, Pickaway Co.
Wiley Beckett, Pickaway Co.
John Mundell, Pickaway Co.
James H. and Ann (Burnley) Burnley, Pickaway Co.
Joel Burnley, Pickaway Co.
John and Elizabeth (Wertenbaker) Walker, Pickaway Co.
Isaac W. Durrett, Pickaway Co.

INDIANA.

John and Elizabeth (Woods) Humphrey, Parke Co.
Jacob and Elizabeth (Sharp) Razor, Jefferson Co.
John T. and Mary (Jeffries) Bishop, Dearborn Co.
Benjamin and Rachel Norvell, Franklin Co.
John Dollins, Harrison Co.
Susan (Dollins) Polson, Washington Co.

ILLINOIS.
William B. and Nancy (Kinsolving) Wood, Washington Co.
William L. and Ellen (Craven) Craven, Morgan Co.
Dr. William A. Harris

APPENDIX. No. 9.
NECROLOGY.

1744.
Nicholas Meriwether

1745.
Matthew Jouett — Charles Blaney

1748.
Charles Hudson

1749.
Richard Damron — Robert Baber — Lazarus Damron
William Phelps

1750.
John Tooley — Robert Hamner — James Williamson

1751.
Andrew Reid — Rev. Robert Rose — Benjamin Franklin

1752.
Arthur Osborne — Mark Lively — James Robertson
Abner Abney — Edward Maxwell — John Henderson
James Nevell — David Reese

1753.
Charles Lynch — Andrew Brown — Thomas Goolsby
Samuel Birk — Samuel Birk Jr.

1754.
James Ireland — Thomas McDaniel — Joshua Fry

1755.
Robert White

1756.
Robert McNeely

1757.
Arthur McDaniel — Peter Jefferson

1758.
James McCann — Henry Martin

1759.
John Cocke — Joseph Thompson

1760.
James Daniel — William Horsley — James McCord
Davis Stockton

1761.
William Morrison — Thomas Cobb

1762.
Benjamin Brown	Joseph Martin	Alexander McKillecat
Michael Woods	William Mabe	Philip Joyner

1763.
James Kinkead	Larkin Smith	Thomas Sowell

1764.
William Fitzpatrick	Peter Lyon	John McCord
David Mills	Abraham Childress	

1765.
Robert Harris	Joseph Thompson	Samuel Arnold
Charles Smith		

1766.
Michael Dougherty	Arthur Hopkins	Robert Lewis
William Wallace	Thomas Sowell	

1767.
David Watts	Timothy Dalton

1768.
John Harvie	John Hudson	Obadiah Moore
Rev. James Maury		

1769.
Edwin Hickman	Matthew Jordan

1770.
Rev. Samuel Black	Rev. John Ramsay	David Thompson

1771.
John Hammock	Archelaus Carver	Charles Smith

1772.
Andrew McWilliams	Nicholas Meriwether	Terisha Turner
William Venable		

1773.
James Wharey	Mrs. Mary Fry

1774.
Micajah Clark	Thomas Goolsby	Joseph Huckstep
Joseph Kinkead	Hugh Rice Morris	Joel Terrell
Thomas Tindal	Richard Dalton	

1775.
John Coffey	Patrick Napier	John Rodes
Richard Stockton	Rev. Samuel Leake	William Blackwell

1776.
James Mayo	Reuben Terrell	John Watts
William Harris	Giles Allegre	Alexander Cleveland
John Moran		

1777.
George Martin	John Michie	Jeremiah White
William Garland	John Wood	

HISTORY OF ALBEMARLE

	1778.	
Richard Flint	Henry Head	Henry Randolph
John Fry	Robert Thompson	
	1779.	
Thomas Hughes	Col. Charles Lewis	David Lewis
Christopher Shepherd	Tucker Woodson Jr.	Samuel Brockman
John Woodson	Nicholas Gentry	
	1780.	
Daniel Ferguson	William Lewis	Manus Burgher
John Ballard		
	1781.	
James Garland Jr.	James Tooley	Thomas Ballard
James Defoe		
	1782.	
Charles Lewis Jr.	Edmund Massie	James Michie
Thomas Burch		
	1783.	
Samuel Bowcock	Silas Melton	Thomas Stockton
Thomas Smith	William Dalton	William Via
Nathan Woods		
	1784.	
John McCord	William Watson	Tucker Woodson
Richard Durrett	Samuel Woods	
	1785.	
Thomas Johnson	John Moore	Andrew Wallace
Oliver Cleveland	Robert Bain	George Douglass
William Hamner		
	1786.	
Benjamin Colvard	John Hunton	Thomas Salmon
John Cleveland		
	1787.	
Callum Bailey	Nicholas Caine	Thomas Fitzpatrick
John Henderson	Thomas Moorman	Richard Sharp
John Dalton		
	1788.	
William Hamner	Samuel Jameson	Andrew Leake
Daniel Maupin	Henry Washington	William Harris
Thomas Smith		
	1789.	
John Eubank	Claude de La Cour	William Gregg
James Kerr Jr.	George Murrell	William Shelton
John Spencer	Jeremiah Yancey	Charles Turner
	1790.	
Thomas Emerson	John Fortune	Martin Hackett
Isham Lewis	William McCord	William Reynolds
James Reid		

1791.

John Henderson	Benjamin Huntsman	Martin Key
Jame Minor	John Woods	Thomas Smith
David Anderson	Robert Greening	

1792.

Edward Carter	Thomas Martin	John Gilliam
John Dunn	James Harris	Joseph Morton
John Bailey		

1793.

Richard Davenport	Nathaniel Garland	Stephen Hughes
Charles Irving	Orlando Jones	Joel Perkins
Samuel Shelton	Bennett Henderson	Nicholas Hamner

1794.

Gideon Carr	John Henderson	Gabriel Maupin
David Rodes	Giles Rogers	John Shiflett
James Travillian	Thomas Walker	Thomas West
Joshua Grady	Christopher Harris	Bradley Berry

1795.

Henry Foster	John McCulloch	William Dowell
Valentine Wood Jr.	John Clarkson	Giles Tompkins
Peter Marks	George Gilmer	

1796.

Samuel Gay	Robert Jouett	William Gooch
James Coleman	Nathan Barksdale	William Barksdale
John Newcomb	Thomas Grayson	John Slaughter
Philemon Snell		

1797.

Obadiah Britt	James Minor	Charles Patrick
Hugh Alexander	James Harris	William Simms
Leonard Drumheller	Nathaniel Watkins	John Dowell

1798.

Alexander McKinzie	John Pritchett	John Scott
Samuel Taliaferro	John Simms	Thomas Walker Jr.
Charles Rodes	Nelson Thomson	David Buster

1799.

Micajah Chiles	David Epperson	Henry Shelton
James Jones Jr.	Robert W. Wheeler	Stephen Southall
Thomas Massie	Thomas Jones	George Martin
Peter Davie	Patrick Michie	John Lewis

1800.

Thomas Bell	Maxey Ewell	Samuel Dedman
William Moon	James Suddarth	Samuel Burch
William Clark	Bernard Brown	Robert Alcock
William Thurmond	John Childress	Thomas Smith

HISTORY OF ALBEMARLE

1801.
John Hudson	Joseph Sutherland	Waddy Thomson
Richard Woods	Joel Wheeler	Samuel Scott
Swanny Ferguson	William Smith	Ephriam Seamonds

1802.
William Cole	George Eubank	John Jouett
William Jordan	George Goodridge	Michael Thomas

1803.
Peter Lott	William Shelton	Henry Burke
Charles Wingfield	Schuyler Harris	Benjamin Norvell

1804.
Thomas Ballard	George Blain	Andrew Brown
John Fitz	John Lewis	James Burnley

1805.
Richard H. Allen	Isaac Davis	Alexander Gordon
Lain Jones	Bartholomew Kindred	Owen Lewis
Henry Karr	William Davenport	Joseph H. Irvin

1806.
John Hudson	John Maupin	Holman Snead
Thomas Carr	Francis Walker	Jacob Morris

1807.
Richard Farrar	William Fretwell	Thomas W. Lewis
Edward Wingfield	John White	Claudius Buster
Jeremiah Cleveland	David Clarkson	Jacob Spiece
Joel Smith	Hancock Allen	

1808.
John Coles	Harwood Bacon	Peter Keblinger
Samuel Irvin	Nicholas Lewis	Rev. Matthew Maury
Wyatt Mills	Edward Moore	William Wood

1809.
William Brockman	Bland Ballard	John Carr
Moses Gentry	Rev. William Irvin	Bezaleel Maxwell
John Old	Robert Sharp	Richard Moore
Benjamin Taylor	Micajah Wheeler	William Wallace
Meriwether Lewis	Henry Austin	John Gilliam

1810.
Robert Carter	Madison Breedlove	William Garrison
George Gentry	Taliaferro Lewis	Rev. Thos. Lumpkin
John Rodes	Cornelius Schenk	Edmund Anderson

1811.
James Burnley	William Leake	Jacob Moon
William Michie	John Walker	Martin Railey

1812.

Nathaniel Anderson	James Powell Cocke	Micajah Carr
James Garland	Thomas Garth	John P. Watson
Joseph Cole	Julius Clarkson	Harmer Gilmer
John B. Magruder	John Old	Richard P. Watson
John Martin		

1813.

David Burgher	Mask Leake	Robert Morrison
Jacob Oglesby	David Wood	James Hays
William Jarman	John Wilkinson	Robert Moorman
William Hughes	Kemp Catlett	William S. Dabney
William Watson		

1814.

Joseph Brand	Peter Clarkson	William D. Fitch
Clifton Garland	William Maupin	Charles L. Thomas
John Wingfield	James Harrison	Martin Key

1815.

James Brooks	Rev. Bernis Brown	Samuel Black
Peter Carr	Isaiah Humphrey	Jeremiah Hamner
Lawrence Suddarth	James Turk	Jonathan Browning

1816.

Jason Bowcock	William Elsom	John Michie
Epaphroditus Rodes	William G. Garner	George Carter
David Wood		

1817.

Edward Garland	Elijah Garth	Samuel Hamner
Nicholas Page	William G. Arms	Richard Anderson
James Barrett	Jacob Morris	

1818.

John Alphin	Daniel White	David Humphrey
West Langford	William Moore	Charles Massie
Andrew Squair	Joseph Sutherland	George Twyman
David Watts	Chapman White	Cleviers Duke
Francis Browning	Robert Barclay	William McCord
Charles B. Hunton	Benjamin Richards	Sabrit Hoy

1819.

Samuel W. Anderson	Rice Garland	Milburn Hogg
Robert Leitch	Richard Moon	Charles Wingfield Jr.
William Goolsby	Lewis Johnson	Reuben Herndon
Jechonias Yancey	James Reynolds	Charles Burrus

1820.

John Buster	Isaac Hardin	Robert McCullock
Hugh Rice Morris	William Wood	Daniel Tilman
Wilson C. Nicholas	William Hopkins	John Timberlake

1821.

Richard Durrett	Rev. Martin Dawson	John Eubank
Joseph Gilmore	James Mayo	David Maupin
Christopher Wingfield	James Eubank	Benjamin Martin
James Old	Rev. Jacob Watts	Benjamin Norvell

1822.

Rev. Benj. Burgher	James Durrett	John Grayson
Richards Woods Jr.	Whitaker Carter	Peter Garland
Christopher Gentry	Jesse Davenport	Elijah Sowell

1823.

John H. Carr	John C. Ragland	William Fretwell
Rev. Samuel Wydown	Andrew Leitch Sr.	William Smith
John Rodes	Charles Douglass	Daniel Black

1824.

John Eubank	Joseph Field	Robert Field
Mrs. Mary W. Lewis	Dabney Minor	William Tompkins
Jesse Wood	Alexander Blain	Francis Browning

1825.

Douglass Bowcock	Christopher Hudson	William Ramsay
Bezaleel G. Brown	Robert Wingfield	Joseph Bishop
John A. Michie	Alexander Fretwell	Henry Wood

1826.

Francis Gilmer	Joseph Brand	Berry M. Hardin
Thomas Jefferson	Francis Modena	Samuel Shelton
Michael Thomas	Chapman White	Matthew Watson
Benjamin Thurman	Joel Harris	Pleasant Dawson

1827.

John Bolling	Charles Goodman	Horsley Goodman
Benjamin Lacy	Littlebury Moon	John Neilson
Rev. Hugh White	Richard Price	John Hudson
Thomas Martin		

1828.

John Irvin	Robert Draffen	Abraham Eades
Claiborne Rothwell	George Eubank	James Fowles
Thomas M. Randolph	Andrew Monroe	Jeremiah Yancey

1829.

James Powell Cocke	Bezaleel Brown	Robert Davis
William Grayson	Thomas Goolsby	James Kinsolving
David Young	Jesse Wood Jr.	James Clarkson
Manoah Clarkson	Rev. John Barksdale	John Fagg
Richard Bruce	Philip Watts	Joseph Goodman

1830.

John Kelly	Francis Birckhead	James Dinsmore
George Divers	Charles Massie	Nicholas Merritt
Benajah Gentry	William C. Wren	Lindsay Martin

1831.

Reuben Lindsay	Jonathan Barksdale	John Jordan
Thomas W. Wood	Joseph Wingfield	Stephen Woodson
Richmond Walton	Robert Rea	William Tooley

1832.

Andrew Hart	John S. Farrar	Richard Wallace
William Hopkins	George Eubank	Hugh Rice Morris
John Harris	Goodman Barksdale	John Patrick
William Suddarth	William Morris	Charles C. Lacy
John B. Benson	Edward Ferneyhough	Ison Walton

1833.

Stephen Moore	Rice W. Wood	J. Watson, High Top
John Early	Christian Wertenbaker	John Dettor

1834.

Benjamin Harris	Marshall Durrett	Matthew Rodes
Thomas Garth	Charles L. Bankhead	Hudson Fretwell
Rev. Thornton Rogers	Joel Shiflett	Peter U. Ware

1835.

Martin Dawson	John Gilmer	James P. Henderson
Peter Minor	Horsley Goodman	Henry Price
William Leake	Pleasant Moon	William Piper
Andrew Zigler		

1836.

Hugh Nelson	Jesse Garth	Peachy R. Gilmer
Parmenas Rogers	George Gilmer	Ephriam Seamonds
Isaac Simms	Norborne Powers	William Via

1837.

Craven Peyton	Jesse Jopling	Reuben Lindsay
Micajah Woods	William Woods B. C.	John Winn
John Fretwell	Micajah Wheeler	John Yergain
John N. C. Stockton	Horace Bramham	Charles Hudson
David Isaacs	Mace Pickett	Ezekiel Wilhoi

1838.

John Rogers	Garland Carr	Rev. John Goss
Thomas W. Gooch	Francis B. Dyer	Roger Thompson
James Jones	Louis Leschot	J. Addison Carr
Sabrit King		

1839.

John Rodes	Robert W. Wood	Jeremiah White
Opie Norris	Joshua Wheeler	Anderson Shiflett
James H. Grinstead		

1840.

Samuel and Celia Dyer	Abijah S. Old	John H. Goodloe
Mrs. Elizabeth Clark	James Tooley	Zachariah Wood

1841.

Charles Bonnycastle	John Rogers Jr.	Drury Wood
John Watson, Milton	David Anderson	Isaac A. Coles
Samuel Leitch	John Minor	Michael Catterton
Howell Lewis	David Michie	Thomas Grady
Samuel Powell		

1842.

Ira B. Brown	Jonathan W. Beers	Thomas W. Maury
Gilly M. Lewis	John Pollock	E. W. Reinhart
Samuel Barksdale	Reuben Wingfield	Joseph Watson
Charles Smith		

1843.

Garrett White	John P. Emmett	James Oldham
Charles H. Meriwether	Francis Meriwether	Adam Keblinger
James H. Lewis	Joseph Antrim	Lewis S. Poates
Abraham Eades		

1844.

Reuben Lewis	Dabney C. Gooch	Thomas Draffen
Thomas W. Gilmer	Achilles Douglass	James Duke
Carter H. Harrison	Oliver Cleveland	Benjamin Sowell

1845.

W. D. Meriwether	Nimrod Bramham	Stephen C. Price
Henry T. Harris	Michael Wallace	Nathan C. Goodman
John H. Craven	John Brown	

1846.

John L. Thomas	Brightberry Brown	Frances McGee
Joseph Coleman	Rezin Wheat	Blake Harris
William Dunkum	John H. Holman	Samuel Black
Elisha Thurman	John T. Early	

1847.

James Jarman	Daniel F. Carr	Cleviers Duke
John Thomas	John E. Roberts	Wiley Dickerson
George M. Woods	James Michie Jr.	John Lee
Joseph Twyman	Robert Thrift	Samuel Brockman

1848.

John Coles	Charles Harper	Hardin Massie
Charles Everett	William D. Fitch	James W. Drumheller
Henry St. Geo. Tucker	Albert C. Terrell	

1849.

Jesse Lewis	Richard Duke	Thomas W. Fry
Samuel W. Tompkins	Joseph Grayson	John M. Wingfield
Benjamin Mosby		

1850.

Henry White	Edmund Davis	Andrew McKee
William Woods, S.	George Blaetterman	Samuel S. Gay
James Michie	Mann Page	Edmund Broadus
Benjamin G. Peyton	Meekins Carr	James Jeffries

1851.

Willis Garth	Bernard Carr	Joel Terrell
Thomas Macon	Peter N. Meriwether	Philip Edge
Richard Pollard	Anderson Brown	Edwin H. Gooch
Daniel Scott	John Rogers, Lan.	George W. Craven

1852.

George Sinclair	Valentine Head	Zach. Shackelford
John Bowcock	Jonathan Barksdale	

1853.

Edward H. Moon	David Higginbotham	Hawkey Ferguson
Thomas H. Grayson	Edward Wertenbaker	Paul Tilman Jr.
James H. Shelton		

1854.

Bernard Peyton	John Morris	Reese Jurey
Francis Carr	William W. Wallace	Larkin Hudson
Walter Coles	N. Thompson Jr.	George W. Turpin
John Eubank	A. Hamilton Michie	

1855.

John B. Garrett	John Dunkum	Nathaniel D. Goolsby
John Pilson	James T. Early	Alphonso Garner
Andrew Leitch	Meredith Martin	Thomas Daniel

1856.

Clement P. McKennie	Allen Hawkins	John H. Maddox
James H. Terrell	William M. Woods	Matthew P. Walton
G. W. Kinsolving	Rev. Albert Holladay	George O'Toole

1857.

Andrew Stevenson	John T. Hamner	James A. Watson
Samuel W. Martin	Benjamin L. Johnson	Burwell Garth
Richmond Terrell	John B. Hart	Jeremiah A. Goodman
Daniel Perrow	Charles Massie	William McCoy
Claudius Mayo	John Terrell	

1858.

Robert L. Jefferson	Lewis McGee	Boswell P. Yates
David Hancock	William Woods, B. C.	Gabriel Maupin
William F. Gordon	Hugh Minor	Thomas C. Keller

1859.

Thomas L. Shelton	William T. McCarty	Charles A. Smith
James W. Saunders	Rev. John S. Abell	Henry Morris
John B. Gilmer	Isaiah Stout	Caleb Abell
John J. Wingfield	Samuel Carr	

1860.

Nathaniel Burnley	Tucker Coles	Joseph Miller
Alexander Garrett	John W. Gantt	Hudson Strange
William Garth		

1861.

M. L. Walker	Abraham Wiant	Zachariah Lewis
Nelson Barksdale	Tucker Coles Jr.	Buckner Townley
Chapman W. Maupin	Twyman Wayt	Chiles M. Brand
Valentine W. Southall	Joseph Sutherland	John B. Douglass
Peter F. Jefferson	W. B. Phillips	

1862.

Charles Minor	David Carr	Thomas Woodson
A. Hamilton Rogers	Dabney Carr	Robert Coles
John Timberlake	Chapman C. Maupin	M. L. Anderson
William M. Wade	Luther M. George	Richard D. Simms
Thomas F. Lewis	James S. Leitch	William B. Harris
Francis K. Nelson	Thomas Staples	James H. Minor

1863.

St. George Tucker	Thomas W. Meriwether	Ira Harris
James B. Rogers	George H. Geiger	Thomas Ammonett
James D. Watts	Ralph Thomas	Garland A. Garth

1864.

Rev. W. Timberlake	Lewis Teel	Robert N. Price
Octavius G. Michie	Rev. Charles Wingfield	Archelaus Robertson
Benjamin Ficklin		

1865.

Beverly Staples	Alfred C. Wood	Peter White
William A. Bibb	Frederick Gilliam	George W. Spooner
Charles A. Scott	George Martin	James C. Carter

1866.

Joseph Sutherland Sr.	Leland Blackwell	Ralph Barksdale
John White	William H. Foster	John C. Hughes
William G. Barksdale		

1867.

Robert Rives	H. Carter Moore	Prior Woodson
Franklin Minor	Edward J. Timberlake	George A. Farrow
James R. Watson	John S. Martin	David R. Goodman
Charles Carter	William H. Brown	John D. Carr
David Jeffries	Charles W. Maupin	Peter F. Jefferson
John A. Wilson	Daniel P. Lewis	Paul Tilman

1868.

James Woods	Edmund I. Thompson	William M. Peyton
John R. Jones	Clifton G. Sutherland	Peter Harman
William C. Rives	John Jones	Robert B. Nelson
William Crump	Bland Rea	Willis White

1869.

John D. Moon Sr.	Reuben Maury	Elijah May
William P. Farish	George L. Williams	

1870.

James Hart	Peter A. Woods	William Cowherd
Ira Garrett	Richard Moon, B.	Benjamin Snead
Samuel O. Moon	Rev. James M. Goss	Eli Ames

1871.

Nathaniel Massie	Benjamin F. Randolph	Benjamin F. Ficklin
John H. Coleman	Magill O. Douglass	John Vowles
Socrates Maupin	Roland H. Bates	James C. Lupton
Shepherd Moore		

1872.

Benjamin Wood	Thomas J. Randolph Jr.	Winston O. Purvis
M. L. Anderson	Reuben Wood	David E. Hancock

1873.

W. Edgar Garth	Edward Ferneyhough	Tucker Woodson
William H. McGuffey	Thomas Durrett	George Norris
George W. Hamner	Ira Maupin	Lewis Sowell

1874.

Henry Howard	Thomas Garland	Robert R. Prentis
Thomas H. Brown	Miletus B. Jarman	Robert Rodes
George Rives	William T. Early	William Summerson
Nathaniel Thompson	Peter Craven	F. M. Paoli

1875.

Richard Wingfield	John C. R. Taylor	David Kyle
Thomas J. Randolph	J. P. Halbach	William Cox
Joseph W. Campbell	Stapleton C. Shelton	Andrew Black

1876.

Teakle W. Savage	Charles Goodyear	London Bruce
J. H. Timberlake Jr.	Wilson C. Nicholas	Cosby M. Robertson
Rev. James Fife	John L. White	

1877.

William D. Hart	William T. Brown	John White
Charles D. Everett	William L. Cochran	David Hansbrough
George W. Harris	Robert W. Lewis	John O. Harris

1878.

Joshua Jackson	J. W. Poindexter	Alfred Carpenter
Marcus Durrett	Henry Massie	Thomas Black
Bezaleel Brown	Jacob Van Doren	John A. Brown

1879.

Charles Brown	Hamilton Potts	Thornton W. Bowen
Rice G. Barksdale	Daniel G. Smith	George B. Young
John S. Cocke	David Strange	

1880.

Henry Shepherd	D. J. Hartsook	Robert C. Rives
J. Frank Fry	W. W. Staton	Moses Maxwell
N. H. Massie	Randolph Harris	Atwell Edge
James M. Bowen		

Richard G. Crank
William F. Gooch
Reuben Lindsay

S. A. Hart
Daniel E. Watson
William Wertenbaker

B. M. Pinkerton
Edward Coles
William D. Boaz
John Cochran
J. Summerfield Moon

Shelton F. Leake
George W. Macon
William A. Rogers

Parrott H. Elliott
Benj. H. Magruder
John R. Woods
John Staige Davis

Slaughter W. Ficklin
Thomas C. Bowen

C. W. Purcell
Egbert R. Watson
William W. Minor
Geo. Chris. Gilmer

Peter McGee
John H. Bibb
Thomas F. Wingfield

John Wood Jr.
James L. Cabell

Rev. Thomas D. Bell
John P. Michie
James G. Alexander

1881.
Robert B. Bolling
John H. Timberlake
Tilman T. Maupin
1882.
John O. Massey
John A. Rogers
Caleb Abell
1883.
Orlando B. Barksdale
John W. Goss
W. W. Dinwiddie
Philip Edge

1884.
John T. Antrim
George M. McIntire
Orville Allen
1885.
Stephen O. Southall
Jerome B. Wood
Stokes Tunstall
Joseph F. Wingfield
1886.
Bernard Peyton
Littleton Waddell
1887.
Fleming Broadhead
Peyton S. Coles
Isaac D. Early
William H. Harris
1888.
John S. White
Bluford R. Eddins

1889.
James H. Shepherd
Alexander K. Yancey
1890.
Miles S. Foster
George C. Omohundro

Joel N. Wheeler
Pleasant Sowell
John O. Wingfield

Joseph W. Lipop
Wilton Head
Ezra M. Wolfe

James M. Smith
John A. Carter
Alphonse Lauve
Thomas W. Wood

Fontaine Brockman
William A. Keblinger
Henry Gantt

Charles Hancock
John J. Winn
John A. Snead
Alexander Rives

John H. Nicholas

Horace George
J. Finks Wayland
John Thornley
Richard H. Yancey

George W. Stark
Andrew J. Brown

John S. Coles
W. O. Fry

James Fitz
A. P. Boyd

INDEX.

Agricultural Society, 101.
Albemarle Academy, 91.
   Declaration of Independence, 365.
   Emigrants, 386.
   Necrology, 395.
   Rangers, 363.
   Representatives, 384.
Alcock, William, 198, 242.
Aldermen, 89.
Alexander, Hugh, 246.
Anbury, Travels of, 33.
Area of County, 14.
Army allowances, 54.
Attorneys for Commonwealth, 80.
   List of, 380.
Bache, Dr. William, 62.
Ballou, Solomon, 106.
Bankhead, Charles L., 302, 305.
Banks, 106.
Baptist Churches, 132.
Barboursville Road, 65.
Barracks Prison, 31.
   Road, 65.
   Supplies for, 54.
Barterbrook, 61.
Batesville, 6, 22.
Bear Creek, 23.
Beaverdam, 18, 21.
Belle Grove, 98, 222.
Bible Society, 102.
Birdwood, 4, 174, 244.
Black's Call, Rev. Sam, 362.
Blaetterman, Prof., 288.
Blair, Justice John, 62.
Bland, Col., 36.
Blue Ridge, 14, 19.
   And Rivanna Turnpike, 70.
Bolling, John, 201.
Boundaries of County, 14.
Breckinridge, John, 230.
Brimmer Road, 68.
British ravages, 25.
Broad Mossing Ford, 65.
Brown's Gap Road, 66.
   Turnpike, 69.
Buck's Elbow, 15, 19.
Buck Island, 17, 21.
   Mountain Road, 64.
Burnt Mills, 65, 161, 181.

Cabell v. Wilkinson, 57.
Camp near Rockfish Gap, 30.
Camping Branch, 21, 24.
Capital Punishment, 75.
Carr's Old Ford, 65, 73.
Carter's Bridge, 71.
   Road, 68.
Cartersburg, 22.
Castle Hill, 2, 271, 335.
Central College, 91.
Charlottesville, 26, 105.
   Hospital, 118.
Chestnut Mountains, 2, 19.
Chiles, Micajah, 276, 324.
Chiswell, John, 7, 214.
Church Erection, 136.
Circuit Court, 79.
Clark, Gen. G. R., 50.
Clear Mount, 11, 163.
Collins' Team, 73.
Colonization Society, 102.
Committee of Nine, 120.
Commissioners at Rockfish Gap, 91.
County Court System, 78.
County Officers, 8, 375.
Court House Building, 80.
   First, 9.
Court Proceedings, 9, 54, 74, 110.
Cow Branch, 21.
Crockett, Maj. Joseph, 284, 356.
Currency, deranged, 53, 118.
Davidson's patent, John, 7.
David Wood's old place, 65.
Davis, Prof. J. A. G., 114.
Dawson's Meeting House, 134.
   Row, 94.
Dean, Adam, 247.
Debating Society, 103.
Districts, 25.
District Court, 79.
   No. 1, 118.
Divers, George, 25, 48, 335.
Divisions of County, 24.
Doyle, John, 53.
Drafts of servants, 117.
D. S., 4, 11, 63, 158, 320.
Early, W. T., 117.
Edge, Atwell, 171.
Edge's Creek, 21.
Edgemont, 3, 61, 77.

INDEX

Education, 85.
Elk Run, 23.
Emigration, 55.
Episcopal Churches, 124.
Epperson's Mountain, 20.
Eppes Creek, 3, 18, 168.
Escheats, 47.
Estes, Capt. T. T., 96.
Families, alphabetically arranged, 137.
Farm, The, 5, 70, 45, 252.
Farmington, 5, 47, 54.
Fish, 23.
Flood of 1771, 71.
Forge Church, 56, 125.
Fortune, 188.
Forty-Sixth Virginia, 117.
Franklin, Benjamin, 62.
Franklins, 82.
Fredericksburg Road, 65.
Fredericksville Parish, 124.
Free Bridge, 72.
    Schools, 89.
Frenchmen, 360.
Gallatin, Albert, 9.
Gambell's Grant, Matt., 7.
Gambling, 110.
Game, 22.
Garland, James, Jr., 44.
Garlick, Samuel, 7.
Gazetteer of Virginia, 101.
Giles, Nathaniel, 56.
Gilmer, Dr. John, 76.
    Papers, 363.
Glebes, 125, 127.
Glendower, 10, 185, 238.
Glover, John A., 114.
Goochland County, 1.
Grier, Andrew, 247.
Grills, Eleanor, 52.
Gymnasium. 88.
Haggard's Road, 68.
Hammock's Gap, 15, 58, 330.
Hanover, Presbytery of, 131.
Hardin's Tavern, 60, 217.
Harrisonburg Turnpike, 71.
Hatch, Rev. F. W., 127.
Harvie, Col. John, 35, 225.
Hebrews, 259.
Henderson's Branch, 21.
    Warehouse, 58.
Hening, W. W., 228.
Henry, John, 5, 322.
    Patrick, 46.
Hickman, Edwin, 4, 9, 255.
Hodge, Dr. Charles, 62.
Holt, Joseph, 233.

Hopkins, Dr. James, 75.
Hudson's Creek, 18.
Hunton, Charles B., 299.
Inglis, Thomas, 51.
Indians, 23.
Indian Grave, 5, 23, 286.
Irish Road, 68.
Iron manufacture, 56.
Island Ford, 73.
Italians, 360.
Ivy Creek, 21.
    Depot, 22.
Jailors, 380.
Jameson's Gap, 20.
    Mountain, 20.
Jarman's Gap, 20.
Jefferson on Barracks, 31.
Jerdone, Francis, 47, 201.
Jones, George, 261.
Jones' Plantation, 33, 238.
Johnson, Benjamin, 286.
    Michael, 256, 346.
Jouett, John, 45, 240.
Joyner, Philip, 206.
Judges, 79.
Keppel, Earl of Albemarle, 8.
Key, Nelson, 188.
Key's Meeting House, 135.
    Mill Creek, 20.
King, Martin, 12, 68.
Kinney, Jacob, 287.
Kosciusko's Will, 361.
Lafayette's Visit, 104.
Legislature in Charlottesville, 45, 46.
Leigh, William, 54, 276.
Leitch, James, 82, 139, 253.
Lewis's Creek, 3.
    Ferry, 72.
    Meeting House, 132.
    Mountain, 5, 15.
Library, Public, 103.
Lick Run, 23.
Limestone, 17, 18, 257.
Little D. S., 67.
    Eppes Creek, 18.
    Egypt, 209.
    Mountain, 19.
    River, 20, 85.
Lumpkin, Rev. Thomas, 131.
Lynch's Ford or Ferry, 10, 258.
Lynchburg Road, 68, 70.
Magistrates, 77, 375.
Map of Virginia, 97.
Marches to Williamsburg, 364.
Market House, 106.
Marks, John, 56, 263.

INDEX

Marriage licenses, 55.
Marshall, C. J. John, 63.
Martin, Capt. John, 45, 264.
Meade's Election, Bishop, 129.
Mechum's Depot, 22.
Meriwether's Bridge, 73.
Merritt, Nicholas, 317.
Methodist Churches, 134.
Military of County, 372.
Miller's Branch, 21.
Milton, 3, 57.
Mine, Betsy Martin, 57.
Monticello, 45, 141, 250.
  Bank Specie, 108.
Moore's Creek Bridge, 72.
  Ford, 20, 72.
Morgantown, 60.
Mosby, Col. John S., 115.
Mountain Falls Creek, 21.
Mount Ed Church, 87, 134.
Names, 19.
Negroes, teaching, 111.
New Haven, 61.
Newspapers, 99.
New York, 59.
Nicholas' Warehouse, 58.
Nineteenth Virginia, 117.
Nixville, 22.
Norris, Opie, 70, 106, 243.
North Milton, 59.
Nutter, George, 115.
Offices, Court Square, 82.
Old's Forge, 57, 68, 291.
Oliver's Store, 22.
Ordinaries, 10, 39.
Organization, County, 8.
Pantops, 4, 88, 139.
Partition of County, 26.
Patents, Early, 2.
Personal Collisions, 110.
Petersburg, 22.
Phillips, Gen., 35.
Pigeon Top, 15, 20.
Pillory, 9, 82.
Piney Mountain, 5, 15, 20.
Pinch-'em-slyly, 61.
Plank Road, 69.
Pleasant Grove, 59.
Plum Orchard Branch, 21.
Plum Tree Branch, 21.
Poindexter, George, 77.
Poindexter's Mountain, 20.
Population, 11.
Presbyterian Churches, 129.
Prison Springs, 28.
Punishments, 12.
Railroads, 115.

Rea's Ford Road, 67.
Reconstruction, 119.
Records, 13, 25.
Red Bank Falls, 3.
Revolution, 29.
Richard Woods Road, 67.
Riedesel, Madame, 37.
Rio Bridge, 73.
Rivanna Navigation Co., 84.
River Road, 64.
Roads, 10, 63.
Rock Spring, 71.
Rockfish Gap, 20, 64, 91.
Rodes's Road, 66.
Round Top Mountain, 22.
Salmon, John H., 122.
Scales Creek, 21.
School Commissioners, 86.
Scottsville, 97.
Secretary's Road, 68.
Settlement of Virginia, 1.
Shelby, Letitia, 49.
Sheriffs, 379.
Short, William, 24, 217.
Signs of War, 116.
Simpson's Tanyard, 67.
Slaughter, John, 329.
Smith, Ambrose Joshua, 7.
Soapstone Works, 18.
Soldiers of Revolution, 367.
South River, 20.
South West Mountain, 14, 19.
Spencer, John, 189.
Sprouse, Hudson, 112.
St. Anne's Parish, 124.
Staunton and James River Turn-
  pike, 69.
Still House Mountain, 66.
Stockton's Creek, 17, 319.
Stony Point, 22.
Swan Tavern, 46, 240.
Tarleton's Raid, 44.
Taylor's patent, William, 6, 324.
Teachers, 85.
Temperance Society, 94, 103.
Three Notched Road, 63.
Todd, Rev. John, 233.
Tom's Mountain, 17, 171, 328.
Tooley's Creek, 332.
Topography, 14.
Tories, 47.
Towns, 57.
Townships, 25.
Travellers' Grove, 59.
Tufton, 5, 260, 310.
Turkey Run, 22.
Turk's Gap, 20.

Underwood Convention, 119.
University of Virginia, 92.
Wade's Spring, 66.
Walker, Dr. Thomas, 51, 334.
War of 1812, 96.
Ware, Peter, 113.
Warren, 58.
Washington, Gen., 70.
    Henry, 299.
Wayland, Jeremiah, 301.
Webb's Mountain, 7, 20.
Webster, John Lee, 56.
West's Saw Mill Run, 68.

Wheeler Road, 68.
Whitehall, 22.
Wilkinson, John, 56, 344.
Wirt, William, 207.
Wolf Pit, 22.
Wolf Trap Branch, 22.
Wolves, 13.
Woodridge, 68.
Woods' Gap, 11, 20, 63.
Woods', Meeting at James, 30.
Yellow Mountain, 20.
Yergain, John, 358.

www.ingramcontent.com/pod-product-compliance
Lightning Source LLC
Chambersburg PA
CBHW071223230426
43668CB00011B/1287